Empire's Children

Empire's Children

Race, Filiation, and Citizenship in the French Colonies

EMMANUELLE SAADA

Translated by Arthur Goldhammer

The University of Chicago Press
Chicago and London

Emmanuelle Saada is associate professor in the Department of French and Romance Philology at Columbia University.

Originally published in French as *Les enfants de la colonie: Les métis de l'Empire français entre sujétion et citoyenneté,* © Editions La Découverte, Paris, France, 2007.

This work, published as part of a program providing publication assistance, received financial support from the French Ministry of Foreign Affairs, the Cultural Services of the French Embassy in the United States, and FACE (French American Cultural Exchange).

The University of Chicago Press, Chicago 60637
The University of Chicago Press, Ltd., London
© 2012 by The University of Chicago
All rights reserved. Published 2012.
Printed in the United States of America

21 20 19 18 17 16 15 14 13 12   1 2 3 4 5

ISBN-13: 978-0-226-73307-4 (cloth)
ISBN-13: 978-0-226-73308-1 (paper)
ISBN-10: 0-226-73307-6 (cloth)
ISBN-10: 0-226-73308-4 (paper)

Library of Congress Cataloging-in-Publication Data

Saada, Emmanuelle.
   [Enfants de la colonie. English]
   Empire's children : race, filiation, and citizenship in the French colonies / Emmanuelle Saada ; translated by Arthur Goldhammer.
      p. cm.
   Originally published in French as Les enfants de la colonie: Les métis de l'Empire français entre sujétion et citoyenneté.
   Includes bibliographical references and index.
   ISBN-13: 978-0-226-73307-4 (cloth : alkaline paper)
   ISBN-10: 0-226-73307-6 (cloth : alkaline paper)
   ISBN-13: 978-0-226-73308-1 (paperback : alkaline paper)
   ISBN-10: 0-226-73308-4 (paperback : alkaline paper)   1. Racially mixed people—France—Colonies—History. 2. Racially mixed people—Legal status, laws, etc.—France—Colonies—History. 3. Citizenship—France—Colonies— History. 4. France—Colonies—Ethnic relations—History. 5. Miscegenation— France—Colonies—History.   I. Goldhammer, Arthur. II. Title.
   JV1817.S2313 2012
   305.8'050171244—dc23

                                      201132762

♾ This paper meets the requirements of ANSI/NISO Z39.48-1992 (Permanence of Paper).

To my parents

CONTENTS

Emmanuelle Saada is part of a small cohort of scholars coming out of French academia who have been opening up the study of colonialism and thereby remaking what we mean by French history. Over the past decade, she has striven through her teaching, publications, and scholarly connections on both sides of the Atlantic to articulate an alternative to the strongly national framework in which French history has usually been written.

Leading French historians have proved themselves perfectly capable of writing about the Revolution of 1789 without discussing the revolution in the French plantation colony of Saint Domingue in 1791–1804 or about 1848 without pointing to the act by which former slaves became French citizens. To a wider public, colonies were "out there"—*outre-mer*—a minor and anomalous part of French history, now expunged by the end of colonial rule in sub-Saharan Africa in 1960 and Algeria in 1962, a bit embarrassing perhaps, but never a true indication of the nature of French society or political values.

A more recent trend has gone in what at first seems the opposite direction: to portray colonialism as an intrinsic part of French republicanism, a story of violent conquest, terror, and racial denigration that is the mirror image of a project that proclaimed itself to incarnate liberty, equality, and fraternity. Yet such an approach can be as *"franco-français"* as the nation-centered one, this time with France as a clearly defined, all-determining force for evil instead of for good. *Empire's Children: Race, Filiation, and Citizenship in the French Colonies* provides a more persuasive alternative, not by grand pronouncements but by telling a complex story well. It forces us to rethink what we thought we understood. The questions of who was French and in what way turn out to be complex, and Saada shows that Vietnamese mothers deserted by their French paramours, the directors of orphanages, and the children of mixed relationships themselves—not just jurists, legislators, and colonial officials—played parts in answering them.

Saada's book combines the moral force of critique with a nuanced and dynamic historical practice. She moves back and forth between the specificity of colonial situations—in Indochina most notably—and the general question of what kind of political entity France was. She provides—as only someone trained in both social science and history could do—a discussion of the changing significance of race, noting that the biological definition of it was complemented by a strong cultural component, in which the relevant unit was not "white," "black," or "yellow," but "French." She explains that the question of the "quality of a French person" requires us to think of France not as a neatly national entity but as a more variegated unit in which the relationship of people in different places to the state and to one another was changing and contested. The clarity of the distinction between a French citizen and a French subject was tempered by the existence of intermediate categories within metropolitan France, the full citizenship rights acquired by colonials in the Caribbean colonies after 1848 and by indigenous people in Senegal after 1916, the possibility (however rarely exercised) of colonial subjects acquiring citizenship, and by the presence of ambiguous categories, notably the mixed-race children who are the primary focus of her book. Legal recognition implied access to different schools and to the army and civil service, and eventually made it possible for *métis* to turn a category into the assertion of commonality and make collective demands.

Empire's Children thus ends up being both a historical text and a reflection on what it means—in law and in social and political practices—to be French, what it means to live in a republican polity, and what it means to be marked as a member of a particular social category. Saada provides her readers with a means of transcending the debates that are polarizing French politics. Whereas some argue that France has long been, is, and must always be a republic blind to the origins of its citizens and others insist that the people who make up that republic, particularly those who at one time inhabited its colonies, deserve collective recognition for the painful histories they lived through, she shows that the republican ethos was never so origins-blind and that the relationship of cultural difference and political belonging was continuously debated. Whereas some argue that certain categories of people living in France are unworthy of membership in French society (by virtue of their supposed antidemocratic, antiegalitarian values) and others claim that the republic (because of the violence and humiliation inflicted on the people it colonized and the discrimination it imposes on their descendants) has proved itself unworthy of the people who believed

in its values, Saada asks us to contemplate the possibility that republicanism is not a given, but an ideological framework that was fought over and
redefined as different people made claims in its name. By focusing on the
appearance and eventually the disappearance of an ambiguous category,
the *métis*, Saada invites her readers to reflect on how social boundaries are
constructed and at times transcended through law and through social practices. The 1928 decree discussed in the opening pages of this book turns out
to be a key moment in initiating a debate on French citizenship that would
play itself out across the rest of the twentieth century, in Asian, African, and
European France. Such debates remain at the center of French politics today,
and Emmanuelle Saada's *Empire's Children* is thus as much about France's
present and future as about its past.

Frederick Cooper

ACKNOWLEDGMENTS

To be able to indulge in the American genre of book acknowledgments—typically longer and more sentimental than its French counterpart—is by no means the smallest satisfaction of seeing this book translated into English.

The warp and weft of *Empire's Children* reflect both a personal trajectory and an intellectual journey. The book owes a debt to relatives and friends, as well as teachers, colleagues, and students on both sides of the Atlantic. This book had its earliest origins under the auspices of the joint interdisciplinary program in the social sciences run by the École normale supérieure and the École des hautes études en sciences sociales. I am grateful to Gérard Noiriel, whose own work (in many if sometimes indirect ways) has been instrumental in shaping the central questions raised here. In the 1990s and early 2000s, at the "Laboratoire de sciences sociales" of the École normale supérieure, Gérard Noiriel, Christian Baudelot, Stéphane Beaud, Alban Bensa, Eric Fassin, Frédérique Matonti, Michel Offerlé, Christian Topalov, and Florence Weber formed a team of exemplary teachers in the above-mentioned interdisciplinary program in the social sciences. For almost two decades, it was one of the most rigorous and stimulating training grounds for a generation of people who believed in a constructive dialogue among different disciplines within the social sciences. This book is first the product of the lessons that I learned from these exceptional teachers to articulate history, sociology, anthropology, and law. It has also benefited greatly from the comments of the following professors: Agnès Fine, Danièle Lochak, Daniel Nordman, Evelyne Serverin, and Trinh Van Thao.

The book also owes debts to others who facilitated the research on which it is based. The most important of these debts is to the many *métis* who shared with me their memories and some of their documents, often with emotion. Although I can't name them individually because I promised them not to divulge their identities, I would like to thank them collectively.

I also wish to express my gratitude to the many librarians and archivists who have assisted me with generosity and professionalism on three different continents, especially at the Bibliothèque Cujas in Paris and the New York University Library. The following individuals deserve special mention: Madame Fournier at the Bibliothèque administrative de la Ville de Paris; Lucette Vachier and Jacques Dion, archivists at the Centre des archives d'outre-mer in Aix-en-Provence, who were so helpful during several summer research trips; and Vu Thi Minh Huong, who greatly facilitated access to the Vietnam National Archives Center I in Hanoi. Finally, I would like to acknowledge the support of the Paul-Albert Février Foundation in Aix-en-Provence during two summers.

Over the years I spent researching and writing this book, I also worked in three separate institutions: New York University, the École des hautes etudes en sciences sociales, and Columbia University. In these very different places, I accumulated many intellectual debts to generous and inspiring students and colleagues, especially Agnès Antoine, Isabelle Backouche, Edward Berenson, Jane Burbank, Juliette Cadiot, Craig Calhoun, Herrick Chapman, Frederick Cooper, Myriam Cottias, Muriel Darmon, Vincent Debaene, Bachir Diagne, Mamadou Diouf, Madeleine Dobie, Laura Lee Downs, Vincent Duclert, Jean-Louis Fabiani, Agnès Fine, Stéphane Gerson, Nancy Green, Jean Hébrard, Alain Mahé, Gregory Mann, Fabienne Moore, Pap Ndiaye, Michelle Pinto, François Pouillon, Christophe Prochasson, Kapil Raj, Pierre Rosanvallon, Paul-André Rosental, Paul Sager, Jean-Frédéric Schaub, Irène Théry, Frédéric Viguier, and Jean-Paul Zuniga. Many other colleagues and friends provided important help, intellectual advice, and sometimes direction, among them: Romain Bertrand, Jean-Luc Bonniol, Pierre Brocheux, Alice Conklin, Rozenn Couëdic, Baptiste Coulmont, Jasmine El Yabouri, Didier Fassin, Eric Fassin, Nadine Lefaucheur, Mary Lewis, Ana Pairet, Emmanuel Poisson, Jacques Revel, Derek Schilling, Paul Schor, Todd Sheppard, Emmanuelle Sibeud, Ann Laura Stoler, Judith Surkis, and Claire Zalc.

This book has also benefited from the comments of Thomas Benatouil, Laure Blévis, Benoît de l'Estoile, Dominique Gros, Olivier Ihl, Laurent Jeanpierre, Herman Lebovics, Isabelle Merle, Anne Raffin, Sarah Sasson, and Yerri Urban. Frederick Cooper and Patrick Weil have been especially generous with their time and suggestions; Alexis Spire read and commented on the entire manuscript; Gwenaëlle Calvès has been an insightful guide to the world of law, an acute critic of my work, and a wonderful friend during the years it took to complete the book. To this list of friends, I would like to add those who were instrumental in making this a French book: Christophe Prochasson and Vincent Duclert, who welcomed it in their series L'espace de l'histoire, and François Gèze, Elizabeth Lau, and Delphine Ribouchon at les Éditions la découverte.

Finally, I would like to express my gratitude to the institutions and individuals who made possible the last leg of the journey, from French into English. The translation itself would not have been possible without the generous support of the Columbia University Graduate School of Arts and Sciences, the French Cultural Services, and the PEN American Center. Three people have been instrumental in giving an English voice to *Les enfants de la colonie*: Frederick Cooper has been a strong advocate from beginning to end—and has demonstrated his support by providing a foreword; Arthur Goldhammer, whose interest in this work opened many doors, has put his formidable talent to work in giving new life to the manuscript; and Douglas Mitchell has welcomed the book with great generosity at the University of Chicago Press. I also would like to thank Sarah Lazur for translating the notes and bibliography and Maxime Tourbe for helping with the translation of legal terms into English.

But, in the end, this book would not have been what it is in either language without the many loved ones who have accompanied me in this adventure, especially my wonderfully lively children, Joseph and Ava, and my companion, Joe. We have been together long enough that he has been associated with all the many personal and intellectual steps that led to this book, in both its French and English versions, neither of which would exist without his support and love. This book is dedicated to my parents, Raymond and Jacqueline, who, *sans le savoir*, have made me a *métis* of sorts.

This book began many years ago, when I stumbled upon a remarkable contribution to French citizenship law: a 1928 decree "defining the status of persons of mixed parentage (*métis*) born in Indochina whose legal parents are unknown." Published in the November 8, 1928, issue of the *Journal officiel de la République française*, the decree stipulates that

> *Article 1.* Any individual born in the territory of Indochina to parents of whom one, though legally unidentified, is presumed to be of the French race, shall be eligible to obtain, pursuant to the provisions of the present edict, recognition of French citizenship (*qualité de français*).

> *Article 2.* The presumption that father or mother, though legally unidentified, is of French origin and the French race may be established by any means whatsoever. The primary factors to be taken into consideration are the name of the child, the fact that he or she has received a French education, upbringing, and culture, and the child's situation in society.[1]

For a historian of France, the appearance of the word *race* in this decree comes as a profound surprise. And, indeed, the text marks the first occurrence of the notion in French law.[2] The association between "race" and "citizenship" contradicts the most basic representations of the French "social contract," characterized, since the Revolution, by the irrelevance of "origin" for participation in the public sphere. For the most influential French political thinkers, from Jean-Jacques Rousseau in the eighteenth century to Ernest Renan in the nineteenth century, a "people" or a "nation" is an association based on will.[3] The latter defined the nation as a "soul," animated by "the desire to live together," a "spiritual principle" that transcended the objective characteristics of its members, be they race, language, religion, economic interest, or geography. In particular, because there is "no pure race," according to Renan, "to make politics depend upon ethnographic analysis is to surrender it to a chimera."[4]

The republic, in abolishing slavery in 1848, had affirmed that henceforth it would "make no distinctions within the human family"—a principle that was scrupulously obeyed in official discourse and accordingly reproduced in nearly all subsequent historiography.[5] Among historians, it is generally accepted that the "only period in French history in which race was explicitly indicated as the direct and specific referent of a statute was under the Vichy regime."[6]

What, then, do we make of this appearance of *race* in this decree from 1928—over a decade before Vichy? It is, by all appearances, the first use of the word as a legal category, and not in the context of exclusion of racialized others. On the contrary, the intention was to include individuals within the "community of citizens" on the grounds of belonging to a specific race—namely, "the French race."[7]

Another surprise is that *race* is defined here as a matter of civil condition, social status, and familiarity with French culture—not as a biological identity. The implementation of the decree did nothing to clarify these terms; in fact, it made them more confusing. Since the text allowed the use of "any means whatsoever" to establish race, the courts quickly adopted the most convenient form of proof, "the medical certificate of race," and thereby favored a purely biological interpretation of the term. In the debates that preceded the decree, the same confusion is apparent. All signs in the 1920s point to an understanding of the word *race* as both a biological reality *and* a range of social characteristics and cultural competences that revealed themselves through behavior. This conflation of the biological, social, and cultural suggests a way of thinking about society very different from our current tendency to distinguish these domains. One of the purposes of this book is to excavate this earlier mode of social representation and, in so doing, to contribute to the history of the concept of race.[8]

A third surprise is the use of the term *métis*, designating a person of mixed parentage, in the title of the 1928 edict. Does the use of the word indicate the existence of a formally defined group subject to specific regulations?

Archival research reveals that, from the 1890s until decolonization, the word *métis* was used extensively throughout the French colonial empire, from Africa to the Pacific. Tens of thousands of individuals were designated by the term, and their numbers grew steadily throughout the period. But the *métis* was not an organized group with a common identity but rather a category imposed from above by colonial actors—mainly philanthropists, administrators, and jurists. When the *métis* was discussed, it was generally with a certain anxiety, not to say anguish, and took the form of the "*métis* question."

The *métis* was thus a problem. But what was a *métis*? In colonial parlance, the word usually referred to individuals born to a "European" father and a "native" mother "out of wedlock." Most of these children were not recognized by their fathers, and most were ultimately abandoned by them. The colonial *métis* was therefore both a hybrid and a bastard, to use the prevailing term. Such a person was especially difficult to classify in relation to the main dividing line in colonial society that separated "French" from "natives." This indeterminacy was perceived as a danger to the colonial order and figures recurrently in colonial and metropolitan archives.

The *métis* question became a meeting place for a wide range of anxieties about colonial society, touching on racial mixing, illegitimacy, and the definition of citizenship. As the following chapters will demonstrate, the "question" was of particular importance to men, many of whom spent only a brief time in the colonies; to the male children they brought into the world but were unwilling to treat as their own; and, finally, to the colonial officials who ultimately assumed responsibility for these "children of the empire." The "*métis* problem" was an essentially male problem because it raised questions about the reproduction of the full privileges of French citizenship, from which women were excluded until 1944.

The problem was not equally acute in all parts of the French Empire. Some colonial territories, such as Algeria, did not have a *métis* problem. Others, most notably Indochina, were quick to identify and confront the "danger" that the existence of thousands of illegitimate and abandoned children represented. The following chapters explore this geography of the *métis* question in relation to the wider history and political evolution of the empire. This geography reflects differences but also flows as different parts of the empire influenced one another. Indeed, Indochina served as a veritable laboratory for the *métis* question. It was there that the "problem" was first diagnosed and "solutions" were first proposed. It was also there that the first *métis* statute was promulgated in 1928.

Other territories confronted the same issues, and the solutions first worked out in Indochina were adapted to meet other "local contingencies." The Indochina regulation served as a model for similar measures in French West Africa in 1930, Madagascar in 1931, New Caledonia in 1933, French Equatorial Africa in 1936, Togo in 1937, and Cameroon in 1944. This circulation of discourses and legal texts suggests how the empire acquired legal and political coherence through the confrontation with "major colonial problems," of which *métissage* was one of the most urgent.[9]

Within this broad context, this book recounts two histories from three distinct points of view.

First, it tells the story of those who were called *métis* in the various territories of the French Empire. It describes not only the colonial relations that produced this social category but especially the way in which colonial actors sought to resolve it. Indeed, it was not long before certain prominent individuals decided to resolve the *métis* question by "reclassifying" them as French. They actively sought out *métis* in towns, around military garrisons, and in rural areas and persuaded their mothers, in some cases with great difficulty, to place the children in special orphanages, where they tried to turn them into "Frenchmen, heart and soul." This project soon encountered an obstacle: since they were not acknowledged by their fathers, *métis* shared the "native" status of their mothers. Those who championed the cause of the *métis* saw a mismatch between their "truly" French identity and this native legal status and therefore pushed for changes in the law, eventually resulting in the 1928 decree for Indochina, followed by similar developments in other colonies.

The present work therefore retraces the history of a social category, the *métis*, and describes the way in which it was accommodated in law. The existence of these children was seen as a source of disorder—not only social and political disorder but also confusion in the categories of colonial law. In effect, if all the inhabitants of the empire were French, some were nonetheless more so than others. A minority of "citizens" enjoyed the full rights of nationality, including political representation and the benefit of the French civil and penal codes. In contrast, native "subjects" were relegated to an inferior civil, penal, and political status. Hence, it was not long before the difficulty of classifying the *métis* as "French" or "native" became a problem for the law: should they be treated as "citizens" or "subjects"?

Second, this book explores how a "social question" involving abandoned children became a legal controversy in which the most basic issues of colonial rule were at stake. This calls for an understanding of what it meant to be a French citizen or a native subject in the colonies (see chapter 4). The book then shows how the *métis* question became an object of two intersecting bodies of law, that of filiation and that of nationality. Key to this translation into the legal sphere was the practice of "fraudulent recognitions" of persons of mixed blood for the purpose of gaining French citizenship (chapter 5). Next, it looks at the debate over whether the law governing the investigation of paternity (passed by Parliament in 1912) should apply to the colonies. This debate, which took place in metropolitan France as well as in the various territories of the empire, offers a window onto colonial understandings of sexuality, family, and filiation (chapter 6). Finally, the book turns to an exploration of how jurists concerned about the fate of the *métis* set out to revise the law, resulting in a new pathway to French citizenship by way of racial affiliation (chapter 7). In this manner, race, understood as collective filiation, was introduced into nationality law.

In composing this detailed account of the "fabrication" of colonial law, this book pays attention not only to the strategies and practices of the actors involved but also to the specific way in which the law expresses and constructs the social world.[10] In other words, it takes law seriously as a catalyst for social change. How are we to understand the place of law in a colonial system that we tend to think of today as ruled exclusively by force? How did law shape the reality of colonial domination? In a more general sense, the *métis* issue raises questions about how social and legal categories relate to each other. How do we explain the central role of law in the process of social categorization?

Third, the book looks closely at the fates of the individuals caught up in the *métis* question. It looks at the consequences of the decrees that recognized them as French citizens not only on debates about colonial power but also on the ways in which the *métis* constructed their own identities. My premise here is that law is in fact a highly *effective* discourse—arguably the most effective one. Law, from this perspective, does not reflect the social but produces it. In the case of the *métis*, its effects were concrete and considerable at the individual as well as collective level. Once the *métis* became citizens, they were enlisted as *cadres de la colonisation*—the middle management of colonization. After decolonization, upon their "repatriation to France," those who were still minors were separated from their mothers and placed in specially designated orphanages, even though many of them were unaware of the identities of the fathers to whom they owed this "favor" and spoke no French.

But the most important effect of the law was no doubt the disappearance of the category of "*métis*." Those so designated were literally "assimilated" into the community of citizens. No collective *métis* identity emerged during the colonial period or later in metropolitan France. Invisible in today's French society, thousands of the "empire's children" remain French by virtue of their "race": the word appears on their certificates of nationality. As can be seen in the personal testimony of a number of them (reproduced in chapter 10), they remain to this day deeply affected by their transformation from subjects into citizens.

The three sections of this book take up these three perspectives in turn. The chronological division in the text between the period "before" and "after" the change in citizenship law marks a transformative moment in this history, to be sure, but it is also part of the exposition of a larger, complex dialectic: the *métis* question did not exist apart from its formulation as a question of law, and the law addressed the issue only because it raised questions about one of the fundamental pillars of the colonial political order. The law is "always already there."

The decree of 1928 and its later derivatives made race one criterion of the "quality of Frenchness" (*qualité de français*). The *métis* question does not fit in the origin-blind universalist "republican model" of the nation, which since the 1980s has been the touchstone of both scholarly and political discourse about the social matrix in France.

A major tenet of the republican model is the distinction, traceable to the late nineteenth century, between a "political" definition of nationality, supposedly invented during the French Revolution, and an "ethnocultural" conception of the nation, supposedly characteristic of Germany. Such histories usually focused on the fate of immigrants in each country and on the respective laws of nationality.[11]

When they did occasionally look at the colonial experience, proponents of the republican model came away with contradictory conclusions. Some argued that the French Republic's "civilizing and assimilating mission" overseas was comparable to the acculturation of the French peasantry and thus confirmed the fundamentally open character of the French nation.[12] Conversely, others held that the colonial distinction between "citizen" and "subject" was a "juridical monstrosity" because natives of the colonies were subject to French sovereignty "but not allowed to exercise it."[13]

The fact that the "republican model" admits of such divergent interpretations of the history of nationality in the colonies implies either that the model itself is deficient or that the history was more complex. I would like to suggest that both propositions are true and that nationality was also conceptualized and practiced at the imperial level.

The point is therefore not to show that the republic "contradicted" itself in the colonies. Rather, it is to suggest that the situation in the colonies revealed (in the photographic sense) deep tensions in the *practices* by which nationality was defined—tensions that were largely invisible in the metropolitan context.[14]

Foremost among these tensions was the notion of "race." Historians of the republican model have of course recognized the ambivalence of its principal agents with respect to "the biological, the ethnic, the racial. . . .

Of all the words introduced by the Revolution—'Republic,' 'people,' 'sovereignty,' etc.—the word 'nation' is the only one that was not a legally-based abstraction but a term that, etymologically speaking, derived part of its significance from the biological, like the German word *Volk*."[15] But these same historians argue that the republic was able to overcome the "racist danger" thanks to the "providential crisis" that followed the loss of Alsace-Lorraine, which forced France to counter German claims by adopting a contractual definition of the nation formulated by Ernest Renan. This argument from the history of ideas is largely undermined by the reality of social regulatory practices in the colonies, where republican bureaucracies implemented racial criteria not only to exclude and discriminate but also to include some of their subjects in the community of citizens. With the decrees of 1928 and after, France discovered itself as a race.

Without denying that racial difference served primarily to justify discriminatory practices in the colonies, I will argue that it also encouraged what might be characterized as "dynamic" racism, or, perhaps better, "racism of expansion," to borrow a phrase from Michel Foucault, who used it to discuss the connections among what he called "biopower," "populationism," and "imperialist expansion."[16]

The dialectic of inclusion and exclusion, which lies at the heart of the *métis* question in the colonies, points the way toward a different perspective on the history of French colonization. This field, which for years thrived on celebration of the French "colonial adventure," was marginalized after the colonies gained their independence. Today the colonial past is once again an object of debate. Usually this takes the form of denunciation, which is obviously justified, but many questions remain. Denunciation merely stands the old hagiographic history on its head, and in many respects these analyses of "*la fracture coloniale*" retain a narrow "Franco-French" focus. They fail to notice the contribution of native populations to political change within the empire, condemning natives to passivity, just as the old colonial history did. Like earlier work centered on the violence of the wars of conquest and liberation, this line of work considers the entire colonial period through the lens of war. The history of the *métis* question, like that of other instances of mediation between "colonizers" and "colonized," forces us to look beyond this reductionist perspective, which is really just a version of the "clash of civilizations" thesis.

Looking beyond the fundamental violence of the colonial relation, which was first and foremost a spoliation, the *métis* question offers a glimpse of other areas of domination that were more intimate and therefore probably more pervasive. Because this history involves men, women, and children, it points to the importance of sexuality, as well as of gender, race relations, and domestic organization in colonial power relations. The American historian and anthropologist Ann Laura Stoler has explored this field in depth. She has mapped the "emotional geography of empire" from Indonesia and Indochina to the United States and transformed colonial historiography by analyzing the ways in which the private and public spheres are intertwined. This work is greatly indebted to hers, and the focus on law in many respects extends it.[17]

The history of the *métis* question also helps us to understand the dynamics of French colonial rule in terms of interactions among the various social groups in the colonies.[18] Indeed, the very categories that were used to describe colonial order were shaped in part by the presence of thousands of the "empire's children." The early determination to "reclass" them in French society made it necessary to redefine the terms *French* and *indigenous* and therefore to redraw the central dividing line of colonial social classification: the *métis* joined the *convertis, évolués, petits blancs,* and *décivilisés* that mark the history of colonial interactions.[19] The categorization process became enmeshed in local and imperial power struggles, and certain of its technical features spread from one colony to another and even to other empires.[20] Both the colonial and imperial strands are woven together in this work, which explores not only the way in which the *métis* question was presented as a general "problem" of colonization but also its particular local inflections. The latter will enable us to see how native actors helped shape the "question" through the ways in which they handled sexual contacts with the colonizers and elaborated their own categories for describing *métissage* and its products.

In opposition to an ahistorical and often functionalist vision of *métissage,* which posits the "hybrid" as a universal type fulfilling the role of social mediator—a *Homo métis* produced by all societies—the example of colonial France shows that the very existence of the *métis* category depends on the way in which social identities are defined, and therefore on power relations.[21] What is more, the *métis,* whose presence throughout much of the French Empire was unmistakable, "disappeared" with decolonization: our history is therefore a history of the "dissolution" as well as the "construction" of a social category.

This book focuses on a population that was thought of as straddling the boundary between the society of the colonizers and that of the colonized and thus threatening the coherence of the whole colonial social structure. One can therefore think of social boundaries not as residual categories but as sociologically primary sites—focal points for the deployment of countless techniques of classification and thus social configuration. Social science is familiar with this idea,[22] but placing it once again front and center is a valuable exercise at a time when French politicians and social scientists are celebrating a "*métis* France" and thereby reinforcing the very racial identities they claim to be undermining.

coherence
in
colonial
structure

PART ONE

Le Métissage: A Colonial Social Problem

ONE

An Imperial Question

In the late nineteenth century, *métissage* ("racial mixing") was not a new phenomenon in France. Representations of it go back a long way, to the early days of European colonization. Perceptions of *métissage*, however, changed significantly in the second half of the century, with the formation of the new French Empire. These were shaped by increasingly influential social sciences, especially anthropology. By the end of the period of colonial conquests in the 1890s, *métissage* had become an issue of the utmost importance throughout the empire. Its forms varied from colony to colony, yet colonial actors clearly felt that they were dealing with an issue of imperial scale and significance.

New Empire, New Question

As early as the seventeenth century, people had begun to use words drawn from the lexicon of animal breeding to describe the offspring of Europeans and the natives of the New World. In French the most common terms were *métis*, *mulâtre* ("mulatto"), and *sang-mêlé* ("mixed blood").[1]

In the first half of the nineteenth century, men and women of color in the colonies became familiar figures in popular literature. In a volume entitled *Les Français peints par eux-mêmes* (1842), for instance, the *mulâtre* appeared among the classic types of provincial Frenchmen—the Breton, the Roussillonnais, the Béarnais, and the Dauphinois.[2] A *métis* was the tragic hero Alexandre Dumas's novel *Georges*, published in 1843 and set in Mauritius. Serialized popular fiction featured plots built around the ambiguous appearance of mulatto characters: in the volumes of Eugène Sue's *Mystères de Paris* that came out in 1842 and 1843, Cécily, a former slave from the American South, plays a major role passing as an Alsatian. The mulatto doctor in Ponson du Terrail's *Rocambole* (published between 1857 and 1870) knows the secrets of various medicinal plants, including some that can "erase the most indelible tattoos."

In the nineteenth century, however, it was above all anthropology that appropriated the theme of *métissage*. At midcentury, *métissage* played a central role in a debate between monogenists, proponents of the unity of the human race, and polygenists, who argued that different races have distinct sources. The arguments of both camps can be traced back to the naturalist Georges-Louis Leclerc de Buffon, who had argued that species are defined by the ability of members to produce fertile offspring: monogenists insisted that racial hybrids were viable, fertile, and therefore valuable, while polygenists argued that interbreeding led to sterility and deformity and therefore that the distance between the races was insurmountable.[3] The physician and anatomist Paul Broca revived this debate with his early work and used the rejection of a paper on *métissage* by the Biology Society as a pretext for founding the Paris Anthropological Society in 1859.[4] This society played a central role in the development of physical anthropology as an autonomous discipline.[5]

A confirmed polygenist, Broca questioned the universality of "interfertility" and suggested that, depending on the proximity of the races involved, hybrids could be either "sterile," "dysgenesic," "partially fertile," or "eugenesic." Using these distinctions, he was able to condemn the mixing of "distant races" and to promote "eugenesic" mixing. By showing that the French population was the result of a harmonious cross between Celts and Kymris, he lent scientific support to the celebration of the "French melting pot," a central feature of the nineteenth-century republican representation of French history.[6] One also finds this theme in nineteenth-century historical writing—in Jules Michelet's description of France as a "person," for example, or Charles Seignobos's characterization of the French as a "people of *métis*."[7]

The general tendency was nevertheless pessimistic: in the final decades of the nineteenth century, the vast majority of the many anthropological studies of hybridization stressed the deficiencies of the *métis*. The figure of the monstrous freak, which had fascinated the eighteenth century, gave way to a new theme: physical and moral degeneracy due to the conflict of heredities. For instance, at the Second International Congress of Criminal Anthropology in 1889, Clémence Royer, a female philosopher and scientist and Darwin's French translator, proposed that an investigation of the genealogy of criminals would reveal large numbers of hybrids: "Indeed, it is only natural to expect that in the offspring of very diverse races, with different habits, mores, and social instincts, the vast difference in moral heredity will result in mutual cancellation, as when forces of opposite sign are added together to yield zero."[8]

Between the two world wars, this argument was enthusiastically embraced by psychiatrists, who appropriated the theme of *métissage* and linked it to the question of immigration, both European and colonial. In the 1920s, Dr. Edgar Bérillon claimed in a series of publications on "the psychobiological problem of racial mixing" that observing the offspring of mixed marriages between French and immigrants had convinced him "that in our European environment, the crossing of antagonistic races, even when the skin color of the individuals involved was the same, yielded offspring of obvious inferiority with respect to health and resistance to disease as well as to morality."[9]

A few years later, Dr. Georges Heuyer, one of the founders of child psychiatry and a pioneer in the field of "maladapted childhood," noted that "the number of offspring of marriages between Arab men and French women is large," so it would be wise to determine "whether it is a good idea or a bad one to encourage natives of the colonies to come to France and marry French women." On this basis, he launched an investigation into "the important question of whether the *métis* is capable of social adaptation." He studied the offspring of marriages between "French" and "Chinese," "Indochinese," "Martiniquais," "Muslim Arab," "Indian," "mixed blood," and "*métis* from Madagascar and Réunion" and found "character troubles" in all of the adolescents he examined.[10]

Denunciation of the consequences of racial mixing grew louder in the 1930s among a small group of doctors who posed as experts on immigration. Among them was René Martial, the longtime director of the Douai department of public hygiene and later marine health inspector, who also began teaching a course in anthropology at the Paris Faculty of Medicine in 1938.[11]

Alongside this dominant line of criticism, another school of thought emerged around the view that racial mixing could produce offspring "superior to the mother races." This idea was first formulated by Armand de Quatrefages, a contemporary of Broca and an ardent defender of the monogenist line, who argued that, among other things, the *métis* was generally more resistant to the tropical climate than his European father. Between the two world wars, another variant of the racial-mixing theme gained currency on the fringes of physical anthropology: a critique of theories of race as static, unchanging formations, which began with a reflection on the "value" of children of mixed race.[12] After World War II, this idea would be taken up by various antiracist groups such as UNESCO (the United Nations

Educational, Scientific, and Cultural Organization).[13] The universality of racial mixing was seen as an important argument not against the existence of races but against the idea that there exists a racial hierarchy.

Yet although these debates agitated scientific circles, they attracted little attention in the colonies. When colonials discussed racial mixing, they rarely referred to anthropological concepts and never cited anthropologists.[14] Evidence that the concerns of Parisian scholars aroused little interest in the colonies can be seen in the low response rate to a "questionnaire on the *métis*" sent out by the Paris Anthropology Society in 1908, even though it was transmitted through the colonial administration.[15] For anthropologists in France, the colonies served mainly as a laboratory, providing a vast reservoir of samples for the study of interbreeding, just like other historical examples of conquests and migratory movements. For the most part, these scholars had little interest in what was distinctive about the history, politics, or social aspects of racial mixing in the French Empire.

Yet colonials were well aware of the phenomenon. Instead of looking at it in physiological terms, however, they were mainly interested in its implications for colonial rule. This was already the case by the middle of the nineteenth century, after Africa had become a focal point of colonization. Colonial administrators like Louis Faidherbe looked to generalized racial mixing as a way of "regenerating" the African races.[16]

Things changed further toward the end of the century: the proximity of the colonizers to the natives lost favor, and the segregation of populations became a stronger norm. Racial mixing ceased to be a desired goal and began to be presented as an "agonizing problem," which was soon subdivided into three subproblems: "human," "social," and "political." In the 1890s, interested actors in the colonies began to describe the situation of mixed-race children, usually abandoned by their European fathers, as an *injustice*. Their status was said to be that of "outcasts"[17] or "pariahs,"[18] caught between colonizers and colonized. Their discontent was perceived as a threat to the colonial order.

In short, the phenomenon of *métissage* acquired a new face: it became the "*métis* question," which, as we shall see, shared many features with the "social question"—the political and moral threat posed by the rise of an industrial working class—that was such a central feature of nineteenth-century culture. The new formula was associated with what is called the "second colonial empire," which historians traditionally date from 1830. Colonial rule was now legitimized by the assertion of a hierarchical difference between colonizers and colonized, the reproduction of which the colonial authorities were constantly at pains to assure.[19] By blurring this crucial dividing line, the existence of the *métis* posed a problem of *classification* and threatened the stability of the most basic categories of the colonial social order. That is why the *métis* question would continue to be raised in more or less the same terms from the end of the nineteenth century to the eve of decolonization. Observers considered it "undoubtedly a human and charitable question, as well as a social question, a question of reason, and a question of politics. Throwing into the colonial mix an individual of mixed race, out of step with both colonizers and colonized, raises serious issues that justified the intervention of the authorities."[20] Over the next decades, actors from both within and without the colonial state intervened continually to resolve these "issues."

Hybrids and Bastards

The new view of racial mixing did not apply uniformly to all offspring of colonial sexual encounters. The *métis* question referred only to hybrids *who were also "bastards"*—unrecognized by their European fathers. The relatively few children who were born from the legitimate union of a colonial male and a native female or, still more rarely, of a European female and a native male, were not a problem. Indeed, they were rarely referred to as *métis* at all. Thus, in a discussion of the *métis* question, the president of the Society for the Assistance of Abandoned Franco-Indochinese Children declared that he was "not speaking here of the children of regular Franco-indigenous unions whose families are taking care of them nor of illegitimate children whose fathers have acknowledged them and not abandoned them."[21] These "unproblematic" *métis* were not very visible in colonial society and have left few traces in the archives.

Still, the condition of the *métis* was not defined solely by their status as illegitimate children: they bore both physical and social stigma and could not hide from "the presumption of bastardy that marked their features."[22] An article published in a popular Indochinese newspaper in the 1920s stated:

> In the home country, legal steps have been taken to counter outdated prejudices and cruel hypocrisy with effective measures to protect illegitimate children—a phrase which not so very long ago was capable of provoking an outcry in certain segments of society. In the colonies, the question is more complex: the illegitimate child, generally born out of wedlock to a native woman and a European father, is also of mixed blood (*métis*). In the battle of life, there is nothing to distinguish the illegitimate child in France from others around him, or later from other men. His status is merely a matter of how his

birth is recorded. In the case of the *métis*, however, the mixing of two races is indelibly inscribed in his features, and diverse emotions will at various times contend within his bosom.[23]

Situated at this intersection of illegitimacy and hybridity, the condition of the *métis* placed the racial question squarely in the realm of law.

[handwritten marginal note: racial question was result a ... legal]

The Law Takes Up a Social Question

In the twentieth century, the ideal type of colonial *métis* combined *illegitimate* birth with *nonrecognition* and *abandonment* by a European father. Although statistical evidence is lacking, most *métis* probably met these criteria. The legal terms used to express these conditions were important. The French Code civil was quite precise about the kinship status of persons. The key distinctions were based on the marital status of the parents (which determined whether the child was *legitimate* or *illegitimate*) and, in the case of illegitimate children, whether or not the child was officially recognized by his or her father at the office of identity records (*bureau d'état civil*). *Abandonment* was also a term defined by law, especially after major legislation concerning child assistance was passed in France on June 27, 1904.

The *métis* problem thus involved children who stood outside the institution of the family as defined by law. This immediately raised a second issue. French law followed the tradition of *patrem liberi sequuntur* ("When the parents are married, the condition of the child is that of the father") to determine the child's legal status and nationality. A legitimate child inherited the father's legal status, but illegitimate and unrecognized *métis* acquired the native status of their mother and were therefore not French citizens. They stood outside both the family and the nation, and it was this double alienation that made the *métis* question so acute. This point was noted by one of the most astute colonial observers, who wrote several books on the subject following a lengthy stay in Indochina at the turn of the twentieth century.

[handwritten marginal note: inheriting legal status]

> When, for example, a Frenchman marries an Annamite women under French law, his wife becomes French, his children are French, and, in general, all is for the best in the best of all possible Protectorates. What is at stake is simply a question of personal behavior and family happiness, which concerns only the two people involved. There is no "*métis* question" because the children of a natural-born Frenchman and a naturalized Frenchwoman are French in law and in fact, and in real life no one has any right to discriminate in any way between them and pure-blooded French offspring. . . . But marriages that count

as legitimate in the eyes of French law are rare. By contrast, what are quite common are unsanctioned temporary unions with yellow-skinned women: our concern is with these relationships and their consequences. . . . If children are born to these couples, of which nothing noble or enduring remains, it is a great misfortune both for them and for the state.[24]

The *métis* question arose where family affairs intersected with affairs of state because the existence of children of mixed race was a sign of moral disorder and a threat to the distinction between "French" and "native." If these children posed such a problem for colonials, it was because their existence blurred the relations among physical appearance, legal status, and position relative to the "great divide" in colonial society. Their condition was marked by a mismatch between "law" and "fact," between legal status and an identity perceived as more "real" based on their appearance and on the "milieu" in which the child lived. The worst case was that of the unrecognized *métis* who was raised by his father for several years before being abandoned. The child's "indigenous" legal status was then in complete contradiction with the effects of early socialization, which, as one administrator wrote in Hanoi in 1912, shaped the child's deepest instincts:

If the mixed-race child was abandoned very young and could ignore its origins, and if its features were not a constant reminder thereof, then it could be raised in the same way as the abandoned child discussed above. In time it could become a good Annamite worker or farmer. But inevitably the child will learn that it is of mixed race. Others will make sure of this. Tendencies, passions, and tastes due to atavism will be awakened in this child and not shared by its Annamite comrades. The case that most seriously transgresses and overwhelms the rules laid down by the Code civil is the common case of the *métis* who knew his father, lived in his home, and was raised by him for several years, only to be suddenly abandoned owing to a death, a marriage, or a definitive return to France. No matter what one does, this child will be truly "of mixed race." The Code may well call him Annamite, but he will nevertheless distinguish himself from the Annamites and seek closer ties with the French society to which his father belonged—a father whom in many cases he will have every right to condemn and curse. And if this society does not lend him a helping hand, rancor and hatred will inevitably grow in him.[25]

In order to avoid what they saw as the disastrous consequences of the *métis* problem, colonials would seek constantly to align status and identity, law and fact.

Paternity and Citizenship

In practice, European men created *métis* by not recognizing the offspring of their relations with native women. Most observers remained silent about the maternal filiation, even though native mothers in the vast majority of cases did not abandon their children voluntarily. We find the same gender asymmetry in the attention focused on the *métis*: colonial actors were far more interested in what happened to boys than to girls. The *métis* problem was therefore a predominantly male affair, which is hardly surprising since it was posed in terms of citizenship.[26] If the problem was seen as troubling, it was because it signaled a flaw in the reproduction of the "community of citizens"[27] in the colonies, as one philanthropist suggested:

> I will say nothing about children of mixed race who are raised entirely and appropriately by a French father in a French setting with French upbringing and education. They are whatever upbringing and education make of them. For them, there is no *métis* problem. They are French, and I hasten to add that their childhood is for the most part every bit as good as that of a one-hundred-percent French child raised in the colony. . . . [Here he mentions a number of *métis* who occupy high-status positions in Indochina: plantation manager, bureaucratic department head, physician.] But if these children, despite being of mixed parentage, owe their enviable situation to their own effort and intelligence, they also owe it, beyond a shadow of a doubt, to their having experienced from birth the vigilant and severe authority of a father or guardian who watched over them.[28]

Consistently, discussions of the *métis* question suggested that "being French" was something that one learned first of all at home, under the authority of a father, in early childhood. We are thus a long way from our current representations of the formation of citizens at the time, which we tend to associate with motherhood and school education.

Lexical Issues

Until the 1930s, the word *métis* was used extensively in both the colonies and France to refer to abandoned children born of the colonial encounter. We find it in philanthropic discourse, in the press, and in the records of the bureaucracy. The word was in use wherever "the social problem of racial mixing" arose, including Africa, where the word *mulatto* was also used, but less frequently.

The word, which bore the double stigma of hybridity and illegitimacy, quickly acquired pejorative connotations, even among the philanthropists who involuntarily contributed most to its negative content. The Society for the Assistance of Abandoned *Métis* Children, founded in Saigon in 1894, affirmed as early as 1903 that "the word *métis*, which figures in the name of this society, spoke of a social stigma that did not need to be shouted from the rooftops" and decided in 1906 to revise its statutes and "erase from its title anything that might serve as a pretext for the humiliation of its wards."[29] It was at this point that it adopted the more neutral name "Society for the Protection of Childhood in Cochin China." In Tonkin, philanthropists were thinking of the stigma attached to the word when they decided in 1925 to transform the name of their group from "Society for the Protection of Abandoned *Métis* Children" to "Society for the Assistance of Abandoned Franco-Indochinese Children."[30] In the 1930s, the colonial bureaucracy adopted the term *Franco-Indochinese* to "avoid ruffling certain sensitivities."[31]

In Asia, the expression "French of Indochina" came into use as a synonym for "Franco-Indochinese *métis*."[32] It suggested a process of *creolization* and that France would remain a permanent presence in the tropics as a result of racial mixing. Philanthropists and representatives of the *métis* preferred this term to *Eurasian*, which was also common in the 1930s and which later, under Vichy, made its way into bureaucratic language before entering the general vocabulary in the 1940s and 1950s. Suitably modified, this construction also caught on in Africa: a "Union of Eurafricans of French West Africa" was created in Dakar in 1949.[33] The terminology reflected a racialized vision of the population, as a 1939 note from the chief of statistics for the general government of Indochina suggests:

> The term *métis* has several meanings in French Indochina. It is sometimes restricted to the first generation of children born to a European or assimilated father originally from outside Indochina and to a native mother, or vice versa. It is sometimes extended to all subsequent generations of mixed blood, resulting from the marriage of a *métis* in the first sense to a European or native. The term *Eurasian* has a narrower meaning, because among the *métis* some were the children of fathers native to the old colonies, such as French India, the Antilles, Réunion, Senegal, etc. (and therefore in many cases European in status only and not in origin), or else of Asian fathers assimilated to Europeans (Japanese, Filipino, etc.).[34]

In other words, when the colonial administration had to deal with the *métis* question, it tended to distinguish among the French according to their origin, thereby posing a challenge to the unified status of citizen.

Geography of the *Métis* Question

The "distressing problem" of racial mixing did not arise in all the colonies with the same acuity—far from it. It was in Indochina that the issue developed earliest, mobilized the most energy, and shaped subsequent practice elsewhere. It attracted much less attention in the two African federations, French West Africa and French Equatorial Africa, as well as in Madagascar and New Caledonia, and was not discussed in the "old colonies" (Guadeloupe, Martinique, Guiana, and Réunion) or in North Africa at all.

Since children of mixed parentage were born in all these places, in some cases in large numbers, this geographical differentiation tells us something about the social conditions that had to be met for a *métis* question to arise.

Acknowledging this diversity also helps us to avoid the culturalist type of explanation that was so common in the colonial period. This was based on the idea that there was "a" French colonial style and a French "attitude" toward the *métis* grounded in a Latin "assimilationism," immune from racism. This claim was then used to distinguish France from its rival imperial powers, especially the British, who were said to be resistant to racial mixing. In fact, however, the variety of forms that the *métis* question assumed in different parts of the empire was a function of the nature of social relations in each colony and of the representations and practices of the natives themselves, who were never passive in dealing with the phenomenon of racial mixing.

Because it was not possible in this work to investigate all the variations of the *métis* problem in all the territories involved, what follows are a few hypotheses that may help to explain the observed differences among the colonies.

The "Old Colonies"

The question of racial mixing never arose as a "social and political problem" in the old colonies. The main reason for this was that former slaves were granted French citizenship in 1848. In the absence of an opposition between "citizen" and "subject," illegitimacy was not compounded by confinement within native status. More generally, universal citizenship transformed the significance of race in the old colonies: while race continued to matter tremendously, formal equality delegitimized and silenced the voices that insisted on the persistence of racial inequalities. As Myriam Cottias noted, citizenship was "bartered" against the affirmation of unity and harmony and the denial of race.[35] In particular, equality led to the erasure of the marks of color in administrative practices. Even before 1848, the law of 1833, which granted civil and civic equality to "free men of color," eliminated all signs of origin in vital statistics, census data, and other official records. In 1844, in response to a request from the Ministry of the Navy for a list of voters and eligible individuals in the colony specifying the number of whites and colored, the governor of Guadeloupe responded that "it is difficult for us to satisfy requests of this kind." He noted that "owing to frequently reiterated and religiously observed ministerial orders, all traces of the distinction that once existed between the white and colored classes are daily disappearing" and suggested that to comply with the request "would be to risk provoking the anxious susceptibilities of a class that is apt, at the slightest provocation, to doubt the sincerity of the new legislation and to arouse suspicions whose consequences could well prove dangerous."[36]

After 1848, officials in their daily work engaged in a veritable censorship of signs of race. To be sure, this cleansing of the records did not prevent frequent public as well as private references to color and race in the old colonies.[37] The hybrid and the bastard retained their prominence in local culture. But political equality meant that the two conditions were not combined in a way that would make them a central issue for the colonial powers. The geography of the *métis* question was above all a matter of politics and law.

The Indochinese Laboratory

It was in Indochina that the *métis* question was formulated earliest and most forcefully. It was also in Indochina that the first solutions were developed—social as well as legal solutions that were subsequently exported to the rest of the French Empire. In this respect, Indochina served as a veritable laboratory for the *métis* problem. Although Cochin China did not become a colony until 1862,[38] an orphanage for abandoned girls of mixed race was created as early as 1874, and in 1875 this was followed by a home for "native and mixed-race girls who had been abused and abandoned."[39] The question would continue to mobilize prominent colonials, administrators, and jurists throughout the colonial period. Collectively, they would define the terms of the problem and propose solutions in the form of numerous studies and projects. Their comprehensive efforts would ultimately affect the fate of tens of thousands of individuals.

Yet the contours of the *métis* problem were never fixed once and for all. In particular, the nature of the issue would be affected by modern challenges to the colonial order, which developed quite early in Indochina. For the colonial authorities, the problem was to find a way to secure the allegiance of the ever-growing mixed-race population. Accordingly, efforts to resolve the *métis* question picked up steam throughout the period, becoming a major public concern by the 1920s and still more in the 1930s.

The first attempt to resolve the problem by legal means was led in 1926 by Governor-General Alexandre Varenne, an important figure in the SFIO (the French Section of the Workers' International). Varenne's initiative should be seen against the background of other (limited) reforms that he sponsored and especially of protests by urban Vietnamese youth in the spring of 1926, which spread in the years that followed. Later, the *métis* question would reemerge as a major issue in the decolonization of Indochina—their fate an issue in the negotiations leading up to the Geneva accords. The French-Vietnamese nationality agreement of 1955 devoted considerable space to the issue, and even before the end of hostilities, thousands of mixed-race children were taken from their Vietnamese mothers and sent to France (see chapter 9).

If Indochina served as a laboratory for the *métis* question, it was because the relative number of mixed-raced children born there was larger than elsewhere. This overrepresentation was due to factors that one might characterize as "objective" but for fears of succumbing to the logic of "biological necessity" adopted by many contemporary observers. Because parts of the country were organized as zones of military occupation, the European population of Indochina was disproportionately young and male.

This demographic characteristic explains the prevalence of the *métis* question only when combined with specific features of colonial rule in Indochina. What was chiefly at stake was the organization of sexual encounters: in contrast to other parts of the empire, in Indochina the civil and military authorities did not seek to regulate prostitution. Instead, they tolerated the development of concubinage, an institution already firmly established in the social organization of the region. The nature of the colonial settlement in Indochina also encouraged an abundance of children of mixed race (the adjectives *unrecognized* and *abandoned* should be understood). Relatively few civilian or military officials settled permanently in the colony. Abandonment of women and children was most common when the officials were transferred to another colony or sent back home, often leaving their

Indochinese families with a small sum of money and entrusting them in some cases to a colleague or successor, who would take over the home as well as the concubine and offspring of the departing father.

Last but not least, the attitude of Vietnamese society toward these children was an important reason for the intensity of the *métis* question in the colony: in a strictly patrilineal society, it was hard for the child of an unknown foreign father to find his or her place. The mothers were cast out of their villages and often condemned to "careers" as concubines, passed from one European male to another. Colonials outdid one another in pointing out—and no doubt exaggerating—native hostility toward mixed-race children and called attention to the pejorative names that were applied to them, such as "chickenhead-duck's ass."[40] To outside observers, these children looked like "pariahs" in both colonial and native society. They lived in a no-man's-land and were left "stranded," to use a common term from the period.

The conditions required for the *métis* question—the nature of colonial social relations and the way in which native society participated in its construction—emerge even more clearly when the situation in Indochina is compared with that in other colonies.

The Algerian Silence

There was no *métis* question in Algeria. The term never arose except in a few enclaves in the south after the turn of the twentieth century. The archives of public assistance and private charities, which are so loquacious about the issue in Indochina, never mention it in Algeria except for rare exceptions, to which I will return later. Literature is also virtually mute on the subject: Émile Zola, though not generally stingy with racial observations, discreetly limits himself to commenting on the "black eyes" and "African blood" of Thérèse Raquin, who was born in Oran to a Frenchman from Vernon and a native beauty.[41]

This silence is surprising: the dividing line between "subject" and "citizen," which we have seen was a necessary condition for the emergence of "the question," existed in Algeria. One might even say that it was invented there and more systematically employed than in any other colony (see chapter 4).

Observers of the colonial situation in Algeria were, moreover, intensely interested in the question of racial mixing. Geographers and demographers offered lengthy descriptions of "the fusion of the races" through "mixed marriages," in terms that varied little from the 1880s to the 1940s. But they applied this language solely to marriages between Frenchmen and women from other Mediterranean countries (primarily Spain, Italy, and Malta), who constituted what they called the "neo-French" people.[42] For the most part, they ignored the possibility of miscegenation with the local inhabitants, as if it were inconceivable in the Algerian context. They nevertheless drew on tropes of racial science in their reflections—tropes that were elsewhere applied to colonial *métissage*. For instance, "mixed marriages" were discussed in terms of "acclimatization," which was seen as essential for the establishment of durable French colonies overseas: "On these Mediterranean shores, a new people, better adapted to the climate, is coming into being through the mixing of the three great Latin races."[43] The monstrous figure of the *métis* was stood on its head: the "Algerian" was instead a harmonious mixture—harmonious because composed of "closely related races"—that was often compared to the product of the American melting pot:

> The better acclimated race confers its resistance and physical vigor on the less acclimated one. It has been said that the French find it difficult to tolerate the African climate, with its debilitating warmth, its hot siroccos, and burning African sun; that families find it difficult to raise their children there; and that individuals grow anemic. By contrast, it has also been said that foreigners such as Spaniards, Italians, and Maltese from countries situated at the same latitude as North Africa prosper in Algeria as in their home countries, and that they are more prolific there and suffer fewer deaths. If these assertions are correct, how can one not hope for mixing that would give our compatriots the qualities they need to ensure the destiny of France in Africa? . . . One race would gain in physical strength and fecundity, while the other would benefit from the moral prestige attached to the French name. . . . As a product of mostly Latin elements, the Algerian people would combine the clarity, common sense, and precision of the French spirit with Spanish tenacity and Italian ardor. It would have the spirit of initiative, the taste for novelty, and the love of risk. It would always look ahead. It would feel the vigor of youth and the physical vitality that the crossing of the Latin races will have helped to foster.[44]

Yet Algeria witnessed not only mixed European marriages but also contacts between colonials and natives, from which children were born. If these were less visible than in Indochina, the primary reason was that sexual encounters between native women and Frenchmen were less common. Nevertheless, the absence of statistics compels us to remain very cautious about drawing any conclusions.

Although Algeria always exhibited an imbalance between the sexes, the ratios there cannot be compared with those in Indochina. Unlike Indochina, Algeria was a settlers' colony, with large numbers of colonial families. The importance of this factor is confirmed by the fact that the *métis* question did arise in a limited way in the south of the country, in the military regions where the vast majority of the colonial population was male.

The way in which female sexuality was dealt with in the Maghreb is another possible explanation for why sexual relations between colonizers and colonized were less frequent. Succinctly put, it is often argued that Algerian women had less independence than their Indochinese counterparts. This idea runs through many histories of colonial Algeria and can already be found in the writings of colonial administrators: "Hence the number of mixed marriages is always directly proportional to the freedom and facility permitted to native women in each colony. In Muslim countries, where the women are sequestered, the two races can live side-by-side indefinitely, without appreciable interbreeding. By contrast, in Sudan, Indochina, and Madagascar especially, mixing will proceed rapidly."[45]

The most lucid observers offer similar judgments. For instance, Jacques Berque maintains that in Algeria there "was no intermarriage; there were not even any bastards. Physical exclusiveness was maintained almost absolutely, despite a century of colonization," because "the colonial subject" saw "in his womankind his last hope of autonomy and hence of survival."[46] Yet the same Berque also noted certain fissures in the wall of separation between the two communities: besides prostitution, whether of the "traditional" or colonial type, there were also relations among the urban lower classes.[47]

As early as 1901, Edmound Doutté, an orientalist scholar serving as a government official in Algeria, observed that "irregular unions between indigenous women and Europeans are far more common in the working class than many people imagine."[48] Clearly, sexual relations did cross the colonial divide, and children were born as a result.[49] It is worth noting, however, that no trace of them survives in the archives or the work of historians.[50] In Algeria, *métis* remained invisible. One hypothesis is that these children were integrated into some kind of family structure: although Islamic law does not recognize adoptions, they were in fact commonplace. Anecdotal evidence from colonial sources, which should be handled with caution, suggests that some of these children were adopted by Algerian families. For instance, in the 1950s, Dr. Henri Marchand reported the following conversation:

A very young Muslim woman had indeed avoided the town hall. She was in a relationship with a Frenchman as young as she and without an established situation.

"But the child? If one arrives, how would you raise it?" I asked.

"I would give it to my mother."

"But what would she say?"

"Nothing."

The problem would have been solved efficiently as well as simply. Imagine the same affair in France. . . . And all of this is obviously discussed in French circles, where many look on these types of affairs with envy.[51]

A second hypothesis furthers our understanding of the social invisibility of the *métis* in Algeria: there, race was not the principal criterion of differentiation.[52] Physical anthropologists found fewer subjects to study, no doubt because they saw the country as inhabited by "white races."[53] Their main concern was to explore what differentiated "Arabs" from "Kabyles."[54] Colonial opinion does not seem to have focused on racial difference either, according to a contemporary historian who himself uses highly racialized language: "The resemblance of these 'neo-Latin' French to Maghrebins who adopt the dress and appearance of *pieds-noirs* is striking. . . . Only these people themselves are capable of detecting at once who is Maghrebin on account of their swarthier complexion, curlier hair, and chest thrust forward less confidently than among the *pieds-noirs*, who thereby express their assurance of belonging to the master race."[55]

In this context, the invisible *métis*, like the "tragic mulatto" one finds in American novels around the turn of the twentieth century, could "pass" as white:

As for the mixture of Berber and French blood, the product was usually blond or brunette with blue eyes, in some cases so close to the French type that it would be difficult even for the most perceptive to tell the difference. Many people of mixed French and Kabyle blood who take French first names, speak perfectly correct French, and in some cases convert to Catholicism look for work as servants in the big cities or else seek their fortunes there. Sometimes only their identity papers reveal that they are not native to the banks of the Loire or Seine.[56]

Further proof that the lower intensity of the racial question explains the absence of a *métis* problem in Algeria can be seen in the fact that the "problem" did occur in southern parts of Algeria. There, a portion of the population was classified as "Negro" by observers who, throughout the colonial period, used this word to refer to both descendants of former African slaves, who could be found throughout the colony, and the native populations of the Sahara.

In the Algerian south, a *métis* question did arise in terms quite close to those found in other territories of the empire. Indeed, the first response was to establish charitable institutions to take charge of raising children born to unknown fathers and native mothers. In 1921, the White Fathers founded an orphanage for boys of mixed race at El Goléa. In 1923, the White Sisters created a parallel institution for "native orphans and girls born to unions between European males and women of the country."[57] They later established a workshop for girls and young women. Assistance did not end with childhood: these religious orders encouraged men and women of mixed blood to marry each other and tried to persuade the couples thus formed to remain in El Goléa. In 1955, there were only 193 Europeans at this outpost, compared with 366 *métis*. Thirty-six families were responsible for raising 169 children.[58] As in other territories, the solution to the *métis* problem also involved the law. The *métis* of El Goléa, who had long been classified as "indigenous," were granted full citizenship in 1926 by Governor Maurice Viollette, who had to circumvent provisions of the Code civil in order to do so.[59]

Since these children were raised as Christians by the White Fathers, however, their fate was inextricably intertwined with the history of several thousand Algerian converts.[60] And since in Algeria religion was a more prevalent criterion of differentiation than race, it was the convert rather than the *métis* who straddled the divide between colonizers and colonized.

If the *métis* was invisible, "mixed marriage" between indigenous men and Frenchwomen was nonetheless of great concern to the colonizers. Although their number remained small throughout the nineteenth century, mixed marriages increased sharply after World War I, both in France and in Algeria.[61] Contemporaries attributed this phenomenon to male immigration to France during and after the war, as a result of which indigenous males became "accustomed" to "European life"[62] and to relationships, whether legitimate or not, with Frenchwomen. Given the nationality laws in force until 1927, a Frenchwoman who married an indigenous male should have assumed her husband's status, and the children should have done the same. But this principle was superseded by two others, which eventually took precedence in Algerian legal practice: a European could never become "native" from a legal point of view, and French law was the common law and took

precedence over native law in case of conflict (see chapter 4). At the turn of
the twentieth century, doctrine and case law[63] both held that the child of
a Frenchwoman and an indigenous father should enjoy full citizenship. In
1922, at the request of the general government, the attorney general of
Algeria drafted a bill to define the status of individuals from families of
mixed marriages, the number of which was growing rapidly.

> It is *a priori* repugnant to our French way of thinking that this woman and
> these children can be assigned the status of Muslims. Despite the generally
> accepted principle that children inherit the status of their father, it is not easy
> to accept the idea that children raised by a French mother should be assigned
> the status of indigenous Muslims. It is difficult to accept that they should be
> subject to the right of *djebr*,[64] or forced matrimony; or that they may later
> be authorized to practice polygamy and repudiation; or that they should be
> subject to judgment by special repressive courts and the Native Code.[65] All of
> these are consequences that shock our most honorable feelings, all the more
> so in view of the fact that many of these native husbands, after marrying in
> France, abruptly abandon wives and children to return to their native tribes,
> lured home by nostalgia for the sun and for Muslim ways.[66]

The bill was passed by the Chamber of Deputies in 1928 but never voted
on by the Senate.

Madagascar, Africa, and New Caledonia

Algeria and Indochina therefore represent the two extremes with respect to
the status of the *métis* question. Between these two paradigmatic cases, other
colonies had debates that were in some respects similar to those that took
place in Indochina, and many experimented with similar practices, particularly in the realm of law. These included Madagascar, New Caledonia, and
sub-Saharan Africa (French West Africa and French Equatorial Africa—here-
after, FWA and FEA, respectively—as well as Togo and Cameroon, which
became French mandates after World War I). The diversity of colonial situations and the variety of attitudes of the local populations toward racial
mixing was reflected in variations in the formulation and handling of the
métis question.

In this respect, Madagascar was very much like Indochina: a minority of
settlers formed a stable group among the colonizers early on, but there was
a good deal of turnover in the French population, and the military was over-
represented. Many soldiers openly entered into relations with the natives.

Children were born. As in Indochina, most of them went unrecognized and were ultimately abandoned by their fathers, but many of them were taken in by the families of their mothers. In 1900, a Society for the Assistance and Protection of Mixed-Race Children was created in Antananarivo. At first, it distributed funds to the mothers and children under the supervision of the women who headed the group.[67] With the help of government subsidies, the society built a school in 1905 and later an orphanage, which apparently never served more than a hundred children.[68] Other organizations also concerned themselves with the fate of these children of mixed blood, most notably the local section of the League for the Rights of Man and the Citizen.

In FWA and FEA, children of mixed blood were born with some frequency—the vast majority of them illegitimate, unrecognized, and abandoned by their fathers. Many were integrated without difficulty into local society. To a greater extent than elsewhere, officials insisted that these children must remain part of the native population, of which they were destined to become the elite.[69] Nevertheless, numerous philanthropic enterprises, at first religious but later secular as well, emerged for the exclusive purpose of assisting this group. In FWA, the first orphanage was created in 1904.[70]

In the half century that followed the French seizure of New Caledonia in 1853, many children were born of relations between Frenchmen and native women, particularly in the bush.[71] Yet the *métis* question did not emerge as a "human, social, and political" problem of the same order.[72] Although such children were often ostracized by lower-class white colonists, who, being "isolated in a strange and foreign country," sought to "protect their status as members of the 'civilized world' at any price,"[73] the broader practice, observers agreed, was for children of mixed blood to be taken in by families of both colonizers and colonized.[74] In 1948, when the central government ordered the governors of the various territories to report on charitable and other organizations whose purpose was "to provide children of mixed blood with the material and moral assistance that their abandonment often requires," the chief administrator for New Caledonia justified the absence of any specific institution there on the grounds that "in New Caledonia the fate of the *métis* is decided quite naturally on the basis of the environment in which they grow up. . . . Because they are dispersed in many different settings in which they are perfectly assimilated, it is impossible to count them both for practical reasons and out of respect for privacy."[75]

The primary reason why there was no *métis* question in New Caledonia was that both colonizers and colonized were willing to care for children of mixed blood. In Caledonian societies, foster parentage and adoption were common: for example, the fathers of unwed mothers could adopt their grandchildren.[76] These practices were no doubt encouraged by the serious demographic crisis that the island faced after the conquest. Meanwhile, colonists who had settled permanently may have included women and children in their strategies for passing on their patrimony.[77] In this respect, New Caledonia resembled Algeria. Both were settler colonies, in which inheritance of the land played a central role in the organization of family life. Both colonizers and colonized had good reasons to keep the children born of their encounters.

One can also argue that there was no *métis* question in New Caledonia because there was no common stage on which it could have played out. In most respects, the populations were kept rigorously apart,[78] above all through the system of reservations established for the Kanaks. Interactions were limited, as were social situations in which the woes of mixed-race children would have been visible to both colonizers and colonized simultaneously. As we will see, the "sentiment of horror" produced by such sights was at the heart of the *métis* question.

In the Metropole

The overseas territories were not the only theater in which the drama of the *métis* was visible. After World War I, it also played in the metropole, but there the roles were reversed. During the war and the years that followed, colonial workers, many of them from Indochina, formed relationships with Frenchwomen, usually workers in the same factories.[79] In so doing, they defied the intense surveillance to which they were subjected in the workplace and in the barracks to which they were confined. These unions alarmed government officials, especially when they led to plans for marriage. The minister of justice therefore issued a confidential directive in February 1917, asking mayors to do whatever they could to thwart such plans. The mayors took it upon themselves to warn "compatriots too imprudent or credulous in the face of dangers they do not suspect," which include the practice of polygamy among the colonials as well as their standard of living, "since the wages paid to natives [were] insufficient to allow a European woman to live decently."

Beyond the protection of these "special interests," however, the emphasis was placed on the "political point of view," because in the opinion of the ministry, such unions "can only damage our prestige in indigenous milieus."[80] Above all, the administration in Indochina feared that these couples would return to the colonies. The governor wrote to the ministry: "It will not have escaped your notice that there is an issue of French honor and national influence at stake."[81] Indeed, these couples embodied an intolerable inversion of the relation of colonial domination, because they placed a Frenchwoman "in a position of dependence on one of our protégés."

The moral paternalism toward the lower classes, which the authorities practiced throughout the nineteenth century in their "policing of families,"[82] was thus forgotten. To discourage marriages, colonial officials on leave in France were sent to visit the families involved. They were told to explain to the young woman and her parents the difficulties of living overseas. Colonial officials also conducted investigations in the colonies to try to prove that the indigenous member of the couple was already married. In some cases, they sent the young woman photos of her future in-laws posed in rags in front of a rudimentary hut.[83] Both the central and local bureaucracies would do everything in their power to prevent "the downfall of women and children."[84] When all attempts at persuasion failed, bureaucrats were resourceful in creating obstacles to issuing the needed permits, or they would deny free passage to the new family and search vessels for the presence of children. These practices led many young working-class women to apply directly to the Ministry of Justice or of the Colonies for authorization to marry.

The bureaucracy worried even more about the status of children. Here, too, the situation was the reverse of that which prevailed in the colonies. In order to maintain the French citizenship of the children, officials sought to dissuade fathers from recognizing their offspring. By the end of the nineteenth century, colonial case law held that the child of a Frenchwoman and an indigenous male was still a French citizen, but these decisions were not known in France. In the absence of legislation, bureaucrats in France drew an analogy with the principle of the law of nationality, according to which, in case of simultaneous recognition by both parents, the child was assigned the nationality of the father; otherwise, the child was assigned the nationality of the first parent to recognize it.

> For the child of mixed blood born in France to a French woman and an indigenous father . . . the mere fact of recognition by the presumptive father would make the child's fate more precarious. It would lose the French citizenship so prized by our protégés. It would retain the bitterness that is found in *métis* not recognized by their French fathers. And, if it remained in France, its Annamite name would perpetuate the memory of the mother's fleeting liaison with an indigenous male. If, moreover, the mother failed to recognize the child, it could be separated from her at an age when maternal care is essential, and it would be introduced into an Annamite family, in contact with the indigenous

wife, the concubines, and the father's other children, who would treat it as an intruder and in many cases subject it to abuse.[85]

In order to avoid unprecedented family troubles of this sort, public officials therefore sought to influence attitudes toward kinship, but they also attempted to change the law. In 1917, the appellate courts of Hanoi and Saigon were convoked to propose changes to the law in force in the colonies in regard to marriage (creating new grounds for prosecuting natives for bigamy), nationality (so that women could retain their nationality in case of union with an indigenous male), and filiation (in order to allow French mothers to exercise paternal authority). With the end of hostilities, the matter was dropped. Guest worker programs were ended, and the authorities were eager to send home colonial workers who had become a little too well integrated into French society.

An Imperial Problem

Despite this uneven geography, the *métis* question was seen as an inevitable product of the colonial situation itself and therefore as an imperial problem. In the late 1920s, Georges Hardy, director of the École coloniale, in a book that explained the outlines of French policy to the general public,[86] presented the *métis* question as one of the "great colonial problems," along with "pacification," "education," "public health," the "property regime," and the "fate of woman." This observation figured in two broad processes of popularization of the *métis* question: the diffusion of debates within the empire and the "politics of comparison" in which the European colonial powers were engaged.[87]

Discussions of the *métis* question initially circulated through scholarly networks in which many civil and military administrators participated.[88] Some of these administrators married native women and had children (who, because they were raised in stable families, were not *métis* in the strict sense of the word). One such official was Lieutenant Colonel Auguste Bonifacy, a correspondent of the Anthropological Society, member of the Society for the Protection of Abandoned Children of Mixed Blood in Hanoi, and the author of a long report on Franco-Tonkinois *métis* that was published in 1911 in the *Bulletins et mémoires de la Société d'anthropologie de Paris*.[89] This text would become a classic study of the *métis* question and was often cited in both scholarly work and administrative literature on Indochina.[90] The article embodied all the tenets of physical anthropology. Although it dealt with the still-burning question of fertility and with physical characteristics such as "facial features" and "resistance to disease," it also treated "intellectual and moral" characteristics. It inventoried "aptitude for study," "amour-propre and vanity," "frankness and sense of honor," "tendency to steal," "sexual morality," and so on. Above all, it ventured into the realm of politics, remarking on the dangers of racial mixing and calling for help in dealing with them:

> It would be impossible to overstate the importance of this question. It is un-just and inhuman to leave men and women with our blood in their veins to fend for themselves. It is politically unwise to allow an anti-French party to be created and to provoke the contempt of Annamites who blame us for abandoning those whom they consider to be our sons. . . . *I beg you to have pity* on these unfortunate children, who are helpless and have little choice but to lead lives of crime and dishonor. I beg you to use the substantial influence that you derive from your scientific work to help dispel the prejudices against them and to facilitate their entry into the extended French family in the name of justice, logic, and political self-interest.[91]

This politics of pity, though quite alien to the technical tone of the jour- nal, rapidly bore fruit. The society alerted the minister of colonies, who responded by sending a memorandum concerning the abandonment of illegitimate children to the senior official in every colony. Echoing the demands of the philanthropists, the minister called upon administrators to "remind the civilian and military officials under them of the duty im-posed on them by the strictest humanitarian principles." He added that "from a political point of view, it is clearly in our interest to avoid any measure or irritation that might alienate the mixed-race population. The abandonment of illegitimate children is one possible cause of misunder-standing among the various elements of the population, in addition to which it is likely to undermine the moral foundations on which our civili-zation claims to rest."[92] The network of anthropologists was paralleled by a network of administrators: a channel of communication was thus created, whereby the *métis* question found its way from Indochina to the metropole and from there to the rest of the empire. At the central level, the agents of this network separated the "social problem" from its local conditions of possibility and then imposed the question on territories where it was still marginal.

In addition to scholarly and administrative networks, the *métis* question mobilized the vast, nebulous network of social reformers.[93] Just after the turn of the twentieth century, the League for the Rights of Man intervened in the matter, having been alerted by certain of its colonial sections, which were themselves often members of the societies for the protection of children of mixed blood. Last but not least, elements of what was then called the "colonial party," which brought together people with a political and/or economic interest in colonization, also became involved. For instance, the French Colonial Union, the most powerful group of this sort, became interested in the "social question" of the *métis* in 1911.[94] In 1928, it officially petitioned the ministry to resolve the issue of the legal status of children of mixed blood.[95]

Additional channels of transmission included the press and the colonial novel, a genre that was in vogue in the period between the two world wars. Albert Londres, who in 1928 reported on West Africa for *Le Petit Parisien*, devoted one of his pieces to the social situation of the *métis* in the region, painting a rather bleak portrait of the situation of these *mulots* (slang for "mulatto," the word also means "field mouse").[96] In the 1920s and 1930s, a number of novels and short stories appeared in which *métis* figured as characters. These drew on the portrait painted by the anthropologists and exaggerated it: the characters were filled with resentment toward the society of their progenitors, weak willed, disoriented, incapable of establishing themselves in life, and often delinquent or debauched. In many of these stories, the plot hinges on uncovering the identity of the father. This is true of one (quite bad) story, "Le métis," by Albert de Pouvourville, a public advocate of colonization, specialist on Indochina (where he lived at the turn of the century), and a prolific writer on the *métis* question. It features the trial of the murderer of a French colonel, who turns out to be the victim's own son.[97] A feminine version of the *métis* tragedy appeared in a novel by Clotilde Chivas-Baron entitled *Confidences de métisse*: a young girl is entrusted by her father to an unscrupulous friend who pays the girl's mother to marry him and legitimizes the child. She is witness to her mother's degradation and undergoes a series of humiliations and disillusionments.[98] Penniless, she is unable to find a decent way to support herself and ultimately sinks into prostitution.[99] The *métis* question served as a vehicle for transplanting the descriptions of social misery that were common in French popular fiction into an exotic setting.

This process of diffusion was reinforced by "a politics of comparison" within the French Empire and beyond. This practice was a common feature of modern imperial formations and was particularly intense with respect to the *métis* question. In 1905, a prominent citizen of Madagascar returned from a stay in Indochina with information about how the *métis* situation was handled there. Persuaded that "the facts here are the same as there and that the same consequences will eventually follow," he warned "against the dangers that experience has revealed in Cochin China."[100]

In due course, Indochina became a model to imitate. In 1934, Jules Brévié, then governor-general of FWA, asked his counterpart in Hanoi to "let him know what has been done in Indochina to assist and educate children of mixed blood." He indicated that "any information you are willing to share will serve as an inspiration."[101] Administrators and jurists in other colonies paid close attention to Indochinese case law concerning the legal status of the *métis*.[102]

The politics of comparison did not end at the frontiers of the French Empire but concerned larger geographical areas. For instance, colonists in Indochina observed and analyzed how the large mixed-race population was treated in the Dutch West Indies. In 1901, the French consul in Batavia sent a voluminous report in response to a "request for information about individuals of mixed race" from the Society for the Protection of Abandoned *Métis* in Cochin China, relayed by the governor.[103] He mentioned not only the legal aspects but also the care, upbringing, and social development of children, differences within the mixed-race community, relations with "European colonists," and political preferences of the *métis*. In 1938, the supreme commander of the army in Indochina, who was quite concerned about *métis* born in the vicinity of military posts, also collected "a large volume of information about measures taken in the Dutch West Indies on behalf of *métis*."[104] The case of the Philippines was also mentioned, but as a counterexample in order to highlight the dangers that could arise if the *métis* question were not dealt with effectively. Similarly, in FEA, the policy failures of the Belgian Congo were discussed as lessons about what to avoid.[105]

Soon all the European imperial powers were debating the issue,[106] convinced that "this question is among the most sensitive and difficult that colonial governments face."[107] As was the case with social reform, international congresses were convened to define the scope of the problem, gather data, and make international comparisons.[108] The most important of these was the International Colonial Institute, headquartered in Brussels. Founded in 1894, it functioned as a club where administrators, colonial scholars (especially doctors, geographers, and lawyers), and journalists could come together to discuss problems and study what had been done and what still remained to be done.[109] Members included Belgium, Great Britain, France, Italy, the Netherlands, and Portugal, as well as the United States and Japan. Between 1911 and 1923, the institute devoted three sessions to the *métis* question. It also sponsored a vast survey, responses to which were published in 1923. Representing France, the colonial administrator turned ethnologist

Maurice Delafosse contributed a "note concerning the *métis* in French West Africa," while "the question of the *métis* in Indochina" was treated by the ubiquitous Marquis de Pouvourville. A long discussion about the best ways to deal with the *métis* question ensued. Each nation set forth its own position in regard to a problem that all believed they faced in common.[110]

Statistics on *Métissage*

Like everyone who attempted to do something about the "social question" from the time it first arose in the nineteenth century, those who became interested in the fate of the *métis* relied on numbers. Indeed, modern "governmentality,"[111] to borrow a word from Michel Foucault, assumes a "politics of large numbers" bearing on "cohesive objects that exist apart from special interests in order to act on them."[112] Although the category "*métis*" regularly appeared in census data in the colonies, numerical estimates for individual colonies varied widely over short periods of time. Constantly in search of more accurate estimates, the colonial officials involved multiplied their efforts over time, but it was as if the phenomenon of *métissage* resisted all attempts to measure it. No exact count of *métis* in the French Empire can be given, but we can at least try to explain how the counting was done and what difficulties were encountered.

Let us begin by looking at colonial censuses more generally. The first point to underline is that natives were reluctant to be counted. This may have been due to their having a different conception of the individual or to their wariness of numbers, as colonial administrators believed, but it was above all a conscious strategy in the empire where taxes were assessed by head count.

Another obstacle to the counting of *métis* was confusion between the categories of nationality and race. The choice of one criterion or the other made a big difference in the results. The first general census of imperial populations was carried out in 1906, and the exercise was thereafter repeated every five years, in parallel with the census in metropolitan France. At that time, "Europeans and assimilated" were counted as one group (often under the heading "white race and assimilated"), while "natives and assimilated" formed another group. Each of these groups was then broken down by nationality, which was of course the primary criterion in the metropole. The *métis* were then listed in a third column: in this racial breakdown of the population, they were treated as a residual element.

Clearly, then, the agents of the colonial administration did not censor the topic of race, despite what commentators said then or now. Here is Maurice

Delafosse on the legalism of administrative practice: "In the official view, which admits no distinctions of color, the *métis* is either a French or foreign citizen and therefore included in the numbers of Europeans of one nationality or another, or else he is a native and counted with them."[113] Against assertions of colorblindness we might apply to the racial question what Michel Foucault said about the "repressive hypothesis" in regard to sexuality: what the historian faces is not silence but a proliferation of discourses, not to say a cacophony.[114] Indeed, the notion of race used in the census was far from unequivocal. It changed with time and place and administrative level, and with it the content of the category "*métis*" also changed. The word *race* usually refers to the groups denoted "European" and "indigenous," but sometimes it also refers to what was called the ethnic group or tribe (*ethnie*). The latter term first appeared in the data in the 1920s, sometimes as a synonym for race and sometimes as a subdivision of it. For the statistician, it was a more "sociological" notion than race and therefore "easier to recognize," because it was "characterized by a certain homogeneity of language, mores, and social organization."[115]

Another source of ambiguity was the fact that *race* never referred solely to a perceived phenotypic or anthropological difference but also reflected political power relations. For instance, in Indochina, the Japanese were legally included among Europeans and counted with them. Nevertheless, Delafosse was not entirely wrong: if the *métis* were initially counted separately, the tendency in the long run was to include them among either Europeans or natives depending on their legal status. From the late 1920s on, for example, "European *métis*" were included among "persons of European status," a group that included, in Indochina, "French born in the old colonies, European *métis*, naturalized natives, Japanese, and Filipinos."[116] They became statistically invisible.

Finally, we must mention one difficulty that was specific to the *métis* population: for a long time, children of unknown fathers—that is, the vast majority—were given indigenous status and therefore remained invisible to the census agents. Their numbers could not even be estimated from the registers of vital statistics, because for a long time the recording of native births was optional.

In the absence of numbers certified by the state, people involved in dealing with the *métis* question regularly produced their own estimates. They did so when applying for funding or proposing solutions to the "problem," often in the context of communication with the metropole. Of course the numbers were always said to be "growing constantly" in order to demonstrate the "importance and gravity of the question."[117] For Indochina, between 1904 (when the president of the Society for the *Métis* of Indochina stated that there were "approximately 500 *métis*," both recognized and un-recognized) and 1952 (when the Eurasian Federation proposed the figure of 300,000 Eurasians, of whom 50,000 had French nationality),[118] one set of figures succeeded another without any consistent logic: sometimes all *métis* were counted, other times only unrecognized ones or just those in need of assistance. One sign of growing mobilization around this issue was the fact that from the 1930s on, the number of counts increased, to the point where we find nearly one a year in Tonkin between 1937 and 1945. Counts were usually made for a province or city, seldom for the whole territory. Hence, the numbers were never comparable. For example, while the general gov-ernment's Directorate for Political Affairs stated that there were 18,000 *métis* in Indochina in 1932,[119] a 1933 École coloniale thesis mentioned the figure of 2,340 "at the last census."[120]

It is therefore impossible to arrive at a reliable number of *métis* in each colony. We see from this how vague and variable the category was, depend-ing on whether one counted only its "core" (illegitimate, unrecognized, and abandoned children) or a broader group including all children born of co-lonial encounters.[121] Note, moreover, that people involved in the issue at the time, who had strong motives for trying to obtain accurate numbers, could not do better. And all of these ambiguities would heighten the anxiety that surrounded the *métis* question.

Still, we can say that estimates were on the rise everywhere in the first half of the twentieth century, and they were systematically higher in Indo-china than elsewhere. In 1906, eighteen thousand *métis* of all statuses were counted there, including twelve thousand foreigners, children of Chinese and natives, concentrated for the most part in Cambodia.[122] In 1939, Dr. Pierre Huard, who was very prolix on the question, alluded to six thousand French *métis* and did not even try to estimate the number of indigenous *métis*.[123] He did, however, point to the increase in the number relative to the "pure white" population and predicted a "creolization" of the French population of Indochina. West Africa (especially Senegal), Madagascar, and Equatorial Africa followed in that order, with several thousand *métis* in each case. We have no figures for New Caledonia, which illustrates the island's special place in the geography of *métissage*, or for Algeria, where the *métis* remained socially invisible.

Finally, we should of course point out the small sizes of the popula-tions involved, including in Indochina during the two world wars, where the numbers were highest. At most, only a few tens of thousands of *métis* coexisted there with some twenty million natives and twenty-five thousand to thirty-five thousand French.[124] If the *métis* were a problem, it was not because of their numbers but rather because of the symbolic threat they represented for the colonial order. In order to gain a better grasp of the place of the *métis* question in the colonial societies of the first half of the twentieth century, we turn next to an examination of how various colonial actors—notables, administrators, and jurists—perceived this danger throughout the French Empire.

TWO

A Threat to the Colonial Order

The intense mobilization around the *métis* question reflected the importance of the perceived threat. Because the *métis* blurred the distinction between French and natives, they undermined the foundations of the colonial social and political order.[1] Their existence jeopardized efforts by the colonizers to maintain the "proper distance" from the colonized—a distance conceptualized in terms of both race and class.[2] This imperative was reflected in constant attention to the "prestige" of the colonizer and the "dignity" of French citizenship.

The philanthropists and government officials who devoted themselves to resolving the "tragedy of the *métis*," and thus to upholding the colonial order, were members of the local elite. Many felt nothing but contempt, tinged to one degree or another with pity, for the men, women, and children responsible for the "problem." These judgments were often only tenuously related to the behavior of the men, women, and children whose lives were at issue. This chapter explores the perspectives of the range of actors involved, drawing most of its examples from Indochina, the principal "laboratory" for the study of the *métis* question.

Legionnaires, Women of Ill Repute, and Pariahs

In the many source documents dealing with the etiology of the *métis* problem, fathers play a more important role than mothers. Both were usually characterized in pejorative terms. One observer described children of mixed blood as the offspring of encounters between "drunken soldiery and women of easy virtue of the sort found hanging about well-nourished heroes in every country in the world."[3]

The language of class, never far from the language of race, was ubiquitous. Observers of the *métis* question used the class distinctions that were current in the metropole not only to describe native society but also to explain relations between colonizers and colonized.

The mothers of *métis* were systematically presented as women of "low extraction,"[4] and this seems to have been a necessary condition for a woman to grant her favors to a colonial outside the bonds of matrimony. The fathers were also usually described as men of modest social background. Finally, it was generally believed that "mixed couples combined the most mediocre elements of the population."[5] These social characteristics mixed freely with racial categories: the products of such unions were said to exhibit various hereditary pathologies. In Indochina, a priest who headed an orphanage maintained that the vast majority of fathers were legionnaires and *therefore* often alcoholic or syphilitic: the *métis* "therefore bear a rather heavy burden of atavism, which weighs on their future."[6] Administrators also translated social position into hereditary capital: "Based on all the surveys we have done, it appears that many mixed-race children, perhaps the majority, are of very low origins, and their innate qualities match those of their parents. They are unfortunately condemned by heredity to vegetate if one subjects them to the living conditions of normal children."[7]

These judgments suggest a fissure in masculine colonial society. According to the rhetoric of the *métis* question, the fathers of "abandoned *métis*" were mainly military men or officials temporarily stationed in the colonies, often young and of lower-class origin. By contrast, men who had established themselves in the colony as settlers, officials of the colonial civil service, and private-sector personnel were portrayed as more likely to acknowledge their children or even legitimate them by marriage.[8] This distinction was reinforced by the social geography of the *métis* problem, which was always more intense in military territories from Tonkin to Algeria. But a closer look reveals that this picture is in many ways misleading. Although the fathers were de jure "unknown," their identities were in fact often known, as is clear from many long lists of names of *métis* drawn up by philanthropists or government officials. In Indochina, these lists usually include the names of the fathers and less frequently those of the mothers.[9] They suggest that fathers who abandoned their children included "not only soldiers but also French government officials in prominent positions."[10] In 1948, a report was published with results of a study of 199 "Eurasians." Its conclusions should be treated cautiously, given the small size of the sample, but it, too, suggests that fathers of *métis* came from all segments of the colonial population: not only soldiers and isolated officials (such as customs officers and public works inspectors) but also white-collar workers in commerce, industry, and government; planters and rice growers; and other professions in urban and rural settings.[11]

Women were less closely scrutinized. When their "immorality" could not be explained by their origins, contacts with "colonial kitchens or infantry" did the job.[12] In Indochina, the mistresses of Frenchmen were described as outcasts from Vietnamese society. In order to survive, they embarked on careers as concubines serving one colonial male after another, with each new partner contributing to the upkeep of his predecessors' children. Observers argued that the repeated adventures of these unfit mothers had consequences for their children:

> These women are, and inevitably will remain, uprooted and outcast, deprived of their position in society. In the best of cases their fate is to have several white "husbands" before ceasing to be young and ending up in a more permanent union with an interpreter, who is "flattered" and attracted by their somewhat Frenchified manners and elegance. In such cases, what becomes of the child, whether male or female, whose health is more fragile than that of a pure native, who learns from some obscure atavistic trait how different he or she is from other children, and whose "family" consists of a frequently changing cast of "fathers"?[13]

It was also alleged that these unworthy native mothers took no interest in their children or even that they profited from them. One of the myths that pervaded more anguished formulations of the *métis* question was that some mothers sold their children, especially girls, when they reached puberty. In October 1899, an article in *L'avenir du Tonkin* went so far as to report the sale of the child of an official "who served a dozen years in the colony, known to everyone in Hanoi and Haiphong, who adored his little daughter and who died nearly two years ago in Hanoi before he had time to acknowledge the child! . . . This child was everything to him. . . . She was raised at Sainte-Enfance and spoke good French. A death as sudden as it was unforeseen took her father from her within a few hours, leaving him no time to acknowledge her, although he stated his firm intention to do so on several occasions in the presence of a number of witnesses."[14]

Not all accusations went this far, but it was common to blame mothers for raising their children badly. In 1942, for example, one soldier claimed that "the mothers of *côs* generally abandon their children.[15] They usually don't care about them, although some do love them. Mothers raise children in a very rough environment, filled with scenes of conjugal violence and obscenities, and these things are indelibly engraved in the children's memory from the age of two or three."[16] Clearly, the congenital defects of the *métis*, who were "unstable" by virtue of their dual heredity and "oppressive atavisms," were only magnified by the supposed lack of maternal care. In 1936, the president of the Société d'assistance aux enfants franco-indochinois stated the problem in terms that naturally justified philanthropic intervention:

> Time has shown that the *métis* left in the care of a mother of lower-class origins and lacking both the desirable educational training and moral qualities, is doomed to a mediocre existence. No one can teach the child to correct the original imperfections that would lead it to vegetate, scorned, on the fringes of society. No one will nurture in its soul, at the age when impressions are indelible, the essence of all child-rearing, namely, the basic principles of all education and the sentiments that serve as rules of conduct throughout life.[17]

Yet quite apart from these catalogs of social and racial pathology, the fathers and mothers of mixed-race children did leave a record of their thoughts and feelings. To be sure, such traces are rare and are often constrained by the rhetoric of the "social question," yet they nevertheless allow us to glimpse a very different kind of emotional investment.

The Ambivalence of Paternal Abandonment

The behavior of some fathers was far more ambivalent than the simple image of "abandonment" suggests. In an episode from 1914, for example, we see the role of networks of solidarity between colonials and natives, specifically in the lower classes. When a French game warden lost his position, he entrusted his little boy to an indigenous woman, a butcher. The warden left the woman with a "certificate of abandonment" of his own composition: "I, the undersigned, declare that I am abandoning a child of mixed blood, aged four, to one N.T.B., aged forty, residing in Kien Anh, who has agreed to raise the child, provide him with the necessary care, and adopt him."[18] Ten years later, the woman to whom he had entrusted the boy found that she could no longer accept this responsibility and turned him over to the Société de protection des enfants métis. The society in turn declared that it "reserved the right to take any steps necessary to find the father, whose neglect is truly extreme, and if need be to bring this case of deliberate abandonment to the attention of the state prosecutor." We can, however, read the father's action not as a sign of "neglect" but rather as an indication of concern, of a wish to see that the child was well cared for, and, finally, as an acknowledgment of paternity that sought to leave a public record through the use of administrative style in the document.

Many fathers sought, moreover, to "regularize the civil status of their children" and asked for information about how this could be done.

In 1916, one soldier, after recognizing his son, asked to be "oriented" as to his "child's rights during [his] presence in the colony and during [his] absence," because he thought of "some day returning to France. . . . Being a mere private and very concerned about the well-being of [his] child [but] receiving very minimal pay," he asked to be granted "a small stipend so that the child might be raised properly."[19]

Other fathers arranged placements for their offspring on their own, with the help of charitable organizations. In 1943, a sergeant assigned to Hanoi, who had fathered and recognized a three-year-old boy, sought to take the child away from his mother, whom he deemed to be a woman "of dubious morality." He called upon the Société de protection des métis for assistance. The president of this group sternly advised him either to keep the child with him or to place him "with a French family" or "with the nuns of Saint-Paul de Chartres," which would allow him to "maintain contact with the boy" and "see him as often as [he] might wish."[20]

In 1940, the mother of a legionnaire contacted the superior resident of Tonkin on behalf of her son. The young man was worried about the fate of his twenty-one-month-old daughter, whom he had recognized. A letter "from over there" had allegedly made him aware that his former concubine was of "low morals." He therefore wanted the resident to take "little Georgette" away from her unfit mother and give her to the nuns. His plan was to bring the girl to France when his fifteen-year enlistment period was up. The resident ordered an investigation into the behavior of the young Vietnamese woman, the mother of two children of mixed blood. He reassured the grandmother that the woman was "living decently on the benefits that [her] son was sending" and that "her two daughters are very well cared for and seem to be in good health."[21]

Clearly, then, some fathers were more attached to their children than the champions of the *métis* cause were willing to admit. They sometimes relied on networks of masculine solidarity: a father about to leave the colony would entrust his child to the protection of a comrade slated to remain at his post. Or, if a father died before making provisions for his child, his comrades might look for assistance or entrust the child directly to a philanthropic society.[22] In Tonkin in the 1930s, an association of Frenchmen born or permanently stationed in Indochina even created a subgroup of "fathers of children with Asian mothers."[23] Such solidarity networks were not just horizontal or limited to the colonies: if a father died, his family might take an interest in any children he had left behind and see to it that they received their share of his inheritance[24] or even invite them to join the family back in France.[25]

Mothers' Assimilation of the Rhetoric of the Métis Question

The sentiments that animated women are harder to read in the archives left by those who defined the *métis* question. Socially and culturally more distant from these prominent colonials than the fathers, the mothers often took an instrumental approach to the categories in which the question was posed. Quite a few women asked for assistance, especially in cases where the father recognized the child before abandoning it. Mothers in this situation were familiar with the various legal forms of kinship and knew their rights, so they turned to the highest levels of the bureaucracy in order to compel the fathers to contribute to the upkeep of their offspring even after their return to France, or, if the fathers had died, to apply for benefits.

In 1932, one particularly enterprising woman requested assistance from the colonel in command of the regiment in Aix-en-Provence to which the father of her little boy was assigned. Explaining that the child was born during their "married life" (she attached the child's birth certificate to her letter), she noted that the father had made a promise of financial assistance, which he had kept only very sporadically. She suggested that "he ought to know quite well that this is not enough. I sent him several letters, to which he did not respond, so I find myself forced to ask respectfully for your assistance in achieving a satisfactory resolution of this matter, because the very precarious situation in which I find myself no longer allows me to sat-isfy the needs of our growing boy." Required to respond, the father, Corpo-ral L., proposed bringing the boy to France if the military authorities would pay for his passage. If the mother refused, he suggested that "she place the child with the home for abandoned children of mixed race in Hanoi."[26]

Vietnamese mothers were well versed not only in the terms of French law but also in the rhetoric of the *métis* question. In 1941, for example, one mother asked an orphanage to accept her child lest "he become a 'bad boy.'"[27] In 1936, another woman "sought the assistance" of the administrative mayor of Hanoi to obtain "a place for her daughter Nini, born in 1931, in the girls' or-phanage." In her words, this favor "will protect my daughter from *pernicious influences* and enable her to acquire a proper upbringing and education."[28] Another woman also drew on the standard imagery of the *métis* question:

I lived as man and wife with M.C., an employee of the forest service, and from this union a son was born. After his birth, the child was abandoned. Born without a father, this poor creature was obliged to live with the Annamite name "Phuc," which I gave him. We have lived in most unfortunate circumstances since being abandoned. Lacking funds, I have not been able to meet the educational needs of this abandoned child of mixed blood. I would therefore be most grateful if you would take note of our difficulties and admit my unfortunate eight-year-old to your orphanage.[29]

In all these requests, the mastery not only of French codes for writing supplicant letters but also of the rhetorical tropes of the *métis* question indicates the existence of forms of solidarity that transcended the colonial divide.

Mothers were not limited to instrumental strategies in approaching people in a position to provide them with assistance. Between the lines of administrative documents and philanthropic reports, we find them adopting various forms of resistance to the way in which the *métis* question was handled. Not all mothers sought to place their children in institutions—far from it. In 1931, one mother tried several times to retrieve her daughter from the Orphelinat des enfants franco-indochinois abandonnés, where the girl had been placed at her father's request, with backing from the state prosecutor. Her requests were denied because she was "identified as having a very bad reputation, not working and living off the earnings of prostitution."[30] In addition, it appears that some mothers thwarted the will of philanthropic societies by changing their address or even abandoning their place of residence and returning for a time to their native village in order to avoid an inspector's visit (see chapter 3).[31] Finally, efforts to deal with children of mixed blood did not always succeed in breaking the bonds of affection between mothers and their offspring. We see this in the fate of one adolescent who was expelled from the École d'enfants de troupe in Dalat in 1943. Rather than go back to his original orphanage as he was asked to, he returned to his mother and was permanently excluded from the Société de protection des enfants métis.[32]

Unclassifiable Pariahs

Products of encounters between individuals "of low extraction," growing up uneducated and undisciplined in often "pernicious" environments, the *métis* shared all the faults of their parents. In philanthropic reports, we find a theme favored by physical anthropologists: that of the hybrid who inherits only the defects of both parental races. Indeed, *métis* were outcasts from both colonial and colonized society to an even greater degree than their fathers and mothers. They were *pariahs*, to use a term common throughout the colonial period, rejected on all sides. This commonplace of colonial discourse concerning children of mixed blood can be found in one of the first documents on the *métis* question, an 1898 note entitled "The *métis* question is a social and moral problem whose solution must take account of the special circumstances of the Franco-Annamite case." This was drafted by a certain C. Crévost, an accountant at the Saigon arsenal and one of the founders of a charitable organization:

> Franco-Annamite children of mixed blood currently constitute a class of the population that is generally rejected by French society and banished by the indigenous population. The colonizers are quite wrong to keep these people at a distance because of their origins, being in some cases the offspring of lasting relationships but more often of fleeting ones. This class of people is excluded because of its promiscuous relations with the native element. . . . Finally, the *métis* element is also rejected by the indigenous group owing to our abandonment. The *métis* is therefore considered by one group as a corrupt Frenchman owing to the obscurity of his birth and by another group as a fallen Frenchman, without authority, relations, or support, or, in other words, less than a native.[33]

As a pariah, the *métis* was as impossible to classify socially as anthropologically: hybridity was compounded by loss of class position. It is quite striking that those who were categorized this way were able to turn this rhetorical composite to their advantage. In various requests, usually for financial aid or naturalization,[34] some found it easy to resort to the "politics of pity." They pointed to their status as "unrecognized parentless children of mixed blood" to obtain "a small stipend."[35] As the following request illustrates, the rhetoric of social reformers was perfectly assimilated by some of the individuals to whom it applied. I quote at length from the following document because it reveals the ways in which the terms of the *métis* question could be used by individuals designated as *métis*:

> I, the undersigned, Louis L., a guard at the Superior Residence in Annam, respectfully submit the following petition. As everyone knows, I am an abandoned, unrecognized child of mixed blood. My papa, a certain L., was a soldier in the Ninth Colonial stationed in Hue, when he married N.-T.-H. (*i.e.,*

when she became his concubine), and as you know well, Monsieur le Gouverneur général, it was not my fault that I had the misfortune to come into this world as the fruit of this brief liaison. My father left the city of Hue when I was still in my mother's womb, and I never saw him. Is he still alive? I have no idea. My mother told me that from the day he left until now, he sent us only one note of just a few words and nothing at all to help us survive. Nevertheless, thanks to the generosity of the Société de protection des métis abandonnés, which for ten years (1901–1910) provided me with a monthly stipend of three piasters, I was able to attend the Quôc-Hoc school for a time and was thus able to learn the rudiments of the French language, which should have been my mother tongue.

Facing up to my misfortune, in 1913 I applied for and was granted my present position as guard. Since then, I have always performed my duties conscientiously, and my superiors have been completely satisfied with my work. My salary has risen to twenty-one piasters per month, but I am responsible for my grandmother, my mother, my wife, and my two children. Although my salary and the fruits of my wife's labor are enough to enable me to make ends meet for the time being, the future looks quite bleak because of my special situation, which prevents any village from inscribing me on its rolls.[36] Thus, I live among people whose living conditions I share, in the land in which I was born and will most likely be buried, but as a foreigner, a person from another world. What a misfortune this is for me, I leave it to you to judge, Monsieur le Gouverneur général.

In the hope that the case of a man who is a pariah in spite of himself, who lives on the fringes of society and who, since childhood, has borne the burden of his fate will not seem unworthy of your interest and solicitude, Monsieur le Gouverneur général, I dare to ask you to grant me French naturalization, because I fear that when I am gone, my children will face the prospect of the hardest of labor. They were born in this calm and gentle land but without any definite origin or abode, [and] like little birds that learn to fly only to tumble by accident into a deep abyss, they do not know what path to follow! Have pity on me, Monsieur le Gouverneur général, and grant me the favor that I seek. Your goodness and generosity will never be forgotten if you approve this naturalization. You will find herewith all the documents necessary to initiate this procedure.[37]

Like the philanthropists and bureaucrats, Louis L. emphasized his father's lineage in asserting that French "should have been [his] mother tongue." This was a way of suggesting that he was "already" French and therefore deserved to have his request granted: we will encounter this argument again in the writing of jurists concerned with the fate of these "unwitting pariahs."

Uprooted and Declassed

The "pariah" was also frequently characterized as "uprooted." As a group, the *métis* were "never anything but a class of malcontents, helpless and uprooted individuals. No matter what they are called, the members of this group will inevitably be regarded as socially inferior to the dominant race."[38] Like the characters in Maurice Barrès's novel *Les déracinés*, which was widely read at the turn of the twentieth century and which popularized the term *déraciné* ("deracinated" or "uprooted"),[39] the *métis* did not belong to any "organic community." Born to disgraced mothers and outcasts from the society of their birth, they lived on the margins of the colonized society in a "seminative environment."[40] Stigmatized as illegitimate hybrids, they were also rejected by colonial society. This dual exclusion lay at the heart of the *métis* question. It is reflected in the fact that their lives were not recorded by the bureaucratic apparatus that developed at the end of the period of conquest to establish and track the individual identities of both citizens and subjects.

One of the tools used by the colonial state to control population was a system for recording vital statistics throughout the empire, to establish both records for individuals and, over time, statistical portraits of larger populations. At first, this system dealt only with French citizens and fully "assimilated" individuals, but eventually all the colonies began keeping vital statistics about native populations. This expansion of the record keeping took place in Algeria in 1882, in Cochin China in 1883, in Madagascar in 1897, in New Caledonia in 1908, in FWA and FEA in 1918–19, and in Tonkin in 1921. Except in Algeria, native registration remained optional throughout much of this period, however, and the bureaucracy concerned itself only with the most basic acts of civil life (births and deaths were recorded but not marriages). In most territories, village authorities kept a record of all inhabitants, which was used for calculating the head taxes common to most of the colonies as well as for issuing identity papers—often taxpayer cards that were required for travel outside the village. Children of mixed blood who were unrecognized by their fathers and whose mothers had severed their ties with the organized village community did not appear in any of these records. They were literally "outside the law," in the words of one Indochinese *métis*: "What is the legal status of persons of mixed blood? They have none. As I have shown, they have been rejected by both the Annamites and the French and are in fact outlaws, having no civil status or registered citizenship in any village."[41] They were also characterized as "abandoned" (*épaves*). The image is instructive, and it also had a precise legal meaning. Under the laws of the ancien régime, the term *épaves* was applied to "total strangers," about whom nothing was known, as opposed to *aubains*, whose name and origin could be determined.[42]

The *métis* was even more a *déclassé*—that is, a person who could no longer be readily "classified" as belonging to one of the groups of which the society was composed. In the literature and social commentary of the second half of the nineteenth century, the *déclassé* (sociologically quite similar to the *déraciné*—the "uprooted") was an individual who had a legitimate claim to a place in society but fell short of it. His trajectory was therefore marked by a breaking of the connection between "position" and "aspiration."[43] In conservative writing of the period, the prototype of the *déclassé* was the educated worker, usually an autodidact. Unable to truly assimilate the principles of an education without the accompanying social formation, the working-class autodidact became "semieducated"—enough to claim the privileges associated with education in a meritocratic democracy. Accordingly dissatisfied with his situation, he was quick to join in protests against the social order.[44] We find exactly the same images applied to the *métis* in this text written by the superior resident of Tonkin in 1907: "Given the present state of society and legislation, the *métis* who is orphaned or left in his mother's charge is usually nothing more than a *déclassé*, filled by birth with aspirations that often remain unrealized for lack of adequate guidance and with needs that he cannot satisfy. Reduced to the most common employments, he is predisposed to become an enemy of the state of affairs that is the cause of his suffering, and in particular of French society."[45]

To a greater extent than in the metropole, the discourse on *déclassement* borrowed the vocabulary of race. The aspirations alluded to in the passage above were in fact a product of "the blood," according to Crévost: "I cannot think without sadness of the profound discouragement that afflicts the abandoned and rejected individual who is nevertheless conscious of the hatred and scorn that surround him simply because his blood is that of a generous and proud Frenchman, and the regular beating of his heart powerfully reminds him of his blood ties to the dominant element, which does him serious harm."[46]

The "call of the blood" was compounded by the tyranny of appearances. As one philanthropist put it, "Even after they have become 'nhaqués,'[47] they have only to look at themselves in a well or a pond."[48] *Déclassement* was therefore the result of the disparity between the real identity of the *métis*, who was French by blood and appearance, and his social status, which remained that of a native, as one jurist observed in the 1930s: "Possessing the pride of the white race, he tries to live as close as possible to French society. The people cry out that he is one of the colonizers, so he seeks a place among those he deems to be of his own race, and yet he encounters only mockery and humiliation. Finding no satisfaction for his legitimate aspirations, the *métis* then becomes a *déclassé*."[49]

The figure of the *déclassé* can be compared with that of the "vain mulatto," a stock literary figure of the nineteenth century. Since his "origins cloud his vision with pretensions,"[50] he rejects manual labor as beneath him, but being unqualified for intellectual activity, he is condemned to live on public charity.[51]

The female version of *déclassement* shifted the focal point of "blood pride" toward the profits to be expected from bodily capital, since the body of the *métis* occupied a prime place in the pantheon of colonial fantasies. For women, *déclassement* was associated with prostitution, an activity that was all the more repulsive in that a young woman of "European blood" might find herself delivered into the hands of a native male. This the previously cited Crévost deplored in 1898:

> [Little girls of mixed blood] are glad to learn that their white skin places them well above their little friends among the natives, and they grow up expecting to enjoy a bright future, exemplified by outrageous displays of luxury. . . . The damage is already done: the child has conceived desires of luxury. . . . Since the mother dreams only of riches for herself and for her daughter, whose treasure is placed in her safekeeping, she has already, for quite some time, since the birth of the child, been counting on the large sum of piasters that she will someday receive from a Chinese or a European or Lord knows whom??? (his nationality is the least of her worries) in exchange for her daughter's favors.[52]

The effects of *déclassement* were worse in those cases where the father raised the child before abandoning it. The initial socialization in French ways then combined with blood pride to make it all but impossible for the child to find his or her place in native society after the father departed. The child had, "with consciousness of its origin, acquired a mentality quite close to that of young French children of the same age."[53] Indeed, to have been "raised by a French father as a French child" was said to instill "the aspirations of a French person."[54] In the colonial mind, race was not only transmitted by heredity, it was also a quality acquired by the child from living with his or her father during the first years of life. This plastic conception of race informed the following statement by the president of an aid society in 1913:

> Therefore, the children about whose futures we worry most are those whose fathers, with culpable lack of foresight, initially raised them as Europeans only to abandon them subsequently. Those children are often eight, ten, or twelve years old when they come to us, and sometimes older. At that point they have acquired the pride of their French blood and look down on the "*nhaqué*." It is clearly too late to make honest Annamites of them, and we have no choice but to continue to raise them as Europeans, even though we find that they have neither the attitudes nor aptitudes of French children and will eventually end up as wrecks (*épaves*). We are much more comfortable with the prospects of those who come to us when younger, whom we are then free to guide in one direction or the other, depending on what aptitudes they exhibit.[55]

The political dimension of the *métis* question was a consequence of *déclassement*. Colonials feared that unsatisfied aspirations would turn into resentment and thus foster opposition to the colonial regime, as we see in this statement by the governor-general of FEA in 1932: "The *métis*, as 'children of whites,' are considered as intruders in native families yet rejected by the European community, so they live on the fringes of society and are sometimes treated as people of lower rank. This situation causes them much suffering and builds resentment against their fathers first of all and then against the European community. Gradually and in some cases unwittingly, they become embittered and, rather than support our civilizing efforts, often work against them and sometimes combat them."[56]

These fears echoed an important preoccupation of the republican regime in France in the last third of the nineteenth century, as it tried to reconcile the revolutionary principles of equality among individuals with the existence of social stratification. The educational system served to legitimate inequalities by making them appear to be differences in aptitude and talent.[57] In the colonies, as we shall see, efforts were made to avoid the threat created by *déclassement* by restoring the fit between identity and status, fact and law. Meanwhile, it was very easy to instrumentalize the danger. Every decrease in subsidies revived the worrisome image of the resentful *métis* in the rhetoric of those who made it their "goal to support the unfortunate children who have French blood in their veins and to prevent them from becoming deviants who might later become implacable enemies of our race."[58]

In support of their argument, philanthropists often mentioned edifying cases drawn from novels, the press, and any number of essays about the *métis* question—sources that endlessly glossed one another. They would in any case have found it difficult to cite an actual example in support of the thesis that *métis* were likely to participate in protests against the colonial order. The very rough estimates that one can make on the basis of census reports indicate that *métis* commonly accepted colonial rule, and in fact many of them participated in it. Their mastery of two languages meant that they were sought after as agents of the intelligence services and police (in 1941, 35 percent of the posts in the Indochinese police force were filled by *métis*)[59] and even more as employees of the small colonial bureaucracy.

The Spectacle of Disorder

In the colonial situation, deracination and *déclassement* were intimately associated with the management of appearances. In general, the organization of society closely followed the contours of the color line. The existence of *métis* confused this neat division and provided evidence not only of promiscuity between colonizers and colonized but of a deeper confusion about identities. The *métis* problem was typically incarnated by the child of a French father who had "gone back" to being a native and who was then held up to public view. This exhibition became especially problematic when it took place in shared social settings: wherever colonials and natives interacted, it was considered important to always maintain a "proper distance." There is no need to cite the countless descriptions of scenes in which a colonial visiting a market or a remote village is suddenly confronted with "French blood" transplanted into a "native environment"—an appalling spectacle, which philanthropists repeatedly cited as the reason for their interest in the *métis* question. As one of them explained, "To have seen a child's face gleaming in the French manner, totally European in its features, suddenly appear before you in the midst of so much yellow misery is enough to lay to rest all doubt about the simple and righteous motives that guide us in our work."[60]

In describing the confusion of identities, narrators, posing as spectators, regularly employed the rhetoric of denunciation:

> Listen: two years ago, in the vicinity of the central market, you often ran into
> a noisy, thieving gang of little *nhos* in rags, and among them was a poor lit-

tle lad of seven or eight. This child had a pink complexion, blond hair, and light blue eyes, and he attracted the curiosity of any French who happened to pass by as well as of the natives. He did not know who his father was and probably his mother either, nor did he know a word of our fine French language. I recall writing about this distressing, heart-wrenching case in the *Presse indochinoise*, though to no good end—at least thus far. There are cases that seem, for whatever reason, to hold no interest for either the authorities or our ill-constructed society. Who knows why? Impenetrable mystery? . . . What became of that poor child? Does that sad wretch, abandoned by all, still roam among the stalls of the central market in search of his daily pittance?[61]

Sentimental rhetoric was also common:[62]

From the lives of these poor little creatures come . . . many moving stories. We know any number of anecdotes that reduce us to tears. One day in the streets of Hanoi, for instance, a gentleman approached a child and offered him a few coins and a pat on the head. The child was still too small to attach any importance to the gift of money, but he never forgot the pat on the head. Later, he conceived the notion that the gentleman was his father, and on another occasion he spotted a Frenchman who somewhat resembled the other man and ran after him with all the speed his little legs could muster, shouting, "Papa! Papa!" The Frenchman did not hear him and continued on his way, whereupon the child broke into tears, and for a long time nothing could stanch the flow. Only the promise that he would see his father again the next day was of any avail. We confess that when we heard this story, we felt something welling up in our own eyes, as if a speck of dust had somehow lodged in them, and we turned away as if to remove it. Skeptics may find our sensitivity laughable.[63]

Agents of the state also made use of such edifying descriptions, albeit without the more excessive flourishes of the rhetoric of suffering. For example, one battalion commander, in charge of a military district, justified his indulgence of a child left behind by his predecessor on the grounds that it was important to restore the fit between physical appearance and social status: "I felt that it was important to give this child a French education, so that he could later achieve a position that would keep him from sinking into misery and would in any case rescue him from the rather degrading Annamite environment in which he was otherwise destined to live, for with his white face and blond hair, which made him look like a French child, he would hardly have been in his place there."[64]

The argument always hinges on the most marked European features: blond hair and white skin. The discourse around the *métis* question never depicts children who did not look like their fathers. To see only faces that "glowed with Frenchness" among children of mixed blood is already to make a "choice" of kinship. This selection is an election, a form of adoption of the *métis* by the French community. Here, as is the case with many social contexts, spontaneous theories of resemblance point to the line of filiation that one wants to privilege.[65]

These scenes were not limited to Indochina. In 1941, for example, the governor of Gabon described a "small child of mixed blood [who] roams the [native] village, where people look at him as something remarkable. He is usually either naked or clad only in a filthy loincloth and occasionally covered with pustules, so that he looks even more wretched than the little black children with whom he plays."[66]

In the eyes of colonials, the sight of such a confusion of identities was especially troubling because it was also apparent to natives. This was the case when the Chinese owner of a gambling hall wrote to the superior resident in Tonkin in 1938:

> We are greatly worried about the question of children of unknown fathers. Since they have no papers, no one will hire them. Many of them are vagabonds. That is why we Chinese pay them pennies a day to work as croupiers or to fan the clients in our gambling halls. But our clients insult them constantly. Although they have no papers, they have European faces, which is a source of shame for France. Why is it up to me, a man of the yellow race, to show them compassion, when you, who are of the same race, abandon them? This is particularly surprising since you seem to have money enough to prepare for war.[67]

Among all the sources consulted in preparing this work, this is the only archival document found in the Vietnamese language. Its presence indicates that the colonial administration was very sensitive to the opinion of natives (and others classed as natives) on this issue. They are always assumed to be looking on:

> No sensitive individual can help feeling a violent sentiment of revulsion, pity, and anger on meeting one of these abandoned children living in a filthy straw hut and wallowing, covered with vermin, in the farmyard mud with the pigs, chickens, ducks, and dogs. With their lovely faces, curly blond hair, and tender blue eyes feverish with malaria, the sight of these children totally naked in

such an awful place pains the heart. As you pass, you wipe away a tear and say to yourself that we are all guilty of this disgusting state of affairs. After calming down a bit, you shout, "It's the administration's fault!" and the Annamite stares at us and laughs ironically: "Yes, it's a little French child, they say, the son of X . . . an administrator, magistrate, or officer, who was abandoned by his father and mother and whom I have taken in. He is intelligent. He will look after my water buffalo."[68]

The introduction of the "spectator of the spectator"[69] shows that underlying the threat represented by the existence of the *métis* was the possibility of an *inversion* of colonial domination.

Dignity and Prestige in the Colonial Situation

The recurrent interest in public manifestations of the degradation of "French blood" reveals a key dimension of the colonial relation: domination was based not on the use of force alone but also on "moral influences"[70] or, to borrow a term much used at the time, the politics of "prestige." The importance of this form of legitimacy grew as the conquest receded into the past. It was in part a matter of necessity. Europeans, including both civilians and military, never amounted to more than a tiny minority. They were able to impose their will only by employing various forms of persuasion, or hegemony, to borrow a term from Antonio Gramsci.[71]

It is increasingly common in French historical work to argue that colonial domination was based primarily on the use of force. The politics of prestige, however, was ubiquitous in colonial discourse, and almost always presented as the opposite of the unchecked exercise of violence. In describing the brutality of certain officials, one author described the "deplorable consequences for French prestige of the actions of these men, who were stationed in isolated outposts and hard to control because they operated completely on their own."[72] The importance attached to prestige also contradicts an alternative thesis according to which the colonial situation was a laboratory for bureaucratic modernity, or, as Michel Foucault would put it, "governmental" rationality.[73]

The politics of prestige had many important ramifications for the colonial order. The first was to make sure that the power of colonizers over colonized was constantly visible. Along with the rifle and club, etiquette and every imaginable sign of deference and difference were critical to the enterprise and helped maintain uninterrupted domination. Pomp was sometimes imported from other domains for the purpose. For instance, civilian authorities in some parts of the empire insisted on martial majesty in their relations with natives: in FWA, administrators, called *"commandants de cercle,"* wore uniforms and were saluted by their native charges.[74]

The Native Code (*Code de l'indigénat*—see chapter 4) was an essential instrument of colonial repression and figured prominently in the display of power. Far more drastic in its disciplinary provisions than ordinary metropolitan criminal law, the Native Code also imposed forms of etiquette on the colonized. Wherever it was in force, we find offenses against the prestige of colonial officials defined and sanctioned. In Algeria, for example, the infractions that could be committed by natives under the code included any "act of disrespect" or "insulting statement directed at an agent of authority, even outside his functions."[75] In 1881, a decree establishing a code of laws applicable to natives of Indochina prohibited the following types of behavior: "Irreverent attitudes toward the administration, administrator, or other officials in the village."[76] These were not exceptional measures imposed at a time of conquest. On the contrary, the tendency was for "native codes" to become ever more detailed and elaborate and to offer more and more precise descriptions of offenses against the prestige of colonials. In New Caledonia, for example, an initial list of infractions specific to natives was drawn up in 1887 and gradually extended thereafter. Additional clauses were added in 1915 to punish "any act of disrespect toward a representative of authority or any public statement tending to undermine the respect due to the French authorities."[77] If the French colonial state was initially a military and police state, it was also—and increasingly—sustained by a logic of honor.

Maintaining the "Proper Distance" between Colonizers and Colonized

The first condition to be satisfied by the politics of prestige was to maintain a "proper distance" between colonizers and colonized. Domination assumes, first of all, difference. Because every contact between colonizers and colonized threatened to erode that difference, it was constantly in need of reinforcement.[78] Colonization produced not only *métis* but also converts and different kinds of intermediaries between populations (such as merchants, interpreters, and aides to the colonial administration), as well as "evolved" natives and "decivilized" Europeans. All of these roles tended to make the boundary between colonized and colonizer more porous—despite the efforts of administrators and colonial notables.[79] Throughout the territories, a variety of techniques were used to keep populations distinct. For instance, one author reported from Indochina in 1898: "We have heard Frenchmen forbid native employees of their offices to speak to them in French. Others order natives working under them not to wear European clothes. All such measures, as humiliating as they are arbitrary, are intended to serve one purpose and one purpose only: to maintain 'Prestige.'"[80] In another example from Algeria in the 1920s, officials of the identity records office denied Christian converts the right to register their children with Christian first names.[81]

Maintaining colonial difference also had to be reconciled with *la mission civilisatrice*, through which the colonial enterprise was legitimated in metropolitan political arguments, if not always in the rhetoric of colonial administrators.[82] Natives were therefore asked both to maintain their "nativeness" and to "become civilized." In other words, they were to maintain a proper distance, neither too close to nor too far away from colonial society. This double bind is particularly apparent in educational policy after 1930. For instance, from 1933 on, the curricula of Franco-Vietnamese schools limited the teaching of French and emphasized instead Vietnamese language, history, and literature along with practical instruction in the trades and farming.[83] In Algeria at about the same time, teachers trained in normal schools learned what Fanny Colonna has aptly termed a "hidden rule": they were expected to absorb Western culture but within implicit limits, making sure not to become either too Westernized or not Westernized enough. In other words, they were to cease being Arabs (or Kabyles) but without cutting themselves off from their "roots," so that they could serve as useful intermediaries between France and "the Muslim people."[84]

The need to maintain a "proper distance" did not apply solely to natives. Colonials were also expected to be "proper," to remain what they were, or again, to borrow from the colonial lexicon, to maintain their "dignity." This was an essential element of prestige. Anthropologically, we are close to the aristocratic logic of the ancien régime, where *honor* referred both to virtue, understood as conformity to a certain code of conduct, and to the prestige associated with it.[85] Maintaining the "dignity of a Frenchman" meant that one always had to behave properly, in accordance with the norms of French civilization as set forth in the Civil Code, which was originally published under the title "The Civil Code of the French." In the colonies, this difficulty was compounded by distance from the metropole and by isolation, which reduced or eliminated the informal but omnipresent control exercised on individuals by their fellow citizens. This threat was made explicit by Georges Hardy, the director of the École coloniale from 1926 to 1933, in a note to future administrators on preparing for colonial life: "There are . . . what I will call risks of endosmosis, by which I mean the subtle influence on the European of certain unfortunate features of the native environment and the disappearance of certain scruples after coming into contact with a morality different from ours. It is clear that, in order to maintain perfect self-control in this confluence of deleterious currents, the colonial needs to have a re-markably firm backbone and very clear awareness of his duties."[86]

With the slightest failure of "self-control," the colonial was in danger of slowly shedding his French attributes and turning into what some began to refer to anxiously in the 1920s as a "decivilized" European—one who had "gone native."[87]

On the Risk of "Decivilization"

The colonial's obligation to maintain his rank was especially strong in the private realm, where there were no institutions of social control to preserve the colonial difference. The maximum feasible segregation was essential there. Evidence of this can be seen in a comment in the file of one offi-cial: "Frequents natives. Even invites them to dinner. Not made for colonial life."[88] Sexuality, which had become a central feature of social identity in bourgeois Europe, represented an opportunity for mixing and therefore loss of propriety.[89] Even more problematic than sexual relations, however, was the sharing of domestic space and especially concubinage, as Ann Laura Stoler has powerfully demonstrated.[90] Indeed, a colonial male was most likely to become decivilized by sharing his bed and his life with a native woman. This was the point made by Victor Augagneur, the former governor of Madagascar, in a 1913 brief in favor of sending large numbers of French-women to the colonies:

> I want to consider the moral state of our compatriots after years of cohabita-
> tion with *ramatoas* or *congaies*. I have often been struck, and deeply saddened,
> by the sight of their psychic transformation, their intellectual and moral de-
> cay. One might assume at first that the white man would impart to the native
> women some measure of the tastes, habits, manners, and pride of Europeans,
> that he would raise his companion up and bring her closer to the European
> type. In short, one might assume that he would teach her civilization. But if
> there is any education, it amounts to little more than a few changes of ap-
> pearance and a few stabs at adopting European attitudes. More commonly,
> not even this rudimentary Europeanization takes place. The native woman

remains totally native. Soon she fills her mate's home with countless members of her family, and the white man is plunged into the midst of native life. The woman does not become a European. Rather, the man gradually changes and adapts and becomes part Malagasy or Annamite. Unless you have visited some hut in the outback, many days from the cities and far from the eyes of superiors and peers, you cannot comprehend the depths to which some of our officers, officials, and colonists have sunk.[91]

Anxiety about sexual relations and cohabitation never resulted in the banning of either, in contrast to what happened in the German and Dutch Empires at the turn of the twentieth century.[92] Bureaucrats and especially judges were, however, strongly advised not to enter into sustained relationships with native women. In 1897, the chief prosecutor for Indochina, alluding to a subject that he "takes up only with the greatest reluctance," called attention to the "unfortunate consequences of these illicit cohabitations, which degrade the magistrate, compromise his authority and prestige, and, worse still, in some cases, impugn his honor." In a memorandum sent to all the magistrates in Indochina, he assured them of "the great value [that he attached] to the dignity of the private lives of magistrates." He took disciplinary steps to ensure that "throughout Cochin China the magistracy sets an example of propriety, conduct, and morality."[93] In 1901, the governor-general of Indochina took up the issue and sent a warning to all public officials via the provincial administrators:

> It has recently come to my attention that it is not only magistrates who are guilty of such misconduct. Such behavior is scarcely less serious on the part of administrative officials, who represent the central government in the cities and provinces of Indochina and who in that sense exercise a measure of public authority. It is imperative that the private lives of administrators be beyond reproach and that there be no question about their integrity and impartiality. Experience has shown that the influence of native concubines is nearly always harmful to the reputation of officials who allow them into their most intimate circle.[94]

The problem was not so much the existence of such relations as the fact that they were visible in the space shared by colonizers and colonized. The superior resident in Laos was under no illusions: given "the special circumstances of most posts in Laos,"[95] he was inclined "to be more tolerant" but still refused "to go so far as to officially countenance the permanent and public presence of a native woman in a government residence paid for by the administration. Furthermore, such permanent cohabitation can only undermine the official's dignity and moral authority."[96]

The combination of dignity, prestige, and domination was one of the linchpins of colonial policy, but it was not unique to the overseas territories. Public officials have been required to maintain their dignity ever since the modern civil service was created in the nineteenth century, and the obligation still exists today. Although the word *dignity* does not figure in the Comprehensive Civil Service Statute, numerous court decisions attest to the reality of the requirement, which does figure explicitly in the Statute of the Magistracy.[97] What was distinctive about the colonies was that the obligation seems to have extended to all French citizens, who were seen as representatives of the colonizing nation and thus, like it or not, agents of the state in prosecuting the politics of prestige. The large literature on the training of prospective colonists echoed this idea. For instance, in the text cited earlier, Georges Hardy wrote: "Colonial life increases moral responsibility. The colonial is responsible not only for his personal actions but also for setting an example. He is responsible for the influence he exerts. It is therefore essential that he be trained methodically for his social role and that everything possible be done to ensure that his actions as an individual have only positive effects."[98]

We are now in a better position to grasp the nature of the threat posed by the *métis* question. It was twofold. Like "evolved" natives and "decivilized" Europeans, the very existence of the *métis* dissolved the boundary between dominant and dominated. But it also laid bare a lack of dignity on the part of male colonizers, since it revealed not only sexual promiscuity between colonizers and colonized but also immoral behavior on the part of fathers who abandoned their offspring to sad lives as pariahs in colonial society. In the view of colonial notables and philanthropists, these men, many of whom were "soldiers serving with our Indochinese forces, forget that they have a very noble role to play in the colonies; that they represent the mother country and the race that preceded the native on the path to civilization and that has the duty to raise the native up to its own level."[99] Colonials "wanting in moral influence" therefore had a duty to "take themselves in hand" in order "to preserve national society and our good reputation."[100] Efforts to resolve the *métis* question were thus part of the logic of honor, which in the colonies rested on a racial foundation. As the president of the Society for the Protection of Abandoned Children of Mixed Blood put it in 1917: "Race, gentlemen, is the nobility of peoples, and *race obliges* even more than *noblesse*."[101]

Consequently, the response to the *métis* question was subordinated to the desire to maintain colonial domination:

> Children born to French (or European) fathers and Asian mothers—half whites, who are always recognizable no matter what people say—quite simply confront us with a twofold duty in Indochina: a duty of charity and a duty of policy. Charity, because every profound misfortune must elicit appropriate compassion, an effort of succor and kindness. Policy, because in Asia especially, misfortunes and abandoned children inevitably cause scandal, and scandal undermines the very essence of the rulers' prestige and authority. And given today's ideas, shouldn't that authority be increasingly moral, based on the esteem and affection of the natives and less characterized by force and oppression?[102]

In order to put an end to the scandal, it was necessary to "reclassify the *métis*" as part of French society. And for more than sixty years, that is what colonial philanthropists, administrators, and jurists would attempt to do by applying techniques of social engineering in the colonies where the *métis* question posed a threat to the colonial order.

THREE

"Reclassifying" the *Métis*

The need to intervene to resolve the *métis* question was not immediately apparent. At the turn of the twentieth century, there was a real debate about the wisdom of dealing with the *métis as such*. Subsequently, not only in Indochina but also in Madagascar and Africa, colonial notables attempted to "reclassify" the *métis*, taking them from their mothers and placing them in special institutions in which they could grow up to be "French in soul and character," to borrow a phrase from one philanthropist. Techniques for "training" souls and bodies were based on a view of the individual as a product of the combined influence of "heredity" and "environment"—an idea borrowed from the triumphant neo-Lamarckianism of the late nineteenth century. This reclassification effort soon collided with the legal status of unrecognized *métis*, however: although they became French *in fact*, they remained natives *in law*. Hence, the debate soon turned to the legal status of these children.

Producing *Métis* by Helping Them

Throughout the empire, various observers initially claimed that any effort aimed specifically at children abandoned by Europeans would have the effect of creating a separate category of "*déclassés*." In other words, one would "manufacture" *métis* where previously there had been only children born of the colonial encounter. These observers invoked the argument of "perverse effects," which Albert Hirschman has identified as one of the three main tropes of reactionary rhetoric.[1] For instance, the colonial publicist Albert de Pouvourville wrote the following in 1911:

Métis is a grammatical term, and it denotes a child born of relations between individuals of different races and pigmentation. It is also an ethnic term, when because of ignorance or even charitable encouragement, one of the races involved, the superior one, allows an intermediate caste to form and differentiate itself educationally. Finally, it is also a social term. . . . It is above all important . . . not to allow the members [of this caste] to establish themselves as an ethnic order. Then the *métis* will exist in grammar and in grammar only and must never stray beyond its limits. . . . It is by no means in our interest to encourage the birth of a middle class—let us not mention the word *métis*—between the white race and the yellow race. . . . No such class has ever been anything but a bunch of malcontents, failures, and people without roots. . . . In dealing with our *métis*, we should take only individual measures and grant only individual favors.[2]

In other words, Pouvourville favored only ad hoc generosity to children of mixed blood. The *métis* question was a matter for private charity rather than public assistance. On the scale of merit, the *métis* therefore did not rank as high as abandoned children in France: *métis* were comparable to "able-bodied indigents" and thus to the "undeserving poor" (mainly unemployed workers) rather than to invalids (such as sick children, the elderly, and the infirm).[3] Accidents of colonial history, they had no claim on the generosity of the national community.

Soon, however, those arguing on the basis of unintended consequences were confronted with a very different view of the matter. In 1912, charitable organizations requested an increase in their subsidies, and this led to a high-level debate within the Indochinese bureaucracy. The head of administrative affairs proposed that municipalities be required to contribute funds toward these subsidies. He noted that although the indigent in France enjoyed no "right to assistance," the state had the "duty to offer social assistance and solidarity to the needy, the ill, the elderly, the infirm, the insane, and abandoned children."[4] But the director of finance refused to make local contributions compulsory on the grounds that "legally the *métis* does not exist. He cannot be created as a legal person by issuing an order or a local ordinance."[5] His position reflected that of most colonial administrators, who, prior to World War I, systematically dealt with *métis* on the basis of their individual legal status: only legitimate offspring or children recognized by their fathers counted as citizens and were therefore entitled to stipends. The others were to be treated as natives. Colonial authorities had no basis to intervene in the "classification" of *métis*, which should be based solely on the kinship status of individuals. Let us listen again to Pouvourville:

There is generally no ambiguity as to the actions of the father, who is the primary interested party and the best informed. We have only to heed his intentions. He knows better than anyone else the value of the native union in which he engaged and the fruit that it bore. These are family and personal matters, which are very subtle yet all-powerful, and which it would be presumptuous of us to judge. When a Frenchman has done what is necessary, either by legal means or by other avenues when legal means are unsuitable, to make it known that a child is his, that child should sooner or later become French, and if the father, voluntarily or not, someday fails in his duty, then it is up to the state to replace him. There can be no doubt on this point. But if the father disappears without having made known his wish that the child born of his union *take his race*, then he has his reasons, which we do not need to know, and we do not have to take his place. In such cases, the child should be left to the mother, and the mother will almost always try to make the child a native so that it cannot be differentiated from the others.[6]

The father's role in colonial social reproduction is the main issue in this debate. When it was finally resolved in the late 1920s, it was determined that the father could not be the only one to decide whether or not his child ought to "take his race": the state, by way of the judiciary, also became the judge. Accompanying this change was a major shift in the meaning of *race*. The original idea, that the father alone decided the race of the child, relied on an older meaning of the word as synonymous with *lineage* (*lignage*), which was common during the ancien régime.[7] Later, "race" ceased to be a family possession, left to the father's discretion, and became a collective attribute of the nation and a suitable object for state intervention. In the course of this process, the relation between paternal filiation and national affiliation was transformed.

These changes became possible only after the argument of perverse effects had failed. In colonial societies and later in colonial circles in Paris, people gradually came to believe that concerted large-scale action was necessary for the purpose of reclassifying the *métis*. Proponents of intervention adopted a realist perspective, in contrast to the nominalist perspective of those who saw any reform effort as involving a risk of producing a group of *déclassés*. For defenders of the *métis*, the *métis* was not merely a "grammatical category." Even without intervention, the group had a coherence of its own owing to the effects of "atavism" on the one hand and various forms of discrimination in colonial society on the other. This position was clearly set forth by Charles Gravelle, the founder and head of the Société de protection des métis of Cambodia, in a response to the Marquis de Pouvourville:

Let us be wary of demonstrations so "mathematical" that they neglect the laws of pity and forget that races are made not by statutes or social regulations but by the facts of birth and atavism. . . . The advice to help such children without characterizing them as "*métis*" is both pointless and morally and socially untenable. The mere fact of their birth, the suffering inflicted on them by the natives, and the rather inadequate and almost shameful aid that they receive from the French classifies them as "semiwhite" and keeps them in that position, whether you like it or not, as do their complexion, eyes, hair, and other physical characteristics.[8]

The thesis here is the converse of the perverse effects argument. It holds that the problem is the result of inaction by the public authorities and elites of colonial society: "Not dealing with children of mixed blood is the surest way to turn them into *déclassés*. To take an interest in them, as we do and as we would like to be able to do better, is the only way to bind them to us and turn them into people useful to the country."[9] Starting with philanthropic circles in the first decade of the twentieth century, colonial societies thus gradually convinced themselves of the need to intervene.

On the Need to Intervene

As time went by, the scope of intervention expanded. In the early years in Indochina, charitable ventures limited themselves to distributing material and financial assistance to mothers. Only children who were abandoned by both parents or who "needed to be removed from an unsavory environment" or who displayed "aptitude for study" were sent to residential facilities, usually run by religious institutions.[10] Philanthropists quickly came to the conclusion that these practices should be extended to all children of mixed blood. As early as 1909, they arranged for the building of an orphanage in Hanoi. There, orphans found "room and board as well as a 'home' to make up for their absent families."[11] From then on, the goal was to eliminate home aid except for very young children and to welcome all children of mixed blood, regardless of their legal status or talents. As one representative of the colonial state put it, the aim was "in a sense to reclassify [these children] by placing them in the European environment that is theirs by virtue of their European blood."[12]

Subsequently, dozens of similar proposals were seen throughout the empire—some more utopian than others. Their goal was to teach, rear, train, and more broadly reclassify children of mixed blood. The most ambitious programs envisioned using *métis* as agents of agricultural or industrial colonization, especially in Indochina, where candidates for these posts were rare. Some of these ideas were actually put into practice: for example, an agricultural school for young *métis* was created in Hung Hoa (Tonkin) in 1907, although the project came to an abrupt end after some of the students caused a disturbance. But most, like the plan proposed in 1938 by Governor-General Brévié to use *métis* to colonize the Darlac Plateau, were never acted on.

Although assistance projects proliferated during the years between the two world wars, some in the colonial elite continued to refuse to deal with the *métis* as such. This was especially true in FEA, where the colonial press criticized a politics "of difference [that] only awakens totally inappropriate appetites and illusions."[13] This attitude was related to a representation of the *métis* as being deeply tied to the native world. Listen to the words of one "honest official" in Cameroon discussing the case of his adoptive daughter in 1948, whose behavior confirmed "the *métis*'s taste for native life":

> F. never smiles except when blacks are around, and we have a hard time getting her out of the native kitchen, where she yammers away in Touricou and laughs raucously with the boys, even though they are very primitive and crude. This has always worried us and seems to confirm F.'s true nature. She is 95 percent black, and probably nothing can weaken her instinctive attraction. . . . Raised in a native environment until the age of ten, when she was abandoned by her mother, she was shaped too late, I believe, to experience the reactions of conscience that are perhaps the essential characteristic of the "civilized," who are separated from black Africa by centuries, where instincts alone reign.[14]

In 1941, Governor-General Félix Éboué expressed similar reservations about a proposal to "reclassify *métis*." This was in an important memorandum on native policy at a time when it was crucially important for Free France to win the support of the African population. Criticizing the practices of orphanages for *métis*, he proposed that they "refrain from always separating [the *métis*] and keeping them apart from their black emulators."[15] It was probably under his influence that the organizers of the Brazzaville conference (held between January 30 and February 4, 1944, to discuss the future of French Africa after the war) once again raised the *métis* question. In a questionnaire circulated prior to the meeting, they asked colonial leaders whether *métis* should be "assigned a place of their own in native society"—a sign of the continuing importance of the issue as an "imperial problem." The governors of Madagascar and FEA said no, arguing that *métis* should be reared in families.[16] In 1944, René Pleven, colonial minister in the provisional government, also argued that it was better to see to it that the child of mixed blood became a well-integrated native rather than an ill-adapted European. It seems to me that the principal stumbling block to avoid is the constitution of a mixed-race society standing between blacks and whites, contemptuous of the former and incapable of assimilating with the latter. The presence of such a society places the question of race squarely on the agenda and makes it a permanent irritant, impossible to eliminate, which is absolutely contrary to our inclinations and interests.[17]

Like previous regimes, the newly established Fourth Republic relied on the logic of race while denying its pertinence in the French context.

Toward Assumption of Responsibility by the Colonial State

This view remained confined to the territory of FEA. Everywhere else, authorities opted for a "social treatment" of the *métis* question. Religious organizations almost always preceded secular ones in providing care for *métis* children. Such organizations were early arrivals in the colonies, and many offered broad programs of assistance for the local populations: most often, they did not distinguish the *métis* from the rest of those in need.

Throughout the colonial period, various orders, especially the Sisters of Saint-Paul of Chartres, would provide homes for children of both sexes.[18] In Cochin China, which had been a French colony since 1862, the first such institutions were founded in the mid-1870s.[19] The religious orders also established high schools, such as the Taberd school in Saigon.

Secular organizations dedicated to the *métis* problem emerged a short time later: the Société d'assistance des enfants métis abandonnés was founded in Saigon in 1894,[20] the Association de protection des enfants métis of Tonkin in 1898, the Société de protection de l'enfance au Cambodge shortly after the turn of the twentieth century, and the Société de protection de l'enfance in Annam in 1918. Religious groups and secular groups often worked together in these contexts. In Madagascar, the Société d'assistance et de protection des enfants métis, founded in 1900, shared responsibility for the protection of *métis* children with the Oeuvre des Paulins, founded in 1905 by Father Joseph de Villèle, and with the schools of the Sisters of Saint Joseph of Cluny.

In Africa, by contrast, secular charities did not emerge. This lack of mobilization can be attributed in part to the lower density and stability of the French population, which made the *métis* problem less acute. There, religious orders and the official bureaucracy directly shared responsibility for children of mixed blood. In French Sudan (present-day Mali), the Sisters of Saint Joseph of Cluny accepted girls of mixed blood into their school at Dniguiraye as early as 1896. After some of the students caused trouble, Governor William Ponty created a Homemaking School for them in 1912. Boys were treated similarly: the White Fathers took in mixed-race orphans at Ségou as early as 1896, well before orphan boys were welcomed into a special section of the government-run School for Leaders' Sons at Bamako in 1904. In the Ivory Coast, special sections were created in 1910 for boys at Bingerville and for girls at Mossou. We find the same organization in Dahomey (now Benin), at Porto Novo and Cotonou.[21] Any child of mixed race in FWA could be admitted to these orphanages, with the cost of upkeep charged to the colony from which the child came.[22] In FEA, *métis* were most commonly received either by religious missions, especially those of the Congregation of the Holy Spirit, with expenses borne by the local administration, or by public orphanages.[23] In Algeria, where the *métis* problem was limited to southern regions, the White Fathers and Sisters took in children of mixed race at El Goléa from 1921 on.[24]

Where religious orders and secular groups coexisted, they usually collaborated.[25] In some cases, the secular groups were content to locate children and turn them over to the religious orders for care. Still, there were clear differences between the two types of organizations. The philanthropic societies were interested in all aspects of the *métis* question, which they helped to formulate as a "human, social, and political problem." The religious orders simply took care of children. They treated *métis* as needy natives and did not physically segregate those of mixed race from other native children in need.

Both religious and lay organizations maintained various ties with the colonial administration. Initially, the administration took the position that the issue was not an immediate concern of government. It allowed the charitable groups that it subsidized to deal with the problem. This practice was the result of initial indifference to the issue, of confusion between "public assistance" and "private charity" (which endured far longer in the colonies than in metropolitan France), and of the lack of enforcement of the separation of church and state in the colonies, enabling the administration to turn the problem of social assistance over to religious organizations.

As the problem came to be seen as a "major colonial issue," the state's involvement gradually increased. The system of subsidies was institutionalized, and the private organizations dealing with the problem were recognized as public service organizations. Eventually, the government took more direct charge, especially in Indochina. In 1939, this led to the creation of the Jules Brévié Federation, named for the governor of the Indochinese union from

1936 to 1939. This was an umbrella organization whose role was to coordinate both secular and religious charities dealing with "the education and placement of children of mixed Franco-Indochinese blood." It distributed public funds and directed efforts to deal with the *métis*. The role of the state also increased in Africa: in 1941, the Oeuvre de protection des métis of Free French Africa was created. Its goal was to "locate and identify" children of mixed blood, provide them with "moral and material assistance," give them "instruction sufficient to facilitate their placement and establishment," "to help them acquire state concessions," and to prevent the "prostitution of girls and women of mixed blood," while ensuring that "*métis* do not lose contact with the native environment in which they are destined to live and do not form a caste within this society."[26] The tension between the desire to intervene and the wish to avoid creating a separate *métis* group, noticeable in all the colonies, was most intense in Africa.

Notables and Proletarians of the Empire

The notables of colonial society were the first to become involved with the *métis* question, and were the most deeply interested. Most were either government officials or professionals. In Tonkin in 1894, the founders of the Société de protection des enfants métis abandonnés included the postmaster, the head of the legal office in the department of public works, and a pharmacist from Hanoi. Among the forty-six all-male members of the Société de protection de l'enfance (founded in 1918) in Annam, thirty-four were government officials with significant responsibilities. Lawyers practicing in both the public and private sectors were also common in these organizations. In the 1930s in Saigon, for example, we find the chief prosecutor, the assistant chief judge of the court of appeals, and a prominent attorney.

Although a majority of the founders of charitable organizations were unmarried men (a fact that should be seen in relation to the small number of Frenchwomen in the colonies prior to World War I), fathers of *métis* soon joined the ranks of the philanthropists. The vast majority of these were married to the mothers of their children, however, and therefore not among those responsible for the "problem." These philanthropists had established local roots, started families, and invested in social reform: all these aspects of their personal trajectories were connected as different modes of what they called their "love for the country." It was also one of the many ways in which individual social trajectories intersected with France's imperial project.

Consider, for example, the case of Commandant Révérony, who arrived in Tonkin in 1886. An early member of the Société de protection des métis, he eventually became its president and served in that post until 1924. "Won over by the country, he settled there and started a family." He was "an exemplary father."[27] Such notables were often the most ardent proponents of the politics of prestige.

Many of those married to native women were also men of science and learning, and in particular local historians and ethnographers. *Libido sciendi* and libido *tout court* were strongly connected. Particularly enlightening in this respect is the career of Lieutenant Colonel Auguste Bonifacy, an ethnographer and local historian of Indochina, respected by his peers as well as his superiors.[28] He belonged to a society to assist *métis* and wrote a widely read article on the subject, which appeared in the *Bulletins et mémoires* of the Société d'anthropologie of Paris in 1911 (see chapter 1). He, too, married a Vietnamese woman and started a family. This connection between the realm of learning and that of philanthropy was not an isolated case. Another example was Georges Coedès, who served as head of the École française d'Extrême Orient from 1935 to 1946 and as president of the Société d'assistance aux enfants franco-indochinois from February 1940.[29] Government officials were not the only ones so involved. Businessmen, judges, and planters also published in scholarly reviews.

Noticeably absent from the ranks of philanthropic organizations, however, were natives. For the entire period under study, we find only two Vietnamese names in the records of the three main Indochinese charities. Once again, the *métis* question and the necessity of reasserting the coherence of the colonial order were a "problem" only from the French perspective.

Women, too, were rare among the members of charitable organizations before 1920. In part, this absence reflected their small numbers in colonial society, especially before World War I. But it should also be seen in light of women's general lack of involvement in reformist circles around the turn of the twentieth century in France.[30] After 1925, the Société d'assistance aux enfants abandonnés franco-indochinois made it a rule to include three women among the fifteen members of its board of directors, in view of the "maternal assistance" they could provide.[31] These women were usually the wives of male members of the group, and they were effectively assigned the status of patrons of the organization. Ultimately, the exclusion of women stemmed from the fact that the *métis* question was a man's affair, touching as it did on issues of paternity, citizenship, and above all the relation between the two. Thus, the men involved in dealing with it described their work as a "manly effort"[32] to restore the prestige of the colonizers and thus the dignity of France. If the *métis* problem indicated a "deficiency of moral influence," dealing with it allowed the community of men to "take itself in hand" and "revive its sense of decency."[33]

This was a genuine form of social work, based on a distinction within the colonial population between philanthropists and those who were responsible for the *métis* problem, or, in other words, between prominent settlers and mostly younger men of more modest social background stationed in the colonies for relatively short periods of time, whom the former accused of lacking "dignity and morality."[34] This class contempt for the "drunken soldiery"[35] responsible for the *métis* issue was linked to a determination to maintain "group boundaries—that is, limits beyond which no substantial exchange, commerce, social intercourse, or marriage shall take place."[36] The prominent settlers who trumpeted the issue were primarily concerned with maintaining the integrity of colonial society over time: in other words, with social reproduction. Hence, it will come as no surprise that we find among them a certain number of offspring of colonial encounters—legitimate children who were therefore legally French and not *métis* in the strict sense of the word but for whom the trace of the boundary between the two groups within colonial society was an issue of particular importance. Some of these individuals, mostly low-level bureaucrats, founded one of the first aid societies in 1894, and the new organization quickly merged with another created that same year by leading citizens of the city: "Proud of their origins, [they were] eager to organize a group to provide for the heirs of French blood who had been left without protection and exposed to risks of all sorts—troubling reminders of acts of cowardice and desertion that had to be erased from the memories not only of the small children involved but also of the contemporaries of the men responsible."[37]

This division between colonial notables and proletarians was one of many cleavages in a colonial society that was anything but monolithic.[38] It also reminded everyone involved of the fragility of the mechanisms by which colonial society reproduced itself. This evidence weighs against recurring interpretations of colonial domination as confident and undivided.

Identifying, Reporting, and Assisting

First philanthropists and later administrators sought to ward off the political danger that the *métis* question posed to the future of the colonial project.

The logic of their actions was racial: "It is clearly French blood that pre-dominates in their veins. In their behavior and psychological reactions, they instinctively demonstrate their attachment to France."[39] The same "blood ties" made the *métis* an object of concern for others: "It is unjust and inhu-man to allow men with our blood in their veins to live as vagabonds."[40] On this view, blood was said to take precedence over law, which led certain well-intentioned men to denounce the granting of rights to certain "natives" who were less "French" than their own protégés. Indeed, they considered the situation of the *métis* to be "shocking and unjust, not to say somewhat paradoxical, when we have made natives of the Four Communes of Senegal French citizens"[41] (on this example, see chapter 4). Note that the racial cri-terion was here part of a gesture of inclusiveness: the idea was that anyone who was to any degree "of French blood" should enjoy full French citi-zenship. In an inversion of the "one drop rule"[42] that was prevalent in the United States at the time, "a single drop" of French blood was enough for inclusion in the "community of citizens." Blood ties were associated with certain rights, the most basic of which was the "right to life," to borrow an expression from the president of the Amicale des métis of Gabon.[43] The application of racial logic to the *métis* question and the concern with pre-serving life probably represent the most complete colonial application of what Michel Foucault has called "biopower," which he identified as the basis of modern racism.[44]

Race was not used only to justify assistance to *métis*. It also served as a practical criterion for identifying which individuals to help. This was not always easy. Philanthropic associations in all the colonies nominated repre-sentatives to identify and keep an eye on children.[45] In this context, they did *not* refer to the "scientific" indexes developed by physical anthropologists at the Paris École d'anthropologie after 1860: these included straightforward measurements (size of limbs, circumference of the skull) and more com-monly ratios of these measures (such as the "cephalic index" and "facial angle"), along with very detailed "chromatic scales" of skin and hair color developed by Paul Broca.[46] These metropolitan forms of scientific racism, which have been at the center of the historians' agenda, simply did not in-form colonial behavior. The emphasis was rather on a semiology of racial signs, part of a local visual culture that enabled "a moderately practiced eye" to identify *métis*.[47] Such practical knowledge, a product of experience and "habit" rather than scientific rationalization, was never made explicit by the philanthropists who relied on it. They also relied on reputations and testi-mony about fathers from mothers and neighbors, or even on the father's own report when it was he who entrusted them with his child. The local administration often assisted in the task of identification.[48]

Heredity and Environment

The idea of race on which people involved in the *métis* question relied cannot be reduced to blood alone. It figured in a dialectic of "heredity" and "environment," which was ubiquitous in late nineteenth-century social discourse in the metropole as well as the colonies and particularly important in the case of *métis*. In the absence of a dominant hereditary influence, the role of environment became especially important:

> The problem of the definitive formation of the mentality of the *métis* is a delicate one, because in them the hereditary element, which is the basis of character, is complex. Ancient European heredities and still more ancient Asian ones, profoundly different from one another, clash and mix uneasily. In the course of the child's intellectual development, these opposing tendencies interfere, giving rise to periods of crisis and indecision. At some point, however, the child, whether unconsciously or not, ends up making a choice for one or the other, depending on whether, under the influence of education and environment, the paternal or maternal heredity wins out. . . . Discipline must be applied in a timely and methodical manner. Certain tendencies should be encouraged and developed, others attenuated, in order to ensure that one of the heredities predominates to the maximum extent possible.[49]

The "discipline" in question was a matter not of formal education but rather of early influences. That is why philanthropists wanted to take charge of children at the earliest stage possible:

> Above this age [seven years], the character is formed, and habits have set in. Regardless of the child's heredity, it is shaped from birth by the environment in which it grows up. The more malleable the child, and the more faithfully it preserves the impressions it receives, the greater the influence of the environment. If it learns very quickly, it imitates even more promptly. And whom is it most likely to imitate when its sensibility is awakened, and reason along with it? The individuals in its milieu, those whom it loves best or whose superiority it recognizes. In other words, the child reflects its milieu. Hence, it is impossible to stress too strongly the need for the moral climate in this first milieu, where the child will acquire the vices and virtues that will leave an indelible imprint on it, to be as healthy as the physical climate.[50]

This is a long way from the Durkheimian notion of socialization via the school, the centerpiece of the republican educational project. The colonial concept of individual formation drew instead on the work of one of Durkheim's principal rivals, Gabriel de Tarde. Tarde developed a notion of imitation that was closely tied to the milieu "in which it proceeds by way of refraction" and "relies essentially on heredity."[51] More important still was the neo-Lamarckian synthesis that influenced the thinking of many republican reformers in the last few decades of the nineteenth century. Many were doctors who divided their time between the academy and politics and, like Paul Bert and Jean-Louis de Lanessan, were particularly active in the colonial administration.[52] The adepts of this school rejected Darwin's theses and in the 1870s embraced Lamarck's transformism. Adding a mechanistic twist to Lamarck's vitalism, neo-Lamarckianism stressed the adaptation of living things to their environment and the transmission of acquired characters.[53] In order for a change in the milieu to transform an organism, it had to induce some repetitive action to create a habit.[54] This line of argument had direct political consequences, because it suggested that individuals could be improved by improving their milieu and inculcating "good habits." Neo-Lamarckianism thus inspired any number of efforts to achieve social reform by transforming the body, such as social hygiene, gymnastics, and child-care practices (*puériculture*), which later figured in the inception of eugenics in France.[55] The goal of all of these schools was to shape "habits" by influencing the education dispensed both in the schools, at home, and in the "social environment." Neo-Lamarckianism thus gave rise to a "total" educational project that contributed to what Jacques Donzelot has called "the policing of families."[56]

Making "Frenchmen in Soul and Character"

In the colonies, the dialectic of heredity and environment would have a profound influence on the *métis* question. It was used first of all to justify separating children from their mothers at an age that decreased as time went by. Indeed, philanthropists from Asia to Africa agreed that "it is best to remove them from what is often an unhealthy environment while still in infancy, before they have acquired unfortunate habits of mind and body that would be impossible to eliminate at a later stage."[57] In a broader perspective, the neo-Lamarckian synthesis opened the way to a wide range of social engineering projects that sought to transform these "Frenchmen by blood" into full-fledged members of the national community. This goal was made explicit in the 1917 program of the Société de protection de l'enfance in Cambodia:

The very delicate case that concerns us calls for psychologists and others aware of Asiatic atavisms, which one finds in combination in these children of mixed blood, who bear the marks of two races in varying proportions. The hereditary influence on both physical and moral characteristics is undeniable. Our task is above all to shape characters, to adjust the mechanism of the heart. But since we are the absolute masters of this process, there is in principle nothing to prevent us from gradually allowing the Asiatic element to atrophy and developing only the white side of these still virgin natures, devoid of ingrained penchants and habits. The entire purpose of our program is to make "French souls."[58]

This conviction, shared by reformers throughout the empire, was based on a concept of socialization as the product of interpersonal interactions: "Our duty as Frenchmen is . . . to turn these de facto Frenchmen into Frenchmen in soul and character. Only education can accomplish this. That education must therefore be French, provided by French teachers, alongside children of French origin, because *contact* is still the best teacher and the quickest way to shape feelings and consciences."[59]

The guiding principle of the social reformers was thus to immerse the *métis* in a "French environment" as soon as possible. That is why orphanages based on a family model were built throughout the empire. Children were supposed to be able to "find food and lodging, a 'home' to replace their missing families."[60] Philanthropists stressed the emotional side of child rearing and sought to give children of mixed blood "teachers and devoted protectors (both male and female), whom they could love [and with whom they could form] sincere, absolute, supple, and lasting bonds—not rigid bureaucrats concerned only with their programs and coming and going like birds."[61] When the administration took direct charge of the *métis* question, its goal was the same: to make sure that the orphanages were "true homes" in which the children could find a "familial atmosphere."[62] Within this re-created family, the philanthropists always presented themselves as "adoptive fathers,"[63] "excellent heads of family" who not only inculcated a sense of discipline but also, "with tenderness in their hearts," offered "counsel and encouragement" from which "gratitude would arise."[64] Again, much more importance was ascribed to the paternal role and its emotional aspects than to "maternal care," which was mentioned far less often.

The role assigned to "the familial environment" was not specific to the *métis* question. Similar arguments could be heard in the metropole in the debate concerning the placement of children with families by the Office of

Public Assistance.[65] In the case of the *métis*, however, the goal was explicitly "national": it was a matter of reclassifying these children as members of the French population, turning them into "Frenchmen in soul and character." The most important traits of character were the moral virtues, especially "dignity," which, as we have seen, was an essential attribute for Frenchmen living outside the metropole and a prerequisite for colonial domination. Thus, the statutes of one of the first philanthropic societies stipulated that the group "shall watch over all its wards with equal solicitude and strive to inculcate in them our sense of honor and probity."[66] As one observer recalled, "associations . . . have always sought to . . . develop in them a sense of their *dignity*."[67] Implicit in the goal of reclassifying the *métis* was thus a veritable sentimental education[68] to instill a "love of France, with the ambitions of whites."[69]

In the late 1920s, the philanthropists summed up their enterprise by describing "the policy of 'assimilation' that [they intended] to apply to their wards, the *métis*."[70] In the 1930s, the use of the word became increasingly common, without the distancing quotation marks. A very specific concept of nationality was at work in this project to turn *métis* into "Frenchmen in soul and character." Instead of a "daily plebiscite" or "contract" formalizing the acceptance of a political project,[71] nationality was the product of the dialectic between "heredity" and "environment," especially the family environment, in which the role of paternal care was paramount.

Producing Coherence

As we have seen, one of the major problems raised by the existence of *métis* was that it blurred the dividing line between colonizers and colonized. One primary purpose of the reclassification of *métis* was thus to restore the colonial order, which meant reestablishing the "coherence"[72] of various features of the children's identity by working on their appearance and guiding their social trajectory. Here again, philanthropists were influenced by neo-Lamarckian thinking, which persuaded them that they could transform both souls and bodies—the former by way of the latter. In Indochina, where the natives were usually described in terms of "feminine" attributes ("delicacy," "weak constitution"), the representatives of charitable organizations congratulated themselves on the robustness of their charges, which made them more like the French: "It is worth noting that most *métis* are sickly, weak, and frail when they are admitted. This must be ascribed to their origins, to poor hygienic conditions, and to the privations to which some of them were subjected before entering our orphanages, where their health improved rapidly. Changes in diet, a healthy lifestyle, and strict hygiene transform them before our very eyes."[73]

According to the "environmental paradigm," both bodies and souls are shaped by the material features of their environment. Philanthropists therefore paid close attention to clothing, given the marked differences in dress that distinguished Europeans from natives. Between the two world wars, the adoption of European garb by a Vietnamese was taken as a sign of "evolution," but a Frenchman could not decently wear the local costume without losing status and marking himself as an irredeemable renegade from civilization. When charitable organizations finally opted for a policy of reclassifying children of mixed blood as French in the 1920s, all assisted children were given a wardrobe of European clothing.

The same "orthopedics of the soul" was applied to the diet of the *métis*: orphanage rules stipulated that the food must be European. Only during the Depression of the 1930s was it decided that girls in Indochinese orphanages should "eat Annamite-style three or four times a week." This meant that they were served a bowl of rice with vegetables, which allowed for substantial savings.[74] Here we see additional proof that the reclassification of *métis* was primarily concerned with reproducing male identities. Government efforts were guided by the same ideas: in the late 1930s, when the colonial administration became more directly involved with the *métis*, inspectors were assigned to visit orphanages in order to make sure that, among other things, the food served was "French."[75] Diet, like clothing, was one of the "technologies of the body"[76] that fostered objective ties among members of the group while distinguishing them from others. To eat Vietnamese meant not only consuming a particular type of food but also adopting a particular posture (generally crouching or sitting at a low table), objects (bowl and chopsticks), and gestures. Eating was therefore an important sign of membership in one community or the other. It also shaped identity: in terms of the paradigm of habit—close to that of Pierre Bourdieu's habitus—technologies of the body transformed body and soul by sheer force of repetition.[77]

Philanthropists also mobilized around names, which they took to be both *signs* of belonging and *generators* of a sense of identity.[78] In Indochina, the "spontaneous" naming practices of the *métis* were complex. The vast majority took French first names, which accorded with local theories of resemblance: both French and Vietnamese stressed affinities with the father.[79] By contrast, last names could be either Vietnamese or French. A child who was legitimate or recognized by his or her father naturally bore the father's last name. Otherwise, the child used the father's last name preceded by the prefix *dit* ("known as"), a practice that was tolerated by the government: fathers "unknown" to the law were nevertheless "known" to everyone in practice. Philanthropists, who thought of themselves as surrogate fathers, often assigned last names. When they took a child in, they gave him or her a name. Usually, this was the name of the father, with a few letters changed or syllables reversed to make the child's last name sound similar to the father's: for example, *Robin* might become *Rimbault* and *Delarue* might be transformed into *Dulerat*. These attributions of French-sounding names, subsequently approved by the courts,[80] indicated that even if the individual filiation remained unclear, the child was recognized as a child of the nation.

Finally, the insistence on coherence was applied to the relation between appearance, race, and social status.[81] Philanthropists and administrators therefore paid particular attention to the professional orientation of the children they assisted to make sure that it matched the "aptitudes" of their race: "Because they are raised in conditions that bring them closer to the race of their father than to that of their mother, a large gap could develop between the faculties of these young people and their social rank if we neglect these aptitudes rather than cultivate them."[82] It was also important to avoid the danger of *déclassement* by allowing *métis* to achieve the "standing of Frenchmen" without fostering "hopes" beyond their actual rank. The internal regulations of one charitable society stipulated that "only modest tastes and humble aspirations [will be suggested] to them."[83] The entrepreneurs who took charge of the *métis* question had every intention of regulating the desires of their charges.[84] Concretely, the goal was to train skilled workers, who were expected, especially after 1930, to become the agents (*cadres*) of colonization. Philanthropists therefore hoped to inculcate "simple habits and . . . encourage them to follow the path of manual labor rather than anything else."[85] They favored primary schooling followed by occupational training or apprenticeship. As good fathers, they drew on their social capital to win places for their charges in state and private workshops. But they also took account of individual "aptitudes," and it was with great paternal pride that the annual reports of the society remarked on those rare few who earned a school certificate, high school diploma, or perhaps even admission to a teachers academy.

Reclassification in France

The ultimate reclassification of the *métis* was the decision to send a few to metropolitan France, where they would enjoy the largest number of interactions with French people, the closest possible "contact," and the most French "environment." According to the philanthropists, this was "the most effective way to help them adapt to a culture and mentality very different from the ones they knew in their early years. . . . [This is] the quickest way to incorporate them into French society."[86] But the strong association between Frenchness and location did not apply uniformly to the metropolitan territory. For philanthropists, Frenchness was not evenly distributed:

> The circumstances and ambience are too hostile here, however. Education in France, in a purely national environment, can provide a better chance of success. . . . Provence, our original idea, does not seem on reflection to be absolutely preferable to all other possibilities. Its blessed skies conceal too much laxity and easy living and probably too much in the way of tall tales and cosmopolitanism. In such a place, the young do not readily acquire energetic characters. Algeria and Corsica, though attractive at first sight, are still "special," apparently, too remote from the French heartland. . . . Perpignan, Montpellier, Pau, Toulouse, Bordeaux: these places offer us a somewhat more severe southern environment, but also more positive (less "lazy" than Provence), a better environment. In the end, I think that Bordeaux would be preferable in terms of culture and acclimatization, with Arcachon as a home base, if we opt for a Colonial House as familial as possible.[87]

World War I provided the first experience with reclassification in the French environment. Philanthropic societies sent their wards as volunteers.[88] Many *métis* were requisitioned as native troops at a time when French and native soldiers were completely segregated. They often served as skilled workers or interpreters for Vietnamese troops. After the war, when the government hastened to send colonial workers back where they came from, "benevolent measures" were taken to allow those of mixed blood to remain in the metropole.[89] Fiftysome adolescents sent by the Society of Tonkin remained in France. In 1919, the society expanded this program, taking its inspiration from the experience of public assistance with placing children in foster homes, in order to ensure the "fusion" of the *métis* into the "mass of the French population."[90] Believing in the virtues of imitation, philanthropists assumed that if their young charges were "placed in a new environment at an early enough age, so that they are exposed to examples of courageous toil, honesty, uprightness, and dignity of the sort that one finds in most French families, they [would be able] to become . . . respectable citizens contributing as much as possible to the prosperity of the nation."[91] The colonial administration supported this project by paying for the children's transportation. The system was institutionalized in 1924, when the vice president of the Society of Tonkin retired and returned to France. He took up residence in Coutances and placed fifty-nine children in the surrounding region (La Manche), mostly with farmers but some as apprentices to artisans, in state workshops, or, if their educational level allowed, in the upper grades of primary schools and later in teachers schools.[92]

This experiment, which everyone involved judged favorably, came to an end in 1931. The economic crisis, which hit Indochina particularly hard, forced the colony to cut its budget drastically and end its policy of paying for the transportation of children to France. The Indochinese administration revived the program at the end of the 1930s. With France in the midst of a profound demographic crisis, the argument was that sending children to France to stay would yield two benefits: "There is a human interest in saving abandoned French children, who would otherwise all too likely swell the ranks of juvenile delinquents and prostitutes, and there is a political interest in sending them to France and turning them into Frenchmen."[93] Since xenophobic sentiment was increasingly common in France in the 1920s and 1930s, this consensus regarding the advantages of sending *métis* to France may seem surprising. There was only a single discordant voice: one colonial inspector general observed that "it may not be desirable for these *métis* to establish roots in France, where the exotic and foreign element has already grown too large since the end of hostilities."[94] By this time, however, thanks to the efforts of the philanthropists, these children of mixed blood were no longer regarded as "exotic and foreign elements" but as potential Frenchmen.

Crossing Borders

The reclassification effort soon ran up against legal limitations. After being raised as young Frenchmen "in soul and character," *métis* not recognized by their fathers were still classified as native subjects, with all the attendant social consequences. In the colonies, many social institutions bore the imprint of the great divide between Europeans and natives. This was particularly true of the institutions of socialization whose mission, according to republican doctrine, was to produce citizens: the school and the army were marked by more or less overt forms of discrimination. *Métis* were a priori excluded from French military regiments and had to serve in indigenous units. Philanthropists, joined by others who saw these *métis* as de facto Frenchmen, developed ways of getting around the legal restrictions. Colonial functionaries themselves often hesitated when it came to classifying the *métis*.[95]

French Schools and Native Schools

The French Empire never had a uniform educational policy. Practices varied from colony to colony depending on the local features of colonial society.[96] Yet almost everywhere, French and native students were fairly strictly segregated. In Indochina, alongside the public and private French schools, certain traditional educational institutions were tolerated to one degree or another by the colonial administration. The public school system itself was dual-tracked: the curriculum for Europeans was identical to that offered in France, while a so-called Franco-native curriculum was offered to the local population. The native curriculum was first adopted in Cochin China in 1879 and then extended to other territories of the confederation. In 1917, it was reorganized: several tracks were established, and a minority of students received a local baccalaureate degree and admission to the University of Hanoi, which opened its doors in 1917. The Franco-native schools thus paralleled the French system and echoed the similar dual track in France established for children of the working class. The barrier separating the two systems was fairly difficult to cross. French children did not attend Franco-native classes, and natives rarely attended French schools.[97] It was not until 1912 that the Lycée Paul-Bert opened its doors to children of the local native elite.[98] Curricula were different and the prestige of a diploma from one system did not match that of the other, nor did it open the same doors. For instance, the Hanoi Faculty of Medicine trained only "auxiliary physicians," who were allowed to practice only in the colony. Natives were prohibited from applying for French diplomas, especially the *certificat d'études*. In 1920, the administration gave in to pressure from native parents demanding an exception but limited this to children "admitted to French schools" in order to avoid a surge in the number of native candidates.[99] Under the circumstances, the assignment of unrecognized *métis* to one system or the other posed a problem: were they to be educated with the French or with the natives?

In 1901, the Hanoi school committee considered the admission of *métis* to the municipal school but decided that "only French children may attend." However, the principal was granted the power "to accept certain Asian students whose aptitude and intelligence suggest that they might be capable of being pushed. These students shall nevertheless be taught separately from the Europeans." A special class was then created for twelve unrecognized *métis*, who received instruction in Vietnamese from a native instructor. In 1904, growing numbers of families of settlers from Tonkin insisted that the public school in Hanoi accept their sons and offer a curriculum based on that of the metropole. To meet this new demand, the class for *métis* was eliminated. That same year, "Franco-Annamite" instruction was formally established in the protectorate. The educational committee stated that henceforth "French schools will accept only European children or recognized *métis*. Since unrecognized *métis* belong to the same category as natives, such children must receive the same instruction as Annamite children in the protectorate's Franco-Annamite schools." After a period of "waiver" (*tolérance*), to use the term employed by the resident mayor of Hanoi, the provisions of the law would be enforced. Nevertheless, the affair caused something of a stir and led to a debate in the Hanoi city council. Not everyone accepted the legal distinction: one city councilor asked "how one distinguishes between a recognized *métis* and an unrecognized one."[100]

In 1913, another episode illustrated the interplay between administrative and legal classifications. The head of the Tonkin department of public education observed that, of the ninety-one students in one Haiphong school, "fifty are French (pure blood or recognized *métis*), twenty Annamites, fourteen unrecognized *métis*, and seven of various races, including Chinese, Indians, Macanese, and so on." The principal of this school was thus violating the rule established by the government "not to admit more than one Annamite for every four Europeans in the Henri Rivière School and, in the girls' school, to take only those unrecognized *métisses* whose French sponsors' situation and relationship to the child make it reasonable to count on a French upbringing." This infraction could not be tolerated for long without "risk of the native element overwhelming the French element":

> The schools of Haiphong are French institutions with French curricula to which only French or assimilated children can in principle be admitted. I have permitted certain waivers in favor of Annamite families whom we have reason to prefer owing to their social situation or services rendered to our cause, as well as for certain unrecognized *métis* with French sponsors who have assumed responsibility for their upbringing. In regard to the latter, the issue is sensitive in the extreme, but I do not think that we can admit them all indiscriminately, especially those who are raised by native mothers in the Annamite environment, where they acquire the ideas, mores, and habits of those around them. Our influence during the brief hours of the school day cannot become preponderant in such cases.[101]

From this it is clear that the criterion of legal status was in competition with other practical schemes of classification, especially that of *race*—a term that top officials used freely. The use of race as a criterion did not diminish with time but rather increased.

Given these circumstances, the philanthropists were obliged to circumvent the law. Depending on "aptitude," most of the children they raised were directed to Franco-native schools, which sought to provide a "short, functional, utilitarian"[102] education that was perfectly suited to the goal of reclassifying the *métis*, but a small minority were sent to "European" schools. Because investment in Franco-native schools was limited, these schools could accept only a small number of pupils. After 1910, *métis* received "preferential" admission: school administrators signed blank admission orders to accommodate them. Thus, *métis* were treated as natives somewhat "more equal" than others. For the more gifted students, the government formally agreed to accept them into French schools without "demanding any proof of legitimacy, recognition, and so forth." The only condition was that the children were able to follow the instruction and were wards of one of the philanthropic societies.[103] In the absence of recognition by a French father, acceptance by a philanthropic organization was taken as proof of affiliation with the nation.

The case of Madagascar offers an even clearer illustration of the interplay between *law* and *fact* that was a constant feature of the *métis* question. There, discrimination in the schools was made explicit by local ordinances in 1904 and 1906. These were quickly denounced by prominent natives as well as by the Ligue des droits de l'homme.[104] The result was a polemic regarding the school assignments of *métis*: should they be sent to European or native schools? The governor of Madagascar put this question to the minister of colonies, who responded by proposing to reconcile the imperatives of the local politics of domination with "republican principles":

> This matter is one that calls for local judgment, which you are particularly competent to provide. The department cannot object on principle, since the principle of a legal hierarchy of races is not accepted in republican law. Hence, only educational and social considerations come into play, and they are not without importance. For instance, it is up to us to judge whether differences in the rate of physical, intellectual, and moral development that could be the result of ethnic differences between students attending the same classes might be of a nature to disrupt the common educational process to one degree or another.[105]

In any case, even if "republican law" prohibited consideration of "ethnic differences" in theory, it could not prevent their consideration in practice. After much debate, the solution finally adopted was that only recognized *métis* would be admitted to European schools. In 1928, the director of education modified his position and agreed to accept unrecognized children. He then raised the question of how one identifies *métis* among children classified as natives. The political affairs department proposed to take account of "the public notoriety and, if need be, the ethnic characteristics of the individual in question."[106] Clearly, practical problems of classification led to circumvention of the legal framework and to innovation in French practices of identification.

Incorporating the Métis

After its 1870 military defeat by Prussia, France's primary strategic objective was continental defense. Colonial conquest was left to expeditionary forces assembled for that purpose and complemented by professional soldiers, primarily from the Foreign Legion. Few of these professional soldiers remained on the scene after conquest. The long, slow job of "pacification" therefore required a standing colonial army. It was finally organized in 1900 after lengthy debate in the metropole and drew heavily on indigenous soldiers: the revolutionary model of the "nation in arms" was at odds with the disconnection between citizenship and military service that prevailed in the colonies. The law of 1900 envisioned an army composed of volunteers; professional soldiers, especially from the Foreign Legion; and regiments of troops born in the colonies, including both Europeans and natives.[107] In all the colonies, "native troops" were to be strictly segregated from "white troops." Like school segregation, this form of discrimination raised practical difficulties when it came to assigning *métis* to one component or the other of the colonial army.

In this instance, the philanthropists were the first to criticize the inadequacy of the legal criterion. At the height of World War I, for example, the president of the Cambodian society took steps to ensure that two of his charges would be enlisted as French citizens. These two men, "for regrettable reasons of vanity," recoiled at the idea of enlisting as "native volunteers." He asked that the decision be based not on their legal status but on their "appearance, blood, and sentiments." He then offered a veritable "calculus of color" to borrow an expression from Werner Sollors, providing the number of "quarters" of white blood, which counted as "quarters of nobility" in colonial society:[108]

> I have the honor of begging you to intervene to secure the prompt departure for France of two of our wards: Jean N., age twenty-two, employed by the

department of public works (Phnom Penh), French father, Franco-Cambodian mother; Louis H., age twenty-three, an employee of the land survey office in Battambang, French father, Annamite mother. Both, *entirely French in appearance*, ask to serve the Fatherland. . . . Perhaps, *especially in regard to Jean N. (three-quarters white)*, your sovereign will (which in such cases amounts to princely powers) could grant our wish. . . . His physical appearance is entirely French, and his attitude is excellent.[109]

The military bureaucracy was itself embarrassed by the question of enlisting *métis* in the colonial army. Applying the "environmental paradigm," it quickly came to the conclusion that "there may be serious drawbacks to incorporating young *métis*, who have usually adapted to European habits and customs either through their parents or as a result of the efforts of private charities, into native regiments, where they would come into contact with individuals from an entirely different social environment and an essentially different mentality."[110] Everyone involved felt that one possible solution might be to allow *métis* to join the Foreign Legion. The legion, which maintained a large presence in Indochina throughout the colonial period, did not accept native French subjects. It therefore rejected unrecognized *métis* but accepted "foreign Asiatics," including "Chinese, Siamese, Japanese, and Hindus from English possessions." To get around this rule, some *métis* passed themselves off as Filipinos, Americans, or Spaniards.[111] Certain officers, including the chief of staff, were aware of these practices and in some cases encouraged them.[112]

In the metropole, a law of April 1, 1923, made it easier for the French army to recruit *Heimatlosen*—stateless individuals whose fate had long been of concern to specialists in private international law, thus opening a privileged path to naturalization. This immediately raised the possibility of applying the provisions of this law to *métis* whose fathers were unknown and who therefore had no civil status, just like the stateless. Against the wishes of the Indochinese administration, the minister of war decided in January 1928 to extend the law to Indochina, FWA, and Madagascar, for the express purpose of recruiting unrecognized *métis*. A circular of January 5, 1928, stipulated that "the French colonial corps may enlist . . . unrecognized young males of mixed blood who have declared . . . their intention to seek French naturalization in due course . . . and who have been raised for at least eight years in a French family or school."[113] The purpose of this circular was to open a path to French citizenship for unrecognized *métis* by eliminating the formal criterion of recognition by a French father in favor

of actual upbringing in a "French environment." This would later be superseded by legislation on the status of *métis* born to unknown parents (see
chapter 7).

The Demand for Law

In the eyes of the law, the social reformers were thus in an ambiguous situation. They insisted on applying the letter of the law when it was to the advantage of the *métis*. For instance, they fought the colonial administration's
habit of paying for the passage only of legitimate children of government
officials. In 1912, they succeeded in obtaining free passage for illegitimate
children who had been recognized by their fathers and who were therefore
French citizens. More often than not, however, they invoked "real" identities (defined by blood, feelings, and habits) as opposed to "formal" legal
status. The law thus seemed to define the limits of their enterprise. Not
only did it threaten the project of reclassification by assigning native status
to children who were French "in soul and character," but it also hampered
the philanthropists' activity for decades. Indeed, they would have liked to
rely on provisions of the law of July 24, 1889, concerning "abused and
morally abandoned children," which would have authorized them to "remove" children of mixed blood from the "native environment"—that is, it
would have allowed children to be taken by force from mothers deemed
unworthy, regardless of their desires for custody. Although an 1890 decree
made this law applicable to French citizens in most of the colonies, it was
not until 1924 that natives—and unrecognized *métis*, who were natives in
the eyes of the law—were covered. Thus, the philanthropists' sphere of action—their "jurisdiction," to use the terminology of the sociology of the
professions[114]—was limited by the legal framework.

Social reformers discovered the power of law in the course of their
practice. From the beginning of the twentieth century, but especially in
the 1920s, they made legal status the cornerstone of their project of reclassification. The president of the Société d'assistance aux enfants franco-
indochinois put it clearly in 1926: "If the authorities in France see things
our way, if [they grant] this child French citizenship, all the related issues
will be resolved at one stroke."[115] The philanthropists therefore asked for a
change in citizenship law that would make it possible to reduce the gap between a person's real identity, produced not only by ties of blood but also
by environment and education, and his or her formal identity—between
fact and *law*.

It appears to be . . . illegal that . . . natural children, the sons of Frenchmen, should not be governed by French law . . . ; that boys should not be listed on the recruitment rolls, and that they should not even be allowed to enlist as French soldiers. I would point out that among the unrecognized *métis*, many are raised French, in their father's home and in French schools, and bear their father's name, even though the father has not recognized them, either because it was impossible,[116] or because the man was negligent, or because of some calculation. *These French children are not French.*[117]

As we will see next, this demand was very effectively translated into the language of law. Indeed, the existence of *métis* represented a social and political threat, not only because it erased the distinction between "French" and "native" but also because it disrupted the legal foundations of colonial domination, which depended on the opposition between "citizen" and "subject."

PART TWO

The Law Takes Up the "*Métis* Question"

FOUR

Nationality and Citizenship in the Colonial Situation

Once the *métis* question had been established as a "human, social, and political" problem, it was not long before it became an issue for the law as well. As we saw in the previous chapter, the legal treatment of the problem originated with a veritable insistence on the need for new laws by people who were attempting to resolve the uncertain social status of the *métis*. Jurists were forced to respond because the existence of *métis* posed a challenge to the basic categories of colonial law, especially the categories of "citizen" and "subject." To understand why law took up the issue, we first need to reconsider the colonial interpretations of nationality and citizenship. Only then can we look at the various ways in which the *métis* question encountered the law, first in connection with a controversy over fraudulent recognitions (chapter 5), then in the context of a debate over the application to the colonies of the 1912 law concerning investigations of paternity (chapter 6), and finally in relation to the status of children born in the colonies to unknown parents (chapter 7).

The Stakes of Legal Status

In order to grasp what was at stake in debates about the legal status of the *métis*, we must first consider the gulf that separated the condition of citizens from that of native subjects. Until the end of World War II, this "great divide" was inscribed in both civil and criminal law as well as in the rules governing participation in the public sphere. Denial of voting rights was part of this divide but not a simple or decisive part. Most colonies had no representation in the national parliament, making this political right moot for citizens as well. Native subjects generally did enjoy some local political rights: they could be appointed or elected to local assemblies, for example, even if the powers of these bodies were often quite limited. Ultimately, it was not so much participation in sovereignty that distinguished the subject from the citizen; it was the way in which the power of the state was exercised.

Consider criminal law: the definitions of crimes, sentencing rules, the jurisdiction and composition of the courts, and the penitentiary regime all varied depending on whether the accused was a citizen or a subject. What is more, these differences grew larger over time.[1] In Algeria and Cochin China, a special Native Code (Code de l'indigénat) was established in 1881 and subsequently exported to other colonies.[2] Under the code, infractions specific to natives were punished by administrative procedures. This violated the principles of French law in two respects: in constitutional terms, it violated the separation of powers, since the colonial administration assumed judicial powers; and it violated the principle of universality inherent in the penal code, since the Native Code defined a range of crimes that only natives could commit.[3]

The distinction between "citizen" and "subject" also determined who was eligible to serve in what parts of the civil service: from the inception of the colonial regime, subjects could apply only to posts in the "native section" of the bureaucracy. Posts in the "European section" were closed to them until 1919 in Algeria and until the late 1920s elsewhere.[4] The magistracy and high civil service remained off limits.

Natives were also subject to compulsory labor and to head taxes (*capitation*) reminiscent of the ancien régime. The principle of this tax was sharply contrary to the goal of "emancipating the individual" that characterized the more modern aspects of the colonial project.[5] In most territories, subjects' movements were strictly controlled: the tax card served as an identity card, and natives generally had to have their tax cards stamped whenever they left their home village. By the 1920s, these cards included photographs and fingerprints.[6]

Finally, the private law governing interpersonal relations was different for subjects and citizens. French citizens in the colonies were covered by the Code civil, but natives were governed by local "custom" or, rather, by colonial jurists' interpretations of local customary law.

This legal pluralism is evidence that the revolutionary ideal of producing community through law had been abandoned in the colonies. The French Code civil was the traditional embodiment of this ideal, which Jean-Étienne-Marie Portalis, one of its main authors, characterized in terms of unifying the "diverse nations" that composed ancien régime France in order to foster a "common homeland."[7] The multiplicity of legal codes in the colonies reflected, rather, the evolutionary view of law held by colonial jurists, whereby every legal system is associated with a specific stage of "civilization."

The principle of respecting the institutions of native private law, which figured in the treaties establishing French control over various territories, was in practice subject to a number of limitations. First, French law was applicable if a citizen agreed to it—for example, when natives opted for French law in some specific area (most commonly marriage)—or if customary law was silent. More important, most colonial legal codes included a provision that "native jurisdictions enforce local law and customs whenever these are not in conflict with the principles of French civilization." This stipulation targeted anything having to do with "human dignity," a concept that was central to the colonial legal regime and to its basic division between citizens and subjects.

Jurists and Natives

Until 1946, one important feature of the legal status of natives was the severing of citizenship from nationality: natives were subjects of the French state and therefore "French nationals," yet they were deprived of the rights of citizens. This distinction ran counter to the general tendency in the metropole in the nineteenth and twentieth centuries, nationality and citizenship became more closely linked with the establishment of "universal" male suffrage in 1848 and the gradual extension of political rights to servants, paupers, and finally, in 1944, women.[8]

At first glance, it might appear that a similar liberalization took place in the colonies, especially with the abrogation of the "Native Code" (Code de l'indigénat) in 1944, and, in 1946, the Lamine-Gueye law and the institution of the French Union: both granted citizenship to all subjects of the empire. But the citizen-subject distinction was to some extent reproduced through a dichotomy between two forms of citizenship defined in the constitution of the Fourth Republic in 1946: the "citizen under local law" and the "citizen under ordinary law." These two statuses were further institutionalized by the creation of a double electoral *college* in the colonies, which greatly skewed voting power toward full citizens.

Nationality and Citizenship

Although nationality and citizenship are closely related, they are not a priori identical and do not have the same status or clarity of definition within French law.

Nationality is a term of recent origin. French jurists began to use it only in the early nineteenth century. By the end of the century, however, it had become a stable concept that no one thought to challenge.[9] By then, its meaning was largely determined by the rules of private international law: the term referred to the legal bond between an individual and a state. The primary question for jurists and legislators, especially around the time that the 1889 nationality law was being drafted, was how to define that bond.

In order to define who was a national (and therefore subject to the sovereignty of the state), the law took account of various subjective and objective social characteristics. What tied the individual to the state was neither pure convention nor legal fiction. Rather, the legal bond was supposed to reflect belonging to a deeper reality, to a *real community*, the nation. In legal language, the vertical dimension of nationality (membership in the state) was defined in terms of the horizontal dimension (inclusion in a "national community"). This view, dominant to this day, is not the only logically possible one. One could also take an entirely "artificialist" or nominalist position, according to which there is no real national community apart from its legal definition and the "nation" is merely the population subject to state sovereignty. This was, for example, the view of Hans Kelsen, who in the 1930s advocated a "pure theory of law" that defined nationality as a strictly legal term without objective foundation.[10]

We find this intertwining of fact and law in the work of André Weiss, the author of the leading textbook on private international law in the late nineteenth century. After identifying the nation with the state, rejecting the principle of nationalities, and stating that nationality "is the bond that links the state to each of its members," he defined nationality not as a purely legal construct but in terms of attachment to a "fatherland."[11] French law, and especially the law of 1889, recognized two ways in which this "attachment" could form at birth: through place of birth, or *jus soli* (the law of territory), and through filiation, or *jus sanguinis* (the law of blood). Law also allowed for the acquisition of nationality over the course of adult life, since naturalization was open to anyone who fulfilled the conditions of residence and "morality," to which the law of 1927 added "loyalty" and respect for the "national and social interest."

At the same time, the concept of citizenship seems to have lost some of its former significance and to have become blurred in the minds of jurists. The notion had been central in revolutionary debates, where it referred to participation in the exercise of national sovereignty as distinct from allegiance to the sovereign, at a time when the legal concept of nationality had still not been clearly defined or differentiated from the concept of citizenship.[12]

In 1804, the Napoleonic Code ushered in a different era in which basic laws served not so much to define the exercise of citizenship as to identify the criteria that defined a Frenchman. The code for the first time invoked filiation as the primary criterion in the definition of nationality and linked Frenchness to the enjoyment of various private rights. Indeed, Article 7 stipulated that "the exercise of civil rights is independent of the status of citizen, which can be acquired and maintained only as specified in constitutional law. Every French person shall enjoy civil rights." Postrevolutionary constitutional texts said nothing about citizenship (except for that of 1848). As the century proceeded, legal categorization focused more and more on nationality at the expense of citizenship. For instance, the law of nationality of 1889, which amended a number of articles of the Civil Code, struck the word *citizen* from the new version of Article 7 and referred only to "political rights."[13]

This shift in focus was contemporaneous with a process whereby an increasingly large proportion of nationals enjoyed the rights of citizenship. Leaving aside the "incompetent" (such as women, the insane, children, and criminals), the "national" tended to coincide with the "citizen," defined as a person endowed with political rights. This new equilibrium, central to the republican compromise, came at the cost of a double exclusion of foreigners, who were placed outside both the national and the political community. It was fraught with tensions, however, and nowhere were these more apparent than in the colonies.

The Algerian Laboratory[14]

In defining the status of natives, the Third Republic was not in uncharted territory. Under the ancien régime, the question of the status of colonials had been raised in the Antilles, Mascareignes Islands (Mauritius and Réunion), and Louisiana. It was dealt with in the "Black Codes" of, respectively, 1685, 1723, and 1724, which characterized slaves as "possessions" (*meubles*) and freed slaves as "subjects" (*régnicoles*), "even though they were born in foreign countries."

The Revolution saw the emergence of the terms that would continue to shape colonial debate throughout the nineteenth century. Equal political rights were granted to freeborn men of color in 1791 and extended to all freedmen in 1792. After much hesitation, slavery was abolished in 1794. These measures, which provoked stormy debates, effectively ratified the successful slave rebellions.[15] They were subsequently challenged during the First Empire, which inherited a much reduced colonial regime after Haiti achieved its independence in 1804. The July Monarchy revisited the question of the status of colonials with the law of April 24, 1833, which restored equality to free men of color and granted them civil and political rights.

The nature of the debate changed profoundly after the conquest of Algeria, however, because it was no longer defined by the opposition between "free" and "slave." The new colonial relation emerged slowly from another opposition, between "citizen" and "native subject." After the surrender of Algiers in July 1830, the government promised to respect "the freedom of residents of all classes, as well as their religion, property, commerce, and industry." This promise initiated an ongoing controversy regarding the status of Algerians.

The categories had stabilized by the 1860s. In February 1862, the court of Algiers, while admitting that it was a "principle" of international law that the "subjects of conquered countries" are "French in the same degree as French born on the soil of old France," held that this rule admitted certain exceptions "of necessity when the two populations are in no way homogeneous but differ profoundly as to religion, mores, marriage customs, and family organization." The court took the 1830 treaty of capitulation as settling the question of distinguishing citizens and subjects: "By deciding to maintain their religion, property, commerce, and industry, the high contracting parties agreed . . . that though the various members of this population became French, they would not be permitted to enjoy the rights accruing to French citizens."[16]

Paradoxically, this invention of the "native" had been precipitated by the abolition of slavery in 1848. Indeed, the Second Republic had with one stroke abolished slavery and granted citizenship to those whose irons had been removed in the "old colonies" (Antilles, Guiana, and Réunion). It had also granted voting rights to residents of those parts of Senegal and India that were under French rule. But by deciding to "make no judgment as to the status of native populations" in Algeria,[17] the commission responsible for drafting the act of abolition transformed the latter into subjects by default. Although this category still lacked the conceptual solidity that it would acquire later in the century in colonial law, it already possessed the negative definition of "national deprived of citizenship."

Debate resumed under the Second Empire with the "Arab kingdom" program of Napoleon III. The severing of citizenship from nationality was confirmed by the senatus consult of July 14, 1865, concerning the status of persons and naturalization in Algeria. This text stipulated that any native, whether Muslim or Jew, was French and could "upon request be granted the rights of French citizenship, in which case he would be subject to the civil and political laws of France."[18] In other words, the distinction between the citizen and the subject was based on a difference of personal status, defined in terms of the norms of private law to which an individual was subject. Still, to renounce native personal status was only a necessary and not a sufficient condition to become a citizen. Along with the promulgation of the law came an administrative procedure for judging whether or not applications for citizenship should be allowed to go forward: only those deemed "worthy" (*dignes*) of citizenship were permitted to proceed.[19] The other colonies would gradually adopt the citizen-subject distinction and its associated administrative procedures after 1880. In this respect, Algeria served as a laboratory for experimenting with the legal definition of native status.

The Crémieux decree of 1870 granted full French citizenship to the "*Israélites*" of Algeria. It thus established a distinction between Muslims and Jews, who since 1865 had been subject to the same legal regime. It also marked a break with the practice of individual acquisition of citizenship. The new measure was immediately challenged because the so-called Lambrecht decree of October 7, 1871, stipulated that only Jews living in Algeria at the time of the conquest and their descendants could benefit from the Crémieux decree. As a result, the Jews of the Mzab region, annexed in 1882, retained their native status.[20] This clarification prefigured the new native policy of the republic, which was less liberal than that of the empire in that it aimed to harden legal distinctions between natives and citizens.

Nationality Denatured

This hardening paralleled efforts to clarify the legal definition of nationality in the metropole. The law of nationality of 1889 combined previously scattered elements of a definition of national status into a single coherent text: greater importance was attached to socialization within the French population, as reflected in a measure known as *jus soli* (attribution of French nationality by birth on French soil), which provided that any child born in France to foreign parents should become, upon reaching the age of majority, a French national provided that certain residence requirements were met.[21]

The law of 1889 stabilized the definition of nationality for some time to come. It was declared applicable to Algeria (excluding natives) and to the colonies of Guadeloupe, Martinique, and Réunion, but its extension to the other territories remained unresolved for many years. Although the law called for an administrative order to adjust its dispositions to the colonies, this was not done until 1897 because of uncertainty about how to apply the distinction between Frenchman and foreigner in the colonies.

The decree of 1897 excluded natives from its provisions and thus confirmed the existence of a "native status" alien to the space defined by the French-foreign distinction. Indeed, Article 17 of the decree stipulated that "the condition of natives in the French colonies remains unchanged."[22]

The decree of 1897 also departed from the law of 1889 in eliminating the two measures pertaining to territorial status, which had been the centerpiece of the metropolitan text. In particular, paragraphs 3 and 4 of Article 8 of the Civil Code disappeared completely from the decree of 1897. These had granted French nationality to any individual born in France to a foreign parent, at birth if the parent had also been born in France or else at majority, as long as certain residence requirements were satisfied. In other words, colonial soil did not have the same power as metropolitan soil to confer nationality. The elimination of all provisions pertaining to *jus soli* was intended to block access to French nationality for all foreigners whose foreignness was deemed to be of a different nature than that of immigrants on metropolitan soil. These, according to the new law, were better classified as "natives."

Indeed, "foreigners" in the colonies did not form a homogeneous legal category. It was necessary to differentiate them according to race, as noted in the late 1920s by Henry Solus, an eminent specialist on the legal status of natives:

> In theory, foreigners in the French colonies should be treated in the same way as foreigners in France are treated: they are deprived of political rights but enjoy civil rights as specified by the Civil Code. . . . This is strictly the case, however, only for foreigners of European race or of the white race, or at any rate foreigners whose civilization and social state correspond to ours. But when it comes to certain foreign citizens of states bordering on certain of our colonies, who therefore share with the natives of those colonies great affinities of race, mores, institutions, and, in short, civilization, it has long been thought more rational to take a different line of conduct. Rather than decide that these foreigners in the colonies in question should be treated as foreigners are treated in France, it seemed logical to regard them as natives and assimilate them to natives, whence the expression used to characterize them: "foreigners assimilated to natives."[23]

Throughout the colonial period, colonial jurists resorted most readily to the category of race in dealing with these populations distinguished by a double alterity—foreigners who were also natives. Here, the notion of race was at once the criterion of and the basis for distinctions between populations. It referred not so much to a biological reality (the "white race") as to a set of characteristics that we would today call "cultural," since it was in fact a matter of "civilization." The notion was also eminently political. Indeed, the racial status of a population was not thought of solely in terms of biology; in particular, it also depended on international relations. In Indochina, for example, Japanese citizens joined foreigners of European nations in being assimilated to French citizens. By contrast, the Chinese, who were very numerous in Indochina, were subject to the same regime as the natives. Protests by successive Chinese governments against this unfavorable treatment resulted in the Nanking accords of 1930, which became effective five years later. These removed the Chinese from the category of "Asiatic foreigners" and assimilated them to French citizens for civil, fiscal, and penal purposes.[24]

In the colonies, then, French nationality ceased to be a monolithic category and began to be interpreted in terms of degrees. For instance, the prosecutor in New Caledonia described the natives as "French to a lesser degree."[25] There were several modes of French nationality within the empire. Citizens lived alongside natives who were directly subject to French sovereignty in the colonies sensu stricto but who maintained a nationality of their own in the protectorates and were considered stateless in the mandates: "In the colonies and protectorates, there exist French nationals of several types. They can be classified in three categories: French in the strict sense, enjoying all the rights associated with that status; French subjects; and French protégés."[26]

In the metropole, the legal status of "French national" was characterized by its unity: observable differences in the right to vote were considered consequences of *conditions* such as sex, age, or morality required for the exercise of that particular function. From the standpoint of civil law after the abolition of "civil death" in 1854, incapacities were always specific to certain rights and always pertained to the exercise rather than the enjoyment of those rights.

In the colonies, by contrast, the concept of nationality lost its stability[27] and much of its substance. In many respects, colonial nationality was denatured,[28] as can be seen in the maintenance of "native customary law," in contradiction to the definition of the Frenchman in terms of the exercise of civil rights as set forth in Article 7 of the Civil Code (discussed earlier in the chapter).

Natives were therefore French only in the minimal sense of being subject to French sovereignty. Nationality without citizenship was an abstract construct, which made sense only in the framework of international law, as the author of a doctoral dissertation in law from the 1930s stressed:

> The fact is that the quality of French national has been granted to certain noncitizens for want of any other quality to assign to them. It is the fallback position for a colonial policy of direct rule, which has led to the elimination of even the appearance of local sovereign authority in the occupied territories. The natives of all these territories must be assigned some status in relation to the law of nationality and foreign authorities. It is because they cannot be assigned either native nationality or foreign nationality that they have been made French nationals for the purposes of administrative practice and doctrine, which is always flexible. This is not so much a privilege or an obligation as a matter of definition, a simple consequence of colonial logic.[29]

In some respects, the colonial situation serves to remind us that citizenship is the truth of nationality.

What Is a Native?

Rather than assert, as the Indochinese court of appeals did in 1910, that natives occupied a "situation intermediate between French citizens and foreigners,"[30] it seems more correct to say that the notion of "native" made no sense outside a novel interpretive space that was not defined by the French/foreign axis. "Native" was a category marked by deep ambiguity, in that it referred to both a legal status and a sociological fact (place of birth or "origin"). It therefore stands out from more unambiguous notions such as "subject," which had no use outside the language of the law.

In strict legal logic, a native could be a "subject," a "protégé," or a "citizen." "The word *native*, which has only a generic sense, calls for another adjective to indicate the legal prerogatives that are associated with it and give it real content in the form of a legal status."[31] In practice, this specificity was often neglected. In most administrative and legal texts, *native* replaced *subject*:

> Colonial legislation refers to the colored population as both "native" and "subject." No law defines the word *native*. It seems that the expression "French

subject native" should be used in law. The word *native* by itself means nothing. A native is an aborigine. An Ouolof is a native in Dakar, a Bambara is a native in Bamako, a Frenchman is a native in France. More generally, in French West Africa, any individual born within the territory of the federation can be called a native. . . . The meaning of the word seems to have been restricted, however, and we tend nowadays to consider native any individual who does not enjoy the rights of a French citizen. The term has therefore taken on a somewhat pejorative connotation, and it is likely that the correct expression "French citizen native" will disappear.[32]

The notion of "subject," which was obviously reminiscent of the legal and political vocabulary of the ancien régime, was little used during the Second Empire. Paradoxically, it was republican law that brought it back into general circulation by giving it a purely negative definition: a "subject" was a French national without French citizenship rights—that is, an individual subject to French sovereignty but unable to exercise that sovereignty.

Late nineteenth-century legal doctrine justified the exclusion of natives from citizenship on the basis of two arguments. The first had to do with the organic nature of law, which implied that participation in political life was intimately intertwined with respect for private norms. The second relied on a connection between race and law.

First, the idea that public law and private law were related through their common anchorage in a specific "environment" and "civilization" resulted from the relativistic and evolutionistic understanding of late nineteenth-century colonial doctrine: "It is a truth based on both reason and experience that the private law of a people is in strict harmony and concordance with its political organization, its social state, and its degree of civilization. Civil law is deeply rooted in the social environment for which it is made and to which the specific character and physiognomy of its institutions are adapted."[33]

In a deeper sense, submission to the norms of French civility was laid down as a necessary condition for the exercise of French citizenship.[34] The basic reason why natives could not be citizens was that in their daily lives, they did not behave like Frenchmen and violated the rules of the Civil Code.

Nevertheless, the idea of an "in-status naturalization" that would have granted political rights to natives while allowing them to maintain their personal status was proposed on several occasions. First put forward during the Second Empire, the idea was developed in "nativist" circles around the turn of the twentieth century. In 1911, the *Revue indigène* conducted a campaign along with a series of surveys of jurists, politicians, philosophers, sociologists, and men of letters, focusing on the case of Algeria. Despite this, the intimate connection of civil and civic rights was reaffirmed in parliamentary debates, culminating in the law of February 4, 1919, for Algeria. This law did not mark much of an advance in terms of the "defense of natives": henceforth, access to citizenship for certain categories of natives was to be controlled by the courts rather than the arbitrary decisions of administrators, but full submission to the Civil Code was still required.[35]

In-status naturalization finally became a concrete reality not in Algeria but in FWA with the law of September 29, 1916. The law contained only one article, which stated that "natives of the four full-exercise communes of Senegal and their descendants are and shall remain French citizens subject to the military obligations specified by the law of October 19, 1915." This measure, whose primary purpose was to extend military recruitment to natives of the Four Communes (Dakar, Saint-Louis, Gorée, and Rufisque), gave rise to an intense legal controversy. The law would remain an exception, and an unfortunate one in the opinion of all colonial jurists who insisted on the intimate connection of civil and civic laws.[36] Here, for example is Pierre Dareste, a member of the Conseil d'État and eminent expert on colonial law:

> No one has ever granted that a Senegalese from Saint-Louis or Dakar could settle in the metropole, live there under Muslim law, practice polygamy, or apply rules diametrically opposed to the Civil Code in establishing his family, determining his civil status, defining the filiation of his children, determining their majority, capacity, matrimonial regime, or inheritances, and yet still be issued a voter's card, influence through his vote the choice of deputies, general and municipal councilors, or even run for these offices himself and sit in the French assemblies where the content and applications of laws from which he himself would be exempt are discussed daily.[37]

Race and Law

Besides rooting citizenship in civility, legal doctrine justified maintaining the subject status of natives due to the relationship between race, civilization, and law. In this perspective, every legal system is merely an expression of the deeper realities of a "civilization," conceived as an autonomous and coherent set of institutions subject to slow transformations that are largely beyond the reach of human will. The reason why natives could not escape their subject status was that their civilization was incompatible with the civilization that produced the Civil Code. In the eyes of colonial doctrine, which had become profoundly relativist, the Civil Code was nothing more than the "customary law" of the "French native": "Human laws are relative and contingent. It is likely, since these particular laws were adopted, that they were the most appropriate to their environment: why should the code of Gia Long, a learned monument to Chinese civilization, not be as good for the Annamites as the Civil Code is for the French? What determines private law has never been revealed. No legislation is naturally destined to rule the world. None contains 'the Law' in its pure state."[38]

Civilization itself, the jurists argued, was merely the product of an even more persistent historical reality: "race." In the language of legal scholars, race was never a matter of pure biology, much less of population genetics, a science still in its infancy at the time. "Race" referred rather to the continuity of generations. The jurists' concept of race was close to that of historians: it designated a population rooted in its territory, to use a formulation made popular by Jules Michelet and Ernest Renan.[39] Colonial administrators as well as jurists availed themselves of this conception of race, which cannot always be readily distinguished from more overtly biological concepts such as "heredity." We see this in the following excerpt from a 1926 report by one high official of the Ministry of Colonies:

> It is easy to understand why there can be only one category of citizens. There is but one right of citizenship, because this right stands above all the other rights that the French possess. In modern parlance, it is the ultimate right, and anyone who is covered by it is in some sense a full-fledged Frenchman. Can the same thing be said of subjects? Clearly not. When we get to the bottom of things, we find that a Frenchman, born in France of French parents whose ancestors always lived on the land cultivated by their fathers (*patria*), is not of the same nature as the subject who was born and settled in a newly annexed territory, even though this country is now an integral part of the national territory. He is different in terms of ethnic origin, heredity, customs, mentality, character, and degree of civilization. One is a subject of a dominant, conquering collectivity and the other of a conquered, dominated collectivity. The first is a member of the guardian people, the second of the dependent people. One further remark: none of the races that inhabit our colonies are kindred to us and therefore assimilable en masse. All belong to collectivities with ethnic characteristics incompatible with ours.[40]

This helps us to understand the close relationship between the legal construct of "subject" and the notion of "native": the former is merely the legal translation of the latter, which refers to a more "real" identity, the historical product of a certain civilization. The native is the (ethnic) truth of the subject, a mere legal category, just as the national is the (sociological) truth of the citizen.

An individual can therefore no more escape "his" law than he can free himself from his race. For instance, in Algeria, French citizens who converted to Islam were denied the right to assume "Muslim personal status": in particular, the marriage under Islamic customary law of a European converted to Islam was legally null and void. Conversely, natives who converted to Christianity—of whom there were a considerable number in Kabylia—and who for various reasons could not become citizens under the senatus consult of 1865 or the law of 1919 were considered "Christian Muslim natives."[41] As one German colonial administrator describing the French system put it, "Personal status is the law appropriate to each individual by virtue of the race to which he or she belongs."[42]

The combination of these two elements—a concept of law as the organic product of a civilization (and, beyond that, of a race) and the rooting of citizenship in civility—explains the increasingly overt refusal to apply French law in the colonies. Specifically, it signified a refusal of the notion of *assimilation* in the sense that was prevalent in the early nineteenth century, when it referred to the exportation of French legal and administrative institutions to the colonies.[43] By contrast, as the empire grew, the colonial state sought increasingly to govern populations by applying local law, or, rather, what colonial jurists and administrators viewed as local law. From the end of the nineteenth century to the Second World War, we see a broad effort to institutionalize native courts and to codify "customary law" in all parts of the empire.

Impossible Assimilation

Keeping natives under native law ran counter to the dominant practice in the first half of the nineteenth century, which was to grant residents of the colonies the full civil and political rights of French citizens. This was reflected in the Civil Code of Senegal of 1830 and in the law of 1833 that recognized the "civil" and "political" rights of "any person born free or in possession of legally acquired freedom."[44] It was also reflected in the granting of voting rights in 1848 to former slaves in the Antilles, Réunion, and Guiana and natives from the French territories of India and Senegal.

From the end of the nineteenth century on, however, this "assimilationist" tendency came in for increasingly vigorous criticism from colonial jurists and administrators, because it assumed that legal institutions suited to the French "environment" would be imposed by necessarily artificial means. In 1848, one commentator argued, "The theory of assimilation reigned supreme. Distinctions of race were ignored. No one was aware of the immense difficulty of treating a Muslim or a Hindu exactly like a true Frenchman."[45]

Hence, the goal of assimilation (in the sense of having uniform legislation applicable to both the metropole and colonies) was postponed to a distant and hypothetical future. For example, the president of the Congress of Colonial Sociology, which brought together leading figures in colonial administration and law in 1900, opened the meeting by asserting, "No assimilation: that, I believe, is the formula that must be inscribed at the head of any program on colonial law in all of its aspects—civil, administrative, political, and private. It is the principle of every study of colonial sociology."[46] Indeed, assimilation could only come as the capstone of an extremely slow global process, whose pace would be determined by the natural rhythm of civilizational development, not by political will.

The meaning of the word *assimilation* therefore shifted.[47] It no longer referred to the application of metropolitan norms in the colonies and took on instead the more global meaning of a transformation of all the social institutions of a civilization and a race, of which law was merely one product. In the short run, this process could apply only to exceptional individuals, whose unusual lives allowed them to "move closer to French civilization," to borrow an expression that appeared often in decrees defining the conditions for access to French citizenship in the colonies. This semantic shift explains the later evolution of the idea of assimilation, which was taken up in the metropole to discuss laws of naturalization: the foreigner's adoption of the host country's norms of civility (and thus implicitly of the Civil Code) became a requirement of citizenship. In this context, measures granting French citizenship collectively to all the natives of certain colonies came under increasingly vigorous attack. This was true of the Crémieux decree of 1870 and the law of December 30, 1880, which had granted full citizenship respectively to the Jews of Algeria and the natives of Tahiti. In 1910, some went so far as to regret the granting of citizenship to former slaves in 1848, "a measure today deplored by many experienced colonials for its fatal effects on a sane and intelligent colonial policy."[48]

Joining the polity was no longer defined, as at the time of the Revolution, in terms of voluntary adhesion to a shared political project; it was rather the culmination of a process of internalizing French civilization and mores. In this view, will was not merely insufficient but suspect: indeed, assimilation implied an unconscious adoption of French civilization. The "will to assimilate" was a contradiction in terms.[49] The decree of September 21, 1881, which made it possible for natives of French settlements in India to renounce their personal status and obtain citizenship merely by expressing their will to become citizens, now seemed excessive by the standards of colonial law. It was challenged by the decree of September 10, 1899, which established two electoral colleges in French settlements in India, one for Europeans and the assimilated and the other for "natives."[50]

Education was no more sufficient than will to "guarantee" assimilation, at least according to one colonial administrator in Indochina who wrote a doctoral dissertation in law in the early 1930s:

> Some jurists believe that they can establish the nationality of origin solely on the basis of education. . . . But even if this thesis is valid for certain individuals plucked from their original environment on the day they are born, it seems absolutely mistaken for individuals who have received, even in early childhood, the imprint of the family environment. The child then bears the indelible mark of the intrinsic genius of his race, with all its virtues and flaws. It is all the deeper for being the first impression on his young brain. Whenever there is an opportunity for the deepest human reflexes to assert themselves, it is the individual's race that dominates, and the veneer of European upbringing that the child may have received has no influence on this more decisive factor.[51]

For the authors of legal doctrine, the influence of "race" therefore exceeded that of education.[52] But the determinism of race could be countered by the influence of environment, and in particular by one of its specific configurations, the "family environment," which figures here as the key site for the transmission of the mores and rules of civilization. Civility, a condition of citizenship, is learned above all in the family. But "environment" also has a broader meaning. It is a space for face-to-face interaction between individuals: "To become French, in terms not only of language but also of intellectual mentality, moral sense, and judgment, requires, except in very exceptional cases, long years of residence among the French population at its most dense—in other words, in the metropole."[53]

The notion of "environment" used here is borrowed directly from neo-Lamarckianism, knowledge of which was extremely widespread among republican elites and in the colonial administration at the end of the nineteenth century (see chapter 3). Neo-Lamarckianism assumes that individuals are shaped by the organic relationship that they maintain with their physical and social environment. In this perspective, "environment" can never be separated from "heredity," and the influence of "soil" can never be separated from that of "blood." This view is far from the Durkheimian idea of socialization through educational institutions, which is often said to be one of the theoretical foundations of the French conception of nationality at the end of the nineteenth century.[54]

In a particularly perverse reversal, it was thus the experience of slavery and two centuries of continual interaction between masters and slaves in the French Antilles that justified, a posteriori, the granting of citizenship rights to former slaves in 1848: "The freed slaves of the Antilles and of the United States of America, who were uprooted from their ancestral environment and, through slavery, intimately involved in the lives of their masters, were slowly and gradually initiated by this cohabitation."[55]

French Citizenship in Practice

In the colonies, citizenship was transmitted by filiation. One was born a citizen. To become a citizen was exceptional, and it could occur only as a result of an objective embrace of French civilization. From the late nineteenth century on, the criteria of such "assimilation" were set forth in a vast corpus of texts dealing with the conditions for access to citizenship.

Each territory had specific regulations determining access to citizenship. Evolutionism, which established a strict hierarchy of races and therefore of civilizations, translated into a fractured body of colonial law. Legislators, seeking to adapt the law to the degree of civilization attained by each population, took up the question of the transition from "subject" to "citizen" on very differentiated timetables. Whereas rules were established for Algeria and Cochin China in 1865 and 1881, respectively, New Caledonia, whose natives, in the minds of colonial observers, occupied the lowest degree on the scale of evolution, had to wait until 1932 and French Somalia until 1937.[56]

There were nevertheless certain constants applicable to the entire period. As in the case of naturalization of foreigners, access to citizenship was predicated on meeting certain age restrictions (majority) and satisfying requirements of "morality and loyalty"—qualities to be judged by an administrator. In contrast to metropolitan rules governing naturalization, which remained evasive, the specific content of these regulations was usually carefully spelled out. Candidates for citizenship had to demonstrate "good living and morals" and to "show definite means of earning a living." Loyalty was reflected by various types of behavior: demonstrated devotion to French interests; ten years' employment in a public or private French enterprise; fulfillment of military obligations (where applicable); meritorious service and devotion to France for a period of ten years in the army, navy, or civil service; or services rendered to France that earned the candidate a high distinction (such as the Legion of Honor, a military medal, and so forth). This last distinction often meant that the candidate was not required to know the French language.

Furthermore, conditions missing from the regulations governing naturalizations before 1927 were present in colonial citizenship laws from the end of the nineteenth century. These related to "proof" of "assimilation" to French civilization. Laws in the various colonies listed criteria indicating mastery of French culture (such as the ability to read and write or possession of a French advanced degree). Local rules specified in great detail the criteria to be used by administrators: for instance, in FWA, the test of mastery of the French language included "(1) The drafting of a letter about some very simple subject taken from the daily life of the native; (2) a conversational exercise of the same type, suitable for judging the applicant's ability to make practical use of the French language."[57]

A second, more extensive list of criteria touched on civil aspects of citizenship: the recording of family events in the identity records registers, marriage to a Frenchwoman (and in some cases having fathered a living child with her), the provision of French education for the children, and the "embrace of French civilization and mores." In the 1930s, the last condition was formulated as follows: "Embraced French civilization in his lifestyle and social habits." Finally, monogamy was considered to be absolutely indispensable.

Meeting all these conditions did not automatically confer the right to citizenship, however. All the decrees envisioned a complex and lengthy process, the outcome of which was left to the discretion of the administration, as was also the case with naturalization. Access to citizenship was a favor, not a right. This constraint was relaxed after 1919 in Algeria and in the 1930s for the other territories, as the law was changed to make access to citizenship a right for certain categories of subjects. But the conditions were so difficult that the change cannot really be seen as a major one. In Indochina, for example, to meet the educational requirement, the candidate had to have attended a prestigious university and received a doctorate or master's degree or attained the rank of officer in the military.[58]

The difficulty and complexity of the procedure account for both the small number of candidates for citizenship and the even smaller number of successes. In Algeria, for example, citizenship was not eagerly sought.[59] The figures were even more modest in the other colonies. Between 1914 and 1922, in Indochina, 70 people were granted citizenship, or an average of 9 per year.[60] The 1920s showed no greater openness: between 1926 and 1930, grants of citizenship or naturalizations were awarded to 160 people in all of Indochina.[61] This is the result of both low numbers of applications and a high percentage of rejections: in 1929, for example, 58 requests were granted, 65 postponed, and 42 definitively rejected.[62] The rejection rate was far higher than the rate for applications for naturalization in the metropole.[63]

To understand the difference between the status of subject and that of citizen, we need to look not only at the regulations and statistics but also at the concrete practices associated with the transformation of the former into the latter. The files pertaining to the "naturalization" of natives in Indochina tell us a great deal about how citizens were made.

In the sample of one hundred naturalization files analyzed for this project, the most remarkable feature is the very high rate of rejection of applications for citizenship.[64] During the entire period (1898–1944), if we eliminate the cases of foreigners who were unusually successful in their applications,[65] the rejection rate for the entire sample was 55 percent. The scrutiny became more severe as time went by. The 1930s were particularly unfavorable to natives (eight rejections versus three positive responses). The tougher scrutiny was due in part to the tense political climate, as opposition to the French presence in Indochina became more overt and organized. These findings completely contradict the jurists' idea of a slow, cautious, but inexorable opening of the gates to the polity to admit natives transformed by a process of assimilation. This evolution also suggests that the historical trajectories of racism and discrimination were far from linear.

The increased severity is all the more remarkable in that it often involved applications from candidates who satisfied all the legal conditions, as the administration conceded. Consider, for instance, the following application, which was initially approved by the resident for Laos but marked for rejection by the governor's staff in 1925:

> The applicant has served in the Post and Telegraph Department since January 1, 1901. He has therefore attained twenty-four years of service and can claim the benefits of Article 1, paragraph 1, of the decree of May 26, 1913, concerning the naturalization of natives. . . . Although he has demonstrated his attachment to France, the applicant has not distinguished himself by any *remarkable action*, nor has he rendered any *important service* capable of justifying the *signal favor* that he is requesting. Nor are his wife and grown children in a better position to *claim this high reward*.[66]

This insistence on exceptional qualities applied not only to the behavior of individuals but also to their *qualities*, which were seen as signs of assimilation to French society. Here, social status was quite fundamental: administrators focused not so much on profession or income as on the more global notion of "social situation." In a highly inegalitarian context, citizenship assumed that an individual occupied a certain rank, which was associated with a certain *prestige* or *standing*, to use terms that appear often in the files. Any deficiency in this respect led to denial of the application, as we see in a 1926 report concerning a soldier, rejected despite high ratings from his superiors: "Although it is undeniably true that L. has demonstrated bravery and devotion, it should nevertheless be noted that his education and social situation do not mark him out as a man destined to occupy a place of dignity in society of the sort he would be called upon to occupy were he granted French citizenship. Furthermore, his excellent conduct under fire has been rewarded by means other than the grant of naturalization, which would merely make the applicant a *déclassé* in the French family."[67]

The candidate for citizenship was expected to demonstrate his "dignity" and therefore his capacity to maintain the "prestige" of the colonial power.

Even more important than "standing" was a whole array of objective and subjective signs of "assimilation to French civilization." From the 1930s on, agents of the colonial administration were required to fill out a standard form evaluating the candidate's everyday activities and "attachment" to France. The first few questions dealt with the social situation of the candidate, his upbringing, and the upbringing of his wife and children, but on the whole, the questionnaire was intended to identify his cultural practices and observance of the norms of French civility:

> Does he dress in the French manner? Is he attached to traditions and old customs?
>
> Does he have French manners? Is his home arranged in the French manner (salon, office, bedroom, and so forth)?
>
> Does he participate in sports? Which ones?
>
> Does he frequent the French cinema or theaters?
>
> Does he visit the sea or mountains from time to time?
>
> Has he any other French habits? What are they?

A final series of questions focused on the nature of the applicant's interactions with French citizens. These called explicitly for affective judgments: "Does he have relations with French people? What is the nature of these relations? Can he engage appropriately in French conversation?"[68] The social, cultural, and emotional dimension of assimilation was more difficult to grasp and thus opened the way for harsh scrutiny.

In the 1920s and 1930s, the applicant's activity in World War I was used as an indicator of his "attachment to France." But it was never enough simply to have volunteered to serve for the duration of the war. Time at the front and acts of heroism were taken into account. In many cases, the applicant had to have earned the Croix de Guerre or a similar decoration in order for the application to be taken seriously. Private behavior could also be interpreted as a sign of attachment to France. For instance, in one report from the Hanoi mayor's office in 1927, a native's attitude toward his French concubine was taken to be a sign of lack of attachment to the French cause: "I will add that the applicant, whose loyalty is doubtful, has an unsavory reputation in Haiphong. He lives out of wedlock with a Frenchwoman he brought back from France, whom he abuses and treats in the crudest manner. He has never rendered any service either to his compatriots or to the French administration, toward which he has never demonstrated the slightest attachment. The favor he is requesting has been denied to far more promising subjects."[69]

Here again, for the agents of the colonial state, access to the public sphere depended on behavior in the domestic sphere. Citizenship was founded on civility.

The *Métis*: Between Subjection and Citizenship

Finding a place for the *métis* in this legal edifice was problematic, however. Where were individuals of mixed blood to be located in relation to the "great divide" in colonial society? Were they to be regarded as citizens or native subjects? As in debates about the social and political dimension of the *métis* question, the legal character of the family tie was essential: only the status of *métis* born out of wedlock was in question. If the parents were married, the child inherited his or her father's or mother's citizenship. Indeed, thanks to the principle that no European could become native, even transgenerationally, from the early twentieth century on, the solution adopted by the courts was that the rare Frenchwomen who married natives would keep their citizenship and pass it on to their children (unlike metropolitan women who married foreigners and thereby lost their French nationality prior to 1927).[70]

By contrast, the status of illegitimate *métis*, which included the vast majority of individuals of mixed blood, was long regarded as indeterminate and gave rise to extensive legal controversy. If the child was recognized by the "fully entitled" French parent, the question was whether the provisions of the Civil Code regarding nationality ought to be applied. Article 8 of the law of 1889 provided that the illegitimate child of parents of different nationality should have the status of the parent recognizing the child. If both parents recognized the child, the recognition could be simultaneous, in which case, the child inherited the status of the father; or it could be sequential, in which case, the child inherited the nationality of whichever parent was the first to recognize him or her. From the organicist standpoint, according to which the tie to the nation is the result of primary socialization in the "family environment," it was assumed that child was more "attached" to the nationality of the first parent to recognize him or her, who had presumably provided the child with more care.

Nevertheless, it was not obvious that the nationality provisions of the Civil Code were applicable in the colonies. There was bitter debate on the issue, as well as about the legal technicalities of recognizing children. In the colonial context, recognition not only created a tie of kinship but also transformed the child from a subject into a citizen. This issue, which was fundamental for the colonial state, led to controversies about fraudulent recognitions (see chapter 5) and about the wisdom of extending the law of 1912 concerning investigation of paternity to the colonies (see chapter 6).

The most important controversy, however, involved children whose fathers were unknown. For a time, colonial figures assumed that such children should logically inherit the status of their mothers. After 1910, however, and even more after 1920, various grounds were advanced for believing that it was unacceptable to maintain the native status of children whose fathers were unknown but nevertheless of "French blood." This controversy and its resolution were at the heart of the colonial process of racialization of French citizenship law (see chapter 7). Before proceeding with the analysis, I want to look at alternative solutions to the problem of deciding the status of the *métis*—solutions that were considered for a time but ultimately discarded. By looking at the paths not taken, we can get a better idea of the process of production of colonial law.

The Rejection of an Intermediate Category

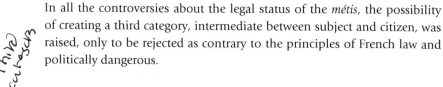

In all the controversies about the legal status of the *métis*, the possibility of creating a third category, intermediate between subject and citizen, was raised, only to be rejected as contrary to the principles of French law and politically dangerous.

The discussion reflected thinking about the social treatment of the *métis* question in that it emphasized the danger of *déclassement*. This argument was invoked in 1900 in one of the first texts to deal with the "status of the *métis*," a report to the International Congress of Colonial Sociology by one of the leading colonial jurists of the time, Arthur Girault. Girault argued that "to create an intermediate situation for them, which would not be entirely equivalent to that of the white but that would not be that of the native, would be an imprudent thing to do, and the consequences might become dangerous. What is to be avoided at all cost is to turn the *métis* into a separate class despised by some and despising others."[71]

This refusal to countenance an intermediate category became the "French position" on the issue, defended at international meetings where a politics of comparison tended to crystallize national colonial styles. At a 1911 meeting of the International Colonial Institute devoted to the *métis* question, the same Arthur Girault countered the views of the Portuguese representative with the following:

> It is essential that the *métis* not constitute a distinct social group. Colonial society is already heterogeneous enough that there is no need to introduce a new *métis* class subject to special rules. If you treat the *métis* as a separate class, ask yourselves what sentiments you will foster in these people. Rejected on all sides, they will become *déclassés*, and, I would add, *déclassés* of the most dangerous sort from the standpoint of maintaining European domination in the country. This is a peril to be avoided at all cost.[72]

The debate about the wisdom of creating a status between that of subject and citizen did not pertain solely to *métis*: various colonial situations gave rise to populations of "mediators" between colonizers and colonized, natives "severed from their environment" whom the colonial state believed it would be difficult to maintain in subject status. In all of the colonies, the emergence of so-called evolved populations was of concern.

In the late 1920s and again in 1944 as preparations were being made for the Brazzaville conference, colonial jurists proposed to create a "new legal classification" for these groups: "elite natives" (*indigènes d'élite*). According to the sponsor of a proposal submitted to the Conseil supérieur des colonies in 1927, "Naturalization [is] dangerous because of the lack of political maturity of the individuals in question, for whom it is difficult to acquire our mentality. . . . In another respect, it is hard for us and inherently unjust not to reserve an enviable legal status for the best elements of our colonial possessions."[73] Brandishing the specter of Bolshevism and colonial revolt, the author of this report, a law professor, noted that it was necessary "to achieve in our native policy a skillful blend of the principle of authority, which must be maintained, with a suitable dose of a certain kind of liberalism."[74]

The ministry fought the proposal, however, not only because it ultimately offered few advantages to the people involved (the right to vote in and be elected to local assemblies and, for their children, the right to attend top schools in France and the colonies as "French" students) but also because it was felt that this intermediate category drained the category "citizen" of its substance.[75] The will to maintain two distinct categories, however, did not prevent the administration from granting exceptions from the most discriminatory measures to certain groups of "subjects." Over time, and particularly after World War I, exemptions from the Native Code were granted to more and more groups: some people were less "native" than others.

Favorable Treatment

Although jurists refused to consider a status between subject and citizen, it was not long before access to French citizenship was made easier for *métis*. This was true, first of all, in law: in Indochina, the decree of 1913 concerning access to French citizenship by natives mentioned that its provisions could apply to those who were "sponsored, taken in, or raised for five years prior to their majority by French families or philanthropic societies and who had obtained an advanced primary or professional diploma or a secondary school diploma." This measure implicitly covered *métis* taken in by charitable institutions. Here we have further evidence of the exceptional character of the *métis* question in Indochina: no similar disposition existed in any other part of the French Empire.

But it was above all in administrative practice that the force of blood took priority over the force of law: in procedures regarding access to full French citizenship, *métis* systematically received favorable treatment. The officials in charge of evaluating applications believed that candidates of mixed race enjoyed "a claim to the status of French citizen greatly superior to what individuals of pure race and equal qualifications could claim."[76] The blood argument was also wielded by politicians: one deputy supported a candidate for citizenship by mentioning that "he is also the natural child of a former high civil servant in Indochina and therefore half French by blood."[77] This favorable bias is reflected in statistics that show a much higher success rate for naturalization requests by *métis*.[78]

In some decisions, claims of justice were based on blood. For instance, one official argued that it was unjust for a child to suffer for the sin of an irresponsible father, particularly when that child demonstrated loyalty to French society:

> Abandoned in childhood to a native mother, he was nevertheless quick to grasp the respect he owed to his European origins, attended French schools, and at the age of sixteen volunteered to serve France, which he regarded as his true homeland. Always evaluated highly by his superiors, loyal, hardworking, and just as productive as his European colleagues, as well as exemplary in the conduct of his private life, he finds himself in an ambiguous civil status only because of the irregularity of his birth, for which he is currently suffering the unjust consequences.[79]

A widespread variant of the justice argument[80] invoked "the premature death of the father before he was able to recognize his child."[81] In view of the high mortality rate in the colonies, cases of early death were to be understood as related to imperial service; hence; the state was merely doing its duty by fulfilling the father's intentions and assuming responsibility for a child born as a consequence of the colonial project.

Finally, officials often referred to the applicant's phenotype in evaluating requests for naturalization: visible signs of European blood were noted as an argument in favor of naturalization. In 1932, for example, the chief of the Tonkin police prepared a report on an "applicant who received very good evaluations in Tonkin and the New Hebrides [where he served as an interpreter], a widower with three children. Furthermore, his physical appearance clearly signals his European descent."[82] Conversely, the absence of European features counted against the candidate: a report filed on one applicant by the security chief in Tonkin, after indicating that he had "no permanent residence," "only very rudimentary education, not fit for military service," was "lazy and without resources," and had "relatives unwilling to care for him," went on to say that he "does not have the characteristic features of a person of mixed blood."[83]

Individuals designated as *métis* were quite capable of deploying these same arguments. In 1922, one of them filed an application for naturalization that based its claims on the arguments of race, justice, and appearance:

> When I returned from France, I applied once for naturalization but received no reply, and what is not explained to me [sic] is that my two half brothers, who are purely Annamite, are today naturalized French citizens. I am not

applying to be French in order to benefit from the advantages available to Europeans, but I cannot understand why, as the son of a Frenchman, I am condemned to remain Annamite despite the services I have rendered.

In the circumstances in which I find myself, I think I can call upon your sense of justice, and I am hopeful that for the sake of France's reputation and in honor of the service my late father rendered in the conquest of Indochina, Your Excellency will not hesitate to take an interest in the fate of a poor *métis* who has placed his trust in your noble sentiments. . . .

P.S. I am attaching a photograph of me taken in France in 1916. My patronym will be Claude Alexandre.[84]

This man's application was ultimately rejected. Having signed up as an interpreter for the duration of the war, he had come into serious conflict with his commanding officer and had been reduced in rank and eventually banned from any further public employment. Despite the blood ties that linked the *métis* to France, naturalization was always a favor, never a right. What was really at stake in the controversy over the status of the *métis* was whether the benevolent treatment of this category of individual in law and in practice should be transformed into a true right to citizenship. As the study of the naturalization records indicates, this debate began when colonial officials started to take account of "blood" in a variety of contexts. What followed was a three-stage process, which we will examine in the next three chapters.

FIVE

The Controversy over "Fraudulent Recognitions"

In the territories in which the *métis* question arose, it was soon linked to the practice of "fraudulent recognition." Colonial administrators and jurists expressed alarm at what they saw as a serious threat to the colonial order, in which unscrupulous individuals flouted the law and granted citizenship to whomever they wished.[1]

In view of the geography of the *métis* problem, it is not surprising that Indochina was the epicenter of the phenomenon—though Madagascar and sub-Saharan Africa were also affected to a degree. In this chapter, we will trace the controversy generated by fraudulent recognitions; the controls on the practice established by the colonial administration (often at odds with existing law); the contradictory decisions of colonial courts; and, finally, the background of the law that was proposed to put an end to "citizenship fraud." In the metropole, under Article 339 of the Civil Code, only individuals with an "interest" in the matter could contest recognitions of filiation, but a variety of local decrees allowed prosecutors in the colonies to file challenges as principal plaintiffs.[2] Within metropolitan France, in other words, the state was required to respect "the tranquillity and honor of families," but in the colonies, it was authorized to examine the veracity of kinship claims. At the same time, certain provisions of Article 8 of the Civil Code were similarly amended: in France at the time, an illegitimate child recognized by two parents of different nationality received the nationality of the first parent to recognize him or her, but the colonial decrees specified that any child recognized by a French parent would become a French citizen even if previously recognized by the native parent. Although these modifications to the law may seem trivial, they opened the way to a far-reaching transformation of the relationship between paternity and citizenship.

The legal controversy over fraudulent recognitions involved courts in Saigon, departments of the general government in Madagascar, the Cour de cassation in Paris (the highest court for French private law), and various departments of the Ministry of Colonies. Above all, it revealed the ways in which administrators and jurists as well as both "real" and "fraudulent" fathers of *métis* participated in the construction of imperial law by way of practices that were at once local and "global." Although these practices operated within localized social networks, they were framed by the mechanisms through which community membership and identity were regulated throughout the empire.

Fraudulent Recognitions and Citizenship Fraud

In the colonies, citizenship allowed a person to escape from the Native Code (Code de l'indigénat) and become subject instead to French law. It also conferred political, economic, and social rights (including preferential access to land concessions). The earliest welfare state measures in the colonies applied exclusively to citizens. More broadly, citizenship gave access to French education and employment in the French sector and therefore to higher social status. But as we saw in the previous chapter, citizenship was acquired in the colonies primarily through kinship. Administrative access was available only under very restricted conditions. The process was long and rarely ended in success. The fraudulent recognitions that the colonial administration deplored, first in Indochina in the early twentieth century and later elsewhere, were a way of circumventing these difficulties.

Intruders in the Polity

Colonial officials denounced fraudulent recognition as "citizenship fraud," because it enabled "undesirables" to acquire full French citizenship through a process the government did not control. Those who chose fraud did so *because* they did not meet the conditions for citizenship. More fundamentally, the fraud itself was a *sign* that they were unworthy of citizenship. One official put it this way: "Devious behavior of this kind not only misrepresents the status of an individual but also brings numerous intruders into the French community and electorate. These intruders obtain all the benefits of naturalization without the approval of the government and without satisfying the strict conditions of the law (including an upbringing and lifestyle that bring the native closer to the European and the rendering of distinguished service to France) (decree of March 26, 1913)."[3]

In places as far flung as Saigon, Tananarive (Antananarivo), and Paris, critics pointed to the "social and political danger" inherent in such "usurpation of the status of French citizen," which they insisted must be fought in the name of "a higher necessity of social defense."[4] No statistics were offered in support of these arguments, however—a remarkable fact in a bureaucracy ruled by the "politics of large numbers."[5] Of course the illicit nature of the practice made any precise statistical accounting impossible. But the absence of even estimated figures in texts denouncing the ever-growing menace of fraudulent recognition, along with the frequent repetition of the same few examples, suggests that the number of cases of fraud was in reality quite limited.

Furthermore, when it became possible for the state to nullify fraudulent recognitions in Indochina after 1918, fewer than a dozen cases a year were submitted to the courts. This number was probably larger than the number of grants of citizenship: recognition was indeed an alternative to a complex and uncertain administrative procedure. Yet it seems quite modest compared with the French population of twenty-five thousand and the native population of twenty million.[6] Once again we find that the logic of law does not follow the principles of statistical reason: transgressing categorical distinctions was perceived as a problematic practice no matter how uncommon it may have been.

The problem of fraudulent recognition overlapped the *métis* question. This was by no means inevitable. Logically speaking, the practice provided a way to establish fictitious ties of kinship between individuals of different *legal status*—namely, citizens and subjects. It soon turned out, however, that it was used to create a bond between individuals with very specific social characteristics: it was primarily citizens *born in the metropole* who recognized subjects of mixed blood. "Naturalized" natives did not use their newfound status for the benefit of native subjects.[7] Nor did French from the metropole recognize children born to two native parents. Although there was no legal requirement, it was as if those who claimed to be fathers felt that they could only recognize children who resembled them sufficiently that "ethnically, kinship [was] possible."[8] Such behavior implies the internalization of socially plausible kinship ties.

The Lure of Money and Solidarity

Colonial officials and jurists believed that many of those who claimed to be fathers were motivated primarily by money. In their view, it was "poor whites" with little to sell other than their status as citizens who made such claims: these were "indigent Europeans" who "actually trafficked in recognitions."[9] Local court records tell a far more complicated story, however, in which we see various practices of solidarity linking different elements of colonial society. We see this, for example, in the testimony of one young corporal, who in 1916 justified his false declarations as follows:

> On August 2, 1916, I appeared at the Bureau of Identity Records (Bureau d'état civil) in Hanoi with Privates X and N as witnesses to recognize a seventeen-year-old boy of mixed blood, whom I knew under the name H. His mother, whom I never knew, was deceased. I recognized this young man for purely unselfish reasons, as a favor to him, because he wanted to join the French army and enjoy the benefits available to French citizens, which he could not do as an unrecognized *métis*. I am thirty-five years old. I have been in Tonkin for only three and a half years. Of course I cannot be the young man's father. I nevertheless declared to the bureau that I was his father and stated that his mother was unknown. In doing so, I did not believe that I was doing anything wrong.[10]

This and other testimonies indicate that not all fraudulent recognitions were done for money. Many were granted as a kind of assistance. Private individuals created informal mutual aid networks in an effort to resolve the *métis* question on their own:

> When I was a young child, my mother and I considered the situation created by the departure of her common-law husband and subsequent marriage. The status of unrecognized *métis* was disadvantageous and inconvenient, and my Eurasian physique was quite apparent. A solution was offered to me by the kindness of ——, the former head of the —— School, where I studied for several years. He knew me and my family well. He knew of our desire that I obtain French nationality. Since I was quite attached to him, I trusted him completely. One of his friends ——, Mr. X., a merchant and himself a *métis* who was very kind to others like him, offered to find a discreet and compliant Frenchman who would agree to recognize me. Mr. X. was a former student of ——, who trusted him completely. Thus, I was recognized in 1920, in H——, one year before the death of my mother. Mr. X. and Y., employees of the city of H——, were witnesses for the formalities and for the recognition by a certain P., who was related to them and whom I did not know. I know only that another Eurasian, recognized by him and therefore bearing the same name as I do, lives in Cochin China and is the father of several children.[11]

Although these practices reveal the existence of networks of acquaintance and solidarity that crossed the "great colonial divide," they are probably best described as circumventions of the colonial order rather than as resistance to it. They suggest that as discriminatory as colonial law was, its social effects were limited, as all laws are, by tactics of avoidance.

Some fraudulent recognitions had purposes other than access to citizenship. Sometimes they were a way of formalizing an informal relationship: such "indulgent" recognitions were in effect fraudulent adoptions of minors, which French law did not permit until 1923. Colonial philanthropists sometimes described these as "acts of charity"[12] or even as private solutions to the *métis* question. The judgment of the colonial administration was often more severe. The prosecutor for Indochina made veiled reference to cases in which the purpose of fraudulent recognition was not pecuniary but rather to "secure control of defenseless children." It sometimes "turned out that this was done with the complicity of unworthy parents," who surrendered their children to every kind of abuse.[13] Clearly, the *métis* question also figures in the genealogy of sexual exploitation of children.

The Fate of a Legal Controversy

Colonial administrators and jurists, keen to avoid fraudulent grants of citizenship, sought to verify claims of kinship and reject applications that proved to be fraudulent. But they had to contend with provisions of the Civil Code pertaining to the recognition of parentage, including a restrictive interpretation of Article 339 that was widely accepted at the time. As we have noted, the article stated that "any recognition by the father or mother can be contested by those who have an interest in the matter." Jurists interpreted this point narrowly, arguing that *only* those whose interests were directly affected could raise such a challenge: the state, in particular, was not permitted to be a party to such cases.

The Honor and Tranquillity of Families

In metropolitan France, identity records (*l'état civil*) were one of the principal instruments of the "nationalization" of French society. Identity records were the responsibility of the Ministry of Justice, which was vigilant in maintaining their integrity. Formal techniques (involving writing, formatting, language, signature, and so forth) were employed to ensure the authenticity of documents.[14] Officials were also permitted to make corrections or "rectifications," but only within strict limits.

The rectification of a document was not the same as the "modification" of an individual's status. A rectification was a correction applied to a "status contrary to law. . . . A true question of status arises, however, when the document cannot be rectified with the help of the law; that is, when it is necessary, in order to establish that certain statements are false, to undertake an investigation and question certain facts."[15] Although this distinction was not always easy to make,[16] the rule was that prosecutors could intervene to bring documents into *conformity* with the law but not to determine their *truth*.[17]

Furthermore, even in regard to rectification, prosecutorial powers were limited by the desire to maintain "family peace." Here, the rule was still ambiguous. In theory, only interested parties (and therefore private individuals) were entitled to seek rectification of documents pertaining to civil status. There were exceptions, however, laid down in particular by the law of April 20, 1810, which provided that prosecutors could intervene in cases in which "public order" was at stake. But this notion was not precisely defined in the Civil Code, Article 6 of which stated only that *"laws involving public order and good morals cannot be derogated from by private agreements."* The notion was therefore quite broad and applied a priori to anything related to civil status, since the recording of individual identity was one of the "fundamental (social, political, etc.) requirements regarded as essential to the functioning of public services and the maintenance of security and morality."[18]

The jurists who wrote and commented on the Civil Code were nevertheless also concerned with preserving "the honor and tranquillity of families." They believed that the ability of the state to intervene in family matters had to be strictly limited. In their view, public order had to be "involved not in an indirect or secondary way but in a primary and obvious way. This was the case, for example, when an incestuous or adulterous relationship was documented. Or, to take another example, in cases where there are grounds for annulling a marriage, and therefore the document recording that marriage, for reasons of bigamy, incest, or absence of puberty."[19] Given this double constraint, the judge had somehow to determine whether public order was threatened in a "primary and obvious" way or merely "an indirect or secondary" way.

In the case of fraudulent recognitions, the tension between "public order" and "family tranquillity" was governed by Article 327 of the Civil Code, which stated that "prosecution of the crime of altering civil status can begin only after definitive judgment has been rendered concerning the question of status itself." After a period of conflicting rulings by courts and debates among legal experts,[20] this provision was interpreted as preventing the state from prosecuting the crime of *supposition* (when a woman faked giving birth) or *substitution* (replacement of one newborn by another) until the question of civil status had been resolved by the civil courts. The ministry could therefore intervene only by joining a civil action brought by private individuals whose interests were affected. It could never take the initiative.

This perspective can be seen in a judgment of the court of Reims in 1890, which rejected the action of the prosecutor's office. A young woman, Berthe Couvreur, lived with her mother, Appoline Legrand. Legrand had remarried a man named Lefebvre. When Couvreur gave birth to a daughter, Lefebvre declared that the child was his by his wife. The Lefebvres were accused of the crime of *supposition d'enfant*, but the court, in a decision rendered on July 24, 1890, rejected this action by the prosecutor's office: "The prosecutor has no right to intervene in questions of paternity, filiation, or disavowal, which constitute the civil status, properly speaking, of citizens and are their property." This decision was confirmed on appeal by the court of Paris in March 1891: "By subordinating prosecution for *suppression d'état* to the decision of the civil courts on the question of status (Article 327 of the Civil Code), the legislator clearly indicated his strict intention to ensure the peace and tranquillity of families above all, even at the risk of compromising the prosecution of certain cases, because prosecution may at times endanger the public order on the pretext of upholding it."[21]

When it came to filiation, finding the truth thus took a backseat to respecting "family tranquillity"[22] and, more broadly, individual wills.[23] Recognition did not even have to respect the rules of plausibility. Even in cases where cohabitation was manifestly impossible or where the difference in age between the child and the recognizing parent was dubiously small, these factors had no influence on the admissibility of the claim.[24] The interpretation of Article 339 of the code ("any recognition by the father or mother can be challenged by persons having an interest in the matter") was therefore quite restrictive in the sense that only private and not public interests could be considered. Indeed, it seems that indulgent recognitions were and perhaps still are common in France, "the typical case being that of a husband who recognizes the child of his mistress or fiancée for the purpose of legitimation."[25] The administration was well aware of this practice, and the courts tolerated it. Indeed, in 1972, when the law of filiation was rewritten, it was said that the legislature "has deliberately accepted fraud because 'the practice is supported by a kind of popular tradition.'"[26]

Colonial Public Order

If questions of paternity and filiation were of concern in the metropole more for their effect on the honor and tranquillity of families than on the public order,[27] the reverse was true in the colonies. There, and especially in Indochina, a different idea took hold: that because fraudulent recognitions made a person not just a member of a family but also a part of the civic community, what was at stake was not so much family honor and tranquillity as public order. In fact, fraudulent recognitions had allowed some of the least "reputable" members of colonial society to exercise one of the most basic prerogatives of the state, that of conferring citizenship: "The most serious consequence—which goes well beyond the honor and tranquillity of families—stems from the fact that anyone, even an individual ostracized by society, can capriciously, *hic et nunc*, without external control of any kind, confer French citizenship on any native he chooses, whereas lawmakers have been extremely prudent in exercising the power to bestow nationality."[28]

In other words, fraudulent recognitions jeopardized not only the sovereignty of the state in the award of citizenship but also the construction of classes and the assignment of particular individuals to those classes. This was what commentators meant when they said that the practice had "consequences" for public order. The word *scandal* was frequently used because the practice of fraudulent recognition blurred the most basic distinctions of the colonial political order:[29] "It is indeed in the highest degree a matter of public order if fraudulent recognition can shield a native from the application of native laws and customs, from the jurisdiction of native tribunals, from penalties specific to natives, and, finally, from the tax known as the *capitation*."[30]

More specifically, public order was affected because fraudulent recognitions created a discrepancy between legal status and the more basic identity that it was supposed to reflect, which in the colonies had to do with race (see chapter 4). This can be seen explicitly in a comment on a 1913 decision of the Cour de cassation, which settled the colonial controversy for a time: "Prosecutors should never have to rely on arguments dealing solely with family matters. They should be concerned only with the question of nationality: let us say the word—with the question of race."[31] The prosecutor general for Indochina was equally blunt: "When a case involves Europeans only, I have never dreamed of intervening."[32]

In these cases, the public order involved was characterized as "colonial." This notion, put forward in 1927 by Henry Solus, an expert on private law, was the colonial counterpart of the "domestic" and "international" public order. It referred to the set of rules "essential for a successful colonization" and was applied primarily to natives. For instance, respect for native customs and religions, which was guaranteed by the treaties governing each of the territories, was limited by the constraints of public order—thus, for example, anthropophagic practices and witchcraft were not authorized.[33] But the *colonial public order* also concerned colonials and referred to the set of rules they could not violate without endangering colonial rule. Colonial domination assumed that the status of "colonizer" and "colonized" would remain stable, which meant that both would "remain in their places" and exhibit the identity attributes of their respective groups. Fraudulent recognitions misrepresented family relationships and disrupted the contours of citizenship. They were an offense against the moral as well as the political order, or, rather, they posed a political problem because they revealed the moral failings of colonials. "Such practices" were described as "absolutely degrading for those who are derelict in their duty and renounce their families"[34] *and* as damaging to the prestige attached to the status of French nationality.[35]

For colonial administrators, therefore, fraudulent recognitions were of concern primarily for the threat they posed to the public order, which it was the job of the prosecutor's office to uphold. Since Article 339 of the Civil Code authorized anyone with an interest in the matter to challenge the recognition of a child, the prosecutor's office believed that it had the power to attack any recognition it deemed to be fraudulent.

In Indochina, starting in 1903, the prosecutor's office issued a number of memoranda addressed to local prosecutors and records clerks asking them to verify European identity records and indicate any suspect documents. The goal was to challenge suspect recognitions under Article 339 of the Civil Code, which in the prosecutor's view included the prosecutor's office among the possible interested parties. The civil court of Saigon sided with the prosecutor in the first case brought before it in 1903.[36] In 1908, the prosecutor sent out a memorandum together with a standardized form that was intended to establish a protocol for identifying fraudulent recognitions:

> I would therefore be obliged if you would ask the administrator of X—— to investigate the circumstances under which Mr. Y. recognized a native child. Is the child's civil status in order? Was he declared to be a legitimate child or perhaps the child of a known native mother and father not joined in wedlock?

At the time of the birth or presumed conception of the child, was Mr. Y. in the colony? Is it possible that the child he recognized is his? Was there any pecuniary compensation for the recognition? The administrator of X—— shall inform me of the results of his investigation and send me a copy of the act of recognition. I shall then take the steps necessary to annul it.[37]

Clearly, the colonial administration and courts did not hesitate to alter basic categories of law, such as that of "public order." Not everyone accepted their interpretation, however.

From the Saigon Court to the Cour de Cassation

After 1910, the Indochinese courts intervened frequently as the number of fraudulent recognitions increased and the scrutiny of them intensified. No clear pattern emerged: between 1910 and 1913, some courts nullified recognitions, while others refused to do so. The administration's efforts to tighten controls thus met with opposition: in this area, too, there were "tensions of empire."[38]

One case in particular tells us a great deal about what was at stake in this legal controversy. This case achieved paradigmatic status as a result of a decision by the Cour de cassation in 1913, which was frequently cited in textbooks of colonial private law, books about the general law of filiation,[39] and other cases involving contested recognitions. Colonial jurists often referenced this case, and we find commentaries on it in many colonial legal treatises.

The professor of colonial law Arthur Girault, for example, described the man responsible for the fraudulent recognitions in this instance as "a clever old European . . . who, in exchange for cash, agreed to recognize any *métis* who wished to acquire French civil status. This modest philanthropist soon acquired imitators, thus giving rise to a veritable industry open to Europeans who had fallen on hard times and wished to set aside a little something for their retirement. The judicial authorities reacted, and the prosecutor's office sought to nullify the fraudulent recognitions."[40]

The decision of the Cour de cassation is even cited in a recent introduction to the study of law as an instance of a "classic controversy" over the prosecutor's freedom of action.[41] It is also included in the online database Legifrance. The case is cited in a standard format ("Civ.,[42] December 17, 1913"), with no mention of Indochina, of the colonial situation, or of the question of access to citizenship, which, as we have seen, are essential elements for understanding the evolution of this case. The publicity given to this exemplary case reveals the existence of an imperial legal space that encompassed both metropole and colonies.

The case in question originated with the recognition of two children of mixed blood by one Honoré Bodin before the civil records clerk of Gia Dinh on June 17 and August 13, 1909.[43] The prosecutor for Cochin China was apprised of these events and quickly asked the civil court in Saigon to declare these recognitions null and void. The court acknowledged the prosecutor's standing to challenge these recognitions in the name of public order and accepted the arguments of the local administration: the recognitions not only created a family but transformed a subject into a citizen; the title of citizen could be awarded only by the government, however; hence, the fraudulent recognition circumvented the law of naturalization and therefore affected the public order, which it was the duty of the prosecutor's office to protect.

As to the substance of the case, however, the request for nullification was dismissed because the prosecutor offered no proof that Bodin was not the father of the children he had recognized. Furthermore, "it does not appear that such proof can be provided." The prosecutor then appealed this decision to the appeals court of Indochina. In a decision handed down on November 18, 1910, this court dismissed the appeal on the grounds, regularly invoked in metropolitan France, that "questions of filiation concern primarily the honor and tranquillity of families, whose secrets should not be disturbed and whose proprieties should be respected."[44]

The prosecutor appealed this decision to the Cour de cassation, which decided on December 17, 1913, that the appellate court of Indochina had properly applied the law. Its decision reaffirmed the principle that "questions of paternity and filiation concern not so much the public order as the honor and tranquillity of families, which must be protected by law against all attacks." It is worth dwelling for a moment on the court's reasoning, because it will enable us to understand the hierarchy of legal principles involved. The court actually found that recognitions within the territorial boundaries of metropolitan France are more family affairs than affairs of state but that this hierarchy was inverted overseas owing to specific features of the colonial situation. The argument rendered by judge Ruben de Couder in his report before the Cour de cassation had four parts:

1   Fraudulent recognitions in colonial societies affect citizenship as well as filiation:

    For France, there can be no hesitation: since all citizens enjoy the same rights, any question of status becomes a question of family, and the public order is concerned with the solution only in a secondary or background way. By contrast, in Indochina, according to the appellant's brief, the population is divided into two classes, natives on the one hand, French on the other. In Cochin China, at least, the natives have French nationality but do not possess all the advantages normally attached to that status. In particular, they retain their personal status, do not enjoy the civil or political rights reserved to French and naturalized citizens, are obliged to pay special taxes, and, finally, are subject to certain special obligations and to specific penalties.

2 Fraudulent recognitions in the colonies do not create family ties:

In this traffic, there is of course no family reason. The contracting parties, who usually do not even know each other prior to recognition, will continue to ignore each other afterward. They are committed only to a transaction and never intended to create a family tie of any kind giving rise to reciprocal rights and obligations. The father gave no thought to acquiring the prerogatives of paternal authority. The alleged children have no idea that henceforth their father can insist that they provide him with alimony or that, should they predecease him, he would become their heir. Their goal was to become French citizens. They achieved that goal by paying cash for citizenship. Their concept of the contract went no further.

3 Hence, no family interest was at stake, and only the public interest was affected by these frauds:

In the absence of any family interest at stake in such recognitions, is not the public order seriously affected? And, if so, which the appellant does not doubt, is not the prosecutor's office authorized to intervene directly under Article 339 of the Civil Code? We do not contest the fact that this question of recognition by a French citizen of natural children born to Annamite mothers is of the utmost importance for Indochina, and the foregoing remarks clearly demonstrate that the authorities charged with enforcing the laws and maintaining good social order have legitimate grounds for concern.

4 However, the interpretation of the law must be uniform throughout the empire. In order to sanction the practice of examining and nullifying fraudulent recognitions in a social and legal context quite different from that of metropolitan France, the law would have to be transformed:

How can the same texts be interpreted in diametrically opposite ways depending on whether they are applied here or there? If differences of location, mores, or civilization required legislative measures more appropriate to the colony, those measures should have been taken, and there is still time to do so. But as long as Articles 327 and 339 govern, they accord the same powers to the prosecutor's office in all latitudes, powers no more extensive in Indochina than in France.[45]

Note that the notion of "differences of location, mores, or civilization" here refers not to the native population but to colonial society itself, whose distinctive character is a result of the coexistence of colonizers and colonized. Ultimately, the court relied on the unity of imperial law, which it ruled should take precedence over the different stakes attached to recognition in the metropole and the colonies. It saw its role as one of ensuring that law was interpreted in a uniform way throughout French territory. Nevertheless, it did acknowledge that public order required maintaining a distinction between "citizens" and "subjects" and that this was threatened by fraudulent recognitions. In the metropole, filiation created a family tie first and an attachment to the state only second, by way of the definition of nationality, whereas in the colonial context, owing to the difference in status between citizens and subjects, filiation was primarily a matter of political order.[46] In the colonies, questions of *status* were above all questions of *state*, since civil status was more closely related to political status than in the metropole. Recognition of filiation was not only an "act of eminently personal character"[47] but also a declaration whose veracity was an issue of public order.

Lastly, as is often the case in legal controversies, what distinguished the colonial from the metropolitan situation in the 1913 decision was not the values at issue but rather the hierarchy of values.[48] The inversion of the relationship between "family honor and tranquillity" and "public order" implied a change in the meaning of the kinship tie, or, more precisely, in the legal definition of kinship, which had become not merely a tie between individuals but a criterion of membership in the national community.

The Modification of Article 339 of the Civil Code

Taking the suggestion of the Cour de cassation to heart, the prosecutor for Indochina proposed in 1914 to amend the law. This proposal was widely debated within the administration both in the colonies and in France. It was also the subject of discussions in Paris between the Ministry of Colonies and the Ministry of Justice.

Since most legislation under the colonial regime of "special laws" took the form of presidential decrees, the prosecutor's proposal ultimately led to a 1918 decree modifying the Civil Code. The delay between the proposal and the amendment of the law was due more to the war than to any hesitation about the proper course of action. Indeed, the various departments of the administration agreed as to the substance of the argument developed locally in Indochina. Everyone accepted the idea that prosecutors should be authorized to prosecute apparent cases of fraudulent recognition. The prosecutor for Indochina produced a brochure on the subject, and in August

1917, twenty-four copies were sent to the minister of colonies and the minister of justice as part of a veritable lobbying campaign by the Indochinese prosecutor's office. This document insisted on the urgency of the question, arguing that the number of fraudulent recognitions had increased sharply since the beginning of the war owing to the availability of pensions for the recognized children of soldiers and above all to certain exemptions from active duty for fathers of large families.

The decree of March 28, 1918, ratified the argument put forward by the prosecutor for Indochina. Article 2 stated: "Article 339 of the Civil Code applicable in Indochina is amended for that country by the addition of the following paragraph: 'The state may on its own initiative seek the nullification of any recognition by a European or assimilated person of a native or assimilated Asiatic child when the fact of paternity or maternity on which recognition is based can be shown to be false.'"

Clearly, only recognitions that crossed the racial divide were at issue. Those that established kinship ties between "Europeans" were not subject to verification by the state. Note, too, that well before "Europe" had any institutional existence, colonial law invented the legal category of "European" in order to maintain the racial boundary.

Of course, the amendment to the law raised the question of how fraudulent recognition was to be proved. Because Indochinese judicial records are difficult to access[49] and colonial case law anthologies did not publish any relevant cases, it is not possible to offer direct evidence of the types of proof that were admitted. Note, however, that the two criteria mentioned in legal writing are resemblance and plausibility, with the latter based on a comparison of the date of procreation with the dates of the putative parent's presence in Indochina: "The presumption that the prosecutor must contend with is very weak, so proof of the impossibility of procreation is all that is necessary. If the child is purely of the Annamite race and the putative father is of the French race, impossibility is manifest. If kinship is *ethnically possible*, it is enough for the prosecutor to prove that the putative father had nothing to do with the birth in question by producing witnesses or even by mere presumption."[50]

The appearance, in this context, of the notion of "ethnic kinship" illustrated the change in the meaning of filiation: it no longer denoted only attachment to a family but also affiliation with a broader community. The relationship between kinship and citizenship was tightened. This process was confirmed by another provision included in the 1918 decree, which modified Article 8 of the Civil Code. That article stipulated that in the event of successive recognitions, the child would acquire the nationality of the first parent to recognize him or her. Article 1 of the decree of March 28, 1918, added the following paragraph, applicable in Indochina: "However, when the father is a French citizen, the child whose filiation with respect to the father has been established voluntarily or judicially after recognition by the native mother or proof of filiation with respect to her will take the nationality of the father."[51] In other words, the child of a Frenchman, if recognized, is always a French citizen.

At first sight, the juxtaposition of the two paragraphs modifying Articles 8 and 339 of the Civil Code may not seem very logical, since they are concerned with different aspects of the recognition procedure: one with the time at which recognition occurs, the other with whether or not it is fraudulent. In fact, the juxtaposition of these two paragraphs reflects a desire to strike a balance. The first paragraph's effects are inclusive: it overrides the rule concerning the order of recognition and thus tends to confer the status of citizen on a larger number of individuals. The second paragraph's effects are exclusive: it eliminates from the community of citizens those who have gained access by fraudulent means.

The Modification of Article 8 of the Civil Code: A Madagascan Genealogy

The process that led to the juxtaposition of the amendments to Articles 8 and 339 of the Civil Code in the decree of 1918 concerning Indochina is worth dwelling on, because it illustrates the process of production of imperial law.

The amendments that the ministry proposed to the governor of Indochina originated in Madagascar. There, a group of colonists had asked in 1913 that citizenship be granted to any child of mixed blood who had been recognized by his or her French father.

In Madagascan law (as interpreted by French officials), a child born out of wedlock always acquired the status of its mother. Maternal filiation was established in childbirth. Illegitimate paternal filiation had no legal status: recognition or legitimation by marriage was impossible. By the end of the nineteenth century, more convinced than ever of the impossibility of imposing the Civil Code on natives, metropolitan officials specified in the law of August 6, 1896, annexing Madagascar that the republic "had no intention of altering the individual status of residents of the island or the local laws, customs, and institutions."[52]

This legal pluralism created a conflict of laws for children of mixed blood born out of wedlock: how could the Civil Code be reconciled with Madagascan custom? Under Madagascan law, recognition by French citizens was impossible. Had it been possible, it would have had no effect on the status of the child, since maternal filiation, established at delivery, was by definition always prior to recognition by the father. Indeed, by the early twentieth century, a number of settlers had acknowledged paternity of their children born to native mothers out of wedlock, but the status of the children remained ambiguous, particularly in the eyes of the colonial administration, which asserted in various documents that these children were "neither French nor Madagascan."[53] This ambiguity created a number of concrete difficulties related to access to various institutions, primarily schools, which in Madagascar were strictly segregated.[54]

Initially, the governor-general of Madagascar, taking stock of the ambiguous legal situation and of "divergent views" within the administration, proposed an ad hoc solution under which a child would be considered a French citizen if, in addition to being recognized by his or her father, the child was also actually placed in the father's care:

> Among these children, the administration should regard as French those who *live with their French father under his roof or behave as French persons* in the ordinary acts of social life. . . . If these children or their fathers claim, upon reaching the age of sixteen, to be treated administratively as French, you should in principle look most favorably on such requests and, after investigation of each case, grant them those privileges to which the dignity of their lives and their place in European society entitle them. In particular, I do not want these young people to be inscribed on the personal tax rolls or to be subject to the Native Code or special contributions. Any infractions they may commit shall not be prosecuted by the native courts, it being understood that once the investigation is complete, the competent tribunals shall remain entirely free to judge the case as they see fit if the question of status should arise.[55]

The Madagascan administration also considered facilitating naturalization procedures for children of mixed blood. This was a form of favoritism, skirting the letter of the law. But as one observer noted, expedients of this sort had the effect of making it official that recognition by the French father had no legal effect: "To employ the subterfuge of naturalization would damage the *dignity and prestige of the French citizen,* who should not need to rely on a law intended exclusively for foreigners to confer on children he recognizes as his own the same rights that his father transmitted to him."[56]

Here we see once again how "dignity" and "prestige" were linked to the truthfulness of identity. We also see a tension emerging between two different concepts of the relation between paternity and citizenship: the notion that citizenship was a possession of the individual, who was free to pass it on or not to his offspring through the procedure of recognition; and the view that it was the role of the state to safeguard the link between paternity and citizenship.

Sometimes, colonial actors held these two views at the same time, as illustrated by a collective plea of a group of fathers of children of mixed blood in Madagascar. The plea was formulated by the Tananarive (Antananarivo) section of the Ligue des droits de l'homme ("League of Human Rights") and conveyed to the Paris headquarters of that organization. Far from abandoning their children, these fathers hoped to secure their future by ensuring that they would have the status of French citizens in the colony:

> A man who has raised his children with all the love of which he is capable, who has worked to educate them in accordance with their intellectual abilities, and who has taken it upon himself to teach them their duties as citizens can only be disheartened by the actions of a society that refuses the right of citizenship to individuals capable of contributing to the welfare of all. What faith can he have in the future when he sees that children whom he had hoped to civilize have been turned into rebels by merciless exclusion from the rank to which they could aspire as semiwhites? Is it more just that pseudo-French elsewhere have the right to representation of their interests in Parliament simply because they were lucky enough to have been conquered two or three hundred years earlier, even though their moral level is undeniably below that of people who for the most part have received a better and more truly French education? The committee shrinks from depicting the shameful condition of the child of mixed blood who is required to pay a fee to obtain and renew his or her identity card and do forced labor, or the pain of the father who is obliged to witness the spectacle of his own children being treated as natives.[57]

Here, the cry for justice does not rely on the republican idea of the civilizing effects of participation in public life: the "pseudo-French" mentioned in the passage are the residents of the old colonies, which had enjoyed parliamentary representation since 1848. The plea instead invokes the principle that blood has its rights and that the home environment fosters attachment to the nation. Little by little, the administration became convinced that "it would be . . . unacceptable for children of mixed blood raised by their fathers as Europeans to find themselves at some point relegated to the native environment on the grounds that the rights of the mother under native law must be respected."[58] The rule that a citizen could not become a native took on an intergenerational dimension. What this incident implicitly reveals is that the preservation of customary law had more to do with a desire to reinforce the boundary between settler and native populations than with "respect" for native mores. Where the two bodies of law conflicted, it was French law and French citizenship status that prevailed. But Madagascan law was not simply rejected; its principles were taken seriously enough that a decree was issued in order to circumvent them. This consideration shown to what the colonizers defined as "Madagascan law" comes through clearly in a preparatory report for the decree, ultimately published with it in the *Journal officiel*:

> *Monsieur le Président [de la République]*,
>
> In accordance with the laws and customs governing the personal status of natives in the colony of Madagascar and its dependencies, a child born out of wedlock acquires the status of his or her mother. The fact of childbirth suffices to establish the filiation of the child with respect to his or her mother. A natural child is called *"zaza mamba reny"* ("the child that follows the mother"). Filiation with respect to the father cannot be established. Madagascan legislation does not provide for the recognition or legitimation of natural children. . . . But no law has yet determined the extent to which the provisions of the Civil Code concerning the recognition of natural children can be reconciled with Madagascan laws and customs. It seems to us that the time has come to fill this gap. Indeed, a large number of natural children of mixed blood have been recognized in the colonies by French fathers, in keeping with the Civil Code, and many of them have reached an age where their fathers are rightly concerned with securing their futures. It is important that no doubt be permitted as to the value of these recognitions. We also believe that a child born out of wedlock to a Madagascan woman and recognized by his or her French father should acquire the status of the father. . . . Finally, in view of the environment for which this legislation is intended, we believe that the recognition of children of mixed blood should be accompanied by certain guarantees.[59]

As the report points out, if citizenship were permitted to follow from recognition, it would be necessary to take steps to ensure the veracity of the recognition. In Madagascar as in Indochina, the administration evoked the "social danger" inherent in fraudulent recognitions. The move to make Article 8 of the Civil Code more "inclusive" was therefore accompanied by the imposition of more restrictive oversight. The decree of November 7, 1916, authorized recognition by the French father of a child born out of wedlock to a Madagascan mother and stipulated that recognition automatically conferred full French citizenship. These liberal measures were followed by fourteen articles detailing the arduous procedures required to obtain such recognition.[60]

In March 1915, the Ministry of Colonies informed the governor-general of Indochina that a decree was being drafted to modify Article 8 of the Civil Code in Madagascar. In June of that same year, the governor-general, deeply concerned by "frauds on citizenship," responded that he agreed on the need to amend the code applicable to Indochina "but that it would be a good idea at the same time to add to Article 339 a clause allowing the state to challenge fraudulent recognitions of children in Indochina by Europeans and other assimilated individuals."[61]

In Indochina, the arguments in favor of amending Article 8 as well as Article 339 also focused on the effects of filiation on citizenship. Here, the governor took up an argument articulated first by the ministry's Bureau of Political Affairs: that "it is desirable to have as many nationals as possible."[62] As always, this involved distinguishing "intruders," from unrecognized "true Frenchmen."

The price of doing so was to amend certain parts of the law of nationality, especially the rule concerning the order of recognitions. A 1918 internal memorandum of the Indochinese bureau of the Ministry of Colonies stated that "it seems illogical to persist in treating as native (and therefore excluding from European schools) the child of mixed blood who can legally establish that he is the son of a French citizen,"[63] and further that "it is just that the status of the child should not depend on a circumstantial fact such as the priority or nonpriority of the father's recognition."[64] But both logic and justice were ultimately subsumed by the superior status of the citizen to the native, and of French law to native law. This point was made explicit in the same note:

> What we fundamentally do not want is for native laws and customs to stand in the way of a measure as important as that which would allow a French citizen to recognize his natural child in order to make that child a French citizen like himself. The provision that we propose to add to Article 8 achieves this in a roundabout way. Ultimately, it comes down to the following: with respect to a child of mixed French-Indochinese blood, French law will always take precedence over native law in determining nationality.[65]

The ministry's March 28, 1918, decree was the product of fifteen years of such deliberation, fueled by the growing concerns of the Indochinese and Madagascan administrations. The new decree stipulated that a child recognized in the colonies by a French citizen was always a citizen—but that such recognition, precisely because it granted citizenship, was also subject to scrutiny by the prosecutor and ultimately to nullification if found to be fraudulent.

The Production of Imperial Law

In the years that followed, several colonies adopted laws copied from the 1918 decree. Madagascar remained an exception, with more restrictive rules in place since 1916. The history of these texts shows the importance of local initiative in the creation of colonial law. The solution to the problem of fraudulent recognitions and many other aspects of what was then called "native policy" did not emerge from a broad overall plan elaborated in France but rather was a series of ad hoc responses based on the legal apparatus available to the administration. The initial impulse was to turn to the courts, and only when that strategy failed did the administration propose to change the law itself. The metropolitan hierarchy readily agreed.

Faced with a local problem, the administration's response depended on what it referred to as "local contingencies," which included native customs as well as French legislation adapted to each territory. In Madagascar and FEA, the administration sought initially to "determine the extent to which the provisions of the Civil Code concerning the recognition of natural children can be reconciled with custom."[66] In both cases, it found that delivery was enough to establish the filiation of mother and child and that recognition by the father was impossible. In the end, it scarcely matters that the administration's description of local practices was not so much an objective account as an "invention of tradition."[67] In any case, the extensive efforts by colonial administrators to collect and codify local customs after the turn of the twentieth century did place real constraints on colonial policy.

Conversely, however, other mechanisms helped to create relative uniformity in colonial law. In their search for solutions, administrators took inspiration from measures already tried in other colonies. For instance, in July 1918, the governor of settlements in Oceania, noting that "the considerations that led to the decree [of March 28, 1918, for Indochina] seem likely to obtain in our settlements as well," drafted a proposal to extend its provisions to the region under his jurisdiction. Through such borrowing, a relatively homogeneous space of shared administrative practices emerged without the help of the central administration. Nevertheless, the Ministry of Colonies was an important node in this network of legal norms and thus a major force for legal uniformity throughout the empire.

Indeed, departments of the ministry regularly universalized what began as local techniques for managing native populations. Through these interventions, colonial problems quickly became imperial problems. For example, in a note from May 1914, the secretariat of the ministry informed the Indochina bureau about the proposed decree for Madagascar and immediately set it in the context of an imperial strategy for dealing with *métis*:

> The complex problems raised by the various solutions envisioned by jurists and sociologists to the problem of deciding the personal status of *métis* are, in a sense, issues of broad general interest. The question is equally acute in Madagascar as in our possessions in the Far East and West Africa. In view of the universality of the issue and the need for the second section of the secretariat to respond to the request that has been submitted to it, I would be grateful if the director of the Indochina department would send me any information that might be useful in facilitating the study of the *métis* question, along with his opinion as to the advisability of such a study.[68]

After the text for Indochina was adopted in March 1918, the ministry sent it to the governors of various colonies to ask for their opinions. It mentioned two objectives of the new rules, which "tend, on the one hand, to increase the number of our nationals in Indochina and, on the other hand, to repress more effectively fraudulent access by natives to the rights of French citizen via the subterfuge of fictitious recognitions of paternity."[69] The ministry sent this circular letter to the governors of French West Africa, French Equatorial Africa, Cameroon, Madagascar, Guiana, New Caledonia, the French settlements in India, and the French Coast of Somalia. It was also sent, apparently in error, to the governor of Guadeloupe.

The list of addressees shows that the colonial legal space was complex and never totally transparent to the actors involved. For instance, the ministry's proposal that Madagascar and FEA adopt the text for Indochina ignored the fact that texts with similar objectives but different specific provisions had already been adopted in those colonies. The governors of both reminded the ministry that the question had already been resolved. Two other colonies, Guadeloupe and Guiana, rejected the text for the obvious reason that where there was no difference in status between "subject" and "citizen," fictitious recognitions did not provide a means of fraudulent access to citizenship. In the "old colonies," the governor of Guadeloupe noted, such a proposal was "inopportune," because it would place them "on the same footing as colonies where residents have not been granted universal citizenship."[70]

In other territories, the supply of new laws created the demand: local administrators were all in favor of applying the text suggested by the ministry, except in the French Coast of Somalia, which gave no reason for its refusal. Most of the colonies—New Caledonia, FWA, Cameroon—justified their acceptance on numerical grounds, citing the large number of fraudulent recognitions they were obliged to deal with or, in the case of recently occupied Cameroon, expected to have to deal with, although no actual numbers were given. In May 1919, the governor of the French settlements in India noted that although fraudulent recognitions were rare in his jurisdiction, it would still be a good idea to apply the new law, "which is useful for reasons of public order." His argument was couched entirely in terms of legal logic and made no attempt to justify itself by mentioning an actual "social danger." In all of the colonies that expressed a positive opinion, the text drafted for Indochina was adopted over the next few years. Except for the term *Asiatic*, subsequent decrees all repeated the provisions of the March 28, 1918, decree word for word.

Toward a Penalization of Fraudulent Recognitions

Throughout the 1920s, the archival record is largely silent on how the new legal measures affected actual practice. By the early 1930s, however, a partial record can be discerned. In 1933, in Saigon, the prosecutor for Cochin China drafted a proposed decree that specified prison sentences and fines for those guilty of fraudulent recognition, a sign that the 1918 decree had not been very effective.[71]

In support of his proposal, the prosecutor listed the nullifications of recognition issued by the court of Saigon during the previous five years. Only seventeen cases were included from this jurisdiction, a number that seems quite small to justify the claim that a "lucrative industry" was "continuing to make worrisome progress and [had] grown to scandalous proportions." The prosecutor general, who headed the legal department for Indochina in Hanoi, acknowledged the "social danger" of fraudulent recognitions but argued that "their number, to judge by the statistics submitted by the prosecutor for the appellate court of Saigon, does not appear large enough to be of particular concern to public authorities." Though he was not "absolutely opposed" to the project, he challenged the need for the criminalization of fraudulent recognitions and justified his position by citing the difficulty of proving the charges in such cases as well as the need for prudence "in the realm of exceptional measures."[72]

Yet even though the prosecutor general for Tonkin shared the misgivings of the director of legal services for Indochina, the proposal was adopted in a decree of March 28, 1934. Henceforth, those responsible for recognitions nullified by the courts would be subject to prison terms of six days to two years, plus a fine. Apparently, this provision was never used prior to the establishment in Indochina of an administration reporting to the government of Vichy. I have been able to find only four cases in 1941 that ended in prison sentences—the year when Admiral Jean Decoux, in charge of the colony, called upon local administrators to undertake "thorough investigations in order to quickly detect any case of fraudulent recognition of paternity."[73]

Paternity, Citizenship, and Political Order

The 1918 decree in Indochina and its avatars in other colonies represent an important stage in the transformation of the relation between filiation and citizenship in the French Empire. Combining mechanisms of inclusion and exclusion, the 1918 decree reinforced the link between these two modes of social affiliation, which in metropolitan France could be taken for granted. The debates about the relation between filiation and nationality, which were related to the controversy over the hierarchical precedence of two principles—respect for "family honor and tranquillity" and public order—led not only to a greater emphasis on filiation in the determination of citizenship but also to a recharacterization of the filial relationship itself. No longer a matter of personal choice, filiation had become an object of state scrutiny.

The fact that amendments to both Article 8 and Article 339 of the Civil Code were combined in a single text shows that the colonial state was subject to a twofold constraint. On the one hand, it sought to enlarge the "community of citizens" as much as possible in order to ensure that the colonial order would endure. On the other hand, it wished to maintain the prestige of the French population, in part by stamping out frauds that misrepresented filiations and usurped the title of "citizen" in a situation where stable identities were essential to the reproduction of colonial domination. Here, as in metropolitan France, legal definitions were the foundation of the political order. Hence, it is not surprising that this type of controversy has recently reappeared in the debate about immigration.

In France, the law of 1972 concerning filiation authorized prosecutors to challenge recognitions of filiation in cases where "indications drawn from the acts themselves make the declared filiation implausible" (Article 339 of the Civil Code), thereby putting an "end [to the] almost religious respect accorded to the freedom of families."[74] The record of parliamentary debate on this legislation does not indicate that it was linked in any way to issues of immigration. It was rather the culmination of a long history, which over the course of the twentieth century had progressively reduced filiation to a question of procreation and made parental will subordinate to "nature." "Rarely used to track down implausible paternities," the new measure was seized on by prosecutors "above all to attack false mothers" and figured as part of the "sanctification of the womb."[75]

More recently, the link between filiation and nationality has come up again in debates about the control of immigration. In debate prior to passage of the law of November 26, 2003, dealing with immigration, foreigners residing in France, and nationality, several deputies raised the need to combat "fraudulent recognitions of paternity," which, in the eyes of the Ministry of the Interior, led at the time by Nicolas Sarkozy, "constituted an increasingly common tactic of foreign citizens seeking to circumvent visa controls or acquire French citizenship."[76] Concretely, this concern resulted in a new condition for the issuance of temporary family visas, requiring parents to "assume responsibility for the maintenance and education of the children." For legislators, the goal was "to discourage fictitious recognitions of paternity by depriving them of their purpose."[77]

In 2006, some legislators once again claimed that fraudulent recognitions had become common in Mayotte (a tiny island near Madagascar) and Guiana.[78] In view "of the special situation" in these territories, the senators proposed to "provide a way to suspend or challenge a recognition of paternity, based on the current procedure for verifying the validity of a marriage," and promised to impose "penal sanctions for fraudulent recognitions of paternity." The possibility of genetic testing was also mentioned.[79]

This concern was extended to the whole of French territory in a proposed July 2006 reform to the law governing admission to France and the right of asylum, which provided among other things that "where there is serious evidence that the recognition of a child is fraudulent, the civil records clerk shall notify the prosecutor of the republic."

This provision, which was aimed (without saying so) solely at foreigners, amounted to a major amendment of the Civil Code, since it established the state as the final arbiter of filiation. Daunted by the magnitude of the reform, the government submitted to Parliament a final bill that retained the procedure only for Mayotte, which, according to a parliamentary report, was particularly endangered by the "social peril" of clandestine immigration and "fictitious recognitions."[80] In this diagnosis, we see elements similar to the colonial debates, in that what was singled out as problematic was the ease of recognition under local law, involving in particular the practice of "name giving." The contemporary treatment of immigration in the overseas territories reveals that the relation between paternity and citizenship continues to be an issue. Immigration to metropolitan France shows similar tensions. New immigration laws were passed in 2005, 2006, and 2007. In the last of these, the French National Assembly attempted to limit the flow of immigrants coming through the "family reunion" program in favor of skilled workers (the so-called chosen immigrants). The proposed Article 5 stated that "the applicant for a visa from a country in which identity records are deficient can, in the absence of a civil status certificate or in the case of serious doubt about its authenticity, seek identification by DNA fingerprinting to provide evidence of affiliation with at least one parent." This article raised much debate both in France and abroad and in the end was never applied: in the fall of 2009, the minister of immigration and national identity decided not to sign it. Nonetheless, the debate signals persistent anxiety over the ability of fraudulent recognitions to introduce unworthy foreigners into the French polity. We find the same concern at work in the debate about whether to apply the law of 1912 concerning investigation of paternity to the colonies—the subject to which we turn next.

SIX

Investigating Paternity in the Colonies

Even as measures to deal with the problem of fraudulent recognitions were being put in place, the *métis* question aroused a second legal debate over the wisdom of applying the law concerning investigation of paternity (*recherche de paternité*, or "paternity suits" in American parlance) to the colonies. Prohibited since the Revolution, investigations of paternity were once again authorized in France by the law of November 16, 1912, which amended Article 340 of the Civil Code. This text introduced an important change in the legal regime of filiation by defining for the first time a mode of filiation independent of the express will of the progenitor. Previously, the legal bond between father and child stemmed either from the marriage commitment or from voluntary acts of recognition.

Like the controversy over fraudulent recognitions, the debate over investigations of paternity in the colonies was mainly about the citizenship implications for the *métis*. As the governor of Indochina made clear: "Practically speaking, the importance of the question for Indochina lies entirely in the new situation that the law would create for children of mixed blood born to a French father and an Annamite mother. . . . The point to notice is that those who are judicially recognized will change status as a result and be entitled to enjoy all the rights of a citizen."[1] It is not surprising, then, that the 1912 law was promulgated without difficulty in the "old colonies": because citizenship there was extended to all, the law's effects were limited to filiation and did not extend to citizenship.

The controversy over investigation of paternity unfolded in a different way from the debates about fraudulent recognitions and relied on different arguments. Indeed, it began not in the colonies but in Paris, and more precisely in Parliament. Only later, in response to an inquiry from the Ministry of Colonies about the wisdom of extending investigation of paternity to overseas territories, did debate begin in various parts of the empire. There, members of the local elite, from elected members of municipal councils and chambers of commerce to colonial administrators, all had something to say about the issue. Their exchanges dealt with the situation of children of mixed blood but also, more broadly, with the nature of sexuality in the colonies, relations between Frenchmen and native women, and the rights, duties, and responsibilities of each, and mobilized a variety of definitions of the family in the colonial situation.

The Investigation of Paternity in the Metropole: A Compromise Text

On November 8, 1912, after more than thirty years of parliamentary controversy (the first bill had been introduced in 1878),[2] the Senate passed a law authorizing the investigation of paternity.[3] Under strictly defined conditions, the law made it possible for an individual to go to court to establish his or her filiation with respect to a father who had not recognized his child.

To avoid awakening unpleasant memories of this lengthy debate, the text euphemistically avoided the expression "investigation of paternity" and substituted "judicial declaration of paternity" instead. Despite the opposition of certain lawmakers, who would have preferred to limit the rights of a child whose filiation had been declared against his or her father's will to an alimentary allowance, the law put in place a second means of establishing natural paternal filiation. In particular, such judicial recognitions had the same legal implications as voluntary recognitions with respect to use of the name of the father, paternal authority; reciprocal duties to provide alimentary support and rights of inheritance; and, pursuant to the provisions of Article 8 of the Civil Code, the acquisition by the child of the father's nationality (if the mother has not previously recognized the child).

Family Affairs and Affairs of State

The new law was part of a broader shift toward state intervention in matters related to families and early childhood. Instigated by the nascent republic, the shift gathered momentum over time.[4] Three major laws mark this evolution: the Roussel law of 1874 introduced the administrative surveillance of children placed with wet nurses, on the assumption that wet nurses treated children badly. The law of 1889 concerning "the protection of abused and morally abandoned children" set forth conditions under which paternal authority could be stripped away. This reform was aimed not only at children placed outside the home but also at those who received inadequate care from their parents. It thereby brought the state into the heart of family relations.[5] And finally, the law of 1904 concerning assisted children served primarily to strengthen legislation dating back to 1811 and harmonize a range of laws on the subject, thereby establishing a veritable code of child assistance.

Parallel concerns with natalism in this period led to the passage of legislation regulating working conditions for pregnant women and new mothers, as well as laws to protect the reproductive capacity of women. The child labor law of 1874, for example, prohibited girls under the age of twenty-one from working at night. An 1892 law extended this prohibition to all women and limited their working day to eleven hours. The maternity leave law of 1909 created a right of unpaid leave by guaranteeing that new mothers would still have their jobs when they returned to work after giving birth. Four years later, these provisions were strengthened to four weeks of mandatory leave after childbirth, plus an allowance "in the period immediately preceding delivery for any woman of French nationality without resources."[6]

Though part of this broader shift in the law, the debate about investigation of paternity was nevertheless shaped by certain specific issues. The arguments on which it relied revealed changes in the social definition of sexuality, the relation between marriage and filiation, and the division of responsibility for the care of illegitimate offspring among men, women, and the state.

The investigation of paternity had been authorized under the ancien régime but at the time led only to a right of alimentary support and not to legal filiation. It was then banned under the Revolution and later by the Civil Code, whose drafters had cited among their reasons the slanderous allegations and scandalous paternity suits that had agitated public opinion during the ancien régime. They also suggested that the right to investigate paternity would encourage immorality among women, who would no longer have to bear the consequences of their actions. Finally, they argued that proof of paternity remained an "impenetrable mystery." They authorized paternity suits only in cases where the man had abducted the woman at the time of conception, considering, in the words of Portalis, that "the punishment for abduction would be the investigation of paternity."[7] Article 340 of the Napoleonic Code therefore provided that "the investigation of paternity is forbidden. In case of abduction, when the time of abduction coincides with that of conception, the abductor may be declared the father of the child upon request of the interested parties."

At bottom, the ban on investigation of paternity reflected a concept of filiation based on will. By excluding unmarried men from paternity, the code reinforced the principle, already inscribed in the definition of legitimate filiation and the many obstacles placed in the way of disavowals of paternity, that the father is the husband (*pater is est quem nuptiae demonstrant*), or, rather, that marriage makes the father. In the logic of the code, a man, by marrying, agrees in advance that any children born of the union will be his. In the determination of filiation, the Napoleonic Code thus privileged marriage over sexuality, and for both men and women, since it authorized married women to become mothers without giving birth provided that they, in accord with their husbands, respected certain appearances.[8]

To be sure, over the course of the nineteenth century, the courts would increasingly circumvent the ban in cases where the issue was not to establish filiation but to repair the damage suffered by a seduced woman. At a more fundamental level, attacks on Article 340 of the Civil Code became more common after 1860. These were generally expressed in terms of the interests of the child, the woman, and society.

The interest of the child would become fundamental in the twentieth century, especially in the debates about divorce reform in 1975. But the issue at the turn of the century was distinctly less important[9] and more often characterized as the *innocence* of the child and the child's natural right to obtain both civil status and material support from his or her father. It was much more common to emphasize the *interest of the mother.* The unwed mother, whom the authors of the Civil Code had treated as culpable in her own misfortune, came to be seen as a victim: a "seduced girl." Although the Civil Code had already authorized investigation of paternity in cases of abduction, the 1912 law included any action by a man to exact sexual relations by force. Paternity suits could initially be brought in cases of rape, abduction, and "deceitful seduction" (*séduction dolosive*), including "abuse of authority, promise of marriage or engagement," provided that there was "preliminary written proof" (about which more will be said later). The introduction of the notion of "deceitful seduction," against which a law was proposed as early as 1902, suggests a movement to make the man at least partially responsible in cases of extramarital sex.[10]

But the arguments that dominated the debate about investigation of paternity had to do primarily with the notion of "social interest,"[11] countering

Napoleon's well-known position during the drafting of the Civil Code that "society has no interest in the recognition of bastards."[12]

Article 340 was criticized initially for its alleged contribution to the "depopulation" crisis. Indeed, the debate about investigation of paternity took place against a background of demographic crisis, which had become a matter of acute anxiety after negative net population growth was recorded for the years 1890, 1891, 1892, 1895, and 1900. Demographers invariably interpreted these results as reflecting a "deficit of births."[13] In view of the high German birthrate, these birth deficits fed fears of "degeneration of the race."[14] In 1902 and again in 1912, "extraparliamentary committees against depopulation" assembled physicians and demographers charged with "studying all national, social, and fiscal issues relevant to depopulation in France and seeking remedies for them."[15]

In this context, a connection was quickly made between the "license to seduce" implied by Article 340 of the Civil Code and the demographic crisis. Indeed, along with the demoralizing consequences of industrialization,[16] the ban on paternity suits was designated as the primary reason for the steady increase of illegitimate births over the course of the nineteenth century. These accounted for 10 percent of the total number of births at the time that politicians seized on the issue of depopulation. The mortality rate of illegitimate children was twice as high as that of legitimate children,[17] and their rate of death in childbirth was also abnormally high due to the fact that unmarried pregnant women were often reduced to misery and delivered their children in secret. Furthermore, illegitimate children often suffered for life from the "deficit of vitality" with which they were born: many were "sick and feeble." Their existence introduced into the population "a very serious and very considerable element of debility."[18]

The interest of society was also threatened by the criminality encouraged by the ban on investigation of paternity. This meant, first of all, the criminal behavior of seduced women, who were said to be forced to seek abortions, commit infanticide, or, in order to feed their babies, engage in prostitution. Even more alarming was the criminality of their illegitimate offspring, who accounted for more than their share of vagabonds, beggars, prostitutes, and criminals.[19] The argument here touched on the role of paternity in the reproduction of the social order. Because illegitimate and unrecognized children were usually abandoned by their fathers, they escaped "the moralizing influence of family life, in the absence of which mischievous instincts and passions more readily enjoyed free rein."[20] Above all, illegitimate children were not brought up to be good citizens, since it was primarily the task of the father "to feed the child, educate him or her, and make the child a good citizen of the French fatherland."[21]

"He Who Makes the Child Must Make Him or Her a Citizen"

"He who makes the child must feed him or her"—so said the adage recorded by Antoine Loisel, which captured the principle of older French law. To this the Third Republic added that "he who makes the child must make him or her a citizen." Indeed, despite the rather too hasty assertion that "the institution of the family did not have a place as such in republican ideology, which gave priority to reflection on the relationship between citizens,"[22] it seems that many republicans assigned the family a leading role as the primary institution for the formation of citizens. Among them were Jules Simon and Jules Barni, whose *Manuel républicain* stressed the necessity of a "cult of the family": "Properly understood, family virtues feed civic virtues. Far from harming the general interests of the republic, they contribute to its prosperity. Those who believe in strengthening the state by ruining the family commit a profound error. . . . If you wish to be a good citizen, first be a good son, good husband, good father, and good brother. You will thereby fulfill your primary duties, and the republic will reap the benefits."[23]

If the father makes the citizen, it was the family that makes the father. This conviction was at the heart of the 1912 law. Indeed, leaving aside cases in which the man was judged to be at fault, other cases in which the "judicial recognition of paternity" was permitted almost always involved situations in which an unmarried man behaved as the father of a family: demonstrating an "unequivocal avowal of paternity," or "notorious concubinage during the period of conception," or "participation . . . in the maintenance and education of the child in the role of father." The law therefore sought not so much to root filiation in biological fact as to broaden the definition of will and marriage to include "quasi-contractual" relationships at the foundation of "quasi families," to borrow two expressions from Louis Martin, one of the most ardent defenders of investigation of paternity in the Senate.[24] Jurists proposed applying to concubinage the maxim *pater is est quem nuptiae demonstrant* while diminishing its probative force, since concubines were not formally committed to fidelity:

> Just as the presumption *pater is est* . . . in marriage rests on the wife's duty of fidelity, its extramarital equivalent, the admissibility of investigation of natural paternity, obviously rests on an enduring pledge of fidelity by the mistress. This pledge, generally tacit but always serious, is the essential feature of con-

cubinage as it is to be understood here. When coupled with sexual relations, concubinage exists. When absent, there is only accidental union, unsuitable as a basis for investigation of paternity. The absence of natural family organization is then complete. By contrast, with open concubinage, there is an embryonic organization that makes comparison with an organized family, a legitimate family, possible.[25]

Even when the family was not legitimate, when it remained "hidden and disorganized,"[26] it was expected to produce legal ties among its members. Thus, proponents of the law could easily counter the critiques of conservatives, who saw the bill as an attack on legitimate families. By imposing obligations on a man who had behaved as a father and therefore had no further interest in avoiding marriage, the law on investigation of paternity encouraged the formation of legitimate families. Nevertheless, the numerous and repeated objections to the law in the name of morality and public order[27] account for both the length of the parliamentary process and the extremely cautious character of the ultimate text, which was a compromise among divergent conceptions of social order, family, and filiation.

In order to reassure those who feared an attack on the institution of the family, children of adulterous and incestuous relationships were not included among the beneficiaries of the law. Only the child—or, if the child was a minor, the mother, acting in the child's name—could bring a paternity suit. In order to ensure that family tranquillity would not be threatened indefinitely, the deadline for action was extremely short. The mother had two years to act from the date of delivery, the cessation of cohabitation, or the end of the man's contribution to the maintenance and upbringing of the child. The child himself or herself could bring suit only in the year following the attainment of majority. To prevent blackmail, applicants convicted of filing false claims were subject to criminal penalties. Finally, in order to avoid scandal, the publication of proceedings was forbidden.

The most difficult argument for the defenders of investigations of paternity to counter was probably the issue of proof. The problem was not simply the impossibility of providing incontestable proof of paternity, which was also the case in marriage, but "the uncertainty stemming from the fact that in the absence of marriage, the mother was not bound by any duty of fidelity."[28] Various steps were taken to limit the consequences. In particular, the plaintiff's case could be dismissed on two grounds: when the mother was "notorious for her misbehavior or had relations with another individual" during the legal period of conception or when, during the same period, the alleged father was "physically incapable of being the father of the child."

But the issue of proof also arose in cases of "fault," where there were "fraudulent maneuvers, abuses of authority, or promises of marriage or engagement." In such cases, "preliminary proof" was demanded "in writing, under the terms of Article 1347 of the Civil Code." This meant that the document had to have originated with the putative father, even if it was not necessarily written in his hand or signed by him.

This should be seen as reflecting a desire to leave the bourgeoisie in charge of marriage and filiation. In fact, the notion of "fraudulent maneuvers" had been introduced to combat "the most general case of corruption, the most common seduction . . . the abuse by an employer or foreman of authority over a worker in his shop or by a master over his servant—in short, domestic seduction or employer seduction."[29] In order to limit the grounds for suits by employees, however, the deputies introduced the requirement of "preliminary written proof": "Otherwise, a master would be subject to blackmail by a cunning woman who had worked for a time under his roof, who might then seek the services of one of the many agents who lurk about the courts."[30] Furthermore, although the most conservative deputies ultimately allowed the shameful word *concubinage* to be included in the text of the law, it was only because it replaced the word *cohabitation*, which they believed would have made it too easy for servants to file suit against their masters. In the final text, the distance between classes was maintained: as Anne Martin-Fugier has observed, "The lover of a maid did not write to her."[31]

Finally, the ultimate precaution against abuse of the investigation of paternity lay in the very structure of the law. The cases cited in Article 1 were merely facts that allowed the investigation of paternity to proceed. These facts alone were not sufficient to result in recognition of filiation, which it was the sovereign privilege of the judge to decide on the basis of his own intimate conviction. In reaching his decision, the judge was free to rely on all the usual measures of civil matters (investigation, subpoena, interrogation, expert witnesses, and so forth).

A Colonial Debate

The long debate over investigating paternity ended in a final round that played out between 1910 and 1912, when the legislature took up the question of extending the law to the entire empire. Because the colonies operated under a special legal regime, laws were not automatically enforceable overseas except in the old colonies of Guadeloupe, Martinique, Réunion, and Guiana. They became enforceable only by virtue of an express provi-

sion of the law itself, a subsequent law, or a decree.[32] Seeking to extend
to the colonies the authority to investigate paternity, the Senate voted in
June 1910 that "the present law is applicable to Algeria and the colonies."
Since it amended the Civil Code, it was to be applied wherever the code
was in force.[33] But the Ministry of Colonies ruled that "undue extension of
the provisions [of this] text may have serious drawbacks in colonies where
there is a large native population" and ordered governors to look into the
"advantages and disadvantages" of applying the law to the colonies and
how that might be done. Opinions were to be based on "the advice of local
assemblies, heads of competent departments, and the personal opinions [of
local heads of the executive] on the issue."[34]

At issue was the possibility that *métis* might file paternity suits against
French citizens. In fact, a consensus quickly emerged in both the metropole
and the colonies on two fundamental points: first, the illegitimate child of
two French or assimilated citizens should be able to file a paternity suit in
view of the equality of all French citizens before the law; second, respect for
local customs, a basic principle of colonial government, strictly prohibited
any application of the law on investigation of paternity to children born to
two native parents. By contrast, the situation of children of mixed blood—
not only their rights but also the rights of their mothers, and more broadly
the definition of sexuality and the family in the colonies—was a subject of
many bitter discussions in the various territories.

The issue did not arouse the same interest everywhere. Debates were
particularly animated in Indochina, where the residents of various provinces, municipal officials, and the members of a number of chambers of
commerce answered the minister's questions. The city of Haiphong and the
colony of Cochin China even set up special commissions to consider the
application of Article 340. In Madagascar, the issue aroused considerable
interest among local elites, but not as much as in Indochina. In other colonies, only the highest level of the administration participated in the debate.
The geography of the responses to the 1910 survey reproduced that of the
métis question, of which Indochina and to a lesser extent Madagascar were
the epicenters.

Other Places, Other Mores

The survey revealed strongly divided opinions among the members of the
colonial elite about applying the law on investigation of paternity overseas—with a clear majority of respondents hostile to the idea. But a consensus did emerge: the coexistence of two distinct populations made the

issue special in the colonies.[35] In a typical formulation, the administrator of Mayotte wrote to the governor of Madagascar that he did not think the law should be applied to his territory, "given the mixture of races and the cohabitation of the white element, both French and foreign, with the native element."[36] Recourse to the vocabulary of race, so often presented as foreign to republican rhetoric, was not limited to colonials: in Paris, a note in the *Revue critique de législation et jurisprudence* in 1913 challenged the application of the law to the empire so as to avoid "the enlistment of the law in racial conflicts."[37]

Colonial actors also insisted that long experience of relations with natives had given rise to a distinctive morality. This was the position of members of the Chamber of Commerce of Haiphong, which transmitted their opinions to Paris:

> In sum, certain measures of this type, which might at first seem highly moral to a European legal mind, will be judged extremely immoral in their consequences by people who know the insuperable gap that separates the European mentality from the Annamite mentality. . . . Thus, the opinion of the Chamber of Commerce of Haiphong, which is based on its members' familiarity with the mentality and morals of the Annamites and on the disastrous consequences to which application of this measure would lead, is distinctly opposed to the application of the law to natives among themselves and to children born of unions between Europeans and natives. By contrast, the chamber sees no reason not to apply the law to the colony if it is strictly limited to children born to European or naturalized parents.[38]

More precisely, for the colonial observers, the nature of relations between French and natives rendered some metropolitan arguments in favor of investigation of paternity nonsensical: in particular, the notions of fault and "quasi family" made no sense overseas.

According to an argument developed in various territories, the native woman could never be considered a victim. Because she offered herself publicly to colonial men in societies where concubinage existed, as in Indochina, there was allegedly no occasion for seduction or rape. Unlike in the metropole, where concubinage was a substitute for marriage and implied fidelity between the partners, colonial concubinage yielded children whose progenitor was of necessity uncertain. The members of the Haiphong Chamber of Commerce shared their view of the matter with the Ministry of Colonies:

In the case of a union between a European male and an Annamite woman, it is fair to say that seduction is extremely rare. . . . Like the Chinese, Annamites have a legitimate wife and may have one or more concubines. The latter may be repudiated, and a woman who lives with a European is considered a concubine by the Annamites. . . . The European nearly always takes the concubine with the approval of her parents, who generally receive a sum of money and who regard their daughter's temporary arrangement as perfectly honorable. In many other cases, the woman is introduced to the European by a female procurer who has bought her from her parents. Rape does not exist, since concubines taken by Europeans are very seldom if ever virgins. There can be no question of seduction, because the Annamite woman will decide to live with a European only where a pecuniary interest is involved. Furthermore, the fact that Annamite women are generally unfaithful and frequently immoral would constitute the greatest danger if they were permitted to file suit against their lovers, since their union with a European is for them simply a profitable venture, which they regard as honorable but in which questions of sentiment play very little part.[39]

In this context, the man is never at fault and, distinct from metropolitan norms, makes no commitment to the woman: "In France, the peasant or worker who wrongs a neighborhood girl makes *reparations*, and the man who takes advantage of his position to abuse a younger or poorer woman contracts an undeniable debt. But leaving aside questions of color and inferior race, social relations are not the same between a young Frenchman who lands in this country and the native women who are generally offered to him."[40]

By contrast, "If, in France, everything tends to magnify the man's responsibility in these situations, here everything tends to attenuate it,"[41] and it would be unjust to make men bear the consequences of the imperial venture.

Here, the colonial difference is above all the result of representations of sexuality. In a period of intense naturalization of male sexuality,[42] people believed that men could not stop themselves from seeking to satisfy their "natural appetites."[43] That being the case, a continuing relationship with a native woman was a lesser evil, as manuals of preparation for colonial life often noted: for reasons of "health safety," it was better to choose a "temporary union with a carefully selected native woman," such women being "generally healthy, whereas [local] prostitutes, not required to be seen by doctors, are almost always contaminated."[44]

But colonials also recognized an equally imperious need for sociability, which concubinage partly satisfied, while also allowing the re-creation of a kind of domestic space. This was a key point in the report submitted by the superior resident in Annam:

> The unmarried European, especially if he is young and finds himself abruptly deprived of his country, his environment, and all emotional support, experiences a moral crisis that makes it difficult for him, in his isolation, to adapt to the new conditions of his existence. If, in addition, and along with the occupations that attach him to the country, he must devote part of his time to domestic chores of which he has no experience and therefore finds all the more tedious, he may begin to lose his grip on things. If, moreover, he is aware of weaknesses that might lead him into some unfortunate temptation, he will want to take steps to avoid entanglements that he might later come to regret, and this naturally leads him to the idea of assuaging his loneliness, an idea that is so frequently the result of such purely pragmatic thinking that it would hardly be reasonable to attribute it to any other cause. In such cases, we must not think only of those privileged individuals whom circumstances have placed in major centers where they may have frequent and varied contact with other Europeans, and where there exist groups with which they can enjoy certain intellectual relaxations, or even in some cases be fortunate enough to gratify their heart's most intimate wishes. There are others who, living in the "bush," at times feel more intensely than their more fortunate colleagues the burden of their isolation, and it is fair to say that after a certain time, the choice of a native companion (let us say the word for want of anything better) is by no means a sign of sentimental or perverted thinking but rather the consecration of a physical and moral necessity.[45]

As Ann Laura Stoler has shown in a magisterial work, it was therefore in domestic space that the "tensions of empire"—domination and dependence, sentiments and needs—were most intensely displayed.[46] In the end, this configuration seems quite close to that of "ancillary concubinage or union with a good, placid, and comfortable woman whose devotion may be that of either a wife or maid [in metropolitan France]." In French society, which at this time was experiencing the triumph of "domesticity" and a marked sexual division of domestic labor, concubinage was paradoxically a way of conforming to new norms.[47]

If ambiguity reigned in the metropole, there was no such doubt in the colonies. All observers agreed that "racial difference" impeded the growth of sentiment. The superior resident in Annam remarked that "no moral principle presides over the formation of these necessarily precarious relationships between individuals of different races, and no idea of sentimentality enters into them." Hence, the possibilities of abduction and seduction envisioned by the law "are not to be feared here, where the racial affinity likely to provoke them does not exist between individuals of the two sexes considered." In the colonial situation, both partners clearly understood their interests, and this was all that mattered. The fundamental inequality between them was forgotten, according to the resident: "Here, the relationship between a European male and a native woman can more properly be characterized as an *association* rather than a *union*. It should be seen not as a case of either overflowing sentimentality or reprehensible cynicism but rather as a shared institution, based on clearly defined conditions and for a limited period and involving mutual interests freely discussed and agreed upon."[48]

The argument in terms of a "quasi-family" relationship, which played a key role in the metropole in support of investigations of paternity, made no sense in the colonies, where families did not conform to the normal pattern. Regular "mixed" unions, which grew more numerous over time, remained an exception about which colonial observers had notably little to say.[49] In their eyes, the goal for the colonial male "was not to join his life to that of a native woman but rather to form a partnership for a limited period of time in order to alleviate the severe monotony of the bachelor life, which frequently offers no other diversions."[50] Reasoning symmetrically, they also believed that "for the Annamite or Asiatic woman in general, union with a European can only take the form of concubinage and can never acquire the character of a marriage, which would require various rites that cannot be performed with a foreigner."[51]

Accordingly, in the empire, the moralizing objective envisioned by advocates of investigation of paternity was rendered meaningless: if, in the metropole, Article 340 could discourage concubinage, which no longer provided a way to escape the obligations of paternity, in the colonies, "the French legal concept of the putative father would allow the development of a family whose origins were of the most dubious and varied sort"[52]—in short, a new threat to colonial prestige.

Opponents of applying investigation of paternity in the colonies pointed out that it would give native women power over French citizens, contradicting the principles of colonial domination: "To give them such a powerful hold over the father of their child would be to emancipate them quite suddenly and imprudently."[53] Critics of the law were especially afraid of the scandals that paternity suits might precipitate. The superior resident in Laos stated that "given the mentality of the Laotians and their still relatively unformed consciences, there would seem to be a real danger in equipping them with such arms. The cases of attempted blackmail, dubious maneuvers, and shabby bargains that would result might well strike a serious blow to our dignity and prestige."[54]

The risk had often been evoked in metropolitan debates: lower-class women and prostitutes were the main objects of concern because they were the primary targets of young bourgeois males looking for sexual partners in the years before marriage. But compassion for "seduced young women" ultimately won out. For colonial actors, as we have seen, "seduction" had no meaning, while fear of scandal was heightened by the belief that little credence could be placed in the testimony of natives.

Even the most ardent defenders of applying the law in the colonies shared this perspective. For instance, the deputy Maurice Viollette[55] agreed "that certain African tribes do not offer sufficient intellectual guarantees to allow us to place credence in their testimony, which they might well see as a mere formality of no significance." His suggestion was to rely only on testimony of "Europeans or assimilated."[56] Nevertheless, this debate also contained assertions of a principle of universal equivalence that was supposed to outweigh differences of mores. Pierre Guillier, the *rapporteur* for the law in the Senate, did not regard the problem of proof as insuperable: "No doubt it will be more difficult to furnish [proof] regarding events in certain remote regions than in absolutely civilized countries, but the difficulty of providing proof in certain circumstances should not be allowed to stand in the way of applying a principle of justice and fairness that is not seriously contested."[57]

As we see in this debate, the French political elite did not necessarily think of the colonies as a separate world. It projected certain "principles of justice and fairness" upon it.

Filiation without Family

All the arguments raised against applying the investigation of paternity law overseas centered on the difference between the metropolitan and colonial situations with respect to sexuality and affectivity. By contrast, the children born in the colonies were described in terms quite similar to those used in the metropole. The responses to the ministerial query focused in particular on the theme of criminality among illegitimate offspring, with girls going into prostitution and boys into criminal activity or political agitation. At no time, however, was the demographic factor, which was so central in the metropolitan debate, raised in the colonial one. In the early 1910s, *métis* were not yet seen as "French elements" that might help to resolve the "crisis of depopulation," as would be the case later in the 1920s and 1930s (see chapter 7).

By contrast, the dominant argument had to do with responsibility not toward mothers but toward children, whose interests were treated as distinct. Thus, the report by the Hanoi Chamber of Commerce pointed out that "racial diversity stands out here as the most worrisome issue. Can we really think of lumping together in the same legislation, especially on such a delicate issue, people whose moral conceptions are so different from ours?" Enumerating all the dangers that militated "in favor of absolute discretion with respect to unwed native mothers," the report nevertheless described the offspring of colonial unions in terms similar to those used at the time in France to describe illegitimate children: "Does this mean that fear of the difficulties involved should cause us to dismiss all feelings of pity and justice with respect to the child? I do not think so. Shouldn't we rather remind ourselves that the law owes its support to these innocent and feeble creatures? . . . We cannot fail to recognize that the rights of the child make the duties of the father inescapable, and to convince ourselves of this we have only to appeal to our sense of probity."[58]

The emphasis here on the responsibility of the father accorded with the spirit of the law: until 1972, recognition (whether voluntary or judicial) only established a bond of kinship between individuals and did not make the child part of his or her father's family. In other words, investigation of paternity gave the child a father but not a family. In an article calling for rapid promulgation of the law in the colonies, Maurice Viollette vehemently pointed out that what was primarily at stake was the legal bond between a man and his offspring:

But why, then, does the color of the child matter? Would the father be allowed in France to cast out the child because he was handicapped or abnormal or even because he was a monster? The essential point is that the child is indeed his and he has recognized the child as such. But it does not matter that the child was born to a Bambara, Peuhle, Hova, Annamite, or Kanak woman. The mother's identity is of no interest. It is of so little interest that drafting committees in the Senate and Chamber were unanimous in finding that the law is applicable even if the child is born to a prostitute, provided that it is well attested that at the moment of conception the mother's behavior was not such as to create uncertainty as to paternity; and there is no need to reveal the ignominious existence she may have led before or after. Such a subject should undeniably be placed well below a native woman of the most backward tribe that would have a normal existence. It cannot be repeated often enough that the issue here is not the woman but the child and that, thanks to the father's avowal, that child is attached to him by bonds that justice need only confirm, regardless of the child's physical, physiological, or racial status. By virtue of the fact that a man has chosen the child to be his son and has done so in an unequivocal manner, that man has assumed moral obligations to the child that the courts, upon verification, are duty-bound to convert to legal obligations.[59]

Some observers then tried to reconcile the notion of paternal responsibility with the perceived constraints on colonial sexuality and sociability. One suggestion was to promulgate the law on investigation of paternity but to eliminate articles indicating fault on the part of the father (abduction, rape, seduction) and retain only the case of the man who had assumed the paternal role in regard to his child. Another was to propose that philanthropic associations assume collective responsibility for the problem, to be financed by public subsidies and private donations: "This is how the European understands his duty today, equitably sharing the human responsibility that he bears personally and the social responsibility that is beyond his control."[60] Once again, the debate touched on the social meaning of paternity in the colonies.

Paternity and Citizenship: Nature and Will

The colonial controversy concerning the investigation of paternity revealed deep connections between the concepts of filiation and citizenship. Indeed, both affiliation to the family and affiliation to the polity were fraught with the tension between nature and will.

In the familial economy established by the Civil Code of 1804, paternity was exclusively the consequence of a demonstrated will, which could be expressed either in marriage (by marrying a woman, a man agreed to be the father of any children born of the union) or through voluntary recognition.

The law of 1912 challenged this logic by allowing children to search for their fathers, even against the man's will. It thus introduced the notion of "truth" into the concept of filiation, in contrast to the regime of appearances that had hitherto held sway. The truth in question was "biological," to use a common distinction in French legal parlance between biological and sociological filiation. This was clear first of all in the way in which the law was implemented: judges were invited to draw their own conclusions based on any evidence that seemed useful, including physical signs such as resemblance and color.[61] As the law evolved, the "biological" conception of filiation became more prominent. Blood tests were first introduced into French law in a 1955 revision to the law of 1912. Henceforth, incompatible blood types provided a third ground on which a putative father could file for dismissal of a paternity suit, supplementing the older standards of "notorious misbehavior" by the mother and proof of "physical impossibility" of fatherhood.[62]

Nevertheless, the law of 1912 continued to root paternity in will, which could be manifested by the admission of the father, by "notorious concubinage" as a substitute for marriage, and by the father's treatment of the child. The last item, which came closest to a demonstration of will, was considered to have the greatest probative force: it was the only indication that did not require corroboration by a written document. The putative father's participation in the child's upkeep and education was considered to be an act that *created* a duty for the man and a right for the child.[63]

This tension between the two conceptions of paternity was noted by jurists at the time. For Ambroise Colin, the most astute observer on this point, the child's situation was determined either "by nature, by ties of blood, by principles prior to, and superior to, any written rule," or by "a construction, if not arbitrary then at least empirical, based solely on indications of individual and social interest."[64] In his view, the law conflated these two conceptions. It would have been better to distinguish the first, which established a "bond of (simple) kinship" between an individual and his progenitor, and the second, which created a veritable "family tie." *Kinship* was the product of procreation alone (a "community of blood"), whereas *family* was a "social grouping organized by law or custom." The modes of proof and consequences should therefore be different: in one case, it was a matter of demonstrating a natural fact, which creates the "duties of procreators [in view of] preservation of the species" (and therefore a simple alimentary subsidy); in the other, proof of demonstrated will was required to give rise to "rights of power and authority" and a claim to inheritance.[65]

The colonial debate concerning application of the new Article 340 revealed a similar confusion about conceptions of citizenship, which involved treating the polity as both a "community of blood" and a "grouping organized by the law," to paraphrase Colin. Two positions emerged, and these differed as much in their definitions of paternity and citizenship as in their conception of law.

The first position, defended by many colonial administrators and notables, might be characterized as "realist." They argued that investigation of paternity should be allowed only for *métis* who had become, thanks to paternal care, "truly French." As such, they should be able to acquire not only legally recognized filiation but also the title and prerogatives of French citizens. By contrast, children raised by their mothers should remain natives among natives. To allow them to obtain full citizenship via investigation of paternity would turn them into *"déclassés,"* enjoying the title of Frenchmen but not the social status. One high official in the Indochinese administration defended this position in the following terms:

> The child, born of a French father and a native mother, acquires a different status depending on whether he is raised by his mother or his father. If raised by his mother, he remains purely Annamite. He has a home that corresponds to his needs and in no way aspires to a civilization that is not that of his chosen family. He will become a farmer, like other Annamite children, and will contribute as they do to the development of the colony's wealth. . . . If we allow full application of the law, we can imagine cases in which a French father would be forced against his will to give his name to a child he had with a native woman. The judgment may have prescribed payment of an alimentary subsidy, but it cannot force the father to give his child a French education. What will become of the child thus granted French citizenship? One of two things: if raised in an Annamite family, he will remain Annamite in heart and race, or else in adolescence he will join the vagabonds who swarm in the depths of Cholon and Saigon. In either case, we will have created a *déclassé*, a "native Frenchman" who, as a voter, will become the prey of the political parties and constitute a real danger for our domination.
>
> Consider now the opposite case, in which the child is raised by his father. If, as a result of the education he has received, the child is freed from his native family . . . it is fair and it is indispensable that he be recognized. The reasons that guided lawmakers in France all continue to speak in favor of this child. In short, I believe that we must limit application of the law to children who have been "raised the French way."[66]

This argument bestowed upon fathers a fundamental role in shaping identities. It can also be characterized as "familialist," in that it takes the family institution to be the producer of identity. Ultimately, it is a realist argument, which leaves little room for the instituting power of law: the law has become merely the means to ratify a fact—namely, the child's attachment to France as a result of the care the child has received from his or her father. This point was stressed by the minister of colonies:

In and of itself, the fact that a child of mixed blood has been recognized by his or her European father is not enough to give that child French habits of thought and ways of being or a French mentality and conscience, which would fully justify the child's exercise locally or *in France* of the rights associated with French citizenship. Indeed, if, after recognizing the child, his or her father does not take care of the child and takes no interest in his or her education, the child will either be raised by his or her native mother or abandoned and, having become a citizen *in law*, will grow up *in fact* as a native—that is, a French subject.[67]

From this perspective, the proper thing to do in the colonies was to limit investigation of paternity to those cases in which "the putative father has provided or participated in the upkeep and education of the child"—the fifth condition of the 1912 law.

In contrast to the realist argument, a second position asserted both the blood tie and the force of law. Proponents of full application of the investigation of paternity law to the colonies gave priority to the case of "the child who is not unaware that European blood, mixed with oriental atavisms, flows in his or her veins and who derives from this fact hope that will turn to anger if not realized."[68] From this perspective, the first priority was to avoid *déclassement,* defined in racial terms, a situation in which the *métis* was truly French by blood but native by status. Proponents of this view emphasized the "community of race," as the governor-general of Indochina did in this reductio ad absurdum:

Alongside the illegitimate children with French fathers and Annamite mothers, there exists in the colony another category of children particularly worthy of interest. These are the children born to a French father and a mother of mixed blood who was not herself recognized by her father. These unrecognized children, who are separated from the Annamite community by racial differences too deep to allow them to be accepted, are nevertheless assigned the personal status of natives. Hence, they cannot be admitted to educational institutions and for want of adequate upbringing and education end up among the *déclassés* who may one day constitute a political danger.[69]

Focusing on the exceptional case of the "three-quarter-blood" *métis* strengthened the force of the racial logic: a question that might have seemed undecidable in the case of the "pure" *métis* (should having a French citizen for a father open the gates of the polity or not?) could be treated as having a self-evident answer in the case of a child with three French grandparents. One might note here a similarity to the arithmetic of the Jewish identity under Vichy, since the Jewish statute of October 1940 defined as a Jew "any person descended from three grandparents of the Jewish race or two grandparents of the same race if married to a Jew."[70]

Here the perspective is nominalist and *legalistic*: the law does not merely reflect identities; it produces them. The title of "citizen" bestowed on those who benefited from judicial recognition of their paternity actually produces the quality of Frenchness. To begin with, the existence of a tie of filiation creates a duty of education: "The law makes it possible to compel the father to fulfill his obligations. In any case, the French father of a child of mixed blood will not want a child who bears his name to wallow in the depths of misery and vice."[71] Furthermore, the title of citizen opens the doors to the institutions in which citizens are formed, especially the schools, which will make it possible to "classify" the child in French society.

In the end, blood and education, title and status became interlocking elements of a circular argument. The argument based on the law's instituting power drew support from the idea of a community of blood: colonial jurists were a long way from making clear distinctions between nature and will or between the logic of blood and the logic of soil. In that respect, they were no different from their metropolitan colleagues, who, to use the terminology of Ambroise Colin, conflated "kinship" and "family."

Paternity and Race

The results of the survey undertaken by the ministry were included in a report by deputy Maurice Viollette in 1912.[72] These spurred a new debate, first in the Assembly, then in the Senate. Initially, the deputies decided to authorize investigation of paternity overseas, with the restriction that the law be "applicable in Algeria and other French possessions. Local governments, in promulgating the law, would nevertheless have the right to apply it only when *both* the mother *and* the putative father were of French nationality or belonged to the category of foreigners assimilated to French nationals."

According to the Senate *rapporteur*, the reason for this restriction was to allay the fears of those who "worried about the consequences of legislation authorizing investigation of natural filiation on men who have resided in countries where morals are lax."[73] The issue gave rise to a vast press campaign orchestrated by the Ligue française pour le droit des femmes in collaboration with the Ligue des droits de l'homme. These organizations mobilized not only their local sections but also Masonic lodges in Paris and the provinces, and they organized several meetings on behalf of children born to French fathers and native mothers. The *métis* question thus entered metropolitan public opinion, extending far beyond ministerial offices and the corridors of parliament.[74]

The proposal to extend the investigation of paternity to all children born in the colonies also invoked racial arguments: "There are no inferior races, and . . . the republic owes it to itself to safeguard and maintain in the colonies, as in the metropole, the principle of equality of all before the law."[75] This formulation anticipated the antiracist rhetoric that would emerge in the 1920s and 1930s.[76] Legislators close to the Ligue des droits de l'homme such as Paul Strauss expressed themselves in similar terms: "We must not give the fortunately inaccurate impression that we make distinctions between races and share the prejudice against inferior races. The child born to a French father and native mother has the same claim on our solicitude as any other child. He or she must be protected from the risks of misery, degeneracy, and death."[77]

The press campaign was unsuccessful, however. The senators followed the deputies, and in the final draft of the law, Article 4 left local administrations discretion over whether the investigation of paternity should be limited to children born to two French parents or opened up to *métis*. In the end, the law was promulgated without restriction in Algeria, Indochina, New Caledonia, and New Hebrides. In Algeria, the *métis* question was quite marginal and not a subject of debate (see chapter 1). In the Pacific and above all in Asia, the permission granted to *métis* to investigate their fathers put an end to a long controversy.[78] In all the other territories, including Madagascar, French West Africa, French Equatorial Africa, and settlements in Oceania and India, the *métis* were excluded from the benefits of the law.[79]

To some extent, these differences reflected the "hierarchy of civilizations" as defined by late nineteenth-century evolutionism, which republican political elites embraced. According to Viollette, "In a country with a real civilization, such as Indochina, it is impossible to create two categories of women, one consisting of those apt to have children legally capable of having a father and another consisting of those for whom the most formal tacit commitments count for nothing."[80] Furthermore, as an internal Ministry of Colonies note made clear, some consideration was given to excluding "other populations of savages such as the Moïs from the benefits of the law."[81]

But the unequal application of the law was also a consequence of the colonial administration's awareness of native customs, of which the minister had made a point: "You shall decide by exclusively adopting the standpoint of our subjects' laws and customs and not the standpoint of the interests of our nationals and assimilated, these having been protected by the legislature itself."[82] In Indochina, native law already authorized investigation of paternity in a spirit very similar to that of the new law. In Madagascar, by contrast, natural maternity was proved by delivery, and paternity had no legal existence outside marriage. As we saw earlier, these provisions were circumvented in the case of voluntary recognition by French citizens. Where there was conflict of laws, the supremacy of French law was reaffirmed. Here, the principle of "respect" for native law was maintained, primarily because the new law would have given native women rights over European men that they did not have over Madagascan men:

> To recognize the applicability of the law in this case would not only have led to the gravest abuses, it would also have established a measure clearly contrary to the legislation and mores of the inhabitants of the island. . . . Under these conditions, full application to the colony of the law concerning the recognition of natural paternity would have led to granting natives in their relations with Europeans a right that does not exist in their own law and of which they could not avail themselves vis-à-vis their own kind.[83]

Once again, in questions of filiation, it was colonial domination that was at issue.

In view of the mobilization of colonial actors in the 1910s, one might assume that any paternity suit launched by a native mother or child of mixed blood in Indochina or New Caledonia would have aroused considerable interest. Yet no trace of any such case can be found in colonial anthologies of legal decisions or judicial archives. If there were such suits, they were few in number and highly discreet. It may be that the procedural requirements of the law made it practically impossible to bring such cases. These included "preliminary written proof," adherence to strict time limits on filing, and especially the rule that suit had to be filed in the local court where the defendant lived (and therefore often in the metropole).

Consequently, the importance of the law in this case has to do not so much with its actual effects as with its role in the history of the *métis* question and in the evolution of the relationship between paternity and citizenship, family and polity. In Indochina, by authorizing the investigation of paternity in cases in which the father never demonstrated any interest in his child, the governor and the jurists who supported him broke with the voluntary conception of paternity established by the Civil Code. For those who hoped to improve the lot of the *métis*, "blood" bestowed the right to citizenship: the concern for justice that animated them was racial.

Finally, the debate about the application of the law to the colonies became the occasion for introducing the *métis* question into metropolitan France. Indeed, the "social problem" was raised in Parliament for the first time in this context. The press campaign, for its part, raised public awareness of the issue. More broadly, the theoretical and practical uses of the notion of race in colonial law were brought back home. A textbook by one of the great private law specialists of the interwar years, for example, included among the factors on which judges could base their intimate conviction "the color and resemblance of the child."[84]

The controversy about fraudulent recognition and the debate about investigation of paternity changed the meaning of filiation in the colonies. Defined above all by its relation to nationality, filiation became an object of state control. These two episodes therefore paved the way for discussions of the status of the *métis* and the advent of citizenship based on race.

SEVEN

Citizens by Virtue of Race

The *métis* problem touched on legal issues associated with fraudulent recognitions and investigation of paternity in the colonies. But it became a legal question proper when colonial authorities had to decide whether children born in the colonies to unknown fathers were to be considered citizens or natives. There was nothing necessary about this dilemma: toward the end of the nineteenth century, when the "social and moral problem" of the *métis* first arose, legal aspects were not discussed.[1] By the same token, although jurists in this period were increasingly concerned with defining the legal status of natives, the *métis* question did not figure in their theorizing.[2] It was only in the 1920s and 1930s that discussion of this question became an obligatory part of theses and essays dealing with native law and the question of nationality in the colonies. How and why, then, did the law come to concern itself with the *métis* question?

This chapter explores the legal doctrines, judicial decisions, and political debates that shaped the struggle over the legal status of the *métis*: we will follow step by step the jurists' "ways of worldmaking," to borrow an image from Nelson Goodman's constructivist philosophy.[3] This conversation began in Indochina, Africa, and New Caledonia; continued in Paris in the Conseil supérieur des colonies (an advisory body), the Ministry of Colonies, and the Council of State (the highest administrative court in the French legal system); and then spread to other parts of the empire. What emerged, little by little, was the idea that French citizenship should be attributed to those *métis* who could prove that they were of "the French race." As we shall see, this idea was based on the argument that the legal means of determining filiation, and particularly the notion of "possession of status" (*possession d'état*), should be applied to race. Race, in this context, began to be legally described as a form of collective filiation, building on existing legal concepts and practices associated with filiation and inheriting their tensions.

The Law before the Law

For a long time, the *métis* question did not exist in law. There were only discrete cases, which were resolved through the application of the Civil Code: a child of mixed blood who was either legitimate or recognized by a French citizen was a citizen. If not recognized by either parent or recognized only by his or her native parent, the child was a subject.[4] As the governor-general of FEA declared as late as 1931, "There are no *métis*. There are recognized children and unrecognized children, children of European status and children of native status."[5] This position followed from the wider claim that racial categorization did not exist in colonial law.

For instance, in the midst of the controversy concerning application of the law permitting investigation of paternity in the colonies in 1910, a high official in the Ministry of Colonies argued that "it is traditional, in our colonial law, not to take racial differences into account. The *métis* therefore do not constitute a special category of the population, and their status depends solely on the status of their parents. Whether a *métis* is of French or foreign nationality or a French subject or protégé must be decided case by case, possibly in the courts."

The author of this note also maintained, however, that it was "nevertheless of some interest to look at the situation of the *métis* in our colonies in fact as well as in law."[6] The ambivalence is obvious: although the legal status (*statut*) of the *métis* was to be decided "case by case," the *métis* nevertheless lived in a certain "condition," collective by definition. They therefore constituted, if not a legal category, then at least a group—a matter of concern for the colonial state. The legalistic position was quite difficult to maintain when speaking of "*métis*" in the plural.

By the early 1920s, the problem of the *métis* had become a common theme in legal doctrine, case law, and ultimately legislation. Between 1928 and 1944, a series of decrees applicable to the empire as a whole would even consecrate "*métis*" as a legal category. What accounts for this reversal?

Initially, colonial actors remarked on the absurdity of applying Civil Code categories to the social realities of the empire:

> To be sure, from the legal point of view one can argue that there are no *métis*. Some children are not recognized and are Annamites, while others are recognized and are French. In practice, however, the fact that the *métis* has a

different hereditary makeup, a different constitution, and a different physical appearance from the Annamite is clearly what matters, and this makes a mockery of the provisions of the Civil Code.

The case that most clearly stretches the rules laid down by the Civil Code to the breaking point is the common one of the *métis* who knows his father, was raised by him for several years, and lived in his house, only to be suddenly abandoned owing to the father's death, marriage, or permanent return to France. No matter what one does, this person will in fact remain a *"métis."* Even if the code declares him to be an Annamite, he will establish a distinction between himself and the Annamites and seek a relationship to the French society to which his father belonged—a father whom he will frequently have reason to condemn and to curse—and if society does not extend a helping hand, rancor and hatred will inevitably gain a hold over him.[7]

Race—seen as a product of both heredity and paternal care—took priority over the logic of the Civil Code. From there it was but a small step to insisting that a revised code was needed. That step was soon taken by philanthropists, many of whom were also magistrates or, more commonly, lawyers.[8] These individuals took their case into the legal arena, anticipating the later practice of "cause lawyering."[9]

As early as 1904, Camille Paris, a lawyer and president of the Société de protection et d'éducation des enfants métis français abandonnés of Cochin China, published a pamphlet calling for the "nationalization [*sic*] of Franco-Annamite *métis*."[10] He proposed a solution that would not violate "the ban on investigation of paternity," which was still in force in 1904: it would be enough if "every individual recognized by a court as having European blood in his or her veins [were] declared French and inscribed as such on the books of the identity records office, upon request by the individual or by a French guardian."[11] He led a campaign on this issue and published large excerpts from his pamphlet in one of the leading newspapers serving colonial interests in the metropole, *La dépêche coloniale*,[12] in addition to lobbying the Ministry of Colonies directly.

His counterparts in Tonkin were no less active. In 1906, the Société de protection des enfants métis of Tonkin wrote the superior resident about the need to shift its "action onto legal terrain." The group argued that *"métis* must at last have a legal status, and, since they have French blood in their veins, we must not cast them out."[13] In 1912, the society pointed out that "the unjustified exclusion of the *métis* from French nationality [is the origin of] all the obstacles that the abandoned *métis* must face throughout the course of his life." Albert Sarraut, the governor-general newly arrived from the metropole, promised to work "diligently to create a *legal status* for our abandoned children that they do not currently possess, a situation that, no matter how much material aid we can obtain for them, inevitably places them in a false situation that is replete with danger and insuperable difficulties."[14]

Philanthropists also acted at the imperial level. The question of the legal status of *métis* was regularly raised at congresses of the Mutualité coloniale ("Colonial Mutual Aid Society"), for example. At the Tunis meeting in 1923, the organizing committee officially requested that *métis*, "owing to the French blood that flows in their veins, be permitted to enjoy French citizenship." It cited "reasons of fairness" and the "private interest of these children" as well "as considerations of a political order" and "the general interest."[15]

The three men who presented papers to the congress treated the "problem" in three quite different contexts—an indication of the nebulous character of the social reform[16] and of the way in which the *métis* question circulated throughout the empire. A physician, Dr. Antoine Maurice Fontoynont, was the founder and director of an important charitable venture that provided aid to *métis* in Madagascar. François de Coutouly, a colonial administrator serving in Africa, was the father of four *métis* whom he recognized and sent to France to be educated.[17] Henri Sambuc, a lawyer who practiced in Saigon from 1894 to 1917, was the leading specialist on legal aspects of the *métis* question. He also served in a number of local assemblies. After returning to France, he continued his career in colonial circles in Paris, most notably as president of the powerful Indochina section of the Colonial Union. He also sat on the editorial committee of the *Recueil de législation, de doctrine et de jurisprudence coloniales*, published by Pierre Dareste, and was elected a member of the Académie des sciences coloniales in 1938.[18]

The first text that he devoted to the *métis* question was written in 1913 in response to a request from a charitable organization to deliver an opinion about whether or not to grant a subsidy to the Société de protection des métis of Tonkin. His report was published in the *Revue indochinoise*, which in 1913 devoted several issues to a broad survey of *métis* on the peninsula. Sambuc took up themes that were of great interest to the philanthropists of the day: the origins of the *métis* problem, the questions of education and *déclassement*, the potential contribution of *métis* to the development of the colony, and the role of charitable organizations. The legal aspect was present but did not take precedence over other approaches.

This first involvement in the issue seems to have awakened in Sambuc a real vocation for the *métis* question, to which he brought his training as a jurist. In 1914, he published a first article of legal theory on the matter in the periodical *Recueil Dareste*. It dealt with "the legal status of children born in Indochina to French fathers and indigenous mothers as well as to unknown parents." In it, he explored the legal aspects of the "problem" and possible solutions and in so doing established the legal foundations on which all of the subsequent decrees rested. He went on to develop these insights in many articles on legal theory published in *Recueil Dareste* between 1923 and 1933, in which he commented on major landmarks in case law and legislation.

The *Métis* Question in Law

Several cases involving the status of *métis* were taken up in the courts before the issue emerged as a major legal controversy. These cases attracted little attention at the time but helped shape the evidentiary norms and legal reasoning that would figure prominently in later discussions.

First Cases

The first judgment in such a case appears to have been handed down in 1896 by the court of Phnom Penh. It concerned H., a young boy of eight, who was a student at the Taberd School in Saigon—a private religious school that at the time accepted a substantial number of *métis*. The head of the school was both the instigator of the case and a witness in it. Relying on a record of baptism, a declaration by the mother and the godfather, and a note from a notable of the village in which the child was born, the court ordered the boy's birth to be recorded as French. It held that the documents offered "sufficient evidence for a presumption that the quality of *métis* [could] be attributed to young H." and that "from a humanitarian and social point of view," there was "a real interest" in not "allowing him to be deprived of [French] civil status."[19]

This judgment would probably have been forgotten had the superior resident of Cambodia not rejected its conclusion in 1915: he came across the case when the question arose of adding H.'s name to the military recruitment list. In the resident's view, "the law had been violated" and young H. was a native, so he refused to register him. While recognizing the authority of a court decision, he chose to circumvent the judgment by arguing that the court had simply ordered H.'s name to be inscribed on the

European list of the identity records office without granting him French citizenship, since citizens of other nationalities were also included on this list. This case suggests again that the legal and administrative registers of the category of "European" were invented in the context of colonial discrimination.

Another case, this one from 1903, had greater influence. Until the early 1920s, it was treated as a legal precedent. Widely known thanks to publication in the periodical *Dareste*, it was frequently cited not only by legal theorists but also in administrative documents. The decision in question was handed down by the court of appeals for Indochina, which struck down a decision by the court of Saigon to grant citizenship to *métis* born to unknown parents. The second chamber of the Saigon court, which heard cases involving "natives," had been called upon to consider the case of one Jean Joseph, known as "Larsalle," who had no civil status and who had asked the prosecutor of the republic to provide him with a birth certificate. The court found that Larsalle was not a native and therefore declared itself incompetent to hear the case.

Indeed, while all parties agreed that the man was the son of a French father and a native mother, his parents were legally "unknown." He therefore could not be "considered as native" via his mother. Nor was he permitted to seek a court judgment concerning his paternity: the year was 1903, before investigations of paternity were authorized. The court therefore held that Article 8, Section 2, of the Civil Code applied in this case: that "children born in France to unknown parents or parents of unknown nationality" were French. The prosecutor then appealed and the appellate court overturned this decision, ruling that Larsalle was a native. Although his father was unknown and could not be sought, this was not the case with his mother. Opportunistically invoking the authority of native law, the court held that "the legal bond that ties the child to its mother in Annamite law is none other than the natural bond itself." Furthermore, the court pointed out that investigation of maternity was authorized under Annamite law. Finally, it noted that Larsalle "himself stipulated that his mother was Annamite."[20]

For a time, this decision was regarded as authoritative[21] because it confirmed the majority view of the colonial administration at the time that *métis* were natives. For example, in 1902, a circular from the attorney general for Indochina ordered prosecutors to ensure that all children born to native mothers were registered as natives and if need be to investigate the mothers' identity as authorized under Annamite law.[22] The central administration took the same position. Gradually, however, a different view emerged to challenge this consensus.

The Circle of Law

From a legal standpoint, the *métis* problem was understood as a lacuna or contradiction in the law—in other words, as either an absence of norms or an incompatibility between two norms.[23] This was the fruit of reflection by colonial jurists on the possibility of applying to *métis* Article 8, Section 2, of the Civil Code, which provided that children born in France to unknown parents were French. Here, the constraints of legal reasoning combined with colonial practices of social classification.

Article 8, Section 2, was inserted into the Civil Code by the nationality law of 1889. It was the result of a growing preoccupation of nineteenth-century jurists with the question of stateless individuals at a time when nationality was becoming an increasingly central feature of social identity.[24] This section broke with the logic of the Napoleonic Code: after 1804, since birth on French soil no longer sufficed to confer nationality on the child, the offspring of unknown parents could no longer be considered French at birth. The child could invoke Article 9 of the Civil Code, which made it easier for a person born in France to acquire French nationality. The child could also avail himself or herself of a tradition inaugurated by the decree of July 4, 1793, which designated foundlings "natural children of the fatherland," or by the decree of January 19, 1811, which required such children to perform military service.

The 1889 law went beyond these "favors" to create a genuine right to French nationality for children born in France to unknown parents. This measure was conceived as an application of both jus soli (in the absence of known filiation, soil took precedence) and jus sanguinis (birth in France made French filiation probable).[25] Far from being contradictory, as they are often described, the two principles were combined in practice.

The 1889 law was made applicable to the colonies by a decree dated February 7, 1897. Largely copied from the metropolitan text, it declared French "any individual born in the colonies to unknown parents or to parents whose nationality is unknown." This should have settled the fate of the *métis* once and for all. But Article 17 stated that "nothing was changed regarding the status of natives in the French colonies." In reality, the text extended to the colonies a law of nationality applicable exclusively to "French and assimilated"—that is, broadly speaking, to "Europeans."

The problem concerning *métis* thus lay entirely in determining a priori whether they were native or French in order to decide whether they were eligible to benefit from the new law's provisions on nationality. In 1914, Henri

Sambuc was the first to identify the "vicious circle" this created.[26] Later, others pointed more technically to a lacuna in the law. As one critic observed, "The texts do not permit a resolution of the issue, because in order to apply them, one needs precisely that information which is unknown."[27]

One way to break this vicious circle would have been to treat every child born to unknown parents as a French citizen or, alternatively, as a native subject. Sambuc dismissed both of these options:

> It is sometimes said that, given the large size of the native population and the small number of European colonists living in the colony, every child born to unknown parents should be presumed to be native. . . . This . . . would lead to profoundly shocking results. For instance, assume that a child who by all appearances is of pure white race has parents who are legally unknown yet in fact both known to be French. Would it be possible to declare a priori, against all justice and truth, that this child is native, that the decree of 1897 cannot be applied to him or her, and that the child's status shall be that of subject or protégé? We do not think so. Nor is the opposite assumption any more acceptable. No one would think for a moment of presuming to be French, regardless of physical appearance, all the children born in Indochina to unknown parents, and of applying the decree of 1897 to grant them the rights of French citizens. This would transform a host of purely native children into citizens.[28]

This double refusal, rooted in racial logic, can be found not only in all the doctrinal arguments concerning the status of *métis* born to unknown parents but also in administrative practice.[29] For one thing, jurists felt that it was unacceptable to include children born to two native parents in the body of French citizens: in such cases, they invoked the fear of "repugnant errors."[30] This fear was particularly strong because native identity records were very badly organized in most of the colonies, and quite a few natives had parents who were legally unknown.[31] For another, concern with maintaining colonial prestige made it impossible to ascribe "subject" status to the offspring of two French parents: "Would it not be a sinister joke to declare [a child of pure white race] a native?"[32]

Hence, it would be necessary to identify children born to unknown parents as "native," "French," or "*métis*." The solution envisioned was to have recourse to a notion previously regarded as "extralegal"—namely, race.[33] This was the system proposed by the same commentator, Sambuc. In order to decide which law applies to an individual born to unknown parents, it should suffice to decide whether or not the person is "native" based on his or her racial identity:

Imagine a child born in the colony to unknown parents, unknown not only in law but also in fact, there being no information available about the child's progenitors and no possibility of determining his or her filiation according to either native law or French law. In order to decide whether the decree of 1897 is or is not applicable to this child, one has to decide whether or not the child is native. . . . We believe that, given our hypothesis, the court will find itself *obliged* to see and determine, in a sense prejudicially, the child's *race*, in order to draw such conclusions from this finding.[34]

Here, the recourse to race can be seen as the logical solution to a legal problem. But if we follow the progress of Sambuc's thinking about the *métis* question, we find that the idea was introduced in the premise of the argument rather than deduced in the conclusion. Indeed, one year earlier, in 1913, in his report to the Colonial Union, he had already taken a stand in favor of classifying *métis* as French. On that occasion, he drew on the moral and political arguments put forward by the philanthropists:

We must begin with the idea that France, as the conqueror and civilizer of Indochina, is bound to take in and *protect* in a truly effective way all those who, as a result of various circumstances attending the conquest and occupation, were called into being by her soldiers, officials, and colonists, and that she must not allow the *corruption* and thereby the loss of even a small amount of *French seed* under the indifferent or ironic gaze of her Annamite subjects. She must secure the future of her half-breed children by providing them with the same care, the same education, and the same upbringing as her pure-blooded offspring. . . . *It is also urgent that legislation currently applicable to* métis *be modified in a very liberal direction,* so as to allow us to treat these children *with French ideas and inclinations* as true Frenchmen before they reach the age of majority, in anticipation of ultimately granting them that status *by way of a regular naturalization or some other equivalent procedure.*[35]

It seems clear that Sambuc found a technical legal argument to support an inclusive goal that he had formulated independently beforehand. Legal pragmatists are right to underscore that law is indeed "another world" in that it radically transforms the social and political objects that it treats. Nevertheless, the forces that animate it are never completely independent of external social and political dynamics.[36]

Sambuc's argument relies on a principle established in the Middle Ages according to which, in case of a conflict of laws applicable to a particular individual, the law most advantageous to the individual should prevail.

Here, the status of citizen is "superior" to that of native. Furthermore, since "under our law, one normally acquires citizenship at the same time as nationality," the *métis*, "claimed on the one hand by citizenship and on the other by subjection, . . . should be granted the status of citizen, which is the normal status of the Frenchman."[37] Sambuc did not hesitate to translate this old legal principle into explicitly racial terms: "Is it not normal that, when a child embodies a double race and a double quality, the superior race and quality—or, if you prefer, the race and quality most advantageous to the child—should take priority and determine his or her status?"[38]

Ultimately, in order to decide whether an individual born in the colonies to unknown parents was subject to Article 8 of the Civil Code, it was enough, according to Sambuc, to prove that Article 17 of the decree of 1897 did not apply to that person. In other words, it was enough to prove that he or she was not a native. What we see here is thus a sort of inversion of the "one-drop rule" in use in the United States as racial identities hardened in the late nineteenth century. According to this rule, any person whose ancestors were not exclusively "white" was considered "black," even if this led to findings that contradicted the person's physical appearance.[39] For instance, the "Plessy" who figured in the famous Supreme Court decision *Plessy v. Ferguson*, which established the "separate but equal" doctrine for many years to come, was "white" in appearance.[40]

In the French colonies, by contrast, any individual who was not a "pure native" came to be considered a "French" citizen. Here again, we find the translation into legal categories of a prescription that originally arose outside the law, as suggested by this passage from a doctoral dissertation in law on *métissage*: "One must keep in mind the necessity imposed by racial pride: not to lose one drop of national blood; even if but a single drop flows in the child's veins . . . that drop ennobles all the others and is binding."[41]

This inclusive racism had two legal implications. First, from this perspective, the act by which *métis* became French citizens was considered to be a *recognition* and not an *attribution*. *Métis* were already French "in potential," one might say, by virtue of their race; the law was required to sanction this fact. That is why Sambuc was critical of the favors granted to *métis* in regard to naturalization: this should have been a right, not a favor. Furthermore, naturalization came much too late, in Sambuc's view, because "the mentality of the child is formed well before the age of majority, and this is when the child must be directed in his or her studies and choose a career."[42] If the individual were "declared to be French in childhood and treated as such, it will be easier for him to become a good Frenchman upon reaching adulthood."[43] We might characterize this as a "constructivist" view of nationality as well as a psychologizing conception of legal status. One finds the same type of reasoning today in French judges who seek to participate in the "construction of personality."[44]

Another consequence of this inclusive racism was that the new link between race and citizenship affected the nature of the evidence required by the court: judges were now called upon to decide an individual's "race," a novel concept in law. To guide judges in this position, Sambuc and his colleagues might have decided to draw on physical anthropology, a field that had shown considerable interest in the question of racial mixing and techniques for identifying the components of a mixture.[45] They did not do so, however. On the contrary, Sambuc believed that anthropologists had little to offer,[46] which confirms the limited impact of racial science on the colonial enterprise.[47] He and his colleagues took "race" to be a matter of common sense, obvious to everyone. It could be determined in the same way as any other legal fact, using the various methods of proof employed in civil procedure. Although scientific expertise might be called upon, it was not necessary:

> But, someone may object, how can a court determine the race of a child supposed to have been born to parents unknown in law and in fact? The answer is that, in the absence of any other source of information, the court will have to judge on the basis of the child's physical appearance, which is generally an accurate guide, while if need be turning to medical-legal expertise for help in identifying the ethnic characteristics of the subject. Usually, however, in addition to physical appearance, which will always be an important clue, it should be possible to rely on incidental information concerning the identity or nationality of the parents, information that can enlighten the court hearing the case. Generalizing, we can therefore say that in order to determine the race of a child born to unknown parents, courts will have to gather whatever information they can about each particular case, and the child or his or her legal representatives will need to be allowed to prove the child's race by the usual methods, including written evidence, witnesses, and simple presumptions—in particular, the physical appearance of the individual.[48]

This legal doctrine, which based citizenship on race, made its way throughout the empire. Philanthropists were quick to make use of it for their own purposes as well as in their efforts to promote awareness of the problem of the *métis*. It also gained currency in the legal world thanks to Sambuc's publication of six articles in *Dareste*, the leading periodical on colonial law, between 1914 and 1933. These proved highly influential: a decision by the court of appeals in Hanoi dated November 12, 1926, that marked a decisive turning point in legal decisions on this issue, for example, repeated passages from these articles verbatim, without attribution. Unlike the classic accounts of the operation of the French legal system, the doctrine was not simply a commentary on positive law but also a reservoir of arguments that judges could use to justify their decisions.[49] First conceived in the Indochinese context, Sambuc's system was adopted by other writers, who applied it to other colonies. The seemingly endless ability of jurists to cite one another helped to shape these legal practices across the empire.

A Turning Point in Case Law

In the second and third decades of the twentieth century, as legal doctrine concerning the status of *métis* was slowly elaborated and circulated throughout the empire, colonial judges found themselves increasingly called upon to decide the status of children born to unknown parents. Although their approaches to the problem varied widely, the aforementioned 1926 Hanoi case in which Sambuc's doctrine figured quickly set a precedent in introducing race into judicial practice.

Hesitations

The first decision favorable to *métis* was taken in 1913 by the court of Saint-Louis in Senegal.[50] In the case in question, the recruitment board of Senegal had declined to decide whether the three petitioners, all "born to an unnamed father and a native mother" known in fact but not in law, could join the French army until the question of their nationality was resolved. The court held that the circumstances of this case were particularly favorable: "They never assumed that they were not governed by the French Civil Code, and . . . the most striking proof that they can give of this is that today they are asking for the right to pay the blood tax."[51] The court therefore found that they could benefit from the provisions of Article 8 and declared them citizens.

In 1920, however, the civil court of New Caledonia took the opposite tack in the case of a man who claimed to have been "born to an unknown mother and father" and added that he was "European, never having embraced native mores." Note in passing that colonized populations may have adopted administrative uses of the notion of race and especially the connection between race and civility. The court refused to "declare him European, and [furthermore] that characteristic would not have afforded him French nationality."[52] The judge held that citizenship could derive only from legally established filiation. He refused to treat the category "European" as a legal classification, believing (wrongly, as we have seen) that it had no place in law.

A year later, the justice of the peace with jurisdiction over Phnom Penh found otherwise on grounds quite similar to the arguments put forward by Sambuc. In this case, the Société de protection de l'enfance of Cambodia had asked that citizenship be granted to eleven of its wards. Witnesses testified that the children had been born "in Cambodian territory to nondesignated French fathers and unknown mothers." Furthermore, the court noted "that they were not declared at the identity records office and were taken in and raised by the Société de protection de l'enfance of Cambodia and received a French upbringing and education." On these grounds, the judge decided that the children should be registered in the "French register of identity records."[53] This oft-cited case demonstrates the role played by philanthropists, who were not only the plaintiffs in the case but also offered assurances that the children were indeed part of the French nation.

In this unusually tortuous lineage of cases, another milestone was reached with a judgment in favor of a *métis* by a court in New Caledonia in 1923—a first for that colony. The court decided to inscribe the petitioner in the European civil register of the town of Ponérihouen because "the information gathered about the plaintiff is excellent, he has no criminal record, he married a young Frenchwoman, and he has always lived in the European manner and is now living in Témala, where he is raising a large family of six girls and three boys. For him, it is a point of honor to make them French." For the court, it was a matter of avoiding an "extreme solution," which would have the effect of transforming all children born to unknown parents into French citizens, and "to include in the European family only those persons who are worthy of such an honor by virtue of their upbringing, education, and culture so as to satisfy both the spirit of fairness and the need to maintain good order."[54] The "case-by-case" logic that we see at work here was similar to the logic of naturalization, since only the most "worthy" individuals were admitted to the community of citizens. This reasoning rejected the uniform granting of citizenship on the basis of race.

At the same time, some jurisdictions reverted to the old solution, holding that any child born to unknown parents on colonial soil should be treated as a native. This was the case in the March 12, 1920, decision of the court of appeals for West Africa, for example, and of the April 29, 1924, decision of the civil court of Phnom Penh.[55]

Hanoi, 1926

Among these decisions, a ruling by the court of appeals of Hanoi in 1926 stands out. In finding in favor of citizenship for *métis* born to unknown parents, it relied on much more specific grounds than judges in previous cases and provided a richer justification, citing verbatim certain passages from Sambuc's articles. Viewed as a decisive precedent, the ruling was mentioned in the local press and sent to administrative and judicial counterparts in Madagascar, New Caledonia, sub-Saharan Africa, and other colonies facing a *métis* problem.

The decision concerned the status of a man named Victor, also known by two surnames, "Lisier" and "Barbiaux." Born in Tuyen-Quang (Tonkin) in 1889, Victor was recognized by Félicien Barbiaux in 1910. In 1913, the court of Hanoi nullified this recognition "as untruthful and fraudulent," but Victor was not notified of the court's finding until 1920. In 1924, he petitioned the resident of France in Haiduong for recognition of his French citizenship status. On behalf of the administration, the prosecutor general asked the court of Tuyen-Quang to register Victor, "born to a European father and a native mother, both legally unknown," in "the European register of identity records." In 1926, the petition was rejected by a judge, who found it "insufficiently justified, there being no proof that Victor, known as 'Barbiaux,' had a European father." The petitioner was advised to seek naturalization instead.

The prosecutor appealed this decision, and the court of Hanoi eventually found in Victor's favor. To recognize Victor as a citizen, the court could have relied on the delay in notification of the judgment of 1913. Between 1910 and 1920—that is, between the ages of twenty and thirty when "the personality is formed," to borrow Sambuc's formulation—Victor was a citizen. This situation, it was argued, "created rights corresponding to his duties (had he not been required to perform military service as a French citizen?) and could make his return to native status particularly painful."[56]

The court chose not to take this path, however, and instead embraced Sambuc's argument for racial identification. Again, the key provision was Article 8 of the Civil Code concerning the nationality of children born in France to unknown parents. In order for an individual to benefit from the citizenship provisions of Article 8, he or she could not also fall under Article 17 of the decree of 1897: in other words, the individual could not be a native. But this determination could "be established only by investigating the race of the child." Following in Sambuc's steps, the court held that "proof of race may be achieved by all the usual methods" and ultimately found that Victor was "a French citizen under Article 8, Section 2, of the Civil Code":

> In view of our findings and of information furnished in debate, we hold that Victor, known as "Lisier" or "Barbiaux," is of mixed race, one of his parents being neither native nor assimilated to the natives; that Victor, known as "Lisier" or "Barbiaux," having appeared in court on September 3, 1926, the court found that he possessed beyond any doubt the physical characteristics of the European-Annamite *métis*; that, moreover, he received a French education and upbringing and has always lived in a European environment; that his status of French citizen was never challenged; that he did his military service in a French regiment, the Tenth Colonial Infantry, from October 1911 to July 1912; that he is currently employed as a European by the Société des anthracites du Tonkin; that in the social milieu in which he lives, he has always been recognized as being of Franco-native race; that he therefore possesses the status of a French individual.[57]

In this decision, two kinds of proof of race were admitted: the court relied on both the evidence of appearance and factors that we would today characterize as social or cultural, by invoking the "possession of status." This latter notion is an old concept in French filiation law that can be traced to Roman law: legal "ways of worldmaking are to be understood in the *longue durée*."

Filiation, Nationality, Race: Possession of Status

As defined by Article 321 of the Napoleonic Code, the possession of status "is established by a sufficient number of facts to indicate a relation of filiation and kinship between an individual and the family to which he claims to belong. . . . Foremost among these facts are the following: that the individual has always borne the name of the father to whom he pretends to belong; that the father treated him as his child and in that capacity provided him with his upbringing, sustenance, and place in society; that he was continually recognized as such in society; that he was recognized as such by the family." The notion originated in Roman law, which accepted as proof of filiation the combination of bearing of the father's name (*nomen*), parental and filial behavior (*tractatus*), and reputation in the social milieu (*fama*).

Under the Napoleonic Code, possession of status was considered to be the best proof of filiation, superior to a birth certificate:

Of all the proofs justifying a person's status, the most solid and least dubious is public possession. Status is nothing other than the place that each individual holds in the larger society and among families, and what more decisive proof of that place can there be than public possession of it throughout the person's life? Human beings know each other only through this possession. He has known his father, his mother, his brother, and they in turn have known him. The public has witnessed this uninterrupted relationship.[58]

These long-standing practices of personal identification predated the involvement of the state in the recording and monitoring of individual identities.[59] Rather than diminish over time, the importance of the possession of status increased. Throughout the nineteenth and twentieth centuries, it was extended to other statuses—that is, other "qualities that the law takes into consideration in ascribing certain legal consequences, such as the qualities of French citizen, adult, spouse." Since 1961, French law has explicitly taken possession of status to be proof of French nationality; in 1972, it was declared to be proof of "natural" filiation as well.[60]

In 1926, however, the subject before the court of Hanoi was the application of possession of status to race.[61] Through this extension, race became one of the elements of status—that is, a personal quality, like filiation or nationality, to which legal consequences were attached.

The decision of the Hanoi court of appeals relied in part on the way in which the petitioner had been treated not by his father but, more broadly, by "European society" ("French education and upbringing," life in "a European milieu," military service and "employment as a European"): these were aspects of *tractatus* as envisioned under Article 321 of the Civil Code. The final point noted by the court—constant recognition "as being of Franco-native race"—was a matter of *fama*. The *nomen* was not explicitly invoked, but the repetition in the text of the name "Victor, known as 'Lisier' or 'Barbiaux,'" speaks volumes.

It is tempting to think that, based on the role that "possession of status" plays in family law,[62] "possession of racial status" might be intended to demonstrate a "sociological" rather than a "biological" fact. Just as filiation, far from being reduced to procreation, is *instituted* by the public recognition of the parents, the care that they provided, and the attitude of the individual's milieu, so, too, might race be not so much a fact of nature as a product of upbringing, education in a certain "environment," reputation, and the psychological effects of marks of nationality (in particular, the name).

However, the court's decision does not mention factors pertaining to possession of status until it has verified by visual examination that Victor, known as "Barbiaux," "possessed beyond any doubt the physical character- istics of the European-Annamite *métis.*" The proof of French race needed to join the community of citizens was also a biological reality. This reality was manifested in both an individual's physical appearance and his "sociocul- tural" characteristics, to use the terminology of our time. This complemen- tarity was pointed out in a comment on the decision of the Hanoi court and published in the prestigious *Recueil Sirey* in 1927, thereby affording the decision publicity and authority that stretched well beyond the Indochinese context: "Because race is a simple fact, all methods of proof must be admit- ted. It is therefore proper that along with physical indications (complexion, body type, and general appearance), whose probative force is especially de- cisive, the Hanoi court also made room for possession of status. Indeed, the possession of status served to corroborate these other elements. In addition to the physical certitude of race, there was also moral certitude."[63]

The recourse to race as a criterion of citizenship thus gained acceptance in legal circles in both the colonies and the metropole. Among the many published commentaries on the matter, only one discordant voice spoke out in criticism of the ambiguity and indeterminacy of the notion of race invoked by the court:

> Concerning the possibility of "proof of race" by all available methods, in- cluding if need be medical-legal expertise, is there not a terrible likelihood of uncertainty and arbitrariness? It is all too readily forgotten that in Indochina, several hundred Annamites have been naturalized French citizens, making it certain that in the near future we will have a large number of French citizens of color. In addition, certain races, such as the Cambodian, are themselves mixed races. . . . Under such conditions, what does the criterion of race sig- nify? In fact, the court limited itself to saying that B. exhibited, in its words, "the physical characteristics of the European-Annamite *métis.*" It would have been desirable if these characteristics had been enumerated, even in summary fashion.[64]

With doctrine on the subject virtually unanimous after 1926, the Société d'assistance aux enfants franco-indochinois in Tonkin won many favora- ble judgments based on the decision of the court of appeals of Hanoi. The "sympathy of the judges" had been enlisted in their cause.[65] The solution proposed by the court also gained adherents in other colonies. For example, in 1928 in Madagascar, a decision took into account both physical signs and evidence of "possession of racial status." It relied on a medical certification of race, which—apart from the intent to include rather than exclude—is more likely to make us think of Germany in the 1930s than of the French Republic:

> Given that, in order to enjoy the benefit of Article 8, Section 2, of the Civil Code, a child born to unknown parents must have at least one parent who is French or assimilated and worthy of that title—that is, must have the physical appearance, upbringing, mentality, life, and, in a word, the blood of the French—and must have transmitted it to the child; and given that . . . Gabriel Antoine Samat was ordered to appear personally in court in order to allow the court to assess the physical appearance of said Samat and his manner of expressing himself in French; and given that the court has examined the findings of an investigation undertaken by the prosecutor, who obtained from Dr. Lardillon a certificate indicating the ethnic characteristics of Samat, together with all the information developed in debate: we hold that Gabriel Antoine Samat is a European-Madagascan *métis*; that he has always borne the first, middle, and last name Gabriel Antoine Samat; that he has been employed by the customs service of Morondava as an official in a post reserved for Europeans; that he writes and speaks French correctly; and that, despite his current position as native guard, he has always enjoyed the consideration due to a French citizen.[66]

Despite all this, case law remained uncertain. Although the decision of the court of appeals of Hanoi, along with Sambuc's doctrine, definitely influenced the way people thought, judges were not bound by it. They could do as the highest court in Madagascar did in 1928, when it reaffirmed that proof of filiation was necessary for anyone seeking to be recognized as a citizen.[67] It was at this point that a number of colonial jurists and high administrative officials took steps to have the decision of the Hanoi court[68] and the legal doctrine on which it was based[69] enshrined in law.

The Fabrication of Colonial Law

In Hanoi, these actors drafted a document that would become the matrix of an imperial law concerning *métis*. By following its course from Indochina to Paris and then to the other French territories, we can see the interplay between political concerns and the constraints of legal reasoning, the tension between local and global interests, and the confrontation between different meanings of the term *race*.

From Colony to Empire

Before the Hanoi court made its ruling in Indochina in early 1926, colonial administrators, legal professionals, and philanthropists collaborated in drafting a proposed decree concerning the status of unrecognized *métis*. This coincidence is explained by the fact that the same actors were involved in both the legal and legislative processes.

The attorney general for Indochina, who for several years had been defending the position ultimately ratified by the court, initiated the action on behalf of Barbiaux. He also drafted the first version of a decree applicable to all children born to unknown parents: *métis* "with a European parent of any nationality," regardless of whether or not they were recognized by their mothers.[70]

The governor-general, Alexandre Varenne, a Socialist, then invited notables involved in the *métis* cause to participate in discussions regarding the proposed decree.[71] Varenne's concern with the fate of the *métis* grew out of his desire to calm tensions in both colonial circles and nationalist groups. Appointed to his post in 1925, during one of many periods of intense political agitation, he saw a resolution of the *métis* question as a way of quelling one source of anticolonial sentiment. He submitted the draft decree to the Ministry of Colonies on August 22, 1926, before the Hanoi court of appeals delivered its decision in the Barbiaux case. With it he sent a letter emphasizing the "social implications" of a decree that devoted three of its six articles to the guardianship of abandoned children of mixed blood: the problem of legal status was intimately intertwined with the "social question."[72]

The text proposed by the Indochinese jurists was rather poorly drafted. Its stated goal was "to facilitate *access* to French citizenship status for unrecognized Franco-Indochinese *métis* of European origin." The logic of the proposal was close to that of naturalization, because the decree was intended to help *métis* "who have received a Western culture and who have repeatedly manifested their desire to become French *in law* as they are already *in fact*."[73] This condition, which denied the determining power of race, reflected ambivalence in the discourse of the philanthropists. At times, they invoked the "right of children of mixed blood to claim, on the basis of the French blood that [flows] in their veins, access to French citizenship."[74] At other times, they justified their legal request by noting that their wards could offer "credible moral guarantees," moving away from the language of rights.[75] These ambiguities would persist as the proposed draft wended its complex way throughout the empire.

After the ministry received Varenne's proposal, it sought advice from the legislative council of the Conseil supérieur des colonies, which offered the government guidance in drafting colonial law. One of its members, Arthur Girault, probably the leading specialist in colonial law at the time, was assigned to prepare a report and a new draft. He sought help from three eminent colleagues of the Faculty of Law at Poitiers: Eugène Audinet, an expert in international law; René Savatier, an expert in civil law; and, the youngest of the group, Henry Solus, who had returned from a stay in India and was working on an important book about the status of natives in private law. These legal theorists also fully embraced the moralizing perspective of the philanthropists. Indeed, the Girault report adopted many of their arguments when it explained that to assign the *métis* the status of the father was "the most humane and politic solution": "If the *métis* is not to become a dangerous *déclassé*, he must be treated fairly and unhesitatingly as a white. Thus, our concern with our security dictates the same solution as our feelings of generosity and humanity."[76] The imperatives of "security" and "humanity" that have combined to shape contemporary French discussions of immigration can perhaps be traced back to these early formulations of a policy of inclusion based on race.

Girault's draft recognized the French citizenship of a child born in the colonies to unknown parents who could claim "to be of French or assimilated race by way of his or her undesignated father or mother" *and* who "benefited from a compatible possession of status." Such possession of status could be determined "from evidence establishing that the child has received a French education, upbringing, and culture." Here, proof of both a "biological" and a "sociological" attachment to the "French race" was demanded: each was assumed to refer to a distinct reality. In contrast to Sambuc's doctrine and to the Hanoi decision, these two realities were independent, and neither could be substituted for the other.

At the same time, the Ministry of Colonies asked the legislative council to examine "the extension [of the decree] to *métis* in other French possessions populated by natives."[77] The Bureau of Political Affairs even proposed a new draft of Article 8 of the Civil Code applicable to all "colonies with natives" that would recognize "*de plano* the citizenship of any *métis* born to legally unknown European parents."[78] This wish to unify the colonial legal space met with the approval of the Ministry of Justice, which wanted to avoid having judges arrive at "various and contradictory interpretations, in all cases regrettable."[79] It encountered an obstacle, however, in the desire to take account of "local contingencies," another principle of colonial policy in the interwar years. Accordingly, Girault's proposal was sent for review to the governors of all French possessions in which the citizen-subject distinction held sway—with the exception of Algeria, where the *métis* question did not arise.

With few exceptions, all of the territories called for a legal treatment of the *métis* question. Only the governors of Guiana and the territories of Oceania saw no point to the proposal, the former because "the few hundred natives who roam the forests have no relations to speak of with Europeans," the latter because most of the inhabitants of his territory, descendants of former subjects of the Pomare dynasty, were already French citizens.[80] We see here the geography of the *métis* question, discussed in chapter 1.

To Recognize or Grant Citizenship?

Some territories supported the proposed decree without reservation. This was the case with Indochina, where the text originated: in 1927 and 1928, the governor-general called for application of the new rule as quickly as possible, pointing to the increase in the number of petitions to the courts and, more broadly, to the urgency of resolving the *métis* problem. The French settlements in India, the French Coast in Somalia, New Caledonia, and FEA also favored application of the decree concerning the status of *métis*. The decree was never published in the first two territories, however, and in the latter two, it was not published until much later (1933 and 1936, respectively), in part because no *métis* question was raised in New Caledonia and because the social problem of the *métis* never achieved very high profile in FEA.

In contrast, the executives of FWA and Madagascar indicated that they had reservations about the proposal. At first, the governor of Madagascar rejected the text outright. Believing that *métis* in the colonies "find their own place" in either native or colonial society, he opposed granting citizenship to *métis* as a group. Natives would inevitably be jealous of such favorable treatment, besides which certain *métis* were not "worthy" of citizenship and might damage the prestige associated with Frenchness. In any case, the administration already had an instrument for selecting the more "interesting" candidates for citizenship: the regular naturalization procedure. In the governor's view, the rules were applied to *métis* with "particular benevolence" and would continue to be so in the future. He also pointed out the similarity between the kinds of evidence accepted as proof of "possession of status" under the new proposal and the criteria that had to be met by applicants for citizenship: in the administrative investigation of prospective citizens, only names were not taken into account. In any case, names would not be a good criterion, since "certain Madagascar tribes are in the habit of naming children after famous men or indeed any European for whom the parents felt esteem, sympathy, or gratitude."

Finally, the governor felt that the conditions in the proposal were more restrictive than in the existing procedure for access to citizenship, because *métis* were required not only to meet the criteria for "naturalization" but also to prove that they were of the French race: "Since we naturalize foreigners, native subjects, there is no reason to require that *métis* who wish to obtain the same favor prove that they are of the French race. In my view, it is less important to verify that the unrecognized *métis* has a French ancestor than to determine whether he has in fact been subject to French influence, is devoted to our cause, and is close to our civilization in terms of mentality, conduct, education, and upbringing."

In short, the purpose here is to *grant* citizenship to natives who are a little more French than others and not to *recognize* the inherent Frenchness of the *métis* on grounds of race. A further advantage of the naturalization procedure, according to the governor, was that it assumed that applicants were adults, which made it possible to avoid granting citizenship to individuals "whose worth cannot be discerned" owing to their youth.[81] A year later, in May 1928, the same governor abandoned these views and accepted the idea that the *métis* question could be dealt with in Madagascar in the same way as in the other colonies.

In Africa, the governors of the territories making up the federation of French West Africa had a mostly favorable reaction to the proposal. Only the lieutenant governor of Mauritania opposed the idea. In his view, *métis* in his territory could easily blend into the native population, which exhibited a wide variety of phenotypes. The problem of a discordance between appearance and status therefore did not arise, so there was no need for special rules governing *métis*:

> The argument of color that generally applies to the child of a European male and a native woman does not exist among the Moors, whose complexions run the entire gamut from the blackest black to white with the merest tinge of bronze. *Métis* raised within the tribe acquire the status of the mother. Their social and moral situation is identical to that of Moors of pure race, and I am not aware that any of them has ever had to suffer on account of his origins. Therefore, I, for one, do not see any reason to claim French citizenship on their behalf.[82]

Given the small number of *métis* born to unknown parents in Mauritania, the legislative council decided to ignore this opposition. The final text, applied to the whole of FWA, distinguished clearly between evidence of possession of status and evidence of race, thereby establishing a division of labor between the administration and the courts. The administration was expected to evaluate "the moral and intellectual qualities, past, and education" of candidates for citizenship, while the courts were to judge "the white ancestry of the petitioner."[83] In this perspective, citizenship was to be granted only to *métis* "worthy of being associated with French society."

The Jurists' Conception of Race

In the extended debate over the proposed decree, it is remarkable that no one mentioned the incongruous appearance of race as a criterion of French citizenship. In Paris as well as the colonies, at the Conseil supérieur des colonies and even the Council of State, this innovation was simply taken for granted in the late 1920s. Only one of the governors whose opinions were canvassed raised an objection, and it was based not on principle but on the practical difficulty of proving that a given individual was "of the French race." In Madagascar, in fact, the great diversity of the population of French citizens tended to undermine the relevance of the notion:

> The courts will face extraordinary difficulties in determining whether the first condition imposed on the *métis* by Article 1 is satisfied: namely, to prove that the unknown father is "of the French race (?)," meaning, I suppose, a French citizen. . . . If it is already difficult, in the simplest case of crossing a white with a native woman, to say, based on the physical appearance of the child alone, whether the father is French or another nationality, it will be much more complicated when the child is the offspring of two parents who are themselves *métis* to claim that the child is of French descent. I do not believe, however, that the legislature intends to exclude from the benefits of the proposed measure the child of a Réunion man or a Mauritian who has been naturalized French, who might be an elite citizen while representing a mixture of diverse races: European, Asiatic, and black.[84]

As the question mark indicates, it was but a short step from discussing the difficulty of proving race to criticizing the pertinence of the notion itself. Interestingly, this legalistic position would be criticized later not as *racist* (still a relatively rare term) but rather as influenced by "the prejudice of color." Indeed, Girault seized on the allusion to children of mixed blood born to men from Réunion, who were numerous in Madagascar, to insinuate that this was "the reason why the governor-general believes that it is better to allow these *métis* to melt into the native mass."[85]

The objection from the governor of Madagascar was one of the very rare challenges to the use of the racial criterion. One might have thought that the problem of proof would have drawn more attention from jurists. In a contribution to one of the debates on the *métis* problem organized by the International Colonial Congress, Dareste, a Council of State member, indicated a certain skepticism: "How does one recognize that an individual is a *métis*? . . . To settle the issue, should one rely on public notoriety, on skin color, or on the shape of the skull?"[86] But the problem came up only once in the meetings of the legislative council of the Conseil supérieur des colonies. It did so in passing, when one member criticized a proposal that would have granted French citizenship "too liberally": "On what basis can it be asserted that an individual is a *métis*? On the basis of signs of race. But none are absolute."[87] Apart from this question, the participants in the legislative debate seem to have entertained no doubts as to the reliability of "outward signs of race" or the ability of judges to recognize them.

The expression "French and assimilated" gave rise to much more extensive discussion. That a "French race" existed and could serve as the basis of a community of citizens posed no problem. By contrast, the extension of the concept was the subject of endless discussion. In Girault's first draft, the unknown parent was required to be "of the French or assimilated race." What he had in mind was a "European foreigner—for example, an Englishman or a German." He alluded to the "cruelty" of excluding such a child, born on "French soil" and "raised as French." He thus extended to the colonies the arguments used in the metropole by proponents of the jus soli. The final draft of the decree for Indochina, however, mentioned only the "French race." The children of "assimilated" fathers were excluded, because as one high official in the Ministry of Colonies had pointed out, in Indochina, the "assimilated races included the white races and the Japanese." The same official therefore argued that a broad interpretation of the notion of French race would be "very dangerous," and this argument won the support of other council members.[88]

This restriction did not eliminate all ambiguity, however. In Indochina, did the "French race" include French citizens of African origin born in the "old colonies" (of whom there were 195 in the province of Tonkin alone in 1931)[89] and Indian "renouncers,"[90] of whom there were a fairly large number among the merchants, clerks, and low-level officials in the colony? The question was not raised explicitly, but one may conclude that the inclusion in the final draft of the notion of "origin" in addition to that of "race" excluded from the benefits of the decree children of parents who were neither of French "race" nor of French "origin." In any case, that was the interpretation given by various commentators on the text, as in the following passage from a doctoral dissertation in law written by a civil service administrator in Indochina: "In fact, the formula in the decree amounted to insisting on a parent of the white race."[91]

In the decree concerning *métis* in FWA, a different logic presided over the introduction of the word *race*: racism cannot be understood in terms of a single, universal model; local considerations mattered. Initially, Governor Jules Carde suggested targeting *métis* born to one "parent of white race of European extraction." In his mind, the goal was not to limit the scope of the decree but rather to expand it to include non-French fathers "of the white race." He insisted that natives did not distinguish between "individuals of the white race" except that they assimilated Syrians and Maghribis to Moors owing to their common use of Arabic. In this context, it was quite difficult for the administration to distinguish among *métis*. The members of the legislative council approved "this assimilation of descendants of foreign whites of European extraction to descendants of French whites, since the goal is not so much to recognize a certain category of individuals as French but rather to save from a false and lamentable situation children born to whites regardless of nationality and to prevent them from becoming pariahs by according them French nationality."[92] We find an even more explicit expression of this racial solidarity in the words of Michel Tardi, president of the War, Navy, Finance, and Colonies Section of the Council of State: "The objective must be defense of the race, and . . . once a child has white blood in his or her veins, we must try to assimilate the child to the superior race and ensure that he or she is adopted by France."[93]

On the other hand, the exclusivity of the formulation came in for serious discussion. A former colonial inspector pointed out that the wording suggested by the governor ("parent of white race of European extraction") excluded French citizens from Réunion and the Antilles and that "this cannot be done." Girault explained that the point was to cover cases in which the father was "a foreign white—American, for example." A lawyer countered that "the word *race* [was] improper in any case." It was therefore dropped in favor of the expression "of French origin or of foreign origin of European extraction," which gained unanimous support because it included all French citizens and, among foreigners, only whites. Syrians, particularly numerous in the region, were excluded.

The governor did not like this version, however, and proposed "of French origin of European extraction or of foreign origin of European extraction."

This awkward wording eliminated all ambiguity by excluding citizens of the "old colonies," who were quite numerous in the African civil service,[94] and of the Four Communes of Senegal. Girault believed that this was "a minor detail, essentially a comment on form," and proposed "of European extraction, of French or foreign origin." His colleagues on the legislative council accepted this suggestion and therefore proposed distinguishing among French citizens on the basis of their "extraction." After further scrutiny by the Chancellery and the Council of State, the final wording was changed back to "of French origin or of foreign origin of European extraction," more in keeping with the principle of equality of French citizens.[95]

Discrimination among citizens would be reintroduced in administrative practice, however. Indeed, to satisfy the first condition in the decree, the government of FWA established a "certificate of possession of status," which guaranteed that the individual was born "to a legally unknown father (or mother), presumed to be of French (or foreign) origin of European extraction."[96] This formulation excluded the natives of the Four Communes.[97] This should not be seen as a cynical action by the high colonial administration in Africa, which silently but stubbornly resisted the principle of equality defended tooth and nail by republican institutions in Paris: this was ordinary discrimination, which very few people criticized or even noticed.

Another point debated while the texts were being drafted concerned the notion of "possession of status." Its use was challenged primarily by members of the Council of State, none of whom protested the introduction of the notion of "race" as a criterion of citizenship. They decided not to make explicit mention of the notion in the decrees in order to leave the judge free to decide, as the Civil Code envisioned. The final text did, however, retain traces of the notion of possession of status in the enumeration of the main types of evidence to be used in deciding the "origin and race" of the unknown parent: "name, education, upbringing, culture, and situation in society."

This list was only a suggestion, however. The Council of State chose to give the judge great latitude in evaluating proofs "of French race," noting that "all methods" could be used, including not only letters, testimony, signs or presumptions, confessions, and oaths but also affidavits, consultations, and expert witnesses.[98] For the commentators, this included "declarations by witnesses and the physical appearance of the party in question."[99] As we shall see, on this point, colonial judges would prove to be extremely faithful to the intentions of the authors of the decree, going well beyond the letter of the text.

In the end, no systematic and coherent imperial project of racial exclusion emerged at any point. The draft of the decree evolved through a series of modifications and numerous exchanges between the metropole and the colonies in which both jurists and administrators were involved. Very few of them challenged the legitimacy of introducing race as a criterion for the attribution of French citizenship.

But this unanimity did not imply that the notion of race possessed the clarity of a scientific concept. In Indochina, the term *French race* was used to exclude the Japanese; in FWA, "French origin or foreign origin of European extraction" was used to include white foreigners while excluding "Levantines" and the citizens of the Four Communes of Senegal. These two original decrees would serve as models for the other colonies. The decree elaborated for Madagascar in 1931 combined the Indochinese text (relying on a single judicial procedure to determine both origin and possession of status) and the decree published in FWA (the unknown parent had to be "of French origin or of foreign origin of European extraction"). All the other texts (New Caledonia in 1933, FEA in 1936, Togo in 1937, and Cameroon in 1944) repeated verbatim the terms of the Madagascan decree. After a period of hesitation, the unity of law once again prevailed.

Antinomies of Identity

Debates about the status of the *métis* were structured around two related pairs of oppositions: first, an opposition between sociological truth and biological truth, and second, an opposition between a conception of law as a reflection of social reality and a conception of law as that which institutes the social.

In regard to filiation, jurists and sociologists frequently contrasted a "biological truth" (generation) with a "sociological truth," which might also be characterized as "psychosociological," since it concerned affects (such as "attachment") as well as bonds recognized by the family and social group.

In many ways, however, these truths were more complementary in legal thinking than opposed. Consider, for example, the notion of "possession of status." As we have seen, Article 321 of the Civil Code defined it as the result of "a sufficient number of facts to indicate a relation of filiation and kinship between an individual and the family to which he claims to belong." In fact, this "indication" was usually interpreted as a "presumption," and "possession of status" was invoked exclusively for its evidentiary value in court. Implicit in this interpretation was the idea that "the only true filiation is biological, of which parental behavior serves merely as a form of proof."[100] It was based on a statistical argument, contained in the maxim *plerumque fit*: if the vast majority of individuals behave as parents toward their children, it is because they are (or at any rate believe they are) the progenitors. Here, the law envisions a certain type of parental behavior as "normal," in both the statistical and moral senses: as one recent commentator points out, the facts defining possession of status "should above all reflect the normal behavior of any parent placed in the same situation."[101]

In this perspective, sociological truth is a product of biological truth, and there are several ways to look at their relationship. In the period that interests us, the latter was based on an extreme naturalization of individual behavior. In 1914, for example, a doctoral dissertation in law defined filiation as a "physical tie," more difficult to prove in the case of the father than in that of the mother. The care that a man contributed to the child nevertheless constituted evidence in proof of paternity: "A man who at the birth of a child seeks a wet nurse for the child, visits him or her, inquires about the child's needs, and later oversees his or her education: such facts are *the cry of nature*, striking evidence of paternity."[102]

Today the connection between these two truths persists, based more on the strength of conviction than on natural determinism. For example, Jean Carbonnier, an important commentator on the Civil Code who was the instigator of major reforms in French family law in the 1970s, interpreted the elements of "possession of status," particularly *fama*, as "the application of Goffman's aphorism: 'It is the gaze of the other that makes me what I am.'" Immediately after asserting the independence of biological and sociological truths, however, he insisted on their complementarity: "The emotional relationship is stronger when it is supported by the conviction that it corresponds to biological reality."[103]

Conversely, one can assume a disconnect between biological and sociological truths by adopting a different interpretation of possession of status emphasizing not its evidentiary function but rather its effect as a "creator of rights." If it continues for thirty years, the filiation that it indicates can no longer be challenged, even by biological truth. Furthermore, under the code in force in the period that interests us here, possession of status made legitimate filiation incontestable. Finally, ever since the debates of the early nineteenth century concerning the investigation of paternity, many commentators have held that the possession of status creates an obligation.[104] The behavior of adults toward children is not a simple "cry of nature." Rather, it produces a form of commitment: "The care and assistance given to the child . . . tighten the bonds of blood that unite child and parent."[105]

In other words, the sociological truth is at least partly independent of the biological truth and can if necessary be *asserted* against it.

In other words, in law, filiation is seen as both an "objective" bond that reflects and is rooted in a preexisting biological reality and as an "institution," produced by a contract (marriage) or a commitment created by care and upbringing. The same hesitation between objectivist and constructivist concepts of social identity is typical of legal debate and practice associated with the notion of race.

As we have seen, the facts that make it possible to decide whether an individual born to an unknown parent is nevertheless "of French origin and race" are collectivized versions of the facts used to establish possession of status: "name" (*nomen*), "French education, upbringing, and culture" (collectivized *tractatus*), and "situation in society" (*fama*). The relation between this "sociological truth" of race and "biological truth" is no less complex than in the case of filiation.

Thus, in Sambuc's doctrinal system, "physical appearance" can be substituted for facts that we would today call "social," because both serve as proofs of race conceived as a fact of nature. Commenting on a decision by the court of Phnom Penh, Sambuc wrote that "absent testimony bearing on the nationality of the father and facts adequate to prove possession of status, the physical appearance of the parties should have allowed the judge to establish their mixed race in order to draw the same conclusions, and in case of doubt, the judge could have turned to medical-legal expertise for an opinion as to the ethnic characteristics of the subjects."[106] And his argument is based on the statistical logic that gave possession of status its probative force in establishing filiation. For him, just as the biological tie affected the behavior of the father, following the "cry of nature," the "law of blood" ensured that *métis* were "children with French ideas and tendencies."[107]

Most colonial courts accepted this cumulative logic: their decisions enumerated social and cultural indicators that invariably corroborated physical evidence proving membership in the "French race." What is quite striking is that we find no cases in which these various indicators diverged. The same complementarity can be found in the 1928 decree on the status of *métis* in Indochina. The text provided that "French origin and race" could be proved by "all means." In the minds of its authors, this formula was intended to authorize the examination of physical signs, which were taken to be indicators as valid as "name," "French education, upbringing, and culture," and "situation in society."

As in the case of filiation, however, "biological and social truths" could also be viewed as independent. A man who might or might not be the biological father of a particular child could create obligations to that child by treating the child as his own.[108] Similarly, the fathers of *métis* incurred obligations to children that they had begun to raise. In a broader perspective, it was the entire colonial society that contracted an obligation toward the *métis* whom it admitted through the intervention of charitable organizations. Here, the focus was not on the atavism of the *métis* but on the fact that they had "been raised French, in the homes of their fathers and in French schools; they bore their fathers' names, even though they were not recognized by them, whether for reasons of impossibility, neglect, or calculation. . . . The same is true for children raised by publicly sanctioned benevolent societies for the protection of abandoned *métis*."[109]

When "biological" and "sociological" truths are independent, each referring to a specific dimension of social affiliation, one can insist on combining the two. This was what Arthur Girault did in the proposal he submitted to the Conseil supérieur des colonies. It was also the spirit of the decree in FWA, which insisted that a *métis* who applied for citizenship must prove both his membership in the French race *and* his possession of French status. In other words, he had to exhibit the physical signs of the race as well as the signs of French "dignity." Thus, the assumption was that the two did not necessarily coincide.

In the 1920s and 1930s, colonial jurists and administrators thus wavered constantly between two visions: in one, filiation and race were above all facts of nature, and sociological truth merely reinforced biological truth; in the other, one looked to the institutional nature of these two types of social bond and thus to a possible interplay between the two kinds of truth. There was no open conflict between these two views, nor were there organized camps in favor of one or the other. Furthermore, the differences between the two positions were never made explicit by the actors, who vacillated between the two. Only in retrospect can we see the tension between the two ways of looking at social affiliation. This ambivalence was coupled with a second, involving a tension between two conceptions of the relation between law and fact. For the vast majority of actors, legal status was supposed to reflect, in the fairest way possible, a fact existing outside the law. The *métis* were French—whether by virtue of "blood" or of care and education is of no importance in this connection—and it was essential that the law take adequate notice of this fact. For others, however, law could create fact, and legal status had real consequences for social identity. This assumption is shared by jurists today who, in considering filiation, take into account emotional ties and "feelings of identity" produced by the title.[110]

Colonial philanthropists also believed in the social effects of law when they asserted that the title of citizen would help to improve the "standing" of the *métis* in French society. Frequently, however, the same analysts relied on both legal normativism and legal institutionalism,[111] arguing in some contexts from fact to law and in others from law to fact. To be sure, law takes its distance from "real" objects when it constitutes them as legal objects, but legal actors are far from conscious of this construction, which is not without consequences for their practices.

Implementation of a Racial Law

The decrees concerning the legal status of *métis* did not go unnoticed. Both the local and national press commented on them. In October 1930, a month after the publication of the new legislation for FWA, *Le petit parisien* expressed satisfaction with the move, describing it as the result of an appeal first made in its pages by Albert Londres.[112] In 1937, one of the most widely read dailies in Indochina pointed out that "recent laws have made it possible for *métis* with French fathers to assert their rights as French citizens, provided that their physical appearance reflects the incontrovertible presence of European blood."[113]

This publicity, along with the efforts of philanthropic organizations, explains the large number of judgments that ensued, which we can do no more than estimate owing to the lack of any complete accounting. Between December 22, 1928, when the decree was published in Indochina, and May 1938, the civil court of Hanoi alone rendered 181 judgments recognizing French citizenship to roughly 200 *métis*. This is far larger than the number of natives of Tonkin who acquired citizenship in the same period.[114] In FWA, 372 judgments recognizing French citizenship to *métis* were rendered between September 1930 and January 1944. The prosecutor felt obliged to account for this large number: "In nearly all cases, these were individuals of appropriate social rank and good moral character belonging to the 'native bourgeoisie.'"[115] In FEA, 178 cases were dealt with in the year following publication of the decree in September 1936. Here, too, the numbers were far higher than the number of natives allowed to acquire citizenship.[116] In New Caledonia, by contrast, "very few *métis* . . . profited" from the decree of 1933. The local administration explained this by saying that "the fate of the *métis* is quite naturally decided as a function of the environment in which they lead their lives."[117]

All these decisions were occasions to affirm the legal existence of the "French race." It is therefore quite interesting to note that among the various forms of evidence on which colonial judges could rely, "physical signs of ethnic origin" were favored by a large margin. As we have seen, such signs were not mentioned in the texts but merely implicitly authorized by the wording of the decree. Circulars clarifying the new regulations were sometimes more direct: in FEA, legal departments explained to magistrates that "if the information as to the European origin of the applicant is incontestable (most notably, physical characteristics and names), Article 2 of the decree of 1936 . . . does not authorize the court to refuse the requested status."[118]

In Indochina, the courts favored the medical certification "confirming the physical characteristics of the *métis*."[119] The practice was attested by many observers, who saw it as an "application of the theory of race, a powerful idea that inspired changes in the law culminating in the decree of November 4, 1928."[120] But the medical certificate was used mainly to bolster the intimate conviction of the judge, based on his own observation of the applicant. The medical examination was in any case not very thorough and made no use of the instruments and indicators developed by physical anthropologists. The ones that I have been able to find are quite laconic, limited simply to confirming that the individual in question was indeed of mixed blood.

When asked about this, one magistrate, who served in Laos from 1950 to 1953, confirmed that for colonial actors, *métissage* was "obvious": "It is clear to the naked eye. We saw quite plainly that the child was Eurasian. People had a more or less vague idea of who the father was." In the case of children born to German members of the Foreign Legion, he acknowledged that it was impossible to determine their *French* race, but for reasons of "humanity," he admitted that he was lenient in such cases, as doctrine required.[121] Other judges were not so lenient and refused to extend the benefits of the decree of 1928 to the children of *métis* even though one might have assumed that the "French race" was passed on from father to son. For instance, the prosecutor's office in Indochina refused, in 1941 and again in 1943, to act on a petition on behalf of an individual born to an "Annamite mother and *métis* father (not European)," citing the "terms of the certificate of Doctor D. dated August 30, 1941, from which it emerges that Mr. C. cannot be considered a Eurasian in the sense of the decree of November 4, 1928."[122]

In FWA, not only was the wording of the decree on the status of *métis* different than in other colonies, but so was its implementation. In keeping with the spirit of the text, the numerous petitions filed by children of Lebanese and Syrian fathers were systematically rejected because the unknown parent was not "of European extraction."[123] In some cases, moreover, the two conditions set forth in the decree were not both satisfied: namely, the origin, determined by the court, and the possession of status, established by an administrative inquiry. Thus, an individual could be found to have "European ancestry" and yet "live like a native," in which case citizenship would be denied. Conversely, the issuance of a certificate of possession of status might not be enough if the court subsequently found that "European ancestry was not sufficiently well established."[124] Over time, however, administrative and judicial practices tended to converge. It proved so difficult to separate the investigation of the sociological circumstances involved in the possession of status from the determination of origin that it was decided to compile a single dossier on each case.[125]

In the end, what we can say is that the decrees granting French citizenship to *métis* stand at the intersection of several developments. They clearly point to a racialization of citizenship in the colonial context. But they also indicate the increased importance of paternity in the transmission of citizenship, since the children henceforth acquired the status of their father and no longer that of their mother. This development was interpreted at the time as "progress" by observers who considered patrilineal systems to be more "evolved." This was the analysis of René Maunier, the leading specialist in "colonial sociology" in the interwar years: "Among the most primitive of primitives, the child of mixed blood—from different clans or tribes if not different races or peoples—therefore belongs to the mother's group and not the father's. Generally speaking, maternal descent preceded paternal descent. . . . In the same way, in the colonies, the *métis* followed the mother, and the mother's group. He was therefore legally a native, slave, or servant. For *métis*, to be classified in terms of paternal descent was progress."[126]

This "advance" was not unambiguous, however. The paternity at issue here was collective, or "national," as contemporaries who participated in debates about "wards of the nation" used to put it: individuals lost their prerogatives in the transmission of citizenship and therefore in social reproduction. Indeed, fathers could no longer choose whether or not to transmit their "race" and citizenship, as colonial actors once wished.[127] The new citizenship of *métis* born to unknown parents was thus the result of two linked processes: the racialization of citizenship and the assertion of state control over paternity.

In the decrees analyzed here, the word *race* designated both a biological reality and a range of social qualities and cultural competences that manifested themselves in behavior. Today it is hard for us to envision this relationship: in the reshaping of ideologies that took place after World War

II, we learned to separate "race" from both "culture" and "history."[128] In the 1920s and 1930s, this superposition was a consequence of the fact that race was conceived as a collective form of filiation. And in the thinking of jurists, it was characterized, like filiation, by the complementarity rather than the exclusivity of the "biological" and the "sociological," of nature and institution.

PART THREE

The Force of Law

EIGHT

The Effects of Citizenship

Most works on nationality and citizenship pose the question "How to be French?" in terms of law alone, on the assumption that the provisions of the law "translate" or "reflect" a certain conception of the nation.[1] They assume rather than demonstrate the effects of the law on individual trajectories and collective destinies. They never ask how individuals perceive the national categories that are imposed on them or how they make use of them.

In the next three chapters, I examine the effects of the new legislation on the category of *métis*. The present chapter explores the impact of the law on the "human, social, and political problem" raised by the existence of *métis*—the problem that the law was supposed to resolve. In other words, how did law shape social categories? In chapter 9, I ask how citizenship status affected the process of identification on both the individual and collective levels. Finally, in chapter 10, I analyze what the introduction of race as a criterion of citizenship can tell us about the history of French nationality and citizenship.

The decrees promulgated in French colonies between 1928 and 1944 marked the end of the legal controversy over the status of the *métis*. But they also heralded a new departure: despite the hopes of their promoters, the new laws did not eliminate all difficulties. Rather, they changed the meaning of old problems and created new ones. In many ways, the *métis* question became entangled in a never-ending dialectic between social categories and legal status.

The Racialization of Administrative Practices

The new legislation contributed above all to the consolidation of "*métis*" as a social category in colonial society and to the diffusion of a racial conception of French citizenship. The philanthropic societies were quick to take up these ideas: in Indochina, they decided in the 1930s not to assist anyone who did not present "a medical certificate issued by a European doctor certifying that the child exhibits the ethnic characteristics of a Franco-Indochinese *métis*."[2] Administrative practice also responded to the new legislation, to the point where identity records clerks in Indochina began in 1928 to record births of children whose fathers were reputed to be European directly in the European registers. In 1930, the prosecutor general had to remind them that recognition of French status could come only by the decision of a court.[3]

More generally, the new legal category was adopted by state agencies involved with the *métis* question. Between 1939 and 1955, for instance, a school for the children of military personnel in Dalat admitted hundreds of boys "born in the territory of Indochina to legally unknown fathers presumed to be of the French race" or "to a native mother and a father of the French race."[4] Local administrators and base commanders were to select prospective students and submit reports "in the case of children whose fathers remain legally unknown, indicating evidence in support of the presumption that the father is of the French race."[5] Most chose to satisfy this requirement with a brief note concerning the "ethnic signs" exhibited by the child.[6] Administrators thus embraced the idea that "race" was the source of certain rights—in this case, the right to an education—as well as the idea that physical appearance was the most obvious sign of race.

This administrative understanding of race explains why the children of the chief accountant of a large firm in Hanoi, a native who had become a naturalized French citizen, were not admitted to the Dalat school, even though he was described as the "deserving father of eight children, two of whom have already died in the service of France." Similarly, when the mayor of Haiphong asked "how the expression 'of the French race' was to be interpreted, and especially whether a French individual from India may seek admission for his children," he received the following response: "The answer can be found in the decree of November 4, 1928, and in the spirit in which it has been applied. It is the *white race* that is intended, not French citizenship."[7]

A more detailed explanation followed: "Since the legislation embodied in the aforementioned decree of November 4, 1928, is based solely on the theory of race, the expression 'French race' can have no other synonyms than 'French blood' and 'French origin.'" Furthermore, "since the number of places reserved for Eurasians is already clearly insufficient, there can be no question at this time of opening admission to the descendants of Indians, regardless of whether or not they are renouncers."[8] The recourse to race was never purely ideological: it was also a practical criterion used in the management of scarce resources.

Managing *Métis*

The decrees adopted between 1928 and 1944 also led to the assumption by the government of increased responsibility for the lives of *métis*. Indeed, this became a major focus of colonial policy. Granting citizenship to *métis* did not resolve the "social question" posed by the existence of abandoned children. Instead, it amplified the political dimension of the problem:

> Pursuant to recent laws, *métis* descended from French fathers can claim their rights as French citizens, provided that their physical appearance indicates an incontrovertible presence of French blood. This generous disposition of the metropole has enabled large numbers of children to obtain French nationality, but the social benefit of this act of charity has yet to be fully realized. . . . Many of these young men find themselves unemployed after completing their military service, without resources, and living in the gutter, where they form a disoriented class that has unjustly acquired a bad reputation, when in fact their difficult situation is due to deficiencies of early upbringing and to profound misery brought on by the difficulties they face in finding work. There is a danger, an ever-increasing danger, that these young men will constitute a misguided class led astray by enterprising vote seekers and thus a source of agitation that would have undesirable repercussions on the social stability of Indochina. . . . Because this category of people has been granted French citizenship, the government of the metropole has assumed a responsibility that it can shirk no longer.[9]

Although philanthropists had hoped that the problem of finding a proper place for the *métis* in colonial society would be resolved by the decrees granting them citizenship, in fact it was only made worse. More than ever, "society is bound to take these children in and raise them," and "legal equality" cried out to be completed by "moral equality."[10] After 1930, throughout the empire, the colonial administration intervened more and more directly to manage the lives of these future citizens.

The change was particularly noticeable in Indochina. In 1938, Jules Brévié, who served as governor from 1936 to 1939, decided to "settle the *métis* question" once and for all. In May of that year, he called a meeting of all the relevant local actors: the top military commander; the heads of the school, legal, health, welfare, and economic departments; and the president

of the Société d'assistance aux enfants franco-indochinois. This group decided not to dismantle the framework put in place by the philanthropists
but rather to expand it. Children would continue to be actively sought out,
with representatives of the administration now taking the place of charity
workers. The charitable organizations remained at the heart of the venture,
and their budgets were considerably increased. Children they could not accommodate were to be sent to religious institutions, which began to play
an increasing role. In the absence of funds to create a large-scale network
of nurseries, religious groups accepted responsibility for infants who were
taken from their mothers and entrusted until the age of five to nuns, especially those of the Order of Saint Paul of Chartres. The major innovation
was the creation of a federation of all these institutions: the Jules Brévié
Foundation, created in July 1939. Its executive committee was composed
of the presidents of the philanthropic societies, representatives of the religious authorities, and the administration. This group apportioned subsidies
among the member institutions and monitored their operation. It also organized the family councils that appointed guardians for the children.[11]

The assumption of increased responsibility for the *métis* did not end with
the onset of World War II. On the contrary, the Vichy government maintained and strengthened the policy of "reclassification."[12] The goal was still
"to turn Eurasians into Frenchmen with roots in the country."[13] A department headed by Admiral Jean Decoux initiated a census of *métis*. A record-
keeping system was put in place in April 1943 to ensure "that no Eurasian
minor in a position to be assisted would escape" the notice of the administration.[14] As before, each candidate was investigated in order to eliminate
"suspect *métis*." There was, however, one difference from the policy of the
colonial administration under the Third Republic—and it was a major one:
the children of the colony were sorted into different groups. Those with
"rickets, the mentally retarded, and blacks" were supposed to be "left in the
native milieu, absent express request to the contrary."[15] The targets of this
order included the offspring of administrators from the old colonies and of
the few African soldiers posted to the Indochinese peninsula.[16]

The policy of assuming responsibility for the *métis* culminated in the
creation of a new status, the "Eurasian ward of Indochina," in November
1943. This was awarded to children "with one parent reputed to be of European origin and the other of Asiatic origin" who had been "left, found,
abandoned, mistreated, morally abandoned, or gone astray" along with
"indigent orphans." In the absence of information as to the identity of the
child, he or she could not be "declared a 'Eurasian ward of Indochina' until
Eurasian origin [had] been verified by a medical examination."[17] In many

respects, this new legal category can be compared to the "wards of the nation" established by the law of July 27, 1917. In the midst of World War I, France had created this new category in order to honor the state's obligation to children whose fathers had been killed or left incapable of assuring their education. The law's promoters had thus seen it as an act of solidarity rather than assistance.[18] When *métis*, the products of colonial expansion, became full-fledged French citizens, they, too, were considered to be people to whom the nation owed a debt, which it proposed to discharge by adopting them. As we have seen, this obligation was formulated in the language of honor, as had been the case in 1917 when the state assumed responsibility for the children of men who had died for their country: "The nation has both the duty and the honor to raise those children whose fathers have fallen in its defense. This is a debt that national solidarity must discharge, a sacred debt that the entire country must share and that neither can nor should be discharged solely by private charity. It is also a patriotic and social act to be performed by the entire country. More than ever, the future of our race resides with our children: it is they who currently constitute France's living treasure."[19]

In the first half of the twentieth century, in the metropolis as in the colonies, the social bond was conceived as a series of nested ties, from "family," to "nation," to "race." And it was a point of individual and collective honor that this continuity be maintained.

The *Métis*: Cadres of Colonization

The grant of citizenship to the *métis* infused new life into a project whose origins can be traced to the early twentieth century: to use the *métis* as "links" (*traits d'union*) between the native and colonial populations, or, in the colonial terminology of the interwar years, to use them as "cadres of colonization."

The Best Way to Establish French Influence

This plan grew out of the sense, repeatedly confirmed in the period between 1890 and 1930, that the French demographic crisis deprived the empire of the "colonizing agents" it needed. It was also based on the theory of "acclimatization," an offshoot of neo-Lamarckian transformism, which influenced the classification of the colonies from the end of the nineteenth century on. The territories under French domination were divided into "colonies of settlement" and "colonies of exploitation" according to the ability of Europeans to "become acclimated" in them—that is, to adapt to local conditions. In tropical zones, "there are few colonists, so that their role and mission will be to oversee and direct the exploitation of the new country by colored labor."[20] Only territories with the mildest climate, such as Algeria, were suitable to become colonies of settlement.[21]

It was soon noticed that *métis* were naturally "acclimatized." In particular, they were "more resistant to malaria than Europeans."[22] The concept of "acclimatization" and the whole biologizing view of the population on which it rested continued to be influential in the 1930s. These ideas were folded into the "theory of association," which became a cornerstone of colonial policy after World War I. Various authors conceived association as a fusion of races: "The paramount goal [of European colonization] is now to improve the species, to expand and consolidate the human family, and to achieve a moral association, firmly established on a foundation of mutual understanding and good faith."[23]

Métissage thus became an object of *biopolitics*, to borrow Michel Foucault's term for the modern form of power that aims to "regularize life, the biological process of the human species." While Foucault suggested only in passing that biopower was associated with the joint emergence of state racism and colonization,[24] we find the concern at the heart of the colonial administration's response to the *métis* question. It structured Governor Brévié's plan to resolve the *métis* question: "No ethnic element is clearly better prepared to receive this natural impregnation, which is the basis of our colonial policy."[25] In the 1930s, a consensus emerged that there was "no better way to establish French influence than to increase the number of individuals in a colony who are French in their heart and in their blood."[26] The high fertility rate of the *métis* and their growing demographic weight in Indochina were cited as indicators of their future importance in the colony.[27]

At the imperial level, the idea of "improving the species" through racial mixing influenced propaganda directed at the metropolitan public. In 1937, the colonial section of the Exposition internationale in Paris sponsored a contest to select the "best colonial marriage." The goal was to draw public attention to colonial issues with a "spectacular attraction," a competition among "ten young colonial women chosen for their beauty." In a competition organized in conjunction with the eugenics section, they would "demonstrate to the public the results of mixing the white race with native races."[28] The purpose was practical. It was a matter of offering a concrete solution to the problem of a declining birthrate:

> The colonial empire of 60 million people offers us perhaps the ultimate [remedy], through the mixing of these prolific races with our own. But should this

mixing be encouraged, and if so, with which races? Should it be discouraged with some others? Spanish colonial doctrine has practiced such mixing, while English doctrine has avoided it as an abomination. Between these two, France could distinguish according to race: a young Frenchman, working as an official or merchant and prepared to settle in the colonies, would know which races marry with ours to produce beauty and which abort in ugliness. As a moral matter, doubts about the wisdom of *métissage* exist, and will continue to exist for some time to come. But as a physical and aesthetic matter, the fruits are already there. One has only to compare them.[29]

In the 1930s, the theory of acclimatization merged with the later theme of the social role of "cadres." The word *cadres* was a recent coinage, used in the metropole to designate an elite with specific skills imparted by special training and certified by credentials, based on the model of engineers.[30] In this narrow sense, it was also used to describe the role of *métis* in the development of colonial capitalism. For instance, one commentator argued that "the industry that develops [in the colonies] can also have cadres, a role for which Eurasians are predisposed by their atavism."[31]

Ties of Blood and Language

In a broader perspective, "blood" and intimate knowledge of the native world were "credentials" that the *métis* could claim to justify their status as "cadres" of French colonization. Indeed, this was the case made by those who posed as their representatives in this period:

> The *métis*, at the crossroads of two races, generally achieve a harmonious synthesis of characters. In their veins, it is clearly the French blood that predominates. In their behavior and psychological reactions, they instinctively display their attachment to France, yet in most circumstances without renouncing their understanding of the people and things of the countries in which they were born. Nearly all of them speak at least two languages: their father's as well as their mother's. They therefore constitute an invaluable liaison between the French and the natives. Indeed, in their role as go-betweens, they ask only to contribute to the grandeur of France.[32]

As in the debates about the legal status of the *métis*, "biological" and "cultural" factors reinforced each other because they were not yet assigned to separate conceptual spheres.

This change was not confined to discourse. It was also reflected in the way abandoned children were cared for. As early as the turn of the twentieth century, there had been some timid attempts to enlist *métis* as participants in European colonization. In 1908, the superior resident in Tonkin created an agricultural college in Hung Hoa for wards of the Société de protection des métis. Scientific experimentation, agricultural colonization, technology transfer, and teaching of European work discipline converged in this project with the resolution of the *métis* question.[33] It proved unsuccessful: after barely eighteen months, the Hung Hoa agricultural college was closed due to repeated incidents, and the children were returned to the protective society.

In 1938, when Governor Brévié consulted the administration and leading philanthropists about the best way to resolve the *métis* question, the agricultural colonization plan came up again.[34] It was also discussed later under Vichy.[35] But nothing came of these discussions. Taking note of this failure, the administration established a school to train low-level officers in Dalat in 1939, thereby demonstrating interest in using *métis* as "lower-level cadres" in the colonial venture.

The decision to create this school was inspired by an institution that grew out of the modernization of the French army. Traditionally, regiments had taken in a few sons of soldiers, usually to serve as drummers or apprentices. Over the course of the nineteenth century, these children were gradually removed from the day-to-day activity of the troops and assigned to special schools. In 1884, a law was passed establishing military preparatory schools for the sons of soldiers, noncommissioned officers, and officers up to the rank of captain. In return for schooling, students pledged to serve in the military for five years. At a time when reenlistment was rare, this was a convenient way of training noncommissioned officers and, more broadly, of assuring the reproduction of the armed forces.[36]

As the size of the French military presence in Indochina was increased in the 1920s and 1930s, it became necessary to recruit more and more natives for the colonial army. The qualities that philanthropists had always vaunted in the *métis*—acclimatization, bilingualism, and the ability to command the natives thanks to their "atavism"—seemed especially well suited to the new mission. In addition, Indochina was in the throes of a serious economic crisis, which made it impossible to find civilian jobs for *métis*. Accordingly, in 1936, the president of the Société d'assistance aux enfants franco-indochinois officially requested that wards of his organization be sent to France to be trained as noncommissioned officers, with an obligation to return to Indochina. The governor and the commander of French forces in Indochina supported this idea, which was passed on to the minister of war with the observation that this plan would make it possible to provide *métis* with "a stable situation, affording them the means of existence and in a sense making a place for them in a milieu that is theirs by virtue of their European ancestry."[37]

The ministry rejected the proposal, however. It pointed out that the 1884 law, amended in 1929, did not include unrecognized natural children among those entitled to admission to preparatory schools and noted that it had already proved necessary to turn away "candidates who were *legitimate* sons of present and former career military personnel."[38] Nevertheless, the colonial civil administration took up the project on its own and proposed to reconsider admission procedures for schools serving military children. In the process initiated by Governor Brévié in 1938, several civil administrators suggested setting up new schools in the colony. They emphasized the urgent need for noncommissioned officers at a time when twenty thousand natives had been newly recruited to the force, and they pointed to the advantages that *métis* possessed for filling this role. They also noted the army's responsibility in creating the problem: it had a duty to take care of the children that it inevitably produced in the vicinity of its barracks and garrisons.[39]

Governor Brévié decided to make the schools the centerpiece of his plan to resolve the *métis* question. He was convinced that *métis* were particularly well suited to the role of petty officers: "The physical development that they often achieve makes them ideal recruits for the army. In addition to this advantage, they know the languages of the country, a very valuable skill in a lower-level cadre. . . . The time has come to call on the loyalty of the Eurasians, on which we know we can count, in order to give our occupying forces, primarily the native and mixed units, cadres ideally adapted to the country."[40]

The location selected for the new school was Dalat, a mountain resort that had been created by the colonizers in a place where the climate was less oppressive than in Hanoi or Saigon and where the government had set up its summer headquarters. The choice was influenced by the "environmental paradigm": Dalat was selected "for its climate and also because everything in the town is a French creation, so that these young Eurasians will find themselves in a *milieu* similar to that which they might have encountered in the metropole."[41]

Once again, the plan to make a place for the *métis* in colonial society ignored the criterion of recognition by the father in favor of a collective conception of filiation. The decree of June 27, 1939, creating the Dalat school stated that it was reserved for children "born in the territory of Indochina to legally unknown fathers presumed to be of the French race" and to those born "to a native mother and a father of the French race." The institution's purpose was thus above all to ensure the reproduction of masculine colonial society, made up largely of military personnel (in Indochina, at any rate).

In Africa, we encounter similar plans to turn *métis* into cadres of colonization. In 1917, at a time when the influx of colonizers from metropolitan France was low, the *métis* were called upon to form "the basis of the so-called European population of FWA. . . . If we so choose, and if we help them, they will become our successors and continuators, our best and most devoted helpers. But if we abandon them, they will become our most implacable enemies."[42] The solution was to make them "low-level employees" who "could exert a civilizing influence on the black population, which is obviously more open to influence by *métis* born in the country than by Europeans, from whom they are far more distant."[43] The administration proposed to take advantage of the experience of *métis* already serving in the army of Africa: "These mulattos are already integrated into the French community, and their success has been as French soldiers. In this particular case, credit is due solely to the mixing of races, which enables these men to better withstand the climate and better understand the native troops they lead. Combining native ardor with French intelligence, they are particularly able pioneers of our colonial conquest."[44]

Nevertheless, it was only in Indochina that the plan to transform *métis* into cadres of colonization was implemented. Once again, this was because the "problem" was more serious in Indochina and social actors there were considered to be more fully engaged.

A Postcolonial Question

As we have seen, the *métis* question was the product of the colonial situation, whose political and social order it threatened. It was posed anew when colonial rule began to be challenged openly, along with status distinctions within the French Union, the federation created to replace the French Empire in 1946, and the French Community, its successor in 1958. It was subsequently an issue in negotiations over decolonization. And finally, certain aspects of the *métis* question were brought home to France when thousands of *métis* from Indochina were repatriated after the Geneva Accords in 1954.

The Métis Question at Stake in Decolonization

The *métis* question was revived when the colonial system was challenged by native populations after World War II. In Indochina, *métis* became targets of hostility, leading some mothers to hide their children's origin—for example, by shaving their heads.[45] They were also targets of violence, as in the 1945 "massacre at the Hérault housing project" in Saigon, where many *métis* cohabited with "poor whites."[46] At a time when French sovereignty was eroding, the *métis* element represented the possibility of a permanent French presence in the colonies. The point was emphasized by philanthropists when Vietnam, Laos, and Cambodia became associates of the French Union: "If [the Eurasians] continue to enjoy French nationality, France has everything to gain in demographic terms. Its children will put down roots in Indochina and ensure its permanent presence in the associated states—and they will also, let us hope with all our hearts, become friends."[47]

In 1947, a bill to grant French citizenship to *métis* throughout the empire from the moment of birth was filed in the legislature, but the Ministry of Colonies immediately protested that it had "political drawbacks," and it was allowed to die.[48] The Assembly of the French Union revived the proposal in 1952 and again in 1955, but to no avail.

Finally, the *métis* question became an issue in the negotiations leading to the Geneva Accords, which established peace between France and the Republic of Vietnam, and it was discussed at length prior to the signing of the Franco-Vietnamese Convention on nationality on August 16, 1955.[49] The treaty distinguished among children of mixed marriages on the basis of age. Those who were eighteen or older at the time the treaty was signed were French but had the option to choose Vietnamese nationality.[50] Under eighteen, the treaty distinguished status based on parentage. Those whose fathers were French were French but retained the option to choose Vietnamese nationality. Those with Vietnamese fathers and French mothers were Vietnamese at birth but were free to opt for French nationality when they turned eighteen.

Because the soldiers of the expeditionary force fathered a large number of children, the *métis* question cropped up yet again. The French government ultimately won from the Vietnamese government agreement that "Eurasians and Africasians" born in Vietnam and assisted by a French charitable organization would be authorized to settle on French territory "in view of the upbringing they had begun to receive." The Vietnamese government did not object to their naturalization as French at the age of eighteen, "in order to facilitate the integration of these children into the French community."[51]

"Repatriates"

One of the most important effects of the citizenship conferred on "children of the colony" in Indochina was undoubtedly their massive "repatriation" to France. Thousands of adults and at least forty-five hundred minors were "repatriated," though most knew nothing of either the father to whom they owed their journey or his language. The movement of these people was arranged primarily by the organization that succeeded the Brévié Foundation. Because the former governor had been a collaborator during the war, the name was changed in 1946 to the Fondation eurasienne and then in 1950 to the Fédération des oeuvres de l'enfance française de l'Indochine (FOEFI) to better reflect the diversity of backgrounds of the children's fathers, who included not only "pure metropolitans" but also "French citizens from other parts of the French Union."[52]

The number of children in the care of the various charitable organizations exploded after 1946, when a French expeditionary force was dispatched to the Indochinese peninsula. The army neglected to "educate its men,"[53] and the *métis* population increased in proportion to the number of troops. The figure of three hundred thousand, suggested by the president of FOEFI in 1952, was probably quite exaggerated, but it does suggest an unprecedented exacerbation of the problem.[54] Welfare workers attached to the army scoured the countryside for children fathered by soldiers. They often met with resistance from the mothers and disapproval from the local population. Any such children were immediately turned over to the federation, usually with no indication of their name, place, or date of birth, so that establishing their identity was not easy.[55] If a child lacked French civil status, the member institutions of the FOEFI were supposed to request a judgment awarding citizenship as soon as the child arrived: at no other time was the decree of 1928 more frequently invoked. As for what became of children who were not, strictly speaking, "of French origin and race," the answer remains ambiguous. In 1951, the president of the FOEFI indicated that "some courts refuse to award French nationality to Africasians."[56] What is more, these children were "victims of a certain ostracism." Consideration was given to the possibility of sending them to Madagascar.

In addition, children of Foreign Legionnaires who could not prove their attachment to the "French race" were not covered by the 1928 decree and remained "stateless."[57] In practice, however, it seems that many magistrates were particularly generous in awarding citizenship to the children of legionnaires, who were presumed to be "European" and therefore eligible for application of the racial logic on which the decree was based.[58]

The repatriation of minor *métis* began in 1946 and concluded in 1976. Children could not leave the colonies without the agreement of their mothers. Archival records and oral testimony suggest that, initially, many of them resisted. Mothers looked to the foundation to care for their children temporarily, while they remained in close contact with them and had no desire to separate.[59] In 1954, the FOEFI established a new condition for accepting a young *métis*: the mother had to sign a "disclaimer" granting "all powers without exception to the FOEFI. The foundation has the right, *without further approval from you*, to send your child to France or any other country of the French Union to continue his or her studies or to acquire professional training."[60]

Thanks to this pressure and to the intensification of the conflict, the number of repatriations increased rapidly, especially after 1955. The children were initially sent to specific institutions: girls to Saint Rambert in Bugey (Ain), boys to various orphanages in Touraine, especially in Vouvray, Semblancay, and Tours. In many respects, the colonial project of finding a place in society for the *métis* was continued in the metropole. Along with it went any number of practices that had not changed much since colonial times: in the early 1960s, anthropologists, researchers, and students measured children in the institutions in Touraine in every possible way, just as in the heyday of physical anthropology.[61]

A plan for dispersal of the children was quickly put in place. In 1955, within less than six months, thirty-five hundred children were placed in seven hundred establishments, both religious and secular. Officials of the FOEFI maintained that "communal life . . . is not very conducive to integration."[62] This assimilationist activism, the product of a deeply rooted "environmental paradigm," also made it necessary to deny children the right to spend their vacations in one of the welcome centers for refugees from Indochina, where they might well have found a friend, a relative, or even a mother. The FOEFI felt that it could "not run the risk of seeing the physical and moral effects of persistent and prolonged effort undone in a few weeks."[63] The group nevertheless resisted any assumption of direct responsibility for *métis* children by the state. In France, *métis* repatriated from Indochina continued to be treated separately.

French Nationality in Question

Some children arrived in metropolitan France without civil status. Since the dissolution of the empire had abolished the colonial distinction between "citizen" and "subject," what was in question was no longer their citizenship but their nationality. The legal aspect of the *métis* problem was thus transported, mutatis mutandis, to the metropole.

Philanthropists proposed a solution similar to the one adopted in the colonies and obtained the support of the chancellery and the magistrates of the superior court of the Seine department (Tribunal de grande instance de la Seine). Between 1955 and 1965, judges of this court handed down more than a hundred decisions applying the decree of November 4, 1928: racially based citizenship became an integral part of the law of French nationality.

In May 1965, the Office of Civil Affairs of the Ministry of Justice put an end to this practice by sending a note to judges of local courts (*tribunaux d'instance*) stating that these decisions had "no value with respect to nationality." The 1928 decree, the ministry argued, applied only to Indochina and had been superseded by the 1955 Franco-Vietnamese Convention on nationality. "As a result," the note continued, "the interested party is a foreigner and can only request naturalization."[64] Subsequently, a number of *métis* repatriated in their childhood by the FOEFI were refused certificates of nationality and had to request naturalization. Some of them had already completed their military service.

The president of the federation, carrying on in France the work that colonial philanthropists had begun, intervened on their behalf with the Ministry of Justice. He relied in part on old arguments, raising the specter that one of his protégés, for instance, might become "a rootless individual, not to say a rebel, when our task should be to facilitate in every way possible his integration into the nation."[65] But he also made one new point, calling it an "act of racial discrimination" to refuse a certificate of nationality to former wards of the foundation.

With the passage of time, the position of *métis* who arrived in France without civil status was resolved by applying Article 57 of the Code of Nationality. This provision accepted as members of the national community individuals who had enjoyed the possession of French status for a period of at least ten years.[66] Well after independence, the relation of *métis* to the nation was still far from clear, leading to convoluted interpretations of the law. These ambiguities had dramatic consequences for *métis* who remained in Vietnam after the first Indochina war.

In the late 1970s, the government of Hanoi, which had always officially identified children of mixed parentage as *métis*, declared the *métis* "unassimilable" and expressed its desire to see them "repatriated." At a time when large numbers of refugees from Southeast Asia were arriving in France, Paris accepted only children born between 1945 and 1957 to fathers serving in the French expeditionary corps in Indochina.[67] The French government took the position that *métis* born before the end of World War II had "passed up the opportunity that was offered to them during the colonial period to have a court recognize them as French."[68] In other words, categories derived from the colonial period remained relevant. Only 1,821 *métis* and their dependents were admitted to France between 1977 and 1980. Those who were denied visas complained on the familiar grounds that blood establishes a right to citizenship. In a petition published in 1980 in *Le monde*, a group of Vietnamese *métis* insisted on this point: "France has agreed to admit tens of thousands of refugees . . . even though they are neither French nor relatives of French. Meanwhile, we, who have French blood in our veins, must wait in anguish."[69]

It might seem that the government's new reluctance to recognize *métis* marked the end of the exceptional treatment of this group and that the relation between nationality and race was essentially an artifact of colonial times. This is not the case. The racial criterion has never disappeared from judicial practice: the 1928 decree continues to serve as the basis of French nationality for individuals recognized as French by a court judgment prior to 1955 and for their descendants. This is true of those who came from Vietnam and from all the other territories that adopted decrees covering *métis*. Even today, courts issue certificates of nationality based on judgments from the colonial period. To this day, they cite decisions "recognizing the status of French citizen [in an individual] born to a legally unknown father presumed to be of French origin and race."[70]

The Disappearance of a Social Category

Still, the *métis* problem was not simply duplicated in France: as a product of the colonial situation, it disappeared with the colonies, even if the legal categories it engendered remained.

The *métis* problem disappeared because there was no reproduction of the *"métis"* population in France, where the citizen-subject distinction did not exist. In many respects, however, this disappearance was also one of the consequences—perhaps the most important consequence—of the earlier decrees. As we have seen, these decrees were soon felt to be incomplete. As one representative of the administration in a small town in Cochin China suggested in 1937, the *métis* "still needed to feel accepted as an emotionally integral part of the group." To that end, policymakers sought to avoid creating a separate *métis* social identity: "That is why measures taken in their behalf must not appear too overtly to be especially for them. It is wise to listen to what they have to say without indicating that any given decision is specifically directed at them in practice, because otherwise, even with the best intentions in the world, you risk irritating them by drawing attention to their condition—that is, to the distance that you must try to overcome, to erase little by little."[71]

Here we see a tension between the definition of a target population and a refusal to discriminate—a tension that persists today in debates about the struggle against discrimination. Recent controversies about the collection of ethnic statistics and affirmative action in France have indeed been driven by the dialectic between the affirmation and the elimination of differences. Ultimately, in the case of *métis*, the assimilative effects of the decrees were also reflected in colonial vocabularies. Once declared citizens, the children of the colony were no longer *métis*: "The term *métis* is . . . an improper term, legally and civilly speaking."[72] Ultimately, the force of law manifested itself in the disappearance of the social category.

NINE

Identities under the Law

After 1928, thousands of individuals throughout the French colonial empire became French by virtue of their race. How did this new status affect their perception of society and their place within it? A wide range of issues involving the relation between law and individual and collective identities are at stake in this question.

Most analyses of citizenship emphasize the link to political participation, especially voting. In the case of the *métis*, however, the consequences of the new law have to be sought elsewhere. *Métis* themselves emphasized the acquisition of rights that one might characterize as "everyday." For instance, in certain provinces of Indochina, *métis* who became citizens appear to have been particularly grateful for their access to hunting permits, which natives could not obtain.[1]

Agents of the administration were aware of more far-reaching effects of citizenship—individual as well as collective. For instance, in response to a question in the large-scale social survey conducted in the colonies in 1937 (the Guernut survey) that asked about "the practical effect of the recent regulations concerning the status of *métis*,"[2] one administrator stressed the social consequences: "Apart from the rights and advantages they obtained with attribution of French citizenship status, in simple moral terms, their prestige in the eyes of the native population was considerably enhanced."[3] Another administrator emphasized the "psychological" dimension instead and proposed a theory of identity according to which legal status shapes one's sense of self: "The decree of November 4 concerning the status of Indochinese *métis* had the best possible psychological effect on this segment of the population. Since many of them had not been recognized by their fathers, their situation was ambiguous, despite the fact that beyond any doubt they exhibited the anthropological characteristics of the *métis*. The status of French citizen granted to them by the aforementioned decree allowed many of them quite properly to regularize their situation."[4]

Beyond these suppositions, how did legal status change individual and collective self-perceptions?

Taking Roots

As we have seen, one of the principal objectives of the effort to "reclassify" *métis* via the law was to prevent the formation of an intermediate class resentful of the colonial project. This objective was largely achieved: nowhere in the French empire did *métis* emerge as a "collective identity." Indeed, *métis* who became citizens presented themselves as the ideal agents of French colonization.

A Category without a Group

All evidence suggests that no *métis* sociability emerged in the French colonies. We find no residential enclaves and no pronounced tendency toward intermarriage, despite the efforts of the philanthropists. Adult *métis* seem to have joined either the "poor white" group or the segments of the native population in closest contact with the colonial authorities, in proportions that varied from territory to territory. In other words, nowhere did *métis* status give rise to an ethnic identity as defined by anthropologist Fredrik Barth: "a categorical ascription [that] classifies a person in terms of his basic, most general identity, presumptively determined by his origin and background [and used by actors] to categorize themselves and others for purposes of interaction."[5]

Furthermore, the "*métis* identity" did not lead to collective mobilization in any part of the French Empire. In some colonies, groups did emerge to defend the interests of *métis*, but these were always quite limited in size and had almost no visibility. In Indochina, philanthropists supplemented their social work by encouraging collective solidarity among adult *métis*. For example, in 1926, one charitable organization envisioned "the creation of a social circle that would include former wards of our institution working in Tonkin or Indochina."[6] In 1927, however, the plan was put on hold "because the people [for whom it was intended] have shown little enthusiasm for meeting and mingling periodically."[7] In response to the Guernut survey's questions about "groups of *métis*" and their demands, nearly all the reports from Indochina indicated "none." Only in large cities was there any evidence of an associative movement, and that was limited at best.

In Cochin China, *métis* did form a few organizations. Among the members of the Indochinese federation, Cochin China was the only colony proper and therefore the only possession represented by a deputy. *Métis* who were French citizens of the colony could therefore vote for their deputy, but even then attempts to mobilize *métis* around special interests of their own proved fruitless. In Saigon, the Amicale des Français d'Indochine was formed in 1927. Later it became the Mutuelle des Français d'Indochine. In its goals and mode of operation, it was not so much a political movement as a mutual aid society of the sort that became common in the French working class during the nineteenth century. The purpose of these groups was to "unite members through friendly solidarity and mutual assistance," to give them "moral support and fraternal aid," and to obtain "effective pecuniary support for members in need and their families."[8] In 1937, however, the membership was still quite small: at most one hundred members in all of Cochin China. Other groups based on the same model were organized in other territories of the federation, but they were not very active.[9]

Philanthropists and administrators displayed ambivalence about these attempts: although they could help with the reclassification of *métis*, they also raised the specter of separatism, which of course contradicted the spirit of the assimilationist project. Hence, their support was far from universal. During World War II, a proposal to create a "Eurasian mutual aid society" with an identity card and insignia for each of its members worried the administration of Indochina, as one high official in Tonkin observed: "Can we accept the emergence of solidarity among *métis*? In other words, can we accept the formation of a social class with its own particular interests, and therefore opposed to other classes? Would that not be the opposite of what is desirable: the blending of the *métis* into the European milieu?"[10]

In French Africa, mutual aid societies were more numerous and more active. In many respects, they took the place of philanthropic associations, which were not very developed in this part of the world. For instance, in 1933 a Mutualité des métis was organized in the Ivory Coast for the purpose of "seeking out abandoned young *métis* and doing what can be done to gain them admission to the orphanage of Mossou or any other public or private school; assisting *métis* temporarily without employment and finding work for them; securing medical care for indigent *métis* who are ill; meeting burial costs in case of death; and aiding the families of the deceased."[11] In Gabon as of 1934, an Amicale des métis set itself the goal of "raising its members' standard of living," although it devoted most of its effort to the fate of children.[12] At the same time, other mutual aid groups formed in Niger, French Guinea, and Senegal.[13] Such organizations do not seem to have existed in other parts of the empire.

Where *métis* social movements did exist, they did not base their claims on the assertion of a specific identity. On the contrary, their demands focused mainly on inclusion in the French community.

The Appropriation of the Métis Question

The groups that formed in the 1930s and claimed to represent *métis* borrowed tropes developed previously by philanthropists and administrators. In particular, they insisted that *métis* were truly autochthonous and therefore authentic "overseas Frenchmen." In Asia, the words *métis* and *Eurasian* were dropped in favor of *French of Indochina* or even *Indochinese*. For those who adopted it, the latter term, like *Algerian* in North Africa, signaled distance from both natives and metropolitan French.[14] Its contours were fluid: logically, it connoted French citizenship together with permanent residence on the territory of the federation. It therefore subsumed a number of categories: "native French, born in the metropole and settled in the colony with no intention of returning to France except for occasional short stays; creoles, born in the colony to native metropolitan parents and permanently settled in Indochina; Eurasians, or Franco-Indochinese *métis*; autochthonous residents who have obtained through naturalization enjoyment of the rights of French citizens, along with their offspring."[15] In reality, however, in the discourse of Eurasian representatives, the term was often synonymous with *métis*. The high birthrate of this group[16] gave statistical legitimacy to this usage while confirming the environmental paradigm: *métis*, better acclimated than whites, reproduced more easily in the tropical setting.[17]

Another idea borrowed from colonial actors involved in the *métis* question was that of a "link" (*trait d'union*) between colonial and native society. This was the pet theme of *Blanc et jaune* (White and yellow), a weekly that appeared in Saigon between 1937 and 1940, whose masthead featured a symbolic handshake. Conceived as an "instrument of Franco-Annamite rapprochement," the paper described itself as the publication "for the *métis* and naturalized Frenchmen who form the indispensable link between France, the protector nation, and Indochina, owing to their privileged situation, 'straddling' two races."[18]

In its discussion of the *métis* question, *Blanc et jaune* took the position that the *métis* ought to constitute the "middle class" of Indochina, and given the fundamentally conflictual nature of the colonial situation, they ought to act with "deliberation," "measure," and "common sense."[19] The idea of a stabilizing *"juste milieu"* in the midst of political crisis was related to that of a "third way" between capitalism and socialism, which spokesmen for "cadres" in metropolitan France were developing at about the same time.[20] This led to demands that certain jobs should be reserved for *métis*. In situations involving "colonial contact," it was argued that they could help maintain peaceful social relations:

> For the Indochinese, a natural job would be that of interpreter. . . . Isn't that the logical role for the children of white fathers and native mothers? . . . Take one example: *may may may* means "You sow with a machine!" Few "French" ears can hear the difference in intonation that distinguishes these three words of one syllable. By contrast, it would be difficult for an Annamite to interpret correctly, on the spur of the moment, if I may put it that way, a sentence as banal as this one: "The communiqué included a final paragraph containing a substantial but not very obvious modification." Yet any Indochinese from a certain milieu would find it easy. Now, to accurately judge someone whose language one does not speak, to remain within the strict rules of fairness, the slightest subtleties of expression must be grasped. That is why I say that we must recruit certified interpreters from the ranks of the Indochinese. . . . When all our interpreters in Indochina are Eurasians, we will be able to say, "Justice has been served."[21]

Here again we see the influence of the neo-Lamarckian idea that the effects of both heredity and environment are important. This is the basis of the representation of Eurasian identity as reflecting autochthonous influences: Eurasians were seen as Frenchmen of a new type because they were the products of a specific environment, radically different from that of the metropole. It was on such grounds, for instance, that one official of an association of *métis* opposed sending the wards of charitable societies to France:

> No child of mixed blood can feel physically attached to French soil in the way that a child from Paris or Béarn feels attached, even though he may indeed think of himself as the heir of twenty centuries of French civilization. . . . In order to be attached to a country, one has to have been born there, to have grown up there, and to have formed a concept of the place in one's mind. By the time the child reaches the age of twelve and the local image has already been fixed in his mind, it is no longer possible to replace it with another

image. A first love cannot be converted into a second love. To think otherwise is to make short shrift of the powerful attraction of one's native land. The influence of the environment affects the child through a kind of physical mimicry, which spills over into the realm of the emotions. The child becomes integrated with the place in the course of acquiring his individuality of birth and race, his well-defined identity as a Frenchman of Indochina.[22]

The *métis* population was destined to remain rooted in Indochina. The notion of "rootedness" was of course essential not only to thinking about national identity at the turn of the twentieth century but also to judicial and administrative practice, particularly in connection with naturalization.

Métis also developed the theme of loyalty, which played a central role in the debate over the criteria of national affiliation.[23] They proposed themselves as guarantors of a "perennial French presence" in Indochina.[24] Combining these two arguments, one *métis* wrote the following:

> The *métis*—to call a spade a spade—is fundamentally French. He is more French than the French themselves. Why? Because if, contrary to all probability, France were someday induced to abandon Indochina, it is obvious that the children of the colony would not be able to resign themselves to follow. They would remain in their own country, where they have put down roots, yet they would literally be drowned in a mass of twenty-five million natives. There is not a single person among us who does not look upon this eventuality with apprehension, so that for the French of Indochina, French sovereignty in this country is a question of life or death.[25]

Hence, the *métis* did not hesitate to demand privileged access to land grants, pursuant to a "policy that one might call a policy of jus soli,"[26] as a *Blanc et jaune* editorial put it in 1937. As in the debates about the status of the *métis*, this conception of jus soli was inextricably bound up with jus sanguinis.

The Reversal of a Stigma

As we discussed in chapter 1, in the 1930s, some physical anthropologists began to attach a positive value to hybridity.[27] Representatives of the *métis* immediately incorporated this into their rationale, invoking "the scientifically proven physical advantages of *métissage*, not only in animals but also in humans."[28] They translated this into political terms by portraying hybridity as the motor of national regeneration. A work intended for a Eurasian audience, whose final chapter was entitled "Don't Blush at Being *Métis*," ended with this exhortation: "And now, to conclude, my friends, a word of advice: don't blush at being *métis*, because *métissage* is a necessity, an essential condition of a nation's vitality. Just as a graft can develop and enhance the strength of a tree, so can the mixing of blood improve the human race."[29]

The theme of "assimilative regeneration" had already been exploited in the first phase of modern colonialism, especially during the conquest of Africa. In the 1930s, as we have seen, it remained a central feature of the politics of "association." More broadly, following Jean-Loup Amselle, it can be considered the touchstone of "French multiculturalism," which originated in the modern colonial empire.[30]

Toward an Imperial Multiculturalism?

The celebration of an "overseas France," as a product of *métissage*, was a double-edged discourse: it contained both a claim of equality at the imperial level and an assertion of specificity stemming from rootedness in a particular "environment." What might be read, from the perspective of the "republican model" of citizenship bequeathed by the Revolution, as a contradiction between equality and privilege was in reality the heart of an alternative political project that figured in constitutional debates about the "French Union" and later the "French Community" after World War II:[31] namely, the project of an empire based on difference within equality.

Claims of Equality . . .

The attribution of French citizenship to *métis* gave rise to numerous social demands throughout the empire. Above all, the language of citizenship made it possible to formulate a demand for equality.[32] Again, the point was not to claim that *métis* were different but rather to insist that they be treated like other French citizens. These demands focused mainly on living conditions, particularly for lower-level civil servants in the colonies. A fair number of these were *métis*, and salary differentials became the basis of complaints.

In Indochina in the 1930s, *métis* protested the fact that officials born in the colony were not paid as well as those born in France or in other colonies: the remuneration of the former was only ten-seventeenths that of the latter. Drawing on a store of ideas associated with citizenship, those who felt mistreated insisted on being allowed to lead "honorable and decent lives" and on their right to enjoy the "dignity" and "prestige" that were the due of all French citizens in the colonies:[33] "If the Eurasian wants to retain the respect of the Annamites, he cannot accept this paltry compensation."[34] The link between citizenship and civility was stressed:

> From the social standpoint, all the citizens of a country form a community of identical mores. Whether born overseas or in the metropole, French citizens have French mores. They are duty bound to raise their children honorably in accordance with French customs. They think and act in French and have no intention of adapting to native life. Indeed, this is a national necessity, and the administration itself, before granting French citizenship to a native, investigates his way of life and mores and naturalizes him only if his way of life is sufficiently close to that of the French. How, then, are we to explain the fact that this same administration would deny a whole category of French citizens the right to live in the French style, that it would refuse to some of its officials the very means of existence and standard of living that it grants to others for an equal quantity and quality of work?[35]

In Indochina and elsewhere, the pensions of colonial officials were another controversial issue (as the pensions of African army veterans have been in recent years).[36] This was the subject of heated debate at both the local and the central level, a sign that granting citizenship to *métis* did not settle all the questions related to their place in the national community.

In 1924, a retirement plan for colonial officials favored those who were natives of Europe. Compared with their locally recruited colleagues, they received a supplement of one-third to one-half of the pension amount depending on the colony in which they had served. In 1930, the governor of Indochina issued a decree stating that the phrase "'native of Europe' applies to an official whose father and mother are both Europeans, whose residence in these regions is temporary, and who does not settle here permanently." This decision was strenuously contested for many years by the *métis*, who used the press to attack these "monstrous laws"[37] and who also availed themselves of the forum offered by the Ligue des droits de l'homme, both in its local sections and at its Paris headquarters. Their argument was based on the principle of equality before the law, as illustrated by the intervention of the league's president: "All French citizens are equal before the law. It is therefore difficult to explain why some of them, whose assigned duties are the same as others, nevertheless do not share the same rights."[38] They also based their case on the link between filiation and nationality that had been at the center of debates about the legal status of *métis*. With respect to equal pay for civil servants, the *métis* had demanded that "the French of Indochina be accorded the same benefits as their white fathers performing equivalent tasks."[39] In the pension debate, the president of the league emphasized equality between brothers instead: "We are told, moreover, that it is not uncommon in the colonies to see civil servants who are half brothers, one of whom is the child of a European mother, the other of a native mother. The difference in compensation is then particularly shocking when it comes time for both brothers to retire to France, where their home is, and where they return to a more clement climate that is equally salutary to both."[40]

Protests combined the familialist conception of the nation with the "paradigm of the environment." The *métis* emphasized their Frenchness by pointing out that "the vast majority of the population whose interests we are defending is as alien to the country as those who were born in France to European fathers and mothers, because the geographical place of birth is of little importance: what constitutes the country for the individual is the family and social environment."[41]

In the end, these arguments would be turned back against the *métis*: the Council of State ruled that the bonuses were compensation for expatriation, for which only "natives of Europe" were eligible. One of the league's legal advisers was more explicit, translating the question of rights into racial language. It is worth citing his argument at length, because it reveals just how influential the paradigm of the environment was in the thinking of jurists in the 1930s:

It does not seem possible to treat the problem solely in terms of legal capacity: it is not a matter of exercising a civil right to which all citizens have an equal claim. The problem is of a physical or physiological order, since it has to do with members of different ethnic groups, raised and educated in different latitudes. It brings us face-to-face with two individuals of different organic constitution, one of whom is physically less able to withstand the climate. Now these two men live side by side, and the additional salary is intended to compensate for the racial deficiency. . . . In fact, the *métis* with a native mother does not experience the same needs or run the same risks as the Occidental with respect to diet, clothing, and health. He has his mother's temperament and resistance: *natura sequitur ventrem.* He subsists on local products (rice, manioc, corn, fowl) purchased at low prices. He is resistant to the assaults of the sun and submits to wearing a hat only if the fancy takes him. He is immunized against the epidemic diseases (yellow fever in Africa). Indeed, it is fair to say that the life, habitat, and behavior of the native are for him a necessity, to which he returns as soon as he is able. For if he is obliged to wear tailored clothing during the day, when his day is ended, he hastens home to don the convenient loincloth of the brush and remove his uncomfortably tight imported footwear.[42]

Although the *métis* had acquired the citizenship status of their fathers, they had retained their mothers' native nature. Here, the citizenship of the *métis* was of little moment and would not prevent the league from discreetly abandoning their cause: equality before the law seems to have been a fragile principle, even for the champions of human rights. When Vichy sought to win the support of *métis* in Indochina during the war, the criteria of European origin were reviewed. In 1943, the order went out that "any official with at least two grandparents of metropolitan origin" would be considered European.[43] Although the mention of grandparents may be reminiscent of the Jewish Statute, its purpose here was inclusive, and it allowed *métis* to receive colonial supplements. It was therefore more "liberal" than the regulations put in place by the Third Republic.

After the war, the determination of origin by place of birth was reinstated and applied more widely. It figured in the award of family allocations and other social benefits under the Code of the Family, which was extended to the colonies in the postwar period and applied to new populations, especially soldiers. Once again, *métis* mobilized, invoking what were generally accepted as benefits of nationality in this period—namely, equality among citizens and human dignity: "We do not understand why, other things being equal, the compensation of workers should vary according to their place of birth or the racial origin of their grandparents. This is contrary to the principle of equality and, what is more, a social injustice and a political error. In social terms, all the citizens of a country form a community of identical mores."[44]

At a time when French colonial armed forces had to rely on *métis* contingents, especially in Indochina, the *métis* groups won the argument in 1946, and the notion of origin disappeared as a basis on which to discriminate among public officials.[45] Similar debates took place in Africa. In 1946, at the height of the "Dakar strikes," the Association philanthropique des métis français of Dakar insisted on equality with "Europeans" in regard to the salary of public officials and family allotments. In both cases, the administration argued that it was impossible to "assimilate [the *métis*] to natives of the metropole."[46]

At the same time, preventive distribution of quinine led to a controversy in which the old theme of atavism became mixed up with the new one of biopolitical rationality. In a restrictive context, the inspector general of the health department argued that "considerations of a political order must give way to therapeutic findings." In his view, "it is medically established that *métis* are chronically infected with malaria from early childhood and cannot expect any benefit from preventive doses of quinine, which are weak and ineffective against chronic infection," whereas "the European is virgin of any malarial affliction before arriving in the colonies."[47]

Representatives of the *métis* countered that they were the victims of discrimination on the basis of having "more or less dark skin, . . . as if malaria cut down only 'Europeans,' when it is a fact that we, who are mixtures of two races, are perhaps more vulnerable than whites."[48] Here the argument is based not on the principle of equality but rather on the rhetoric of difference.

. . . in a Differentiated Empire

Indeed, for the *métis*, equality was not identical to uniformity. The community of citizens was not necessarily a "society of identical individuals."[49] In many respects, they rejected what is often referred to as "the French political model," inherited from the Revolution, and proposed instead a differentiated empire in which abstract citizenship was associated with local rootedness.

For the *métis*, legal status was supposed to guarantee certain specific rights, which in the rhetoric of the Revolution (still in common use today) were called "privileges." For instance, in the 1930s, the *métis* of Indochina asked that the administration grant them preference in hiring and even that "posts that require little education (police, prison and customs personnel, etc.) be set aside for Indochinese, meaning of course low-level positions."[50] In calling for repeal of the law of July 18, 1924, which reserved low-level posts in the colonial administration for soldiers who had served in the colonies, the *métis* called for the creation of "parallel tracks" for themselves. Last but not least, they insisted on priority in the colonization of the land that their fathers had conquered.

At first, the administration took a legalistic position. It insisted on the importance of education and the need to "select candidates for European posts by legally authorized means—that is, on the basis of credentials or competitive examinations."[51] But when it assumed direct responsibility for the future of the *métis*, these principles were quickly set aside. From the time of its creation in 1939, the Brévié Foundation was charged with "coordinating, directing, and supporting efforts to increase the number and quality of administrative posts open to *métis* brought up by charitable organizations."[52] In practice, low- and midlevel posts in the prisons and medical services and in the supervision of native guard troops were implicitly reserved for *métis*.[53]

The rhetoric of difference also began to be heard in the political realm. By the end of the 1930s, in Cochin China, the only part of the Indochinese Union with parliamentary representation, *métis* began to demand representatives of their own. In 1938, some of them insisted that, like military veterans, they should have their own delegate on the Colonial Council of Cochin China, some of whose members were elected, and which had the power to rule on any number of issues. Interestingly, this demand combined the logic of equality with that of ethnicity: "Owing to the principle of equality, which applies to the subjects of the same nation, ethnic groups that live in conditions different from the mass of voters should have the right to designate representatives to the elective bodies in Indochina."[54]

This demand was not acted upon. It can be seen as one sign of an emerging imperial "multiculturalism," which gathered strength before the war. Borrowing a maxim from a home economics textbook of the period, *Blanc et jaune* chose as its motto "A Place for Everyone and Everyone in His Place."[55] Here we also see evidence of the desire to constitute a middle class between the dominant and dominated, which might serve to promote consensus in colonial society. We also discern a political project to create a French empire in which different "ethnic groups" would peacefully coexist.

After World War II, this project was no longer relevant to Indochina, where the armed conflict that would ultimately lead to independence broke out immediately. In FWA, however, demands for equality within difference persisted in the 1950s. *Métis* insisted on being treated the same as people from "the old colonies," which became "overseas *départements*" in 1946: "We do not want the fact that we were born in Africa and have, to one degree or another, members of the black race among our ancestors to force us to drag the ball and chain represented by the adjective *African*. We do not want this to be grounds for special treatment, which we would willingly do without. As adults, we simply want to be treated the same as people from the Antilles and Réunion."[56]

This is a rare occurrence of the affirmation of a common ground for *métis* across empire.

In many respects, the debates about the place of the *métis* in colonial society show that the "republican model," with its Jacobin uniformity, never gained a monopoly over the political imagination of the French Empire. In the 1930s and 1940s, the *métis* question gave rise to alternatives formulated by those who enjoyed citizenship because of their "race."

Legal Categories and Self-Perception

Not all the effects of the post-1928 decrees were collective. Recognitions of citizenship by the courts applied to individuals, often in circumstances that were unique. The social effects of the law must therefore be seen not only in terms of collective identities but also in relation to the self-representations of individuals.[57] This dynamic sheds light on the more general process of the production of the subject, to borrow a phrase from Michel Foucault,[58] of the way in which individuals conceive of the social world and of themselves through institutions, to use the formulation of anthropologist Mary Douglas.[59] Indeed, as Ian Hacking has often suggested, social taxonomies "make up people."[60] In return, they then participate in the "construction of the category" by way of "looping effects."[61]

In the case of the *métis*, individual identity was completely transformed by the recognition of citizenship and a new civil status, which afforded access to the institutions in which social identity is produced—foremost among them, the schools. To appreciate the consequences of these changes, we must listen to what individuals themselves say. For the purposes of this book, I interviewed some thirty individuals born in Indochina between 1928 and 1958 and "repatriated to France" as recently as the 1970s. I met some of them under the auspices of the FOEFI, which has served as a meeting place for its former wards since the 1980s, and others through informal networks. In what follows, I quote excerpts from three of these interviews, which I think are particularly revealing of the way in which the law transformed individual as well as social identities.

The first case is that of René Philipe,[62] who was born near Hué in the early 1940s to a Vietnamese woman and a French soldier. His mother had four sons by different fathers. Her first boy, born in 1932 or 1933, enrolled in the military preparatory school in Dalat and fought in the Indochina war. Her second child died in childhood. René was her third son. After being entrusted to the FOEFI, he was repatriated to France in 1954 and lived in an orphanage managed by the foundation in Touraine. He is today a doctor in the suburbs of Paris. His mother, who never lost contact with her surviving sons, all of whom were raised in institutions, joined them in France in the late 1950s after marrying a soldier from Martinique. René sees her regularly. Their story demonstrates that family and emotional ties were far richer and

more complex than is suggested by the discourse of "abandoned children."
It also shows how powerfully a person's civil status affects his or her sense
of self:

I was born in 1945. Officially, at any rate. Unofficially, according to my
mother, it was 1944. My birth date is completely false, and so is my name.
These were assigned to me at random.

By the FOEFI?

No, it was the sisters who did it. . . . Because the sisters—before the FOEFI
existed, it was the sisters who took care . . . it was the sisters of Saint-Vincent
de Paul. . . .

So it was a sister who came to see your mother. . . .

Apparently, it was a sister. Actually, I don't know. I was told, "a lady." Was it
a sister or a social worker? . . . I don't know who was out in the countryside
and caught a glimpse of my face. . . . She asked where my mother was. It was
my grandmother who was looking after me. "His mother works in a restaurant." So they went looking for her. The sister said, "You must give him to me.
We'll give him an education. He will go to school instead of moldering in the
country looking after water buffalo." Because my mother worked as a maid in
a restaurant, she was poor and couldn't afford to give me an education. She
lived in the country. She had my best interests at heart. So she agreed: "All
right, I'll give you the older one, but the little one is still too young, I want to
keep him." She kept my little brother.

How old were you?

I'm not sure about that either. I was three, or maybe four or five.

Your little brother was a baby?

Yes, he was too young, two or three years younger than me. So the sisters took
me away. To Hué, to an orphanage in Hué. After that, I was transferred to
Turon [Da Nang] and from Turon to Dalat. In each place, my mother came to
visit when she wasn't working. . . . When she came, she was allowed to bring
me things to eat, treats. . . . She always managed to find out where I was, even

though the sisters didn't always give out the information. . . . [*He discusses the words used to describe* métis.] They said "Eurasian." We weren't *métis*. In the colonial period, people were wary of the *métis*. Somebody between two worlds. He was a traitor, he could be a traitor to both sides, one or the other. The word had a very pejorative connotation, whereas now . . . whereas now, *métissage* is tops. . . . I personally suffered a great deal from my situation. Yes, indeed. . . . It's only recently, with my wife's help and so on, that I have begun to liberate myself from my complex. . . . OK, there was the fact that I was a *métis*, and a bastard. Plus I was associated with orphans. Because those who had a father, a normal family. . . When the FOEFI took you in, they had to give you a name, a date of birth, and so forth, so all the birth dates are fake. Nothing corresponds to reality.

Why fake them?

Oh, for practical reasons. Because they didn't know anything. It was very difficult to know the exact date. So it was always for the good of the Eurasian, for the school. . . . Because of my years in school, they put me back two years. . . . I was born in 1943 or 1944, but they put down 1945.

Your name—is it your father's name?

Before entering the FOEFI, we had no identity. We had nicknames: "Bam," "Bang." . . . We had no precise identity before entering the orphanage. Only after the sisters took us in did we get a first name, a last name, and a date of birth.

But *René* —wasn't that your name before?

My mother's version is that from 1948 to 1949, I was "Philippe Renné." *Renné* with two *n*'s. *Philippe* was my first name. When I got to Turon, with the sisters, I was baptized. I had a godfather who was called "René A." Postal address: "Legion." That's in my papers. In the orphanages, when you were baptized, they had to find a godfather, so they went to the barracks next door. I vaguely remember a guy, who may have been my father, who came for me in a GMC truck and took me with him to the barracks, where I spent one Sunday. Turon was also a place where soldiers came on short leaves. And that was his real name: *René A.* So that's how I got that name. They drew up the papers because they had to give me a final identity. By decree, that became my name on

January 12, the date of birth I was given at that time. In 1949, I was assigned a French identity on orders of Colonel D., who said I was to be called "René Philipe."

A second story illustrates both the complexity of emotional and family ties and the violence involved in the attribution of identity. This is the case of Paulette Porcelet, born in 1943, "repatriated" to France in 1954, and today employed in Marseille. The long and rich relationship between her parents suggests that the ties between Vietnamese women and Frenchmen were sometimes closer than administrative reports admit, and that the interaction between colonizers and colonized could create extremely complex "quasi-familial" relationships:

> My mother met my father when she was eighteen. My father was a career soldier in the French military, thirty years older than my mother. This was very common. They didn't marry because my father was already married. He divorced several times. But he was still married. . . . At the time, the law didn't authorize the father to recognize the children, you could say. . . . So we were not only *métis* but also bastards. Most of the time. Not everybody, but . . . it was quite common.
>
> My mother was born in 1924. . . . Plus she came from a very wealthy family. My maternal grandfather was Chinese; he owned a building in Saigon. He had plantations, and my grandmother came from sort of a landlord family. . . . They had just one daughter. They were quite well off for Cochin China. It was a terrible thing that my mother went with a Frenchman and a career soldier. Her father, who was from North China, did not accept the situation at all and disowned my mother. So my grandmother left with her. The two of them. They [left Saigon] and went back to Cochin China, where I was born, because my grandmother owned property there. I was born in Rach Gia, in the southwest of Cochin China. That's a region of streams, close to Cambodia. I was born there. Only at the time in Rach Gia, there were uprisings. It was the beginning of the Viet Minh. So there were constant attacks. And then my father, who was an army doctor, traveled a lot. He must have been in Rach Gia at some point. But he didn't live with us. He came and went. . . . So what else can I tell you? When I left Rach Gia, I must have been two or three. . . .

So they had a relationship. . . .

A regular one. . . . There was a real family relationship . . . because my father had French children by a French mother. . . . And he introduced his *métis* children to his French children. And his French children came to play with us in Cholon. . . . He rented a villa in Cholon because his base was there. . . . He brought his daughter. . . . I think that when I was five, she was fourteen. He came with her regularly. . . . [*Upon the death of her lover, Paulette's mother joined the Viet Minh, after turning Paulette over to her own mother and arranging for a Vietnamese family to adopt her second daughter, one week old.*]

You have your father's name?

No, not at all. The FOEFI really did what was necessary, in every sense of the word. Children who were recognized by their fathers were French. There was no problem. But those who weren't recognized, like me, got French names. . . .

It was the FOEFI that gave you a French name?

Yes. And that baptized us as Catholics. And then my Vietnamese first name was completely. . . Because my Vietnamese first name is My Vinh. I became Paulette [*laughter*].

So at the age of six, you went from My Vinh to Paulette. . . .

Although I think it was my father who named me Paulette. Because he had a daughter named Ginette. So it must have been fashionable at the time, names ending in "-ette." . . . So they called me "Lette" since I was quite small. . . . And it didn't bother me at all. . . . And then they gave me a French name. . . .

And so they took care of the papers. . . . Because until you were taken in by the FOEFI, you weren't French?

Exactly. On my birth certificate, it says, "born to . . . ," and the name of my mother, "and to a father presumed to be French." That was the trick they used. She will now be called whatever. . . .

The birth certificate came after the fact.

Yes, when I was already in the orphanage. Because I had a birth certificate from 1943, which was . . . OK, it had the name of my mother, I was named Tang My Vinh, and then in 1948, when I entered the orphanage, they took the birth certificate and fixed it up.

So they had a lot of power. . . .

I don't know. . . . I'll tell you, when I was a kid, it bothered me a lot. I suffered quite a bit. I said to myself, "They could have gotten married, I wouldn't have had so many problems." Because when I was in school and had to show my birth certificate, I wanted to dig a hole and bury myself in it, because I didn't want to show my birth certificate. OK, so only the nuns had it. At worst, the principal or the teacher would ask to see it, and that was it. But it upset me a lot. And my girlfriends, who were in a similar situation, it upset them a lot, too.

Paulette's father, who was present during part of her childhood, had a hand in choosing her name, or at any rate her first name (since he did not recognize her), as did her mother and later the FOEFI. Paulette's identity was thus not "invented" but simply "fixed." "National influence" again manifested itself first in the imposition of a name.[63] The choice was less arbitrary than in René's case: the father's name survived, in a sense. But the suffering was no less great, even if it was expressed as a consequence of humiliation.

Beyond the imposition of an identity by the postcolonial authorities, a third case will afford us a glimpse of institutional practices and the possibility of manipulating them. Raymond Paoli was born in Hanoi in 1953, and in his story we see that the Vietnamese were not simply victims of colonial policy handed down from "on high." Indeed, they were capable of adopting strategies designed to take full advantage of the possibilities presented by the law. Raymond's mother, the daughter of a Chinese and a Vietnamese, had converted to Catholicism as a child. Employed in a bakery in the capital of North Vietnam, she decided to move to Saigon with her one-year-old in 1954. A colonel in the French air force became her lover and Raymond's "godfather": "She wanted me to become French. He paid the price. I think she forced his hand. She used every weapon at her disposal."

His official father was himself a *métis*, recognized as French by the court of Turon in 1940. In 1960, Raymond was entrusted to the FOEFI and "repatriated" to France, where he rejoined his godfather. Despite resistance from his family, which saw Raymond as "a little Viet, a child of adultery," this soldier took an interest in the boy, got him into a well-regarded Catholic high school in the western suburbs of Paris, and welcomed him into his home on weekends and during school vacations. "By the time I started fourth grade, I did not know how to count. It was hard. My godfather made me work (he was a graduate of the [prestigious École] polytechnique). I did dictation exercises until my last year of high school." Nevertheless, Raymond remained a ward of the FOEFI until the completion of his studies in architecture, which the foundation financed.

> It was not until 1966 that my mother recognized me. She wanted me to be French: I had to be without a father or a mother. That way, the federation could take responsibility for me. When she was certain that I was in France, she recognized me. . . . I learned all this at the age of eighteen, when my mother died. Officially, I was Paoli. My father was a soldier, and he was killed in action. . . . I'm a fraud, or, well, maybe not a fraud, but I am a fake Frenchman, if you think about it. About my mother, I'd say, "She played her hand well. Bravo. She played it well."

> You say, "I stole my nationality," but your father was French.

> How do I know that? Nobody knows. Maybe he was Belgian. Maybe he was in the legion. He might have been German. Nobody can say. True, he certainly wasn't Vietnamese. My godfather worried that I might judge my mother harshly. Because she abandoned me. Legally, that's true. But that's not how I saw it. I thought, "She's smart. She figured out how to play the game. That's extraordinary."

Required on several occasions to prove his French nationality, Raymond keeps all his papers in a meticulously arranged file, which records the various stages of his life. It contains, among other things, a certificate of French nationality issued in 1987 by a Paris court. This document states that he is French "because [he is] born to a father legally unknown but presumed to be of French origin and race and to a mother from Vietnam." Race is thus still today a legal basis of French nationality.

Each of these cases attests forcefully to the arbitrary nature of identity, whether attributed by the state or obtained through the machinations of clever individuals. The emotional and geographical journey of the repatriated *métis*, separated in early childhood from their fathers (if they knew them at all) and taken from their mothers and the land in which they grew up, makes identity a more problematic issue than it is for most of us. More than most people, "empire's children" such as these were subject to the weight of those institutions of identification that play such a crucial role in defining our social presence.

TEN

French Nationality and Citizenship Reconsidered

A third way to understand the "force of law" is to ask whether the legal category of "*métis*" served as a model for other categories. Or, instead, was the introduction of race as a condition of French citizenship limited to the colonies?

Race in Law

Politicians did not wait for the *métis* problem to emerge before availing themselves of the notion of "race." In many respects, race was already ubiquitous in parliamentary debate during the Third Republic.

This was especially true whenever the "colonial question" was discussed. For instance, when Jules Ferry was called upon to defend his policy of conquest, he asserted the "right" of "superior races with respect to inferior races," a right that derived from the "duty to civilize."[1] More generally, race served both Left and Right as a descriptive concept and explanatory variable.[2]

This continued to be the case even after republican social science, led by Émile Durkheim, discredited the use of race as a criterion of social differentiation.[3] The term continued to come up frequently in debates about nationality. In debate prior to passage of the 1927 law, for instance, deputies were particularly interested in the "assimilability" of different nationalities. To illustrate the inherent danger of admitting "Orientals" and "Levantines," one deputy, Léon Baréty, "compiled a voluminous file containing the original nationality and race of every newly nationalized Frenchman based on the lists published weekly by the administration," which he then compared with the names of criminals published in the press.[4]

Even though the notion of race was in common use, the Left and Center

Left sometimes questioned its pertinence.[5] Indeed, prior to the decrees granting citizenship to *métis*, the law did not recognize the concept. In 1912, for example, when the deputies sought to regulate the movement of itinerant populations within France (mostly Romani), they discussed ways of identifying members of this group without confusing them with the less undesirable "itinerants." Some pointed to telltale "signs of race," which could be detected by the police and by experts in anthropometry. The Assembly decided not to include the word *race* in the law, however, even if the concept was fundamental to the "anthropometric passport" that "nomads" would be required to carry.[6]

The 1928 decree concerning *métis* born to unknown parents in Indochina and subsequent, similar measures in other colonies therefore represented a real innovation. What were its precise historical implications? What do these laws, which were mainly enforced locally (they applied only to colonies in which they were promulgated and to individuals born in them), tell us about the connections between race and French citizenship? How deep was the change in the institution and lived reality of citizenship, beyond its effect on the fate of a few thousand individuals?

To measure the magnitude of the change, we should turn our attention to the law of nationality and ask whether the provisions concerning *métis* had a direct impact. The answer is no. More broadly, we find no intersection between the issue of nationality in the metropole and the issue of citizenship in the colonies. For instance, in the debates that preceded passage of the nationality law of 1889, territories under French rule were never mentioned, except for Algeria. In that case, it was the status of large groups of Spaniards, Italians, and Maltese that exercised the lawmakers—not the Algerians. In 1887, the *rapporteur* insisted that there was no need "to take account of the native element."[7] An ad hoc committee was appointed to draft a decree to adapt the law to colonial conditions, and this became the basis of the decree of 1897 (see chapter 4). As we have seen, two separate forms of social and political order emerged in the late nineteenth century: in the metropole, it rested on the distinction between French and foreigners; in the colonies, it rested on the distinction between citizens and subjects.

The law of 1889 was substantially revised in 1927, but once again, the status of colonial *métis* was not discussed. Colonial issues did not figure in the debates, except when a deputy felt the need to add to the "dangers of depopulation" the fact that "our overseas possessions do not have enough colonizing agents."[8] Article 15, which made the law applicable in Algeria,

Guadeloupe, Martinique, and Réunion, was passed without debate. Yet the question of the nationality of women married to foreigners, and of their children, was at the center of the discussion and of the changes made to nationality law. One might expect it to have been influenced by debates taking place at the time in the colonies about the status of *métis*, but this was not the case. Prior to consideration of the law of 1927, the status of women married in France to natives who had arrived during the Great War or shortly thereafter, was indeed discussed by jurists and the press, but the deputies did not go into it.[9]

Colonial and Jewish *Métis*

Vichy's anti-Semitic law was another normative construct that might have looked to colonial laws on the status of *métis* for inspiration. It did not.

In many respects, the Vichy law regarding personal status was similar to colonial law. To begin with, it treated Jews as "subcitizens" or even "noncitizens."[10] In addition, this was the only period in which metropolitan law treated race as a legal category: the "Jewish statutes" of October 1940 and June 1941 mentioned the "Jewish race."[11] Finally, the definition of "Jew" in these laws implied that the main difficulty of classification involved "limit cases," which posed difficulties quite similar to those encountered in the colonies with respect to *métis*. In fact, the law did not enumerate specific attributes of "the Jew" but rather gave criteria of group membership. In other words, it defined the concept in extension rather than in comprehension, to borrow from Aristotle's logic. Doing so, it created a zone of uncertainty around the margins of the group.

The identification of "Jews" was a crucial issue for anti-Semitism in the period—first in policies of exclusion and later in the extermination of the Jews of Europe. Legal definitions of Jewishness accordingly played a pivotal role, as noted by Raul Hilberg. Among the various provisions of Vichy's anti-Semitic law, the identification of Jews was one of the issues most frequently raised in court and discussed in legal doctrine.[12] Although German jurists paid particular attention to the case of "semi-Jews," or *Mischlinge*,[13] this question was approached tentatively in France. The statute of 1940 took one line, while that of 1941 took another, attempting to correct "lacunae" that jurists had identified in the former. Both refused to allow an intermediate category between "Aryan" and "Jew": the "semi-Jew" had to be either one or the other. Yet, as we will see, no one made the connection to the status of the colonial *métis*.

Problems of Identification

The "Jewish statute" of October 3, 1940, counted as a Jew, "for the purposes of the present law, any person with three grandparents of the Jewish race or two grandparents of the same race if the person's spouse is also Jewish." This definition was criticized for being at once too specific and too vague.

On the one hand, since the text defined the Jew only "for the purposes of the present law," it applied only to "certain professional categories" and did not give a "*general* characterization of the Jew."[14] On the other hand, by invoking the race of the grandparents, the law simply pushed the problem of identification back two generations: "How is one to know whether a grandparent is of the Jewish race, and more important, how is this to be proven?"[15] Jurists did not fail to note the difficulties that this formulation created. They therefore proposed to rely on "possession of status" as proof of Jewish racial identity.[16] They did not, however, refer to the concept of possession of racial status in colonial law. Similarly, although the purely generational definition raised concerns that "the introduction of the status of Jew might lead to the recognition of filiation accorded by favor or, conversely, to self-interested cases of retraction of recognition or disavowal of paternity,"[17] colonial debates about "fraudulent recognitions" were not mentioned in this context.

The Jewish statute of June 2, 1941, was interpreted by jurists of the period as an "advance" over the text of 1940. Indeed, it broadened the legal definition of Jew to a "general and absolute category" and clarified its contours.[18] Although the Jewishness of the grandparents remained the decisive factor, Jewishness was now defined in terms of "affiliation with the Jewish religion." Article 1 of the June 2, 1941, law defined "Jew" as follows:

1   A man or woman, whether or not a member of any confession, who is descended from at least three grandparents of the Jewish race or from only two if his or her spouse is descended from two grandparents of the Jewish race. A grandparent is considered to be of the Jewish race if he or she belonged to the Jewish religion.

2   A man or woman who is a member of the Jewish religion, or was a member on June 25, 1940, and who is descended from two grandparents of the Jewish race. Nonmembership in the Jewish religion is established by proof of adherence to one of the other confessions recognized by the state prior to the law of December 9, 1905.

This new statute has often been interpreted as introducing a confessional definition of Jewishness, as opposed to the racial definition of 1940. This analysis is problematic in many respects. It does not take into account the fact that the text combines racial and religious criteria. In addition, race takes precedence over religion when the individual has more than two Jewish grandparents. In fact, as in the case of the colonial *métis*, an identification problem arises only when the individual's heredity is evenly divided between "Aryanness" and "Jewishness." The problem is then to find criteria allowing classification in one group or the other, and the solution is to look to religion and to the choice of spouse. For a person with two Jewish grandparents to be considered "Jewish," "this hybrid individual must prove . . . that he or she has preserved, despite the mixed background, a very particular attachment to the Jewish race."[19] Finally, other provisions of the 1941 statute linked the quality of Jewishness to "biological" filiation. First, "disavowal or nullification of the recognition of a child considered to be Jewish" had no effect, which "prevents anyone from escaping the legal incapacities attached to Jewishness by suppressing the proof of his filiation."[20] Second, adoption also had no effect: "Because [adoption] creates only a purely legal tie indicating no atavistic influence and producing only the limited consequences specified by law, it cannot be considered to be a cause of transmission of the Jewish race of the adopting parent nor grounds for altering that of the adopted child."[21]

Proofs of "Jewish Race"

The definition of Jew in the 1941 statute therefore remained deeply rooted in a racial conception of personal status (*état des personnes*). The administration, in this instance the Commissariat général aux questions juives, then established "presumptions of Jewish race."[22] First among them was the name: "The administration will not easily concede that an individual with, say, the first names Haim and Hersch, and whose parents are named Katz Baruch and Zevi Rachel, is not of the Jewish race."[23] It should be noted that this evidence was not admitted by the courts, which held that "although the patronymic may at times contain certain hints, the law ascribes no presumption of Semitism to either the form or etymology of the name or even to the possession of status."[24]

For the administration, "external signs of race" could also be used to identify an individual, as a doctoral thesis in law on "the quality of

Jewishness" noted: "Thus, the Commissariat général aux questions juives was led to call on experts for help in examining the typological characteristics of the subject. In some cases, these examinations justified positive conclusions as to the subject's biological race and therefore as to the race of his grandparents."[25]

It appears that these expert opinions were not used by the courts. In making its case, the administration could have pointed out that judges in colonial courts relied on names and "external signs of race" in dealing with cases involving *métis*, but I have found no trace of this.

The Jewish statute of 1941 paved the way to both a rich case law and a dense series of doctrinal treatises on the status of Jewish *métis*.[26] The question fell within the jurisdiction of both ordinary courts of law (because the civil courts treated Jewishness as part of a person's personal status, the same as nationality) and administrative courts (the Council of State held that the status of Jews was a question of public policy since it affected a person's eligibility to "occupy a public office, whether administrative or political").[27] The civil courts resolved the issue in a more "liberal" way than the administrative courts.

Indeed, as time went by, civil courts often adopted a position more favorable to "semi-Jews." At first, they held that an individual with two parents of the Jewish race was himself Jewish unless he could prove that he was Catholic or Protestant, these being the two religions officially recognized by the state before 1905. This was the position taken by the court of Rabat in December 1941, for example.[28] This decision came in for harsh criticism in a doctrinal treatise that argued that "an individual with two grandparents of the Jewish race is Jewish only if he himself is of the Jewish confession. He is not Jewish if he does not belong to the Hebraic religion and he can offer any judicial evidence to that effect. This is the case even if he is neither Catholic nor Protestant."[29] The restrictive interpretation of the 1941 statute was later abandoned in favor of the admission of any form of evidence capable of proving "nonmembership of the Jewish race." This position, which was contrary to that of the Commissariat général aux questions juives, was reinforced by an opinion issued by the Commission on the Status of Jews established by the Council of State, which held that it is "up to the competent jurisdiction to judge in each case whether the individual has provided enough evidence to establish that he never belonged or has ceased to belong to the Jewish community."[30]

Another aspect of the "liberalism" of the civil courts in the evaluation of "Jewishness" is also worth noting: they "generously" held that if a grandparent was legally unknown, the Jewishness of that grandparent could not be assumed, nor could it be pursued through investigation of paternity. The courts invoked the principle of "the family's higher interest," which, as we have seen, played a fundamental role in arguments about *métis*.[31] Yet once again the jurisprudence made no reference to the colonial debate.

In fact, French jurists drew most of their arguments from German case law. For instance, the annotator of decisions rendered by the court of appeals in Aix and the criminal court in Bergerac in May and June 1942 concerning individuals with two Jewish grandparents made reference to German law. The French courts had held that it was incumbent on the prosecutor to prove that the individuals in question were Jewish and that he could not do so simply by demonstrating that they did not adhere to the Catholic or Protestant faiths. The commentary pointed out that "this solution [was] in agreement with the German ordinance of April 26, 1941," and noted that "German judicial precedent appear[ed] to require a positive outward manifestation of will to attribute the status of Jew to an individual with mixed ancestry."[32] Similarly, Joseph Haennig, a lawyer attached to the court of appeals in Paris, was sufficiently worried about the status of the "Jewish *métis*" that he wrote two articles about the subject in 1942 and 1943.[33] In them, he conceded that "German case law can be used only as a point of comparison in interpreting French law," which was different, although he still argued that "when it becomes necessary to interpret a provision of French law on racial matters, it is reasonable to think that anyone who seeks clarity in a somewhat obscure text may well find it beneficial to have recourse to German legislation and case law."[34]

The idea that Vichy's anti-Semitic laws can be traced to the colonies therefore does not withstand scrutiny. This thesis rests on the fact that some key figures in the drafting of the Vichy laws were intimately familiar with colonial affairs.[35] But this notion is hard to square with the fact that experts commenting on the Jewish statutes make no reference whatsoever to the colonies. It is also difficult to reconcile with the fact that jurists at the time seem to have regarded the Jewish statutes as an innovation: one of them described the status of Jew as a "new legal notion,"[36] while another wrote of "the first great failure of the principle of the equality of citizens before the law" since the French Revolution,[37] thereby ignoring the profound and continual challenges to this principle in colonial law since 1830. The native was therefore not the model for the Jew, nor the colonial *métis* for the Jewish *métis*.

The *Métis* Question and the "Republican Models" of Nationality and Citizenship

The legal treatment of the "*métis* question" and the relation it established between race and citizenship had no lasting impact on the categories of metropolitan law. Hence we cannot speak of a colonial heritage on this point, unless—and this should not be overlooked—we consider the situation of thousands of individuals who were born in the colonies and who are to this day French by virtue of their race or the race of their parents (see chapter 8). To look at French colonial history in terms of "continuities" is no doubt to engage in the wrong debate. To pose the question of the relation between the colonial forms of racism and contemporary forms of discrimination in terms of "origin" or "heritage," as is increasingly common nowadays, is to forget that nationality and citizenship have been defined in practice in very different ways in different periods and political contexts. To put this in the language of Michel Foucault, the question of colonial *métis* is important not because it directly "influenced" the criteria defining nationality but because it posed a *problem* for the practices associated with nationality and citizenship.[38] It thus reveals their hidden mechanisms.

Paternity, Nationality, and Citizenship

The legal treatment of the "*métis* question" points to the close relationship between two processes that historians tend to treat independently:[39] the increasing state control of both relations of filiation and definitions of nationality.

As we have seen throughout this book, the solution to the "*métis* question" and the threat it posed to the colonial order implied ever greater state intervention in the realm of filiation. In order to prevent "fraudulent recognition" of children and hence "dubious" acquisitions of French citizenship, the colonial state arrogated to itself the right to verify filiation, thereby ignoring the principle of respect for "family honor and tranquillity." With the decrees concerning the citizenship of *métis*, the state also interposed itself between father and son, taking the place of the father in case of abandonment: the texts establishing citizenship on the basis the father's race invented a form of collective filiation, which no longer depended on the will of the progenitor.

A similar increase in the state's involvement in relations of filiation can also be observed in France from the late nineteenth century on. For instance, the law of July 24, 1889, concerning the protection of abused and morally abandoned children profoundly altered family relations. It enabled the state to exclude the father when deemed necessary to protect the child's interests, by removing his parental authority. In 1912, the law on investigation of paternity also created a new involuntary paternal filiation, imposed by the courts. Finally, and more broadly, one can describe the evolution of family law over the course of the twentieth century as a shift toward a greater role for the state in the verification of the "truth" (understood as biological) of filiation at the expense of individual liberty.[40] All of these changes have regularly been criticized as attacks on the freedom of parents (and especially fathers) to choose their children—a freedom guaranteed by the Napoleonic Code.

Meanwhile, the state also set itself the task of defining the nation as a social group—that is, of clarifying what it means to be French.[41] To do so, it relied on an increasingly complex legal and administrative arsenal in which papers and regulations played a growing role in structuring individual identities.[42] The 1889 law on nationality marked a very important milestone in the state's control over the definition of the nation.

These two fundamental processes were in fact related. For example, in the French nationality debates, one very controversial point concerned the "double jus soli" (*le double droit du sol*), which granted French nationality at birth to the child of a foreigner who was himself born in France with no possibility of repudiation or renunciation: this measure was intended to prevent the reproduction of communities of foreigners on French soil, as was common in the second half of the nineteenth century. Simple jus soli, by contrast, granted citizenship at majority to a child born in France of a foreigner, provided that the child had resided in France for five years. French citizenship under these conditions was optional. Double jus soli deprived fathers of the ability to transmit their nationality to their children. Like state intrusions into the law of filiation, this, too, was challenged in the name of the liberalism of the Civil Code.[43] The linkage of these two processes was the result of profound changes in the economy of the family. No longer considered the "basic cell of society," as in the early nineteenth century,[44] it was now seen as the institution through which individuals were linked to the more fundamental social group, the nation. As such, the family was increasingly subject to the power of the state. Émile Durkheim acknowledged this when he observed that the state "is becoming involved in, and indeed becoming a more and more important factor in, domestic life."[45] Michel Foucault made the same point, albeit with a more ample chronology: from the family as "model of good government" in the "classical era" (roughly the seventeenth and eighteenth centuries), society had moved to a model of "government through the family" in the modern era.[46]

For the republicans in power at the end of the nineteenth century, the family was the institution that ensured the reproduction of the nation as both population and polity. The state therefore intervened on issues of demography and the regulation of sexuality, as many historians and sociologists have shown.[47] But the family was also a political entity, because it produced citizens, especially through the education provided by fathers. Republican morality therefore assigned to the paternal function a very important role in citizenship training, as we saw earlier in the discussion of the debate around the investigation of paternity (see chapter 5).[48]

The *métis* question sheds light on the link between these two developments: the growing state role in defining both filiation and the nation. In both cases, state intervention was much blunter in the colonies than in the metropole. To be sure, "racial" difference heightened the stakes with respect to the control of filiation and attribution of citizenship. But the fact that both processes occurred earlier and with greater intensity in the colonies is also explained by the paucity of democratic debate among Europeans in the colonies, which meant that there was no opportunity for "fathers of families" (who in any case showed little interest in their offspring) to mount an opposition to the increased role of the state.

Beyond the Opposition of "Blood" and "Soil"

The examination of the *métis* question also enables us to question the opposition between "blood" (jus sanguinis) and "soil" (jus soli), which sociologists and historians in the 1980s and 1990s presented as fundamental to the various definitions of nationality. Jus soli, they argued, was fundamental to the "civic nation"—that is, a nation based on a political project and therefore open to immigrants. France was almost always the chief example of such civic nationhood. Jus sanguinis, in contrast, reflected an "ethnic" concept of the nation exemplified by Germany.[49] Patrick Weil has recently challenged this dichotomy by showing that the political and legal debates over the criteria of jus soli and jus sanguinis were extremely complex in both France and Germany, and that these debates evolved over time in ways that cannot be reduced to the opposition between civic and ethnic nationhood.

The legal treatment of the *métis* question prompts further reflection on this point. In the debates that led to the decrees concerning their status, blood and soil were not opposed. Indeed, for the majority of those involved, the two were complementary: "French race" manifested itself in "upbringing" and "culture" as well as in "ethnic signs" because all these factors were intertwined through the dialectic of "heredity" and "environment." Put differently, having "French blood" in the colonies was supposed to favor the assimilation of a "French education," which was most effective when dispensed within the family, in close proximity to the father.

This correlation leads us to take a fresh look at the fundamental debate on nationality in the 1880s. Indeed, it is often argued that in 1889, after a battle lasting several years, jus soli finally won out *against* jus sanguinis, even though the latter enjoyed strong support in the Council of State and the Senate. Supposedly, this ultimate "victory," which opened the way to French nationality for the children and grandchildren of immigrants, simply reflected weak support in France for the ethnic conception of the nation along with a "confidence in the assimilatory powers of France" and a "specifically Republican faith in the assimilatory virtues of school and army"—in the power, that is, of republican institutions of socialization.[50]

This interpretation calls for a number of comments. First, it neglects the fact that "the correlation between *socialization* and nationality was not exempt from ethnic considerations," as the exclusion of colonial natives from French nationality shows.[51] The agents of the state who had to apply the law were well aware of limits to the "assimilative virtues" of French institutions, and they explicitly envisioned assimilation in terms of race. For instance, high Ministry of Justice officials asserted, in a text commenting on the 1889 law, that "we must avoid . . . opening the doors too wide to foreigners whose race, too different from ours, might become an obstacle to prompt assimilation."[52]

More significant, to emphasize the importance of socialization is to neglect the complexity of the role that late nineteenth-century republicans ascribed to the family. For example, Rogers Brubaker, in a passage in which he insists that French nationality was not defined in ethnic terms, states that "Frenchness is acquired, not inherited. It is acquired, to be sure, in the family, as well as in workshop and marketplace, classroom and barracks. But it is the family as socializing agency, not the family as genetic unit, that is decisive."[53] But as we have learned, debates about the *métis* suggest that the family was always seen as both a "genetic unit" and an "agent of socialization," or, rather, that socialization was always conceived as the continuation of generation, just as "sociological" filiation was simply an extension of "biological" filiation.

Were these interrelationships pertinent to metropolitan debates about nationality? Further research is needed to answer this question. Still, certain positions taken by members of the republican elite suggest that blood and soil may have been complementary rather than mutually exclusive.

In this connection, it is worth considering the views of André Weiss, an eminent late nineteenth-century specialist in international private law, whose textbook was for several generations the very embodiment of liberal doctrine concerning citizenship and nationality. The first volume of his treatise, devoted entirely to nationality, defends a contractualist conception of the legal bond between the individual and the state.[54] Nationality, based on will and on reciprocal rights and duties, "cannot be imposed."[55] Upon reaching adulthood, an individual must be able to choose his nationality: states cannot require perpetual allegiance and must allow naturalization. Nevertheless, there are limits to this will, "either in the nature of things or in the requirements of social life." First, every person must have a nationality. Belonging to a "more or less dense" group is a law of nature. Here, the family serves as model for conceiving of integration into the nation, which is completely naturalized: "A man without a country is as inconceivable as a man without a family: the idea of fatherland is simply an extension of the idea of family. Social relations are a necessary part of life, and it is within nationality that social relations find their natural form and regulation."[56]

Hence, the contractual character of nationality was more fully respected by the criterion of filiation than by the criterion of birthplace, which had been linked to the idea of imposed nationality since the ancien régime, when it was used to determine who was a subject of the king. Will was associated with filiation, because it was forged through contacts between father and son. After refuting arguments in favor of jus soli, Weiss offers the following argument in favor of jus sanguinis:

> From a theoretical standpoint, the opposite assumption would appear to stand on a firmer footing: namely, that the nationality of the newborn infant is determined by filiation, by the jus sanguinis. Since the infant naturally cannot indicate his or her desire to belong to one country or another, it is reasonable to believe that the infant wishes to be bound to the state of which his or her parents are members and to obey the same laws they do. These laws suit the child as they suit the father, because they are shaped by the characteristics and habits that constitute the race that the father passed on to the child along with his or her life.[57]

In this argument in favor of jus sanguinis,[58] the function of the family is to regulate desire—that is, to regulate "attachment" and "will." The mention of the father rather than the parents should not be attributed to unconscious "phallogocentrism."[59] On the contrary, it was quite explicitly the father-child bond that was at issue: until 1927, a woman lost her nationality if she married a foreigner, so that in this context, nationality was inherited from the father. This bond played an essential role in the socialization of the child, by transmitting to him or her "the characteristics and habits that constitute the race." Here, as in the colonial context, "race" cannot be reduced to biology; it refers, rather, to a normative structure. Like race, nationality was therefore acquired primarily by filiation, which implied the transmission of a biological capital and the formation of specific habits from early childhood on, in a family environment under the aegis of the father. But here, another reason for evoking of the "law of the father" was that in this period, only for men, nationality implied citizenship—that is, active participation in the sovereignty of the state.

Citizenship in Practice

Analysis of the *métis* question in the colonies suggests new ways of thinking about the history of citizenship. In the 1980s and 1990s, a number of intellectuals posited the existence of a "republican model," which in their view could be used to explain modern French history. At the heart of this model was a conception of the nation defined by its ambition of "'*transcending particular belongings*' [which] might include the biological (such at least as they are perceived), historical, economic, social, religious, or cultural" affiliations. The citizen, in this context, was defined as an "abstract individual, without particular identification and qualification, over and above all concrete determinations."[60] This abstract individual, further, was placed in a "face-to-face confrontation with the state" in which "community identities" were dissolved.[61] These thinkers did not ignore the denial of citizenship to natives of the colonies. Rather, they integrated this fact as an objective limitation of the model. Thus, Dominique Schnapper argued that the colonial situation, founded on "nationality without citizenship," was a "juridical monstrosity."[62] The republic contradicted itself in the colonies.

This interpretation is problematic in several respects. First, if there was a contradiction, it was not limited to the colonies—far from it. The same type of exclusion, justified in terms of incomplete participation in civil life, affected women, natives, domestic servants, the insane, and children.[63] This was by no means an exceptional situation.

Furthermore, the "contradiction" appeared at the same time as the "model" and was immediately challenged by its victims. As Laurent Dubois has shown, the slaves of the Caribbean very quickly appropriated the language of citizenship to claim their freedom.[64] The contradiction was therefore always and everywhere present at the heart of the model. For instance, in the period 1944–60, during constitutional debates about the French Union and later the French Community, Africans advanced the idea of a differentiated empire in which equality would go hand in hand with cultural difference. Their arguments did not carry the day, but this was not because they were incompatible with the model of abstract citizenship. Rather, it was because the cost of granting citizenship to Africans was deemed prohibitive for the metropole.[65] Similarly, as Laure Blévis has shown, the exclusion of natives from citizenship was frequently a subject of debate in France, while in Algeria it was often circumvented in various ways. The model was never a political necessity.[66]

The history of the colonies therefore suggests that we should understand citizenship as a political relationship, in practical and historical terms, and that we should be wary of "models." The case of the colonial *métis* suggests that the citizen, far from being an abstract individual, could be defined in terms of the legal parameters of filiation, family milieu, social context, and finally, race.

At the conclusion of this study, what remains of the initial surprise occasioned by the 1928 decree? At a time when a "colonial fracture"[1] in French society is much discussed, isn't it rather naïve to seek the relation between race and nationality in arcane corners of colonial history involving a few tens of thousands of individuals?

Indeed, we are told that race is inscribed in the "genealogy of the French nation."[2] Only now, supposedly, has social science ceased to be blind to this glaring truth. This sudden illumination is said to be the result of challenging the "republican model," whose fundamental contradiction now stands revealed: despite its pretensions to universality, it always bore the stamp of the greatest particularism of them all, race.[3] The republic, it is now argued, was always made by and for whites, as demonstrated first and foremost by its colonial history. This argument, it should be noted, follows closely on work in the social sciences in the 1980s and 1990s, when the "republican model" was developed and popularized. This was a "model" in two senses: both a synthetic description of a historical phenomenon and a norm to adhere to.[4] The new critique, which sees rather a republic in contradiction with itself, simply inverts the terms of the preceding analysis and in many respects reinforces the model by assuming the existence of "the republic" as an abstract agent that shapes history. *republic as abstract agent*

The *métis* question and its relation to colonial citizenship law are tangential to this debate. Rather than denounce the contradictions of a supposedly universalist republic that was in fact "always already" racial, my goal in exploring these issues has been to contribute to a history of the uses of the notion of "race" in the French context—a history attentive to the multiplicity of those uses.

The case of the *métis* suggests, in particular, the ways in which race could figure not only in practices of exclusion and, indeed, extermination but also in projects of national inclusion. In the colonies, in the *métis* question, we see a "positive" use of race by a "populationist" French state seeking to rebuild the "great nation" by integrating as many of its children as possible—including all those "empire's children" who could make a claim on the French race.

In addition, various historical actors attributed different and sometimes contradictory meanings to the word *race*, depending on whether they were anthropologists, administrators, or jurists. Sometimes, moreover, they questioned the relevance of the idea altogether: the dialectic of affirmation and denial was no less complex in the colonies during the imperial era than it is today. As we have seen, the anthropologists' sophisticated theories of hybridity were ignored by administrators and jurists, for whom race was an obvious fact that needed no explicit definition.

If we try too hard to reconcile the various scientific and ideological definitions of race and the no less diverse ways in which the notion was actually used, we will fail to grasp both the meanings that historical actors themselves applied to it and the political strategies of which they were a part. To understand those strategies, we need to examine the social contexts in which those concepts were elaborated—that is, the singular configurations that arose in each colony. In each case, colonizers and colonized stood in a specific relation to each other that depended on the colonial "project" envisioned for each region of the empire as well as on the way that each conquered population reacted to imperial domination.

In this book, I have tried to portray the variety of colonial situations—occasionally emphasizing breadth over depth of local context. I have tried to show how these various situations gave rise to different interpretations of the *métis* question and different uses of the idea of race, and how, despite these differences, a certain way of defining and, through law, addressing the *métis* problem circulated throughout the empire. Legal categories worked as a blanket of rules that structured the empire as a relatively unified social space.[5] The trajectory of the *métis* question is significant in this context. It suggests that the empire existed first and foremost as a legal construct.

The *métis* question also reveals a profound change in the relation of the state to the nation and to the individuals included in it. Indeed, the colonial state, responding to the threat of the social and political disorder inherent in the *métis* question, involved itself in the verification of filiation, authorized investigation of paternity, and ultimately granted French citizenship to *métis* abandoned by their fathers. It thereby arrogated to itself a sort of collective paternity of the "empire's children." It took control of the bonds of filiation because, without the jus soli, which was not applied in the colonies, filiation was the only basis on which to decide who should be included in the nation. Filiation therefore became an object of state intervention.

This process was not specific to the *métis* question. It was part of a broader control of filiation by the state, which can be observed in the metropole as well—most notably in the law on the stripping of paternal authority passed in 1889, the same year in which the law on nationality established an irrevocable double jus soli. Similarly, since the turn of the twentieth century, the state has increasingly involved itself in the verification of filiation, a change from the Napoleonic Code, which allowed married couples more freedom to make their own determinations of filiation.[6] This long-term shift from parental will to biological truth as the basis of filiation has doubtless yet to run its full course. It came earlier and was more pronounced in the colonies: the absence of democratic institutions, even for the colonizers, obviously limited the opportunity for fathers to protest this reduction of their power. This story was quite different in the metropole, where these changes occasioned vehement protest.

The control of filiation by the state was inextricable from the process by which the nation became an object of government. By the end of the nineteenth century, the state played a much stronger role in defining the contours of the nation. The establishment of a legal and administrative apparatus for identifying individuals was a crucial part of this process.[7] This apparatus sought to act on the nation collectively—on the population, in other words—with technologies of social engineering such as child care as well as an arsenal of laws protecting the family, pregnant women, young mothers, and infants. No longer was the family seen as the basic cell of political society, as in the early nineteenth century; now it was rather the group through which individuals were attached to the nation: it produced citizens by combining generation with socialization, with the latter extending the former according to the neo-Lamarckian social thought so prevalent at the time.

It is in light of this complex assemblage of ideas and practices that the social and political function of race should be understood. Filiation and nation were interrelated as bonds that partook of the biological as well as the political, of nature as well as institutions. The new *"police des familles"*[8] that was put in place toward the end of the nineteenth century was associated with two related innovations: the emergence of "population"[9] as a new object of state action and of the nation as a new incarnation of the social and political bond. If the relationship between filiation and nationality was never more visible than in the colonial treatment of the *métis* question, it was because the *métis*, being hybrids and bastards, unraveled the unconscious but essential bonds between blood and soil, heredity and environment, nature and culture.

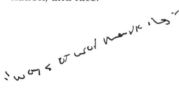

This history, in the wake of many others, therefore compels us to take a fresh look at the oppositions at the heart of the "republican model" developed by French social science toward the end of the twentieth century: "domestic space" versus "community of citizens," for example, or "civic nation" versus "ethnic nation." We must look instead at the dense connections between civility and polity.[10] This excavation also suggests that the historical anthropology of law yields rich dividends. Indeed, as we have seen, legal categories imposed powerful constraints on efforts to define individual and group identities.[11] Hence, any history of group membership must contend with law and its "ways of worldmaking," which hover over other modes of constructing the social and influence the way in which individuals conceive of their lives and their relations with others. The history of the "empire's children" reveals this creative power of law, at the intersection of filiation, nation, and race.

NOTES

INTRODUCTION

1. *Journal officiel de la République française, lois et décrets,* November 8, 1928.
2. By *law,* I mean here not just the usual "statutory law passed by Parliament" but, more broadly, "any rule or regulation promulgated by a competent authority." Similarly, when I use the term *legislation,* I mean "any law (or regulation) applicable to a state or region." Here I am following the definition given by Gérard Cornu in his *Vocabulaire juridique,* 3rd ed. (1st ed., 1987; Paris: PUF, Collection Quadrige, 2002), 516. This extended use is justified by the way in which laws and regulations were made in the colonies: under the colonial legal regime, the vast majority of texts having the force of law in the colonies were presidential decrees and were not voted on by Parliament.
3. Jean-Jacques Rousseau, *On the Social Contract; or, Principles of Political Right,* in *Basic Political Writings,* trans. Donald A. Cress (Indianapolis and Cambridge: Hackett Publishing Company, 1987); and Ernest Renan, "What Is a Nation?," trans. Martin Thom, in *Nation and Narration,* ed. Homi K. Bhabha (London: Routledge, 1990).
4. Renan, "What Is a Nation?" 14–19.
5. See the report by the Commission instituée pour préparer l'acte d'abolition immédiate de l'esclavage, quoted by Charles-Robert Ageron, *France coloniale ou parti colonial?* (Paris: PUF, 1978), 65.
6. Danièle Lochak, "La *race*: Une catégorie juridique?," in "Sans distinction de . . . *race,*" special issue, *Mots: Les langages du politique* 33 (1992): 293. According to Lochak, race functioned as an "implicit" referent in colonial legislation.
7. Dominique Schnapper, *Community of Citizens: On the Modern Idea of Nationality,* trans. Séverine Rosée (New Brunswick, NJ: Transaction Publishers, 1998).
8. This approach takes its inspiration from Reinhart Koselleck's social history of concepts, as developed in particular in *Futures Past: On the Semantics of Historical Time,* trans. Keith Tribe (New York: Columbia University Press, 1990).
9. Georges Hardy, *Nos grands problèmes coloniaux* (Paris: Armand Colin, 1929).
10. Bruno Latour, *La fabrique du droit: Une ethnographie du Conseil d'État* (Paris: la Découverte, 2002).
11. See Schnapper, *Community of Citizens;* and Rogers Brubaker, *Citizenship and Nationhood in France and Germany* (Cambridge, MA: Harvard University Press, 1994). Patrick

Weil has recently challenged this dichotomy with a comparative study of nationality law in *How to Be French: Nationality in the Making since 1789*, trans. Catherine Porter (Durham, NC: Duke University Press, 2009).

12. Brubaker, *Citizenship and Nationhood*, 11.

13. Schnapper, *Community of Citizens*, 126.

14. For a presentation of this perspective, see Laurent Dubois, *A Colony of Citizens: Revolution and Slave Emancipation in the French Caribbean, 1787–1804* (Chapel Hill: University of North Carolina Press, 2004); and Frederick Cooper and Ann Laura Stoler, eds., *Tensions of Empire: Colonial Cultures in a Bourgeois World* (Berkeley: University of California Press, 1997).

15. Claude Nicolet, *L'idée républicaine en France: Essai d'histoire critique, 1789–1924* (Paris: Gallimard, 1982), 405–6.

16. Michel Foucault, *History of Sexuality*, vol. 1, *An Introduction*, trans. Robert Hurley (New York: Vintage Books, 1990), 125.

17. Specifically, Ann Laura Stoler, *Race and Education of Desire: Foucault's History of Sexuality and the Colonial Order of Things* (Durham, NC: Duke University Press, 1995); Ann Laura Stoler, *Carnal Knowledge and Imperial Power: Race and the Intimate in Colonial Rule* (Berkeley: University of California Press, 2002); and Ann Laura Stoler, "Intimidations of Empire: Predicaments of the Tactile and Unseen," in *Haunted by Empire: Geographies of Intimacy in North American History*, ed. Ann Laura Stoler, 1–22 (Durham, NC: Duke University Press, 2006).

18. On this point, see the work of various anthropologists of empire, especially Jean Comaroff and John Comaroff, *Of Revelation and Revolution: Christianity, Colonialism and Consciousness in South Africa*, 2 vols. (Chicago: University of Chicago Press, 1991–97).

19. On the history of colonial categories, see Ann Laura Stoler, "Rethinking Colonial Categories: European Communities and the Boundaries of Rule," *Comparative Studies in Society and History* 31 (1989): 134–61.

20. On imperial circuits, see the introduction of Cooper and Stoler, *Tensions of Empire*, 28.

21. Nelly Schmidt, *Histoire du métissage* (Paris: La Martinière, 2003), 12.

22. See Fredrik Barth, "Ethnic Groups and Boundaries," in *Theories of Ethnicity: A Classical Reader*, ed. Werner Sollors, 294–324 (New York: New York University Press, 1996); Everett C. Hughes, *The Sociological Eye* (Chicago: Aldine-Atherton, 1971); and Andrew Abbott, "Things of Boundaries," *Social Research* 62 (1995): 857–82.

CHAPTER ONE

1. In Jean Nicot's dictionary, published in 1606, the word *métis* applied only to animals (*"métiz: engendered by two different species of animal, such as the leopard, from a male lion and a female panther, or a mule, from a mare and an ass"*). In the first edition of Antoine Furetière's dictionary (1690), the word was extended to humans: *"Mestif. Which has come from two different species. It is said properly of dogs engendered by a male dog and a bitch of different kinds. . . . Mestif can be said in a figurative sense of humans who are engendered by a father and mother of different quality, country, color, or religion. . . . In Spain, the word mulato is applied to a person engendered by a father and mother of different religions and who partakes of both, as a mule partakes of two natures, and it is a great insult. Mestif is also applied to a child born to an Indian male and a Spanish woman, but in the country such people are called crioles. In Peru, one properly applies the word mestif to those*

who are born to a Spanish male and a savage female." See Antoine Furetière, *Dictionnaire usuel contenant généralement tous les mots français et tant vieux que modernes et les termes de toutes les sciences et les arts* (The Hague and Rotterdam: A. R. Leers, 1690–1701).

2. Roseval, L. "Le mulâtre," in *Les Français peints par eux-mêmes*, vol. 3, *Provinces* (Paris: L. Curmer, 1842).

3. Buffon had called his own criterion into question by alluding to experiments that involved crossing different species to produce offspring that remained fertile over several generations (in particular, dogs and wolves and goats and lambs). See Claude Blanckaert, "Of Monstrous *Métis*? Hybridity, Fear of Miscegenation, and Patriotism from Buffon to Paul Broca," in *The Color of Liberty: Histories of Races in France*, ed. Sue Peabody and Tyler Stovall, 42–70 (Durham, NC: Duke University Press, 2003).

4. Paul Broca, "Recherches sur l'hybridité animale en général et sur l'hybridité humaine en particulier considérées dans leurs rapports avec la question de la pluralité des espèces humaines," in *Mémoires d'anthropologie* (Paris: C. Reinwald, 1871).

5. Paul Broca, "Recherches sur l'ethnologie de la France," *Bulletins de la Société d'anthropologie de Paris* 1, no. 1 (1860): 7–15.

6. Ibid. See also Blanckaert, "Of Monstruous *Métis*?"

7. Jules Michelet, *Tableau de l'histoire de France* (Paris: Hachette, 1833). Charles Seignobos, *Histoire sincère de la nation française: Essai d'une histoire de l'évolution du peuple français*, 8th ed. (Paris: PUF, 1982).

8. Intervention de Clémence Royer lors de la discussion générale, *Actes du deuxième Congrès international d'anthropologie criminelle* (Paris: Masson, 1890), 172.

9. *Revue de psychologie appliquée*, 4th ser., 32, no. 7 (July 1926): 114–15.

10. Georges Heuyer and Françoise Lautmann, "Troubles du caractère et inadaptation sociale chez les enfants métis," *Archives de médecine des enfants* 40, no. 9 (1937): 562, 563.

11. For a summary of criticism of *métissage* in the 1930s, see René Martial, *Les métis: Nouvelle étude sur les migrations, le mélange des races, le métissage, la retrempe de la race française et la révision du code de la famille* (Paris: Flammarion, 1942).

12. The principal author on this subject is Henri Neuville. See "L'espèce, la race et le métissage en anthropologie: Introduction à l'anthropologie générale," in *Archives de l'Institut de paléontologie humaine*, vol. 11 (Paris: Masson, 1933).

13. United Nations Educational, Scientific, and Cultural Organization (UNESCO), *Déclaration d'experts sur les questions de race* (Paris: UNESCO, 1950).

14. In all the large number of documents consulted in researching this book, the only explicit citation of works of physical anthropology occurs as an obligatory academic reference in a thesis from the École Coloniale: Robert Cornevin, "Les métis dans la colonisation française: L'hésitation métisse" (thesis, ENFOM [École nationale de la France d'outre-mer], 1941–42) (CAOM, ECOL).

15. On this point, I refer the reader to Emmanuelle Saada, "Race and Sociological Reason in the Republic: Inquiries on the *Métis* in the French Empire, 1908–1937," *International Sociology* 17, no. 3 (2002): 361–91.

16. On this point, see the foundational work by Jean-Loup Amselle, *Affirmative Exclusion: Cultural Pluralism and the Rule of Custom in France*, trans. Jane Marie Todd (Ithaca, NY: Cornell University Press, 2003).

17. Lieutenant Colonel Auguste Bonifacy, "Les métis franco-tonkinois," *Bulletins et mémoires de la Société d'anthropologie de Paris* 6, no. 1 (1910): 607–42.

18. A. Séville, "Les métis parias de l'Indochine: Appel au peuple français," *Les annales diplomatiques et consulaires* (Paris), 1st ser., 2, no. 27 (March 5, 1905): 228–31.

19. On the problem of the reproduction of the colonial situation, see Ann Laura Stoler, "Sexual Affronts and Racial Frontiers: European Identities and the Cultural Politics of Exclusion in Colonial Southeast Asia," *Comparative Studies in Society and History* 34, no. 3 (1992): 514–51.

20. Meeting of the Comité provisoire chargé d'élaborer les statuts de la fédération dite "Fondation Jules-Brévié," Hanoi, July 31, 1939 (ANVN 1, GGI, 4813).

21. "Notice sur la Société d'assistance aux enfants franco-indochinois du Tonkin," April 25, 1937 (ANVN 1, RST, 73758).

22. *Congrès international pour l'étude des problèmes résultant du mélange des races*, Exposition internationale et universelle de Bruxelles (Brussels, 1935), 14.

23. Edmond Laugier, "À la conquête des cœurs," *La presse indochinoise*, September 6, 1926.

24. Albert de Pouvourville, "Mariages mixtes et métis," *La nouvelle revue*, 4th ser., 7, no. 25 (May 1, 1913): 38–40.

25. Service des affaires administratives et contentieuses to the gouvernement général de l'Indochine, July 24, 1912 (CAOM, GGI, 16771).

26. In the much rarer cases in which the mother was French, she passed her citizenship status on to her children whether she was married or not (see chapter 4).

27. Dominique Schnapper, *Community of Citizens: On the Modern Idea of Nationality*, trans. Séverine Rosée (New Brunswick, NJ: Transaction Publishers, 1998).

28. R. Bonniot, *L'enfance métisse malheureuse*, report presented at Congrès de l'enfance (Saigon: Imprimerie de l'union, 1940), 4, 13–14.

29. E. Mathieu, "La protection de l'enfance en Cochinchine, son œuvre, sa portée sociale," in *Semaine de l'enfance du 1ᵉʳ au 7 juillet 1934: Rapports* (Saigon: Imprimerie de l'union, 1934), 37, 39.

30. The gouverneur général de l'Indochine to the ministre des Colonies, August 26, 1925 (CAOM, SG Indo NF, 3141).

31. Gouverneur général Brévié's speech at the meeting of the Comité provisoire chargé d'élaborer les statuts de la fédération dite "Fondation Jules-Brévié," Hanoi, July 1939 (ANVN 1, GGI, 4813).

32. Ibid.

33. CAOM, Aff. pol., 3406/6.

34. Cited by Vu Van Quang, "Le problème des Eurasiens en Indochine" (PhD diss., École de médecine et de pharmacie de plein exercice de l'Indochine, Hanoi, 1939), 39.

35. Myriam Cottias, "Le silence de la nation: Les 'vieilles colonies' comme lieu de définition des dogmes républicains, 1848–1905," *Outre-Mers* 338–39 (2003): 21–45.

36. CAOM, SG Guadeloupe, 133/897.

37. Jean-Luc Bonniol, *La couleur comme maléfice: Une illustration créole de la généalogie des blancs et des noirs* (Paris: Albin Michel, 1992).

38. The Indochinese Union was created in 1887. It was made up of territories conquered from south to north: Cochin China, which had been a colony since 1862, plus the protectorates of Cambodia (1863), Annam and Tonkin (1883), and Laos (1899).

39. Clotilde Chivas-Baron, *La femme française aux colonies* (Paris: Larose, 1929), 92–93.

40. Philippe Franchini, *Continental Saïgon* (repr., Paris: Métailié, 1995).

41. Émile Zola, *Thérèse Raquin* (Paris: GF Flammarion, 1970), 73, 93.

42. Victor Demontès, *L'Algérie économique*, vol. 2, *Les populations algériennes* (Algiers: Imprimerie algérienne, 1923), 401.

43. Victor Demontès, *Le peuple algérien: Essais de démographie algérienne* (Algiers: Imprimerie algérienne, 1906), 241.

44. Demontès, *L'Algérie économique*, 413–15.

45. Albert Billiard, *Politique et organisation coloniales: Principes généraux* (Paris: V. Giard et E. Brière, 1899), 116.

46. Jacques Berque, *French North Africa: The Maghrib between Two World Wars*, trans. Jean Stewart (New York: Praeger, 1967), 304–6.

47. Ibid., 304–5.

48. Edmond Doutté, "Lettre à Augustin Bernard," *Questions diplomatiques et coloniales* (October 1, 1901): 396.

49. On this point, again, opinions differ: Berque says that, "with a few exceptions," illicit relationships did not produce offspring (*French North Africa*, 306), but Émile Dermenghem states that prostitutes had many children. *Les pays d'Abel: Le Sahara des Ouled-Naïl, des Larbaa et des Amour* (Paris: Gallimard, 1960), 73.

50. For instance, the point is never mentioned in the recent volume by Christelle Taraud, *La prostitution coloniale: Algérie, Maroc, Tunisie, 1830–1962* (Paris: Payot, 2003).

51. Dr. Henri Marchand, "Considérations sur les mariages franco-musulmans," in "Le mariage mixte franco-musulman," special issue, *Les annales juridiques, politiques, économiques et sociales* 1, nos. 3–4 (1956): 5–23.

52. This assumption runs counter to recent historical work, which sees the history of colonization in Algeria as a perpetual "race war." See, for example, Olivier Le Cour Grandmaison, *Coloniser, exterminer: Sur la guerre et l'état colonial* (Paris: Fayard, 2005).

53. See, for example, *Rapport général: Exposition coloniale de 1931*, vol. 5, *Les sections coloniales* (Paris: Imprimerie nationale, 1933), 52–53.

54. Philippe Lucas and Jean-Claude Vatin, *L'Algérie des anthropologues* (Paris: François Maspero, 1975); Patricia Lorcin, *Imperial Identities: Stereotyping, Prejudice and Race in Colonial Algeria* (London: I. B. Tauris and Company, 1995).

55. Daniel Rivet, *Le Maghreb à l'épreuve de la colonisation* (Paris: Hachette littératures, 2002), 45.

56. Marchand, "Considérations sur les mariages franco-musulmans," 20.

57. CAOM, GGA, 14/H/72.

58. Ibid., 8/X/232.

59. André Bonnichon, *La conversion au christianisme de l'indigène musulman algérien et ses effets juridiques (un cas de conflit colonial)* (Paris: Librairie du Recueil Sirey, 1931), 24–25.

60. Karima Direche-Slimani, *Chrétiens de Kabylie, 1873–1954: Une action missionnaire dans l'Algérie coloniale* (Saint-Denis, France: Bouchene, 2004).

61. See the estimates in Marchand, "Considérations sur les mariages franco-musulmans."

62. First president of the cour d'appel d'Alger to ministre de la Justice, February 24, 1923, document cited by Henri Bénet, *L'état civil en Algérie: Traité théorique et pratique* (Algiers: Imprimerie Minerva, 1937), 397.

63. In law, *doctrine* refers to "the opinion commonly professed by those who teach law" and by extension to "the authors of legal works taken together." *Case law* (*jurisprudence*) is "the range of decisions handed down during a certain period of time, either in a particular area of law (e.g., real estate case law) or a particular branch of law

(civil case law, fiscal case law, etc.) or in law as a whole." See Gérard Cornu, *Vocabulaire juridique*, 3rd ed. (Paris: PUF, Collection Quadrige, 2002), 311, 506.

64. Right of the father or guardian to compel a child under his protection to marry, up to a certain age.

65. The Native Code—*Code de l'indigénat*—listed special crimes and punishments specific to the indigenous population. See chapter 4.

66. Bénet, *L'état civil en Algérie*, 397–98.

67. CAOM, GGM, 6(10)D4.

68. National Archives of Madagascar, D130.

69. For example, Félix Éboué in a 1941 memo concerning native policy (CAOM, GGAEF 5D202).

70. Owen White, *Children of the French Empire: Miscegenation and Colonial Society in French West Africa, 1895–1960* (Oxford: Oxford University Press, 1999).

71. Joël Dauphiné, "Le métissage biologique dans la Nouvelle-Calédonie coloniale, 1853–1939," in *Colonies, territoires, sociétés: L'enjeu français*, ed. Alain Saussol and Joseph Zitomersky, 217–22 (Paris: l'Harmattan, 1996).

72. Alban Bensa, "Colonialisme, racisme et ethnologie en Nouvelle-Calédonie," *Ethnologie française* 18, no. 2 (1988): 187–97.

73. Isabelle Merle, *Expériences coloniales: La Nouvelle-Calédonie, 1853–1920* (Paris: Belin, 1995), 360–66.

74. See the contributions to "La Nouvelle-Calédonie: Terre de métissages," a special issue of the journal *Annales d'histoire calédonienne* 1 (November 2004). One of the first observers of the phenomenon, a colonist named Moncelon, claims that children were taken back to their tribes by their mothers, to his dismay. See M. Moncelon, "Métis de Français et de Néo-Calédoniens," *Bulletins de la Société d'anthropologie de Paris* 3, no. 9 (1886): 10–19.

75. The gouverneur général de la Nouvelle-Calédonie et dépendances to the ministre des Colonies, April 13, 1948 (CAOM, Aff. pol., 1194).

76. Michel Naepels, *Histoires de terres kanakes: Conflits fonciers et rapports sociaux dans la région de Houaïlou (Nouvelle-Calédonie)* (Paris: Belin, 1998), 167–68.

77. Moncelon, "Métis de Français et de Néo-Calédoniens," 17.

78. Bensa, "Colonialisme, racisme et ethnologie en Nouvelle-Calédonie," 193.

79. Laurent Dornel, "Les usages du racialisme: Le cas de la main-d'œuvre coloniale en France pendant la Première Guerre mondiale," *Genèses* 20 (1995): 48–72; and Mireille Favre-Le-Van-Ho, "Un milieu porteur de modernisation: Travailleurs et tirailleurs vietnamiens en France pendant la Première Guerre mondiale" (thesis, École nationale des Chartes, Paris, 1996).

80. Confidential circular from the ministre de la Justice Viviani to the procureurs généraux, February 2, 1917 (CAOM, SLOTFOM, VI/7).

81. The gouverneur général en Indochine to the ministre des Colonies, January 8, 1920 (CAOM, SLOTFOM, VI/7).

82. Jacques Donzelot, *La police des familles* (repr., Paris: Minuit, 2005).

83. CAOM, SLOTFOM, VI/7.

84. Cour d'appel de l'Indochine, November 29, 1917 (CAOM, SLOTFOM, VI/7).

85. Directorate of Colonial Troops to the Ministry of Colonies, June 16, 1917 (CAOM, SLOTFOM, VI/7). The author is mistaken about the status of children, which illustrates how poorly colonial issues were understood in the metropole.

86. Georges Hardy, *Nos grands problèmes coloniaux* (Paris: Armand Colin, 1929).

87. On the notion of a "politics of comparison," see Ann Laura Stoler, "Sexual Affronts and Racial Frontiers," 528. In another context altogether, refer also to Christian Topalov, "Les réformateurs et leurs réseaux," in *Laboratoires du nouveau siècle: La nébuleuse réformatrice et ses réseaux en France, 1880–1914*, ed. Christian Topalov, 11–58 (Paris: EHESS, 1999).

88. Emmanuelle Sibeud, *Une science impériale pour l'Afrique? La construction des savoirs africanistes en France, 1878–1930* (Paris: EHESS, 2002).

89. Bonifacy, "Les métis franco-tonkinois."

90. For example, it was still being cited thirty years after its publication in a report on the "Eurasian question" dated August 1941 (ANVN 1, GGI, 4810).

91. Bonifacy, "Les métis franco-tonkinois," 635, 641 (emphasis mine).

92. Circular from the ministre des Colonies, May 8, 1912 (CAOM, Aff. pol., 28).

93. On this expression, see Topalov, *Laboratoires du nouveau siècle.*

94. General assembly of the Société de protection des enfants métis abandonnés, February 15, 1911 (ANVN 1, RST, 5547).

95. Union coloniale française to the ministre des Colonies, May 11, 1928 (CAOM, Aff. pol., 1194).

96. Albert Londres, *Terre d'ébène* (Paris: Albin Michel, 1929).

97. Albert de Pouvourville, "Le métis," *Le mal d'argent* (Paris: Éditions du monde moderne, 1926).

98. Clotilde Chivas-Baron, *Confidences de métisse* (Paris: Fasquelle, 1927).

99. These extremely stereotyped narratives might be compared with the late nineteenth-century American theme of the "tragic mulatto."

100. Antony Jully, "La question des enfants métis," *Revue de Madagascar: Organe du Comité de Madagascar* 7 (1905): 509.

101. The gouverneur général de l'AOF to the gouverneur général de l'Indochine, August 1934 (ANVN 1, RST, 71191).

102. For example, in April 1927, the governor-general of FEA cited a decision of the court of appeals in Hanoi dated December 1926 in a letter to the Ministry of Colonies (CAOM, GGAEF, 5D44).

103. Note from the consul général de France à Batavia, December 1901 (CAOM, GGI, 54220).

104. Minutes of the meeting held May 24, 1938, in the office of the gouverneur général in order to examine the "question des métis en Indochine" (CAOM, AGEFOM, 252/376).

105. The inspecteur des affaires administratives du territoire du Gabon to the gouverneur général de l'AEF, February 21, 1941 (CAOM, GGAEF, 5D44).

106. Ann Laura Stoler and Frederick Cooper point out that it was also through comparative discussion of colonial issues that consciousness of a European political community was forged. See Frederick Cooper and Ann Laura Stoler, "Between Metropole and Colony: Rethinking a Research Agenda," in *Tensions of Empire: Colonial Cultures in a Bourgeois World*, ed. Frederick Cooper and Ann Laura Stoler (Berkeley: University of California Press, 1997), 28.

107. M. E. Moresco, "De la condition des métis et de l'attitude des gouvernements à leur égard," *Institut colonial international, rapports préliminaires: Session de Brunswick*, vol. 2 (Brussels: Établissements généraux d'imprimerie, 1911), 447.

108. On the congresses as spaces for elaboration of problems on an international scale, see Anne Rasmussen, "Le travail en congrès, élaboration d'un milieu international,"

in *Histoire de l'Office du travail, 1890–1914*, ed. Jean Luciani, 119–34 (Paris: Syros, 1993).

109. Institut colonial international, "Notice, statuts et règlement, liste des membres et listes des publications" (Brussels: 1937), 5.

110. *Institut colonial international, rapports préliminaires: Session de Bruxelles*, vol. 2 (Brussels: Établissements généraux d'imprimerie, 1923).

111. Michel Foucault, "Governmentality" (1978), in *The Foucault Effect: Studies in Governmentality*, ed. Graham Burchell, Colin Gordon, and Peter Miller, 87–104 (Chicago: University of Chicago Press, 1991).

112. On this point, see Alain Desrosières, *The Politics of Large Numbers: A History of Statistical Reasoning*, trans. Camille Naish (Cambridge, MA: Harvard University Press, 1998).

113. Maurice Delafosse, "Note relative aux métis en Afrique occidentale française," *Institut colonial international*, 82.

114. According to Foucault, what characterizes modern societies "is not that they consigned sex to a shadow existence, but that they dedicated themselves to speaking of it *ad infinitum*, while exploiting it as *the* secret." Michel Foucault, *History of Sexuality*, vol. 1, *An Introduction*, trans. Robert Hurley (New York: Vintage Books, 1990), 35.

115. Gouvernement général de l'Indochine, Direction des affaires économiques, *Annuaire statistique de l'Indochine, recueil de statistiques relatives aux années 1913 à 1922* (Hanoi: Imprimerie d'Extrême-Orient, 1927), 49–50.

116. Ibid.

117. The gouverneur général de l'Indochine to the ministre des Colonies, June 24, 1938 (ANVN 1, RST, 71191).

118. Proposition no. 385 at the Assemblée de l'Union française, 1952 (CAOM, AGEFOM, 252/376).

119. Note from the Direction des affaires politiques, 1932 (CAOM, SG Indo NF, 2374).

120. Cornevin, "Les métis dans la colonisation française."

121. Luc Boltanski, *Les cadres: La formation d'un groupe social* (Paris: Minuit, 1982), 52–54.

122. Ministère des Colonies, Office colonial, *Statistiques de la population dans les colonies françaises pour l'année 1906, suivies du relevé de la superficie des colonies françaises* (Melun, France: Imprimerie administrative, 1909).

123. Pierre Huard and Alfred Bigot, "Introduction à l'étude des Eurasiens," in *Bulletin économique de l'Indochine*, booklet 4, 715–58 (Hanoi: Direction des services économiques, 1939).

124. According to the 1921 and 1940 censuses cited in Pierre Brocheux and Daniel Hémery, *Indochina: An Ambiguous Colonization, 1858–1954*, trans. Ly Lan Dill-Klein with Eric Jennings, Nora Taylor, and Noémi Tousignant (Berkeley: University of California Press, 2009).

CHAPTER TWO

1. The situation of the *métis* was in many respects similar to the situation of immigrants and especially the children of immigrants in French society today. On this point, see Abdelmalek Sayad, *The Suffering of the Immigrant*, trans. David Macey (Cambridge: Polity, 2004), 278–93.

2. On the intertwining roles of race and class in maintaining the boundaries of colonial domination, see Ann Laura Stoler, *Carnal Knowledge and Imperial Power: Race and the Intimate in Colonial Rule* (Berkeley: University of California Press, 2002).

3. Alexis Danan, "Un drame inconnu: Ces Français de hasard que la France aban-
    donne," *Franc tireur*, no. 2292 (December 12, 1951) (article found in CAOM,
    Aff. pol., 1194).
4. Douchet, *Métis et congaies d'Indochine* (Hanoi: 1928), 8.
5. Robert Cornevin, "Les métis dans la colonisation française: L'hésitation métisse"
    (thesis, ENFOM [École nationale de la France d'outre-mer], 1941–42) (CAOM,
    ECOL).
6. Note from the director of the René Robin orphanage in Hanoi, n.d. (ANVN 1, GGI,
    89).
7. The directeur de l'instruction publique to the inspecteur général du travail et de la
    prévoyance sociale, August 24, 1942 (ANVN 1, GGI, 4810).
8. See, for example, Jacques Mazet, "La condition juridique des métis dans les posses-
    sions françaises" (PhD diss., Université de Paris, Faculté de droit, 1932), 8.
9. List of *métis* abandoned by their fathers, March 1898 (ANVN 1, RST, 8419), and list
    of names of *métis* compiled by the city of Hanoi, April 1938 (ANVN 1, Mairie Hanoi,
    3279).
10. Minutes of the May 24, 1938, meeting on the "question des métis en Indochine"
    (CAOM, AGEFOM, 252/376).
11. Médecin-commandant Ravoux, "Aspects sociaux d'un groupe d'Eurasiens," *Bulletins
    et mémoires de la Société d'anthropologie de Paris* 9, no. 9 (1948): 180–90.
12. Victor Augagneur, "Les femmes aux colonies," *Les annales coloniales*, January 18,
    1913.
13. Charles Gravelle, "Les métis et l'œuvre de la protection de l'enfance au Cambodge,"
    Revue indochinoise 16, no. 1 (January 1913): 32.
14. "Bétail humain," *L'avenir du Tonkin*, October 26, 1899 (CAOM, SG Indo NF, 51 bis).
    The case was taken sufficiently seriously in Paris for the minister, at the behest of the
    French Antislavery Society, to order an investigation and request that steps be taken.
    The governor poured cold water on the affair by stating that the reported facts were
    "totally distorted."
15. *Cô* is the Vietnamese word for "young woman," and it was picked up in French slang
    in Indochina.
16. The chargé de l'expédition des affaires courantes du Régiment étranger d'infanterie
    (REI) to the inspecteur du travail et de la prévoyance sociale au Tonkin, November
    12, 1942 (ANVN 1, GGI, 4809).
17. General assembly of the Société d'assistance aux enfants franco-indochinois, 1936
    (ANVN 1, RST, 73758).
18. ANVN 1, RST, 47922.
19. Soldat M. to the résident supérieur au Tonkin, November 1, 1916 (CAOM, RST,
    1098).
20. ANVN 1, GGI, 75.
21. CAOM, RST NF, 6648.
22. For example, ANVN 1, Mairie Hanoi, 5900.
23. The résident supérieur au Tonkin to the général de division, June 1938 (ANVN 1,
    RST, 71191).
24. The chef du Bureau militaire à Mme. G. à Paris, September 1, 1915 (CAOM, GGI,
    26499).
25. The président de la Société des enfants métis abandonnés to the gouverneur général
    de l'Indochine, March 5, 1923 (CAOM, GGI, 16773).
26. ANVN 1, RST, 48405.

27. ANVN 1, Mairie Hanoi, 5900.
28. Ibid. (emphasis mine).
29. Ibid.
30. The résident à Sontay to the résident supérieur au Tonkin, December 24, 1931 (ANVN 1, RST, 48427).
31. The président de la société to the résident supérieur au Tonkin, February 25, 1916 (CAOM, RST, 1099).
32. General assembly of the Société d'assistance aux enfants franco-indochinois, 1944 (ANVN 1, RST, 73758).
33. CAOM, GGI, 7701.
34. In Indochina, prior to 1928, métis whose fathers were unknown were legally classified as natives. If they wished to become citizens, they were required to file a request for "naturalization" with the administration. On this point, see chapter 4.
35. H.-T.-H. to the résident supérieur au Tonkin, August 2, 1932 (ANVN 1, RST, 81130).
36. In Indochina and other French colonies, natives were registered in each commune (more details appear later in this chapter).
37. Louis L. to the gouverneur général de l'Indochine, March 1926 (CAOM, AGEFOM, 272/376).
38. Albert de Pouvourville, "L'Indochine et ses métis," La dépêche coloniale, 4949, September 16, 1911, 2.
39. Maurice Barrès, Les déracinés: Le roman de l'énergie nationale (Paris: Honoré Champion, 2004).
40. Notice sur la Société d'assistance aux enfants franco-indochinois du Tonkin (Hanoi: Imprimerie G. Taupin et cie., 1937) (document found in ANVN 1, RST, 71191).
41. Georges Taridif, "Chronique métisse," Le Tonkin républicain, April 9, 1926.
42. Colette Jandot-Danjou, "La condition civile des étrangers dans les trois derniers siècles de la monarchie" (PhD diss., Université de Paris, Faculté de droit, 1939).
43. To put it in the language of Pierre Bourdieu, whose sociology of social reproduction and its failures would reappropriate these themes, the déclassé was a person who failed to make the unconscious adjustment between "subjective probability" and "objective prospects." His life was then the result of a pathology in "the causality of the probable." See Pierre Bourdieu, "Avenir de classe et causalité du probable," Revue française de sociologie 15, no. 1 (1974): 3–42.
44. Charles Brunot, Les déclassés asolidaires, délinquants de droit commun, mécontents politiques, etc.: Notes présentées au Congrès international de l'éducation sociale (Paris: Librairie polytechnique, 1900).
45. ANVN 1, RST, 12836.
46. C. Crévost, "La question des métis est un problème social et moral dont la solution ne doit envisager que l'élément spécial des métis français-annamites," note, 1898 (CAOM, GGI, 7701).
47. Nhaqué was an extremely pejorative term based on the Vietnamese word for "peasant," which the French used to refer to the Vietnamese.
48. Gravelle, "Les métis et l'œuvre de la protection de l'enfance au Cambodge," 39.
49. Mazet, "La condition juridique des métis," 8.
50. Henri Labouret, "La situation morale et matérielle des métis dans l'Ouest africain français et la législation qui leur est appliquée," in Compte rendu du Congrès international pour l'étude des problèmes résultant du mélange des races (Brussels: Exposition internationale et universelle de Bruxelles, 1935), 23.

51. General assembly of the Société d'assistance aux enfants abandonnés franco-indochinois, 1926 (CAOM, AGEFOM, 900/2652).

52. Crévost, "La question des métis est un problème social et moral."

53. Henri Sambuc, "La condition juridique des métis dans les colonies françaises," *Dareste* II (1933): 62.

54. Albert de Pouvourville, "L'Indochine française: Introduction générale," *L'encyclopédie coloniale et maritime* (Paris: L'encyclopédie coloniale et maritime, 1936), 33.

55. M. Galuski, "Enquête sur la question des métis: Au Tonkin," *Revue indochinoise* 16, no. 4 (1913): 402.

56. The gouverneur général de l'AEF to the ministre des Colonies, April 6, 1932 (CAOM, GGAEF, 5D44).

57. Pierre Rosanvallon, *Le sacre du citoyen: Histoire du suffrage universel en France* (Paris: Gallimard, 1992; repr., "Folio histoire," 2001), 377–79. Citation refers to the 1992 edition.

58. Note on the current situation of the Société de protection des enfants métis abandonnés, May 1, 1912 (CAOM, GGI, 16771).

59. The gouverneur général de l'Indochine to the président du Conseil d'administration de la Fondation Jules-Brévié, July 28, 1941 (ANVN 1, GGI, 4810).

60. Gravelle, "Les métis et l'œuvre de la protection de l'enfance au Cambodge," 37.

61. Edmond Laugier, "À la conquête des cœurs," *La presse indochinoise*, September 6, 1926. *Nhỏ* means "small"; in common parlance, it is often used to signify "young child."

62. For a sociological analysis of the spectacle of suffering, see Luc Boltanski, *Distant Suffering: Morality, Media and Politics*, trans. Graham Burchell (Cambridge: Cambridge University Press, 1999).

63. Ernest Babut, "Le métis franco-annamite," *Revue indochinoise* 61 (1907): 903.

64. The chef de bataillon Edon to the résident supérieur au Tonkin, June 16, 1920 (ANVN 1, RST, 48379).

65. Bernard Vernier, "Prénom et ressemblance: Appropriation symbolique des enfants, économie affective et systèmes de parenté," in *Adoptions, ethnologie des parentés choisies*, ed. Agnès Fine, 97–119 (Paris: Maison des sciences de l'homme, 1998).

66. The gouverneur du Gabon to the gouverneur général de l'AEF (CAOM, GGAEF, 5D44).

67. "Requête émettant le vœu que l'administration s'occupe des orphelins métis qui, abandonnés à eux-mêmes au milieu d'une société qui les méprise, sont souvent obligés d'exercer les plus vils métiers," July 28, 1938 (ANVN 1, RST, 71191).

68. A. Séville, "Les métis parias de l'Indochine: Appel au peuple français," *Les annales diplomatiques et consulaires* (Paris), 1st ser., 2, no. 27 (March 5, 1905): 231.

69. Boltanski, *Distant Suffering*, 39–41.

70. Crévost, "La question des métis est un problème social et moral."

71. There has been a good deal of historical work since the late 1980s on the modes of colonial power. For one of the leaders of the school of "subaltern studies," Ranajit Guha, colonial power was based on "pure" domination, without hegemony. See Ranajit Guha, *Dominance without Hegemony: History and Power in Colonial India* (Cambridge, MA: Harvard University Press, 1997). This interpretation has been criticized by, among others, Frederick Cooper, "Conflict and Connection: Rethinking African Colonial History," *American Historical Review* 99, no. 5 (1994): 1516–45.

72. Henri Bonvicini, *Enfants de la colonie* (Saigon: Imprimerie coloniale, 1938), 45.
73. Very few French historians of empire take their inspiration from Michel Foucault. Most of the references are thus in English. They include Paul Rabinow, *French Modern: Norms and Forms of the Social Environment* (Cambridge, MA: MIT Press, 1989); David Scott, "Colonial Governmentality," *Social Text* 43 (1995): 191–220; Ann Laura Stoler, *Race and Education of Desire: Foucault's History of Sexuality and the Colonial Order of Things* (Durham, NC: Duke University Press, 1995); Gwendolyn Wright, *The Politics of Design in French Colonial Urbanism* (Chicago: University of Chicago Press, 1991).
74. Jean Suret-Canale, *Afrique noire, occidentale et centrale*, vol. 2, *L'ère coloniale, 1900–1945* (Paris: Éditions sociales, 1964), 95.
75. Olivier Le Cour Grandmaison, *De l'indigénat. Anatomie d'un "monstre" juridique: Le droit colonial en Algérie et dans l'Empire français* (Paris: la Découverte, 2010), 181.
76. René Pommier, "Le régime de l'indigénat en Indochine" (PhD diss., Université de Paris, Faculté de droit, 1907), 58.
77. Cited by Isabelle Merle, "De la 'légalisation' de la violence en contexte colonial: Le régime de l'indigénat en question," *Politix* 17, no. 66 (2004): 155.
78. Here I object to a basic line of argument in postcolonial studies according to which imperialism created what Partha Chatterjee calls a "colonial *rule* of difference." See Partha Chatterjee, *The Nation and Its Fragments: Colonial and Postcolonial Histories* (Princeton, NJ: Princeton University Press, 1993). I am following Frederick Cooper, *Colonialism in Question: Theory, Knowledge, History* (Berkeley: University of California Press, 2005), 23, in focusing rather on the plural and dynamic *politics* of difference.
79. On the importance of these "intermediary" populations in the construction of colonial social categories, see Ann Laura Stoler, "Rethinking Colonial Categories: European Communities and the Boundaries of Rule," *Comparative Studies in Society and History* 31 (1989): 134–61.
80. Paul d'Enjoy, *La colonisation de la Cochinchine (Manuel du colon)* (Paris: Sociétés d'éditions scientifiques, 1898), 30.
81. André Bonnichon, *La conversion au christianisme de l'indigène musulman algérien et ses effets juridiques (un cas de conflit colonial)* (Paris: Librairie du Recueil Sirey, 1931), 17.
82. Alice L. Conklin, *A Mission to Civilize: The Republican Idea of Empire in France and West Africa, 1895–1930* (Palo Alto, CA: Stanford University Press, 1997).
83. Herman Lebovics, *True France: The Wars over Cultural Identity, 1900–1945* (Ithaca, NY: Cornell University Press, 1992), 110–19.
84. Fanny Colonna, *Instituteurs algériens, 1883–1939* (Paris: Presses de la Fondation nationale des sciences politiques, 1975), 162–70.
85. Arlette Jouanna, "Recherches sur la notion d'honneur au XVIᵉ siècle," *Revue d'histoire moderne et contemporaine* 15 (1968): 597–623.
86. Georges Hardy, "La préparation sociale des jeunes gens qui se destinent à la colonisation: Fonctionnaires et colons," *Semaines sociales de France*, session 22, Marseille, 1930, 470.
87. "Going native" was a favorite theme of colonial literature from the first half of the twentieth century and can be found in the best-selling novels of Claude Farrère, *Les civilisés* (Paris: Ollendorff, 1906), which received the Prix Goncourt, and especially Charles Renel, *Le "décivilisé"* (Paris: Flammarion, 1923).

88. Cited by Suret-Canale, *Afrique noire, occidentale et centrale,* 401.
89. Robert A. Nye, *Masculinity and Male Codes of Honor in Modern France* (Berkeley: University of California Press, 1993); George L. Mosse, *The Image of Man: The Creation of Modern Masculinity* (New York: Oxford University Press, 1996).
90. Stoler, *Carnal Knowledge and Imperial Power,* and, in French, "Genre et moralité dans la construction impériale de la race," *Actuel Marx* 38 (2005): 75–101.
91. Augagneur, "Les femmes aux colonies."
92. For the Dutch case, see Ann Laura Stoler, "Sexual Affronts and Racial Frontiers: European Identities and the Cultural Politics of Exclusion in Colonial Southeast Asia," *Comparative Studies in Society and History* 34, no. 3 (1992): 514–51; and for the German case, Lora Wildenthal, *German Women for Empire, 1884–1945* (Durham, NC: Duke University Press, 2001).
93. Circular note from the procureur général to the magistrats de l'Indochine, September 18, 1897 (CAOM, GGI, 7770).
94. Confidential circular from the gouverneur général de l'Indochine, September 29, 1901 (CAOM, GGI, 7770).
95. Laos was the least populous country in the union, the least densely colonized, and the least urbanized.
96. Circular marked "très confidentielle" from the résident supérieur du Laos, October 12, 1901 (CAOM, GGI, 7770).
97. Article 43 of the Statute of the Magistracy reads: "Any failure by a magistrate with respect to the duties of his office, honor, tact, or dignity constitutes an offense subject to disciplinary sanction." (See ordinance no. 58-1270 of December 22, 1958, concerning the Statute of the Magistracy.)
98. Hardy, "La préparation sociale des jeunes gens," 470.
99. General assembly of the Société d'assistance aux enfants abandonnés franco-indochinois, 1926 (ANVN 1, RST, 73758).
100. Crévost, "La question des métis est un problème social et moral."
101. General assembly of the Société de protection des enfants métis abandonnés, 1917 (ANVN 1, GGI, 5547).
102. Gravelle, "Les métis et l'œuvre de la protection de l'enfance au Cambodge," 31.

CHAPTER THREE

1. Albert O. Hirschman, *The Rhetoric of Reaction: Perversity, Futility, Jeopardy* (Cambridge, MA: Harvard University Press, 1991).
2. Albert de Pouvourville, "L'Indochine et ses métis," *La dépêche coloniale,* 4949, September 16, 1911, 2.
3. See Christian Topalov, "Les réformateurs et leurs réseaux," in *Laboratoires du nouveau siècle: La nébuleuse réformatrice et ses réseaux en France, 1880–1914,* ed. Christian Topalov (Paris: EHESS, 1999), 14–15.
4. The chef du service des affaires administratives et contentieuses, July 24, 1912 (CAOM, GGI, 16771).
5. The secrétaire général of the general government of Indochina, July 25, 1912 (CAOM, GGI, 16771).
6. Pouvourville, "L'Indochine et ses métis," 2 (emphasis mine).
7. Arlette Jouanna, *L'idée de race en France au XVIe siècle et au début du XVIIe, 1498–1614* (Paris: Honoré Champion, 1975).
8. Charles Gravelle, "Au directeur de la dépêche coloniale," *La dépêche coloniale,* 5040, December 18, 1911 (emphasis mine).

9. General assembly of the Société de protection des enfants métis abandonnés, 1911 (ANVN 1, RST, 5547).

10. General assembly of the Société de protection des enfants métis abandonnés, 1907 (ANVN 1, RST, 5547).

11. Ibid.

12. A general to the ministre de la Guerre, January 18, 1936 (CAOM, GGI, 53523).

13. Letter from the gouverneur du Gabon to the gouverneur général de l'AEF, 1941 (CAOM, GGAEF, 5D44).

14. Statement reported by Claude Pauchet, "Le problème des métis en Afrique" (thesis, ENFOM [École nationale de la France de outre-mer], 1947–48) (CAOM, mémoires ENFOM).

15. Circular "Politique indigène de l'Afrique équatoriale française," November 8, 1941 (CAOM, GGAEF, 5D202).

16. Note for the preparation of the Brazzaville conference, n.d. (CAOM, Aff. pol., 2125/2).

17. AN, GGAOF, 23G22.

18. Clotilde Chivas-Baron, La femme française aux colonies (Paris: Larose, 1929), 92–93.

19. Letter from résident supérieur au Tonkin to général de division, June 18, 1938 (ANVN 1, RST, 71191).

20. In 1906, this became the Société de protection de l'enfance of Cochin China. On the history of this organization, see E. Mathieu, "La protection de l'enfance en Cochinchine, son oeuvre, sa portée sociale," in Semaine de l'enfance du 1er au 7 juillet 1934: Rapports, 32–43 (Saigon: Imprimerie de l'Union, 1934).

21. François de Coutouly, "Note sur les métis en AOF" (CAOM, GGAEF, 5D44).

22. Pauchet, "Le problème des métis en Afrique."

23. CAOM, GGAEF, 5D44.

24. CAOM, GGA, 8/X/232 and GGA, 14/H/72.

25. On the difficult collaboration between missionaries and colonial officials at the turn of the twentieth century, see J. P. Daughton, An Empire Divided: Religion, Republicanism and the Making of French Colonialism, 1880–1914 (Oxford: Oxford University Press, 2006).

26. CAOM, GGAEF, 5D44.

27. General assembly of the Société d'assistance aux enfants franco-indochinois, 1939 (ANVN 1, RST, 73758).

28. Dr. Blot, "L'œuvre scientifique du colonel A. Bonifacy," Bulletins et mémoires de la Société d'anthropologie de Paris, 8th ser., 2 (1931): 9–10.

29. ANVN 1, GGI, 504.

30. Topalov, "Les réformateurs et leurs réseaux," 13.

31. Note on the charitable organizations protecting children in Indochina, 1926 (CAOM, RST, 3920). Brochure for the Société d'assistance aux enfants franco-indochinois, 1938 (ANVN 1, RST, 71191).

32. de Coutouly, "Note sur les métis en AOF."

33. C. Crévost, "La question des métis est un problème social et moral dont la solution ne doit envisager que l'élément spécial des métis français-annamites," note, 1898 (CAOM, GGI, 7701).

34. General assembly of the Société de protection des métis abandonnés, 1911 (ANVN 1, RST, 5547).

35. Alexis Danan, "Un drame inconnu: Ces Français de hasard que la France abandonne," Franc tireur, no. 2292 (December 12, 1951) (CAOM, Aff. pol., 1194).

36. Pierre Bourdieu, "Le capital social," *Actes de la recherche en sciences sociales* 31 (1980): 2–3.

37. Mathieu, "La protection de l'enfance en Cochinchine," 33.

38. Frederick Cooper and Ann Laura Stoler, "Between Metropole and Colony: Rethinking a Research Agenda," in *Tensions of Empire: Colonial Cultures in a Bourgeois World*, ed. Frederick Cooper and Ann Laura Stoler (Berkeley: University of California Press, 1997).

39. Report by the président de l'Amicale des Français d'Indochine, 1938 (CAOM, AGEFOM, 252/376).

40. Lieutenant Colonel Auguste Bonifacy, "Les métis franco-tonkinois," *Bulletins et mémoires de la Société d'anthropologie de Paris* 6, no. 1 (1910): 635.

41. de Coutouly, "Note sur les métis en AOF," 6. The natives of the "Four Communes of Senegal" were collectively granted citizenship in 1916 (see chapter 4).

42. According to this rule, anyone with a black ancestor, no matter how remote, was considered black. See James F. Davis, *Who Is Black? One Nation's Definition* (University Park: Pennsylvania State University Press, 1991); and Virginia R. Domínguez, *White by Definition: Social Classification in Creole Louisiana* (New Brunswick, NJ: Rutgers University Press, 1986).

43. Letter from the gouverneur du Gabon to the gouverneur général de l'AEF, 1941 (CAOM, GGAEF, 5D44).

44. Michel Foucault, *History of Sexuality*, vol. 1, *An Introduction*, trans. Robert Hurley (New York: Vintage Books, 1990).

45. Statutes of the Société d'assistance aux enfants abandonnés franco-indochinois, 1925 (ANVN 1, RST, 73758).

46. On efforts to develop a semiology of such signs in the late nineteenth century, see Carlo Ginzburg, "Clues: Roots of an Evidentiary Paradigm," in *Clues, Myths and the Historical Method*, trans. John Tedeschi and Anne C. Tedeschi, 96–125 (Baltimore: Johns Hopkins University Press, 1989).

47. Bonifacy, "Les métis franco-tonkinois," 618.

48. Note on the charitable organizations protecting children in Indochina, 1926 (CAOM, RST, 3920).

49. Henri Sambuc, "Les métis franco-annamites en Indochine," *Revue du Pacifique diplomatique et coloniale* 10, no. 1 (1931): 262–63.

50. General assembly of the Société d'assistance aux enfants franco-indochinois of Tonkin, 1926 (ANVN 1, RST, 73758). On the uses of imitation in the colonial context, see Emmanuelle Saada, "Entre 'assimilation' et 'décivilisation': L'imitation et le projet colonial républicain," *Terrain*, 44 (2005): 19–38.

51. Gabriel de Tarde, *Les lois de l'imitation* (1890; repr., Paris: Kimé, 1993), xviii–xix.

52. On Jean-Louis de Lanessan, see Damien Deschamps, "Les sources scientifiques et la politique indochinoise de Jean-Louis de Lanessan, 1891–1894," in *Viêt-Nam, sources et approches: Actes du deuxième colloque international Euroviet*, ed. Philippe Le Failler and Jean-Marie Mancini, 279–92 (Aix-en-Provence, France: Publications de l'Université de Provence, 1995); Paul Rabinow, *French Modern: Norms and Forms of the Social Environment* (Cambridge, MA: MIT Press, 1989); and Claude Nicolet, *L'idée républicaine en France: Essai d'histoire critique, 1789–1924* (Paris: Gallimard, 1982), 305–7.

53. Yvette Conry, *L'introduction du darwinisme en France au XIXe siècle* (Paris: Vrin, 1974), 305–17.

54. Georges Canguilhem, "Le vivant et son milieu," in *La connaissance de la vie* (1952; repr., Paris: Vrin, 1985), 135–36.

55. The link between child care (*puériculture*) and eugenics was specific to France. See William H. Schneider, *Quality and Quantity: The Quest for Biological Regeneration in Twentieth-Century France* (Cambridge and New York: Cambridge University Press, 1990), 82.

56. Jacques Donzelot, *La police des familles* (Paris: Minuit, 2005).

57. *Notice sur la Société d'assistance aux enfants franco-indochinois au Tonkin*, 1937 (ANVN 1, RST, 73758).

58. Note on the Société de protection de l'enfance au Cambodge, January 20, 1917 (CAOM, GGI, 16772).

59. Albert de Pouvourville, "L'Indochine française: Introduction générale," *L'encyclopédie coloniale et maritime* (Paris: Imprimerie Lang, Blanchong et Cie., 1936), 33 (emphasis mine).

60. General assembly of the Société de protection des enfants métis abandonnés, 1907 (ANVN 1, RST, 5547).

61. Note from the président de la Société de protection de l'enfance au Cambodge, 1917 (CAOM, GGI, 16772).

62. Letter from Lieutenant Colonel B. to the inspecteur du travail, 1942 (ANVN 1, GGI, 4809).

63. General assembly of the Société de protection des enfants métis abandonnés, 1912 (ANVN 1, RST, 5547).

64. Note from Crévost, "La question des métis est un problème social et moral."

65. Ivan Jablonka, *Ni père ni mère: Histoire des enfants de l'assistance publique, 1874–1939* (Paris: Seuil, 2006).

66. Statutes of the Société de protection des enfants métis non reconnus, 1898 (CAOM, GGI, 7701).

67. Henri Sambuc, "Enquête sur la question des métis," pt. 2, *Revue indochinoise* 16, no. 2 (1913): 207 (emphasis mine).

68. On the notion of the education of sentiments in the colonial context, see Ann Laura Stoler, *Carnal Knowledge and Imperial Power: Race and the Intimate in Colonial Rule* (Berkeley: University of California Press, 2002), chapter 5.

69. General assembly of the Société d'assistance aux enfants abandonnés franco-indochinois, 1929 (CAOM, RST, 3890).

70. General assembly of the Société d'assistance aux enfants abandonnés franco-indochinois, 1926 (ANVN 1, RST, 73758).

71. Dominique Schnapper, *Community of Citizens: On the Modern Idea of Nationality*, trans. Séverine Rosée (New Brunswick, NJ: Transaction Publishers, 1998).

72. I borrow this idea from Erving Goffman. In his analysis of "social identity," Goffman stressed the importance of the "degree of informational connectedness," a notion that applies both to "obvious signs of social information" and to biographical details. See Erving Goffman, *Stigma: Notes on the Management of Spoiled Identity* (Englewood Cliffs, NJ: Prentice-Hall, 1963), 63.

73. *Notice sur la Société d'assistance aux enfants franco-indochinois du Tonkin*, 1937 (ANVN 1, RST, 73758).

74. Petition of the Comité central de l'AMAS (Aide mutuelle à l'assistance sociale), March 1939 (ANVN 1, GGI, 4810).

75. Report by the directeur du travail to the résident supérieur au Tonkin, September 25, 1941 (CAOM, RST, 3942).

76. I borrow the expression from Marcel Mauss, "Techniques of the Body," in *Marcel*

Mauss: Techniques, Technology and Civilization, ed. Nathan Schlanger, 77–96 (New York: Durkheim Press and Berghahn Books, 2006).

77. Similarly, anthropologists who study kinship have shown that "nurturing," in the sense of child care in all its forms, can *produce* filiation, specifically, elective forms of filiation parallel to blood ties. See Agnès Fine, "Introduction," *Adoptions, ethnologie des parentés choisies*, ed. Agnès Fine (Paris: Maison des sciences de l'homme, 1998).

78. Bernard Vernier, "Prénom et ressemblance: Appropriation symbolique des enfants, économie affective et systèmes de parenté," in *Adoptions, ethnologie des parentés choisies*, ed. Agnès Fine (Paris: Maison des sciences de l'homme, 1998), 118.

79. On relations between the attribution of first names, popular theories of family resemblance, and the general structure of kinship, see Bernard Vernier, *La genèse sociale de sentiments: Aînés et cadets dans l'île grecque de Karpathos* (Paris: EHESS, 1991).

80. Médecin-commandant Ravoux, "Aspects sociaux d'un groupe d'Eurasiens," *Bulletins et mémoires de la Société d'anthropologie de Paris* 9, no. 9 (1948), 181.

81. Report by the résident supérieur au Tonkin on the *métis* inquiry, May 31, 1938 (CAOM, GGI, 53500).

82. General assembly of the Société d'assistance aux enfants abandonnés franco-indochinois, February 10, 1926 (ANVN 1, RST, 73758).

83. Statutes of the Société de protection des enfants métis non reconnus, 1898 (CAOM, GGI, 7701).

84. On this point, see the very important contribution of Ann Laura Stoler, who makes "the education of desire" the centerpiece of colonial practices: Stoler, *Race and the Education of Desire: Foucault's History of Sexuality and the Colonial Order of Things* (Durham, NC: Duke University Press, 1995).

85. The président de la Société protectrice des petits métis abandonnés to the résident supérieur au Tonkin, August 7, 1899 (ANVN 1, RST, 5543).

86. General assembly of the Société d'assistance aux enfants abandonnés franco-indochinois, 1933 (ANVN 1, RST, 73758).

87. Note by the président de la Société de protection de l'enfance au Cambodge about the education in France of half-French children, January 20, 1917 (CAOM, GGI, 16772).

88. The gouverneur général de l'Indochine to the Ministère des Colonies, 1921 (CAOM, SLOTFOM, XII/1).

89. The gouverneur général de l'Indochine to the Ministère des Colonies, 1921 (CAOM, SLOTFOM, XII/1).

90. The président de la Société de protection des enfants métis abandonnés to the gouverneur général de l'Indochine, December 7, 1923 (CAOM, GGI, 16776).

91. Commandant R. to the gouverneur général de l'Indochine, 1923 (CAOM, GGI, 16773).

92. General assembly of the Fondation Jules-Brévié, 1941 (ANVN 1, RST, 73758).

93. Report on the Eurasian problem by the résident de Kien-An, March 1938 (ANVN 1, RST, 71191).

94. Note by the inspecteur général des colonies, 1926 (CAOM, SLOTFOM, XII/1).

95. Paul-André Rosental, "Construire le 'macro' par le 'micro': Fredrik Barth et la microstoria," in *Jeux d'échelle: La micro-analyse à l'expérience*, ed. Jacques Revel, 141–59 (Paris: Gallimard/Seuil, 1996).

96. Marie Salaün, *L'école indigène: Nouvelle-Calédonie, 1885–1945* (Rennes, France: Presses universitaires de Rennes, 2005).

97. See Pierre Brocheux and Daniel Hémery, *Indochina: An Ambiguous Colonization, 1858–1954*, trans. Ly Lan Dill-Klein with Eric Jennings, Nora Taylor, and Noémi Tousignant (Berkeley: University of California Press, 2009), 222.

98. CAOM, GGI, 2711.

99. Ibid.

100. ANVN 1, RST, 8459.

101. The chef du service de l'enseignement public du Tonkin to the résident supérieur au Tonkin, March 21, 1913 (CAOM, RST, 3566).

102. Trinh Van Thao, *L'école française en Indochine* (Paris: Karthala, 1995), 100.

103. General assembly of the Société de protection des enfants métis abandonnés, 1908 (ANVN 1, RST, 5547).

104. Yvon Paillard, "Faut-il admettre les jeunes 'indigènes' dans les collèges français de Madagascar (1913)?" *L'information historique* 33, no. 3 (May–June 1971); Francis De Pressensé, "L'égalité devant l'enseignement à Madagascar," *Les cahiers des droits de l'homme* (1905): 1198–99.

105. The ministre des Colonies to the gouverneur général de Madagascar, March 31, 1913 (CAOM, SG Mad, 325/843).

106. The chef des services des affaires politiques to the directeur de l'enseignement, May 14, 1928 (CAOM, GGM, 6[10]D4).

107. Guy Pedroncini, ed., *Histoire militaire de la France*, vol. 3, *De 1871 à 1940* (Paris: PUF, 1992), 43–69.

108. Werner Sollors, *Neither Black nor White Yet Both: Thematic Explorations of Interracial Literature* (New York: Oxford University Press, 1997), 112–41.

109. The président de la Société de protection de l'enfance au Cambodge to the gouverneur général de l'Indochine, February 10, 1917 (CAOM, GGI, 2065) (emphasis in the original).

110. The gouverneur général de l'Indochine to the résident supérieur au Tonkin, May 3, 1912 (CAOM, RST, 3373).

111. Note by the état-major on the situation from the point of view of recruitment of unrecognized Franco-Asian *métis* in Indochina, June 14, 1911 (ANVN 1, RST, 5561).

112. Assembly of the Société de protection des enfants métis abandonnés, 1912 (ANVN 1, RST, 5547).

113. Circular of the Ministry of Colonies, January 5, 1928 (CAOM, Aff. Pol., 1194). In the literature on the question, this law is often referred to as the "Taittinger law." This is an erroneous appellation, because the Parliament never voted on this question.

114. The notion of "jurisdiction" is central to Andrew Abbott's sociology of the professions. He shows that what distinguishes the professions and other forms of expertise is the existence of specific jurisdictions. See Andrew Abbott, *The System of Professions: An Essay on the Division of Expert Labor* (Chicago: University of Chicago Press, 1988).

115. General assembly of the Société d'assistance aux enfants abandonnés franco-indochinois, 1926 (ANVN 1, RST, 73758).

116. Until 1972, children born of an adulterous relationship could not be recognized by their fathers.

117. Bonifacy, "Les métis franco-tonkinois," 636 (emphasis mine).

CHAPTER FOUR

This chapter draws on earlier work: Emmanuelle Saada, "Une nationalité par degrés: Civilité et citoyenneté en situation coloniale," in *L'esclavage, la colonisation et après*, ed. Patrick Weil and Stéphane Dufoix, 193–227 (Paris: PUF, 2005).

1. On penal justice in the colonies, see Pierre Dareste, "Droit public indigène," *Traité de droit colonial*, vol. 2 (Cannes and Paris: Imprimerie Roubaudy, 1931), 486–98.

2. Olivier Le Cour Grandmaison, *De l'indigénat. Anatomie d'un "monstre" juridique: Le droit colonial en Algérie et dans l'Empire français* (Paris: la Découverte, 2010), 181.

3. On the Code de l'indigénat, see Isabelle Merle, "De la 'légalisation' de la violence en contexte colonial: Le régime de l'indigénat en question," *Politix* 17, no. 66 (2004): 137–62.

4. In Indochina, the decree of May 20, 1926, opened some posts in the European section to natives. Similar decrees were issued in FWA on February 23, 1928, and in Madagascar on April 15, 1930.

5. Emmanuel Besson, *La législation civile de l'Algérie: Étude sur la condition des personnes et sur le régime des biens en Algérie* (Paris: Librairie Maresq ainé, 1894), 120.

6. Vietnamese elites called attention to the similarities between the tax card and the anthropometric files used in criminal investigations. See J. Mérimée, "De l'accession des Indochinois à la qualité de citoyen français" (PhD diss., Université de Toulouse, Faculté de droit, 1931), 44.

7. Jean-Étienne-Marie Portalis, "Discours préliminaire prononcé lors de la présentation du projet au gouvernement," in *Naissance du Code civil: La raison du législateur*, ed. François Ewald (Paris: Flammarion, 1989), 36.

8. On this work of universalization, see Pierre Rosanvallon, *Le sacre du citoyen: Histoire du suffrage universel en France* (Paris: Gallimard, 1992; repr. "Folio histoire," 2001), 393–422. Citation is to the 1992 edition.

9. Patrick Weil, *How to Be French: Nationality in the Making since 1789*, trans. Catherine Porter (Durham, NC: Duke University Press, 2009).

10. On Kelsen's definition of nationality, see Olivier Beaud, *La puissance de l'État* (Paris: PUF, 1994), 118–19.

11. André Weiss, *Traité théorique et pratique de droit international privé*, 2nd ed., vol. 1, *De la nationalité* (Paris: Sirey, 1907), 6–7, 46.

12. On the relationships between nationality and citizenship during the Revolution, see Weil, *How to Be French*, chapter 1; Peter Sahlins, *Unnaturally French: Foreign Citizens in the Old Regime and After* (Ithaca, NY: Cornell University Press, 2004), chapter 8; and Serge Slama, "Le privilège du national: Étude historique de la condition civique des étrangers en France" (PhD diss., Université de Paris X, Nanterre, 2003), part 1.

13. On the status of the notion of citizenship in law, see Danièle Lochak, "La citoyenneté: Un concept juridique flou," in *Citoyenneté et nationalité: Perspectives en France et au Québec*, ed. Dominique Colas, Claude Emeri, and Jacques Zylberberg, 179–207 (Paris: PUF, 1991).

14. For an enlightening analysis of the Algerian case, please refer to Laure Blévis, "Sociologie d'un droit colonial. Citoyenneté et nationalité en Algérie (1865–1947): Une exception républicaine?" (PhD diss., Institut d'études politiques d'Aix-en-Provence, France, 2004).

15. Laurent Dubois, *A Colony of Citizens: Revolution and Slave Emancipation in the French Caribbean, 1787–1804* (Chapel Hill: University of North Carolina Press, 2004).

16. "Alger, 24 février 1862," published in Robert Estoublon, *Jurisprudence algérienne de 1830 à 1876*, vol. 3, *1859–1867* (Algiers: Adolphe Jourdan, 1890), 13.

17. *Rapports et projets de décrets de la commission instituée pour préparer l'acte d'abolition immédiate de l'esclavage* (Paris: Imprimerie nationale, 1848), 21–22. In Algeria, the commission did not want to grant more rights to emancipated slaves than to their former masters.

18. Ministère de la Justice, *La nationalité française: Textes et documents* (Paris: la Documentation française, 1996), 228.

19. On naturalization in Algeria, see Laure Blévis, "La citoyenneté française au miroir de la colonisation: Étude des demandes de naturalisation des 'sujets français' en Algérie coloniale," *Genèses* 53 (2003): 25–47. On the question of dignity, please refer to Emmanuelle Saada, "The Empire of Law: Dignity, Prestige and Domination in the Colonial Situation," *French Politics, Culture and Society* 20, no. 2 (2002): 98–120.

20. See Blévis, "Sociologie d'un droit colonial," 83–84.

21. See Weil, *How to Be French*, 52–53.

22. Ministère de la Justice, *La nationalité française*, 196.

23. Henry Solus, *Traité de la condition des indigènes en droit privé, colonies et pays de protectorat et pays sous mandat* (Paris: Librairie du Recueil Sirey, 1927), 59.

24. See Georges Levasseur, *La situation juridique des Chinois en Indochine depuis les accords de Nankin* (Hanoi: Imprimerie d'Extrême-Orient, 1939).

25. Cited in "La condition juridique des indigènes en Nouvelle-Calédonie," *Dareste* II (1919): 14.

26. "La nationalité aux colonies," *Dareste* II (1911): 9.

27. The colonial case offers a good example of the "perpetual imbalance of nationality" discussed by the legal scholar François Terré, "Réflexions sur la notion de nationalité," *Revue critique de droit international privé* 64, no. 2 (1975): 210.

28. Weil, *How to Be French*, 216–19.

29. Auguste-Reynald Werner, "Essai sur la réglementation de la nationalité dans le droit colonial français" (PhD diss., Université de Genève, Faculté de droit, 1936), 15, 41.

30. Cour d'appel de l'Indochine, "27 octobre 1910," *Dareste* III (1911): 170.

31. Solus, *Traité de la condition des indigènes en droit privé*, 11.

32. Paul Moreau, "De la condition juridique, politique et économique des indigènes de l'AOF" (PhD diss., Université de Paris, Faculté de droit, 1938), 194.

33. Solus, *Traité de la condition des indigènes en droit privé*, 230.

34. This point has been noted by Pierre Rosanvallon, *Le sacre du citoyen: Histoire du suffrage universel en France* (Paris: Gallimard, 1992; repr., "Folio histoire," 2001), 424. Citation refers to the 1992 edition.

35. On the stakes of the law of 1919, see Blévis, "Sociologie d'un droit colonial," 151–70.

36. Solus, *Traité de la condition des indigènes en droit privé*, 231.

37. Pierre Dareste, "Les nouveaux citoyens français," *Dareste* II (1916): 7.

38. J. Mérimée, "De l'accession des Indochinois à la qualité de citoyen français" (PhD diss., Université de Toulouse, Faculté de droit, 1931), 67.

39. Gérard Noiriel, "Nations, nationalités, nationalismes: Pour une socio-histoire comparée," in *État, nation et immigration* (Paris: Belin, 2001).

40. Report on the legal condition of French subjects in the colonies and the prerogatives resulting from the quality of the subject, presented before the Conseil supérieur des colonies by M. Tesseron, 1926 (CAOM, CSC, 26).

41. "Alger, 5 novembre 1903," *Revue algérienne et tunisienne de législation et de jurisprudence* 2 (1904): 25. On this question, see André Bonnichon, *La conversion au christianisme de l'indigène musulman algérien et ses effets juridiques (un cas de conflit colonial)* (Paris: Librairie du Recueil Sirey, 1931).

42. Dr. Rudolf Asmis, "La condition juridique des indigènes dans l'Afrique occidentale française," *Dareste* II (1910): 23.

43. Martin Deming Lewis, "One Hundred Million Frenchmen: The 'Assimilation' The-

ory in French Colonial Policy," *Comparative Studies in Society and History* 4, no. 2 (1962).

44. This law did not apply to Algeria, which became officially a French possession only in 1834.

45. Dareste, "Les nouveaux citoyens français," 7.

46. Speech by M. Marchal, in *Congrès international de sociologie coloniale*, vol. 1 (Paris: Arthur Rousseau, 1901), 237.

47. See also Blévis, "Sociologie d'un droit colonial," 289–312.

48. Asmis, "La condition juridique des indigènes dans l'Afrique occidentale française," 19.

49. See, for example, Arthur Girault, *Principes de colonisation et de législation coloniale*, 5th ed., vol. 2 (Paris: Sirey, 1929), 389–90.

50. On this point, see Étienne Antonelli, *Manuel de législation coloniale* (Paris: PUF, 1925), 156; and Damien Deschamps, "La république aux colonies: Le citoyen, l'indigène et le fonctionnaire (vers 1848, vers 1900)" (PhD diss., Université de Grenoble, 1998).

51. Mérimée, "De l'accession des Indochinois à la qualité de citoyen français," 66–67.

52. See, in particular, the debates of the *Congrès colonial international* (Paris: Challamel, 1889).

53. Speech given by Bernard Lavergne, professor at the Faculté de droit de Lille, at the June 2, 1928, session of the Conseil supérieur des colonies (CAOM, CSC, 25).

54. Hence the need to modify the distinction made by Gérard Noiriel and Stéphane Beaud between French thinking about nationality, which supposedly emphasized socialization by way of institutions, and the American position, which allegedly emphasized interactions among individuals as a way of transmitting national values. See Stéphane Beaud and Gérard Noiriel, "Penser l'intégration des immigrés," *Hommes et migrations* 1183 (1990): 43–53.

55. Albert Billiard, *Politique et organisation coloniales: Principes généraux* (Paris: V. Giard et E. Brière, 1899), 8.

56. See Alban Bensa, "Colonialisme, racisme et ethnologie en Nouvelle-Calédonie," *Ethnologie française* 18, no. 2 (1988): 187–97.

57. Decision of October 29, 1912, *Dareste* I (1914): 271.

58. Decree of October 14, 1936, *Dareste* I (1937): 128.

59. Laure Blévis estimated in her dissertation that there were between three thousand and six thousand grants of citizenship during the entire colonial period. Blévis, "Sociologie d'un droit colonial," 412. On the question of "motivation," see Blévis, "La citoyenneté française au miroir de la colonisation."

60. *Journal officiel, débats parlementaires*, Chambre des députés, session of February 1, 1923, 504.

61. The available figures combine the naturalization of foreigners in Indochina with grants of citizenship, and it is impossible to distinguish between the two.

62. Mérimée, "De l'accession des Indochinois à la qualité de citoyen français," 156.

63. Henry Solus reports that in 1926, there were 327 rejections for 8,925 requests for naturalization of foreigners in metropolitan France. Solus, *Traité de la condition des indigènes en droit privé*, 118.

64. What follows is based on a sample of ninety-three files of natives who obtained French citizenship in Indochina between 1898 and 1944. (Thirty-eight of them were *métis*, and thirty-seven individuals had two native parents. In eighteen cases, the files did not contain sufficient information to determine whether the candidate was

of mixed blood.) I also looked at seven files concerning applications for naturalization by foreigners residing in Indochina. Clearly, this sample is not statistically representative. The counts should be taken merely as indicators. For a more detailed analysis, see Emmanuelle Saada, "La 'question des métis' dans les colonies françaises: Socio-histoire d'une catégoire juridique (Indochine et autres territoires de l'Empire français, années 1890–années 1950)" (PhD diss., École des hautes études en sciences sociales, Paris, 2001).

65. All the European applicants in my sample obtained naturalization. The only foreigner whose application was rejected was a Chinese clerk of a notary.

66. Report of the general government of Indochina to the Ministry of Colonies, October 19, 1925 (CAOM, GGI, 42706) (emphasis mine). The governor's recommendation was accepted.

67. CAOM, GGI, 44799.

68. These questionnaires are found in many files from the 1930s and 1940s. Today, the "assimilation evaluations" conducted by the prefectural staff on applicants for naturalization adhere to a similar logic but are more succinct. Apart from notes on linguistic ability, the forms ask only if the candidate "lives in an environment that is primarily French or primarily foreign (family, neighbors, work, and leisure)," "participates in local activities (social, associative, cultural, sports, and so forth)," and "seems assimilated to our ways and customs."

69. ANVN 1, RST, 79378/15.

70. Florence Renucci, "Confrontation entre droit français et droits indigènes: Le cas des mariages mixtes en Afrique du Nord, 1870–1919," *Cahiers aixois d'histoire des droits de l'outre-mer français* 1 (2002): 147–91.

71. Arthur Girault, *Condition des indigènes au point de vue de la législation civile et criminelle et de la distribution de la justice*, report presented at the Congrès international de sociologie coloniale, Exposition universelle internationale de 1900 (Paris: Arthur Rousseau, 1901), 33.

72. Speech given by Arthur Girault in the "Discussion de la question des métis et de l'attitude des gouvernements à leur égard," in *Institut colonial international, rapports préliminaires: Session de Brunswick*, vol. 1, *Discussions et rapports* (Brussels: Établissements généraux d'imprimerie, 1911), 312.

73. Note about the draft decree proposing the creation of a category of "indigène d'élite," presented by M. Bernard Lavergne, April 10, 1927, and minutes of the June 13, 1928, session of the Conseil supérieur des colonies (CAOM, CSC, 25).

74. Lavergne, note about the draft decree.

75. CAOM, CSC, 25.

76. Naturalization dossier of a *métis*, 1918 (CAOM, GGI, 44843).

77. Ernest Outrey to the ministre des Colonies, October 26, 1922 (CAOM, GGI, 45132).

78. In my sample of one hundred cases, thirty-seven concerned native candidates, of which twenty-one were rejected, three postponed, one withdrawn, and only twelve granted. Of thirty-four cases of *métis* that resulted in a decision, eighteen were rejected and sixteen approved. The ethnic origin of the remaining applicants for naturalization is ambiguous.

79. Naturalization dossier, 1921 (CAOM, GGI, 42790).

80. Luc Boltanski, *L'amour et la justice comme compétences: Trois essais de sociologie de l'action* (Paris: Métailié, 1990).

81. See, for example, the naturalization files for 1914 and 1919 (CAOM, GGI, 42807 and 44776).
82. ANVN 1, RST, 79397.
83. ANVN 1, RST, 79378.
84. ANVN 1, GGI, 6564/12. All names have been altered to protect the anonymity of the individuals involved.

CHAPTER FIVE

This chapter draws on a previously published article: Emmanuelle Saada, "Paternité et citoyenneté en situation coloniale: Le débat sur les 'reconnaissances frauduleuses' et la construction d'un droit impérial," *Politix* 17, no. 66 (2004).

1. Ann Laura Stoler offers an illuminating anthropological analysis of the anxiety produced by fraudulent recognitions in Stoler, *Carnal Knowledge and Imperial Power: Race and the Intimate in Colonial Rule* (Berkeley: University of California Press, 2002), 91–96.
2. Specifically, the decrees of March 28, 1918, for Indochina (*Dareste* I [1918]: 231); November 7, 1916, for Madagascar (*Dareste* I [1917]: 48); January 18, 1918, for FEA (*Dareste* I [1918]: 203); April 24, 1919, for settlements in Oceania (*Dareste* I [1919]: 682); and December 15, 1922, for New Caledonia, FWA, and settlements in India (*Dareste* I [1923]: 266–67).
3. Note from the Service de l'Indochine to the Bureau des affaires politiques du Ministère des Colonies, no author, n.d. [1918] (CAOM, Aff. pol., 1194).
4. Raoul Abor, *Des reconnaissances frauduleuses d'enfants naturels en Indochine* (Hanoi: Imprimerie tonkinoise, 1917), 14.
5. See Alain Desrosières, *The Politics of Large Numbers: A History of Statistical Reasoning*, trans. Camille Naish (Cambridge, MA: Harvard University Press, 1998).
6. According to the census of 1921; see Pierre Brocheux and Daniel Hémery, *Indochina: An Ambiguous Colonization, 1858–1954*, trans. Ly Lan Dill-Klein with Eric Jennings, Nora Taylor, and Noémi Tousignant (Berkeley: University of California Press, 2009), 183.
7. To my knowledge, there was only one case of a new citizen fraudulently recognizing a native subject (civil court of Saigon, October 31, 1903, cited in Abor, *Des reconnaissances frauduleuses*, 5). This dearth can perhaps be explained in part in terms of social characteristics of the naturalized (who were selected for their "honorable" character), but in any case, there were very few of them among the population of citizens—perhaps a few dozen in the early years of the twentieth century and a few hundred by the 1920s and 1930s.
8. J. Mérimée, "De l'accession des Indochinois à la qualité de citoyen français" (PhD diss., Université de Toulouse, Faculté de droit, 1931), 201.
9. Abor, *Des reconnaissances frauduleuses*, 5.
10. Ibid., 30.
11. Cited by Médecin-commandant Ravoux, "Aspects sociaux d'un groupe d'Eurasiens," *Bulletins et mémoires de la Société d'anthropologie de Paris* 9, no. 9 (1948): 188–89.
12. Lieutenant Colonel Auguste Bonifacy, "Les métis franco-tonkinois," *Bulletins et mémoires de la Société d'anthropologie de Paris* 6, no. 1 (1910): 641.
13. The procureur général to the gouverneur général de l'Indochine, March 31, 1914 (CAOM, Aff. pol., 1194).

14. Gérard Noiriel, "The Identification of the Citizen: The Birth of Republican Civil Status in France," in *Documenting Individual Identity: The Development of State Practices in the Modern World*, ed. Jane Caplan and John Torpey, 28–38 (Princeton, NJ: Princeton University Press, 2001).

15. Émile Mersier, *Traité théorique et pratique des actes de l'état civil* (Paris: Dupont et Marescq, 1873), 451.

16. Ibid., 448–53.

17. "The Civil Code defined civil identification as the certification of a statement and not research into the truth of an individual's identity." Noiriel, "Identification of the Citizen," 44.

18. Gérard Cornu, *Vocabulaire juridique*, 3rd ed. (1st ed., Paris: PUF, 1987; Paris: PUF, Collection Quadrige, 2002), 615. Citation refers to the 2002 edition.

19. Mersier, *Traité théorique et pratique des actes d'état civil*, 457.

20. See the February 26, 1869, decision of the Marseille tribunal, cited by Mersier, *Traité théorique et pratique des actes d'état civil*, 460.

21. Case cited in Abor, *Des reconnaissances frauduleuses*, 32–33.

22. This became a subject of growing criticism. For instance, André Goguey, "Des reconnaissances et légitimations de complaisance" (PhD diss., Université de Dijon, Faculté de droit, 1958), 123, states: "People say that public order depends on disclosure of the truth. But at the same time, the Cour de cassation asserts that 'family tranquillity' is more important than correcting a fraudulent filiation."

23. See Marcela Iacub, *L'empire du ventre: Pour une autre histoire de la maternité* (Paris: Fayard, 2004): "The codifiers of 1804 . . . wanted to base filiations not on the truth of parentage, meaning the sexual behavior of individuals, but rather on *will*" (17–18; emphasis in the original). The author offers a highly illuminating analysis of various cases of *substitution* and *supposition* (83–101).

24. Goguey, "Des reconnaissances et légitimations de complaisance," 15.

25. Ibid., 10.

26. Cited by René Théry, "Véritable père et paternité vraie" (Paris: Juris classeur périodique, 1979), 1:6.

27. Cour de cassation, chambre civile, audience of December 17, 1913.

28. Abor, *Des reconnaissances frauduleuses*, 39.

29. For a similar analysis of naturalization in contemporary France, see Abdelmalek Sayad, *The Suffering of the Immigrant*, trans. David Macey (Cambridge: Polity, 2004), chapter 6.

30. Note from the Service de l'Indochine to the Bureau des affaires politiques du Ministère des Colonies, no author, n.d. [1918] (CAOM, Aff. pol., 1194).

31. *Dareste* III (1913): 60.

32. The procureur général to the gouverneur général de l'Indochine, March 31, 1914 (CAOM, Aff. pol., 1194).

33. Henry Solus, *Traité de la condition des indigènes en droit privé, colonies et pays de protectorat et pays sous mandat* (Paris: Librairie du Recueil Sirey, 1927), 303–12.

34. Abor, *Des reconnaissances frauduleuses*, 39.

35. Preliminary report on the decree of March 28, 1934, specifying the penalties for fictitious recognition of paternity in Indochina, *Journal officiel de l'Indochine française*, March 31, 1934. *Dareste* I (1934): 489.

36. October 31, 1903, decision, cited by Abor, *Des reconnaissances frauduleuses*, 5–6.

37. September 24, 1908, circular from the procureur général, cited by Abor, *Des reconnaissances frauduleuses*, 8.

38. See Frederick Cooper and Ann Laura Stoler, eds., *Tensions of Empire: Colonial Cultures in a Bourgeois World* (Berkeley: University of California Press, 1997).

39. Goguey, "Des reconnaissances et légitimations de complaisance," 10. Marie-Josèphe Gebler, *Le droit français de la filiation et la vérité* (Paris: Librairie générale de droit et de jurisprudence, 1970), 280–81.

40. Arthur Girault, *Principes de colonisation et de législation coloniale*, 5th ed., vol. 2 (Paris: Sirey, 1929), 523.

41. François Terré, *Introduction générale au droit*, 4th ed. (Paris: Dalloz, 1998), 118n2.

42. Indicating the chambre civile of the Cour de cassation.

43. On this matter, see Abor, *Des reconnaissances frauduleuses d'enfants naturels en Indochine*, 15; and the arrêt de la Cour de cassation no. 59709, from December 17, 1913 (affaire Bodin).

44. Arrêt de la Cour de cassation no. 59709, from December 17, 1913.

45. Report reproduced in Abor, *Des reconnaissances frauduleuses d'enfants naturels en Indochine*, 25.

46. An alternative argument was to abolish the hierarchy between "public order" and "family tranquillity" and assert that both were of *equal importance* in colonial society. We find this argument in a note appended to the 1913 judgment: "Contrary to what the judgment states, it seems to us that in these circumstances, the questions of paternity and filiation concern the public order and defense of society *as much as* the honor and tranquillity of families, which are in any case themselves consonant with the public order." Note on the December 17, 1913, decision of the Cour de cassation, in *Penant* I (1913): 115 (emphasis mine).

47. Jean Carbonnier, *Droit civil*, vol. 2, *La famille, l'enfant, le couple*, 20th ed. (Paris: PUF, 1999), 268.

48. Chaim Perelman and Lucie Olbrechts-Tyeca, *The New Rhetoric: A Treatise on Argumentation*, trans. John Wilkinson and Purcell Weaver (Notre Dame, IN: University of Notre Dame Press, 1969), 81.

49. Judicial records from the colonial era are stored in Vietnam, and access to these archives, particularly those involving provincial courts, was extremely difficult in 1999, when this research was conducted.

50. Mérimée, "De l'accession des Indochinois à la qualité de citoyen français," 201 (emphasis mine).

51. Note that the term *nationality* is here used improperly and that *quality of citizen* would have been more correct. But this confusion reminds us that citizenship was the truth of nationality. On these issues, see Laure Blévis, "Les avatars de la citoyenneté en Algérie coloniale ou les paradoxes d'une catégorisation," *Droit et société* 48 (2001): 557–80.

52. The first proclamation of this type followed the conquest of Algeria, and similar proclamations can be found in all subsequent treaties of annexation (see chapter 4).

53. The gouverneur général de Madagascar to the ministre des Colonies, November 1915 (CAOM, GGM, 6[10]D4).

54. Yvon Paillard, "Faut-il admettre les jeunes 'indigènes' dans les collèges français de Madagascar (1913)?" *L'information historique* 33, no. 3 (May–June 1971): 115–19.

55. February 24, 1913, circular from the gouverneur général Albert Picquié on the subject of *métis* children recognized by their fathers, published in the *Journal officiel de Madagascar*, March 15, 1913 (CAOM, GGM, 6[10]D4) (emphasis in the original).

56. Antony Jully, "La question des enfants métis," *Revue de Madagascar: Organe du Comité de Madagascar* 7 (1905): 516 (emphasis mine).

57. Report to the Comité central on the modifications that could be made to the legal status of *métis* children by the Tananarive section of the Ligue pour la défense des droits de l'homme et du citoyen, November 1912 (CAOM, GGM, 6[10]D4).

58. The gouverneur général de Madagascar to the ministre des Colonies, November 1915 (CAOM, GGM, 6[10]D4).

59. November 7, 1916, decree related to the recognition of illegitimate *métis* children in Madagascar and dependent territories. *Journal officiel de Madagascar*, November 13, 1916, *Dareste* I (1917): 48.

60. The father had to appear in person before the clerk responsible for identity records, who then transmitted the act of recognition to the prosecutor or one of his subordinates. The prosecutor then conducted an investigation and forwarded the results to a court or justice of the peace. The judge then heard the father, mother, and any other witness deemed pertinent to the case before issuing a decision in open court that accepted or rejected the act of recognition.

61. Note from the Bureau des affaires politiques, June 21, 1916 (CAOM, Aff. pol., 1194).

62. Preliminary report on the March 28, 1918, decree modifying for Indochina Articles 8 and 339 of the Civil Code. *Journal officiel de l'Indochine française*, April 7, 1918, *Dareste* I (1918): 231.

63. Note on the draft of a decree related to Articles 8 and 339 of the Civil Code, no author, n.d. [Ministère des Colonies, Service de l'Indochine, 1918] (CAOM, Aff. pol., 1194).

64. Preliminary report on the March 28, 1918, decree.

65. Note on the draft of a decree related to Articles 8 and 339 of the Civil Code (CAOM, Aff. pol., 1194).

66. Preliminary report on the decree related to the recognition of illegitimate children in FEA, *Dareste* I (1918): 203.

67. Terence Ranger, "The Invention of Tradition in Colonial Africa," in *The Invention of Tradition*, ed. Eric Hobsbawm and Terence Ranger, 211–62 (1983; repr., Cambridge: Cambridge University Press, 1996).

68. Note from the Service du secrétariat et contreseing to the Service de l'Indochine, May 27, 1914 (CAOM, Aff. pol., 1194).

69. Circular from the ministre des Colonies to the gouverneurs, March 26, 1919 (CAOM, Aff. pol., 1194).

70. Reply from the gouverneur de la Guadeloupe, July 24, 1919 (CAOM, Aff. pol., 1194).

71. CAOM, GGI, 65316.

72. The procureur général to the gouverneur général de l'Indochine, October 28, 1933 (CAOM, GGI, 65316).

73. CAOM, GGI, 65319.

74. Iacub, *L'empire du ventre*, 177.

75. Ibid., 178, 151.

76. Bill related to immigration control and foreign presence in France, presentation of motives made by Nicolas Sarkozy on April 30, 2003, http://www.assemblee-nationale.fr/12/projets/pl0823.asp.

77. *Immigration clandestine: Une réalité inacceptable, une réponse ferme, juste et humaine,* report by investigatory commission no. 300 (2005–6), submitted April 6, 2006, http://www.senat.fr/rap/r05-300-1/r05-300-1_mono.html.

78. Ibid.

79. Ibid.
80. Ibid.

CHAPTER SIX

1. The gouverneur général de l'Indochine to the ministre des Colonies, July 8, 1911 (CAOM, GGI, 16621).

2. On the history of parliamentary debates on paternity searches, see Nicolae G. Raicovicianu, "La loi du 16 novembre 1912 et l'action en déclaration de paternité naturelle" (PhD diss., Université de Paris, Faculté de droit, 1913).

3. To my knowledge, the only systematic historical study of the law authorizing investigation of paternity is the thesis of Jean Elisabeth Pedersen, "Legislating the Family: Gender, Population, and Republican Politics in France, 1870–1920" (PhD diss., University of Chicago, 1993), which was partly published as Jean Elisabeth Pedersen, *Legislating the French Family: Feminism, Theater, and Republican Politics, 1870–1920* (New Brunswick, NJ: Rutgers University Press, 2003). The author discusses the colonial variant of the debate in "'Special Customs': Paternity Suits and Citizenship in France and the Colonies, 1870–1912," in *Domesticating the Empire: Race, Gender and Family Life in French and Dutch Colonialism*, ed. Julia Clancy-Smith and Frances Gouda, 43–64 (Charlottesville: University of Virginia Press, 1998). Since she relies exclusively on records of parliamentary debates, she cannot take account of the concerns of colonial actors and concludes, no doubt correctly but quite broadly, that "race," "class," and "gender" were interrelated in this debate.

4. On the evolution of policy regarding childhood in the nineteenth century, see Catherine Rollet, *La politique à l'égard de la petite enfance sous la IIIe République* (Paris: INED, 1990); and Catherine Rollet, *Les enfants au XIXe siècle* (Paris: Hachette littératures, 2001).

5. Sylvia Schafer, *Children in Moral Danger and the Problem of Government in Third Republic France* (Princeton, NJ: Princeton University Press, 1997).

6. Elinor A. Accampo, Rachel G. Fuchs, and Mary Lynn Stewart, eds., *Gender and the Politics of Social Reform in France, 1870–1914* (Baltimore: Johns Hopkins University Press, 1995).

7. Cited by Marcela Iacub, *L'empire du ventre: Pour une autre histoire de la maternité* (Paris: Fayard, 2004), 110.

8. Ibid., chapter 2.

9. See, for example, the speech given by Georges Bry, law professor at the Université d'Aix-en-Provence, before the Congrès des sociétés savantes on April 21, 1897, which put the question of paternity searches onto the agenda. The report was published in the *Bulletin du Comité des travaux historiques et scientifiques* (Paris: Imprimerie nationale, 1897).

10. See Marie-Victoire Louis, *Le droit de cuissage, France, 1860–1930* (Paris: Éditions de l'atelier, 1994).

11. See Abel Pouzol, *La recherche de paternité: Étude critique de sociologie et de législation comparée* (Paris: Giard et Brière, 1902).

12. Pierre-Antoine Fenet, *Recueil complet des travaux préparatoires du Code civil*, vol. 10 (Paris: Videcoq, 1836), 77.

13. For an overview of the demographic crisis of the late nineteenth century, see Jacques Dupâquier, ed., *Histoire de la population française*, vol. 3, *De 1789 á 1914* (Paris: PUF, 1988). More closely related to my thesis, see Alain Becchia, "Les milieux parlementaires et la dépopulation de 1900 à 1914," *Communications* 44 (1986): 201–46.

14. See Robert A. Nye, *Crime, Madness and Politics in Modern France: The Medical Concept of National Decline* (Princeton, NJ: Princeton University Press, 1984); and Daniel Pick, *Faces of Degeneration: A European Disorder, c. 1848–1918* (New York: Cambridge University Press, 1989).

15. Becchia, "Les milieux parlementaires et la dépopulation de 1900 à 1914," 207.

16. This was of course a central theme of Frédéric Le Play, one of the most ardent advocates of investigation of paternity, who also criticized "the industrial proxenetism and relaxation of morals that the growth of industry inevitably produced," in *La réforme sociale en France déduite de l'observation comparée des peuples européens* (Geneva: Slatkine, 1982; first published 1864 by H. Plon).

17. Paul Ponsolle, *La dépopulation* (Paris: Baillère et Messager, 1893).

18. Pouzol, *La recherche de paternité*, 119.

19. Ibid., 142–58.

20. Ibid., 151.

21. *Journal officiel, débats parlementaires* (Paris: Sénat, 1910), 1482.

22. Jean-Louis Halperin, *Histoire du droit privé français depuis 1804* (Paris: PUF, 1996), 206.

23. Jules Barni, *La morale dans la démocratie* [1868], *suivi du Manuel républicain* [1872] (Paris: Kimé, 1992), 345.

24. On the "quasi family," see *Lois annotées, décrets, ordonnances, avis du Conseil d'état, etc., avec notes historiques, de concordance et de jurisprudence*, year 1913 (Paris: Larose, 1911–18), 437.

25. René Savatier, *La recherche de paternité: Étude pratique de législation et de jurisprudence* (Paris: Dalloz, 1927), 76.

26. Ibid., 1.

27. In the fourth edition of his course, in 1870, Charles Demolombe, a noted law professor, argued that Article 340 was "based on the most powerful considerations of public order" and deserved to be maintained "given the state of morality in our society." Quoted in Anne Lefebvre-Taillard, *Introduction historique au droit des personnes et de la famille* (Paris: PUF, 1996), 368.

28. Savatier, *La recherche de paternité*, 3.

29. Speech given by Louis Martin before the Senate, November 11, 1910, *Lois annotées*, 437.

30. Ibid.

31. Anne Martin-Fugier, *La place des bonnes: La domesticité féminine à Paris en 1900* (Paris: Grasset, 1979; repr., Paris: Perrin, 2004), 303. Citation refers to the Perrin edition.

32. Pierre Dareste, *Traité de droit colonial*, 2 vols. (Cannes and Paris: Imprimerie Robaudy, 1931), 1:244.

33. For a report on debates concerning the 1912 law in the National Assembly and Senate, see *Lois annotées*, 430–49.

34. The ministre des Colonies to the gouverneur général de l'Indochine, July 27, 1910 (CAOM, GGI, 16621).

35. June 26, 1911, session of the Conseil colonial de Cochinchine (CAOM, GGI, 16621).

36. The administrateur de Mayotte to the gouverneur général de Madagascar, October 18, 1910 (CAOM, GGM, 6[10]D4).

37. "Chronique législative de droit civil en 1912 (filiation)," *Revue critique de législation et de jurisprudence* 42 (1913): 240.

38. Report by the Chamber of Commerce of Haiphong on the proposed application of Article 340 of the Code civil, December 26, 1910 (CAOM, GGI, 16621).
39. Report by the Chamber of Commerce of Haiphong (CAOM, GGI, 16621).
40. *L'avenir du Tonkin*, February 28, 1913 (emphasis mine).
41. Report from the résident supérieur en Annam to the gouverneur général de l'Indochine, February 4, 1911 (CAOM, GGI, 16621).
42. Thomas Laqueur, *Making Sex: Body and Gender from the Greeks to Freud* (Cambridge, MA: Harvard University Press, 1990).
43. The résident supérieur au Laos to the gouverneur général de l'Indochine, January 14, 1911 (CAOM, GGI, 16621).
44. Dr. Louis Barot, *Guide de l'Européen dans l'Afrique occidentale, à l'usage des militaires, fonctionnaires, commerçants, colons et touristes* (Paris: Flammarion, 1902), 328.
45. Report by the résident supérieur en Annam (CAOM, GGI, 16621).
46. See, in particular, Ann Laura Stoler, *Carnal Knowledge and Imperial Power: Race and the Intimate in Colonial Rule* (Berkeley: University of California Press, 2002).
47. Alain Corbin, "Coulisses," in *De la Révolution à la Grande Guerre*, ed. Michelle Perrot, Alain Corbin, Roger-Henri Guerrand, et al., vol. 4 of *Histoire de la vie privée*, ed. Philippe Aries and Georges Duby (Paris: Seuil, 1987), 538.
48. Report by the résident supérieur en Annam (CAOM, GGI, 16621) (emphasis in the original).
49. For instance, in 1928, in all of Indochina, there were 213 marriages between Europeans, 41 marriages between a European male and a native female, and 10 marriages between a European woman and a native man. See Gouvernement général de l'Indochine, Direction des affaires économiques, *Annuaire statistique de l'Indochine: Recueil de statistiques relatives aux années 1923 à 1929*, vol. 2 (Hanoi: Imprimerie d'Extrême Orient, 1931). All my data indicate that before World War I, "mixed marriages" were much less frequent.
50. Report by the résident supérieur en Annam (CAOM, GGI, 16621).
51. Report by the Chamber of Commerce of Haiphong on the proposed adoption of Article 340 of the Code civil, December 26, 1910 (CAOM, GGI, 16621).
52. The résident supérieur au Cambodge to the gouverneur général de l'Indochine, January 23, 1913 (CAOM, GGI, 16621).
53. Report by the Chamber of Commerce of Hanoi, December 8, 1910 (CAOM, GGI, 16621).
54. The résident supérieur au Laos to the gouverneur général de l'Indochine, January 14, 1911 (CAOM, GGI, 16621).
55. Maurice Viollette (1870–1960), a republican deputy from Eure-et-Loir from 1902 to 1914, governor-general of Algeria from 1925 to 1927, and minister under the Popular Front from 1936 to 1938, favored reforms in the colonial empire. In particular, he was the author of the famous Blum-Viollette bill of 1936, which would have granted French citizenship to a "Muslim elite" without requiring renunciation of personal status.
56. Maurice Viollette, "La promulgation de la loi sur la recherche de paternité aux colonies," *Les annales coloniales*, January 6, 1913.
57. *Lois annotées*, 449n23.
58. Report by the Chamber of Commerce of Hanoi (CAOM, GGI, 16621).
59. Viollette, "La promulgation de la loi sur la recherche de paternité aux colonies."
60. Report by the résident supérieur en Annam (CAOM, GGI, 16621).

61. Savatier, *La recherche de paternité*, 162.

62. On this law, see Jean Carbonnier, *Droit civil*, vol. 2, *La famille, l'enfant, le couple*, 20th ed. (Paris: PUF, 1999), 291.

63. See Pouzol, *La recherche de paternité*, 449.

64. Ambroise Colin, "De la protection de la descendance illégitime au point de vue de la filiation," *Revue trimestrielle de droit civil* 1 (1902): 259–60.

65. Ibid., 261.

66. Minutes from the Commission sur la recherche de paternité en Cochinchine (CAOM, GGI, 16621).

67. The ministre des Colonies to the président of the Ligue des droits de l'homme et du citoyen, *Bulletin officiel de la Ligue des droits de l'homme et du citoyen*, no. 22, November 15, 1913, 1267 (emphasis in the original).

68. Report by the président of the commission chargée d'émettre un avis sur l'opportunité de la promulgation dans la colonie de l'article 340 du Code civil sur la recherche de la paternité, May 22, 1911 (CAOM, GGI, 16621).

69. Ibid.

70. Raymond Sarraute and Paul Tager, *Les juifs sous l'occupation, 1940–1944* (Paris: Centre de documentation juive contemporaine, 1982), 19.

71. The gouverneur général de l'Indochine to the ministre des Colonies, July 8, 1911 (CAOM, GGI, 16621).

72. Maurice Viollette, "Rapport fait au nom de la Commission de la réforme judiciaire et de la législation civile et criminelle chargée d'examiner la proposition de loi, adoptée par le Sénat, tendant à modifier l'article 340 du Code civil (reconnaissance judiciaire de paternité naturelle)," *Journal officiel, documents parlementaires*, annexe 796, Chambre des députés, Paris (1911): 1437–44.

73. *Journal officiel, débats parlementaires*, Sénat, November 8, 1912, session, 1345.

74. On this campaign, articles can be consulted in the feminist newspapers *Jus suffragi* and *Le droit des femmes* between the years 1911 and 1913. A compilation of newspaper articles on this specific campaign is available in the collection of the Bibliothèque Marguerite Durand (dossier 347 PAT).

75. Petition of the members of the Congrès de la Ligue des droits de l'homme in August 1912. *Bulletin officiel de la Ligue des droits de l'homme* 16 (August 31, 1912): 942.

76. For a history of racism and antiracism in France, see Pierre-André Taguieff, *The Force of Prejudice: On Racism and Its Doubles*, trans. and ed. Hassan Melehy (Minneapolis: University of Minnesota Press, 2001).

77. *Journal officiel, débats parlementaires*, Sénat, November 8, 1912, session, 1344.

78. The promulgation decree in New Caledonia stipulated that "the law applies only if the mother or the putative father is of French nationality or belongs to the category of foreigners assimilated to French nationals." This formulation, which excluded children born to two French parents, was interpreted in legal writing as a transcription error. In reality, the colonial administration had meant to say "and" and preferred to exclude the *métis* from the benefit of the law. See Henry Solus, "Condition privée de indigènes," in *Traité de droit colonial*, vol. 2, ed. Pierre Dareste (Cannes and Paris: Imprimerie Robaudy, 1931), 362. Against this interpretation, note that the courts of Caledonia and later the governor-general had declared their support for unrestricted application of the law. See Maurice Viollette, "Rapport . . . tendant à modifier l'article 340 du Code civil," 1443.

79. For Madagascar, the promulgation decree was dated February 17, 1913 (*Journal officiel de Madagascar*, February 22, 1913); for FWA, promulgation decree dated Novem-

ber 24, 1916 (*Journal officiel de l'Afrique occidentale française,* December 2, 1916); for
FEA, promulgation decree dated April 4, 1913 (*Journal officiel de l'Afrique équatoriale
française,* April 15, 1913); for the settlements in Oceania, promulgation decree dated
January 22, 1913 (*Journal officiel des établissements français de l'Océanie,* January 23,
1913); for settlements in India, promulgation decree dated January 25, 1913 (*Journal
officiel des établissements français dans l'Inde,* January 28, 1913). In FWA, a 1938 decree
would allow investigation of paternity without restriction.

80. Viollette, "Rapport . . . tendant à modifier l'article 340 du Code civil," 1142.

81. The Moïs are the hill tribes of central and northern Vietnam. See "Note on the
Juridical Relations between Europeans and Natives in French Territories Other Than
Algeria and Tunisia and on the Application in the Colonies of the Bill on Paternity
Searches," December 22, 1911 (CAOM, SG Mad, 325/843).

82. Circular from the ministre des Colonies, November 22, 1912 (CAOM, GGI,
16621).

83. The gouverneur général de Madagascar to the ministre des Colonies, November 27,
1913 (CAOM, GGM, 6[10]D4).

84. Savatier, *La recherche de paternité,* 162.

CHAPTER SEVEN

1. Crévost, "La question des métis est un problème social et moral dont la solution
ne doit envisager que l'élément spécial des métis français-annamites," note, 1898
(CAOM, GGI, 7701).

2. See, for example, Charles Apchié, *De la condition juridique des indigènes en Algérie, dans
les colonies et dans les pays de protectorat* (Paris: Librairie nouvelle de droit et de jurisprudence, 1898), which quickly became a reference. Only Arthur Girault considered
the question briefly in one of the sixteen proposals that accompanied his report to
the Congress of Colonial Sociology in 1900: *Condition des indigènes au point de vue
de la législation civile et criminelle et de la distribution de la justice,* published in *Congrès
international de sociologie coloniale,* 2 vols., *Exposition universelle internationale de 1900*
(Paris: Arthur Rousseau, 1901), 1:45–79. This proposal was not discussed in the
debate following the presentation of his report, however.

3. Nelson Goodman, *Ways of Worldmaking* (Indianapolis: Hackett, 1978).

4. The status of the child recognized first by his or her native parent and then by the
French parent was less clear. The question was resolved by a reform of the Civil Code
that stipulated that a child recognized by a French citizen would always be a citizen,
independently of the order of recognition (see chapter 5).

5. Marginal note by the FEA gouverneur général in a letter from the gouverneur de
l'Oubangui-Chari, August 31, 1931 (CAOM, GGAEF, 5D44).

6. Note on juridical relations between Europeans and natives in the French territories,
Ministère des Colonies, Service du secrétariat et contreseing, December 22, 1911
(CAOM, SG Mad, 325/843).

7. Note from the Service des affaires administratives et contentieuses, July 24, 1912
(CAOM, GGI, 16771).

8. The prosecutor general, Raoul Abor, a leading figure in the controversy over fraudulent recognitions, and Louis-Georges Durwell, a judge at the court of Saigon, were
longtime members of the boards of various societies for the protection of *métis* in
Indochina.

9. On *cause lawyering,* see the contributions gathered by Brigitte Gaïti and Liora Israël,
eds., in "La cause du droit," special issue, *Politix* 62 (2003).

10. Camille Paris, *De la condition juridique des métis dans les colonies et les possessions françaises: Des métis franco-annamites dans l'Indochine* (Saigon: 1904).
11. Ibid., 6.
12. *La dépêche coloniale,* November 20, 1905 (CAOM, Aff. pol., 1194).
13. Note on the Société des enfants métis, March 1906 (ANVN 1, RST, 5545).
14. Minutes of the general assembly of the Société de protection des enfants métis abandonnés, 1912 (ANVN 1, RST, 5547).
15. *Congrès de la mutualité coloniale,* Tunis session (Bordeaux: Imprimerie de l'avenir de la mutualité, 1923), 56.
16. Christian Topalov, ed., *Laboratoires du nouveau siècle: La nébuleuse réformatrice et ses réseaux en France, 1880–1914* (Paris: EHESS, 1999).
17. For his trajectory, see Emmanuelle Sibeud, *Une science impériale pour l'Afrique? La construction des savoirs africanistes en France, 1878–1930* (Paris: EHESS, 2002), 286–87.
18. On the career of Henri Sambuc (1864–1944), see the notice written by Henry Solus in *Hommes et destins: Dictionnaire biographique d'outre-mer,* vol. 1 (Paris: Académie des sciences d'outre-mer, 1975), 552–53, and the "Sambuc" file deposited in the archives of the Académie des sciences d'outre-mer.
19. Excerpt from the records of the tribunal de première instance of Phnom Penh, October 27, 1896, judgment (CAOM, GGI, 1664).
20. Arrêt from the cour d'appel de l'Indochine from May 28, 1903, *Dareste* III (1904): 41.
21. For a description of the social selection of the decisions that constitute precedents, see Évelyne Serverin, *De la jurisprudence en droit privé: Théorie d'une pratique* (Lyon: Presses universitaires de Lyon, 1985).
22. August 1902 circular from the procureur général, cited in J. Mérimée, "De l'accession des Indochinois à la qualité de citoyen français" (PhD diss., Université de Toulouse, Faculté de droit, 1931), 207.
23. On the controversial question of the existence of lacunae in juridical systems, see the studies published by Chaim Perelman, *Le problème des lacunes en droit* (Brussels: Émile Bruylant, 1968). On the legal definition of antinomy, see André-Jean Arnaud, ed., *Dictionnaire encyclopédique de théorie et de sociologie du droit* (Paris: LGDJ, 1988), 36.
24. Gérard Noiriel, *La tyrannie du national: Le droit d'asile en Europe, 1793–1993* (Paris: Calmann-Lévy, 1991).
25. For instance, Charles Auriol asserted that "birth on [French] soil here . . . serves only to justify the presumption of French filiation." See "Du rôle de la possession d'état en droit romain et en droit civil français" (PhD diss., Université de Toulouse, Faculté de droit, 1884), 152–53. On the controversy about the nationality of children born in France to unknown parents, see André Huerne, "La nationalité de l'enfant naturel" (PhD diss., Université de Paris, Faculté de droit, 1903), 31–41; and André Weiss, *Manuel de droit international privé,* 8th ed. (Paris: Sirey, 1920), 75–77.
26. Henri Sambuc, "De la condition légale des enfants nés en Indochine de père français et de mère indigène ou de parents inconnus," *Dareste* II (1914): 5.
27. Arthur Girault, "Rapport au Conseil de législation du Conseil supérieur des colonies sur un projet de décret concernant les métis," December 1, 1926 (CAOM, CSC, 26).
28. Sambuc, "De la condition légale des enfants" (1914): 5.
29. The FEA gouverneur général to the ministre des Colonies, January 24, 1935 (CAOM, GGAEF, 5D44).

30. Auguste-Reynald Werner, "Essai sur la réglementation de la nationalité dans le droit colonial français" (PhD diss., Université de Genève, Faculté de droit, 1936), 76.

31. Henry Solus, *Traité de la condition des indigènes en droit privé, colonies et pays de protectorat et pays sous mandat* (Paris: Librairie du Recueil Sirey, 1927), 74.

32. Jacques Mazet, "La condition juridique des métis dans les possessions françaises" (PhD diss., Université de Paris, Faculté de droit, 1932), 78.

33. Werner, "Essai sur la réglementation de la nationalité dans le droit colonial français," 203.

34. Sambuc, "De la condition légale des enfants" (1914; emphasis in the original), 5, 6.

35. Henri Sambuc, "Enquête sur la question des métis," pt. 2, *Revue indochinoise* 16, no. 2 (1913): 205 (emphasis mine).

36. Marie-Angèle Hermitte, "Le droit est un autre monde," *Enquête* 7 (1998): 17–37.

37. Pierre Lampué, "Note sous arrêt," tribunal de première instance de Tamatave, December 26, 1928, *Penant* I (1929): 176–77.

38. Sambuc, "De la condition légale des enfants" (1914): 8.

39. James F. Davis, *Who Is Black? One Nation's Definition* (University Park: Pennsylvania State University Press, 1991).

40. Homer Plessy was carefully chosen by political activists in Louisiana who wanted to attack the arbitrariness of racial categorizations. On this case, which played a fundamental role in the legalization of racial segregation in the United States, see Charles A. Lofgren, *The Plessy Case: A Legal Historical Interpretation* (New York and Oxford: Oxford University Press, 1987).

41. Mazet, "La condition juridique des métis," 112.

42. Sambuc, "De la condition légale des enfants" (1914): 11.

43. Sambuc, "La condition juridique des métis dans les colonies françaises," *Dareste* II (1933): 66.

44. Daniel Gutmann, *Le sentiment d'identité: Étude de droit des personnes et de la famille* (Paris: LGDJ, 2000).

45. Filippo M. Zerilli, "Il debattito sul meticciato: Biologico e sociale nell'antropologia francese del primo novecento," *Archivio per l'antropologia e la etnologia* 125 (1995): 237–73; Emmanuelle Saada, "Race and Sociological Reason in the Republic: Inquiries on the *Métis* in the French Empire, 1908–1937," *International Sociology* 17, no. 3 (2002): 361–91.

46. Sambuc, "La condition juridique des métis dans les colonies françaises" (1933), 59.

47. Carole Reynaud Paligot, *La république raciale: Paradigme racial et idéologie républicaine, 1860–1930* (Paris: PUF, 2006).

48. Sambuc, "De la condition légale des enfants" (1914): 6.

49. Philippe Jestaz and Christophe Jamin, *La doctrine* (Paris: Dalloz, 2004).

50. And thus before the law of September 29, 1916, granted full citizenship to natives (*originaires*) of the four "full-exercise" communes of Senegal (see chapter 4).

51. Tribunal de première instance de Saint-Louis du Sénégal, August 5, 1913, *Dareste* III (1914): 43–48.

52. Tribunal civil de Nouméa, January 7 and 23, 1920, *Dareste* III (1920): 114.

53. Justice de paix etendue de Phnom Penh, October 20, 1921, *Dareste* III (1922): 118.

54. Tribunal civil de Nouméa, March 28, 1923, *Dareste* III (1924): 109–11.

55. Respectively, cour d'appel de l'Afrique Occidentale, March 12, 1920, *Dareste* III (1923): 135; and tribunal de première instance de Phnom Penh, April 29, 1924, *Penant* I (1926): 250–56.

56. *Penant* I (1927): 207.

57. Cour d'appel de Hanoi, November 12, 1926, *Dareste* III (1927): 83–86.

58. Abel Pouzol, *La recherche de paternité: Étude critique de sociologie et de législation comparée* (Paris: Giard et Brière, 1902), 272.

59. On this, see the many contributions to Jane Caplan and John Torpey, eds., *Documenting Individual Identity: The Development of State Practices in the Modern World* (Princeton, NJ: Princeton University Press, 2001).

60. André Weiss, *Traité théorique et pratique de droit international privé*, 2nd ed., vol. 1, *De la nationalité* (Paris: Sirey, 1907), 22; Paul Lagarde, *La nationalité française*, 3rd ed. (Paris: Dalloz, 1997), 247.

61. Arthur Girault, "Rapport sur un projet de décret concernant les métis présenté au Conseil supérieur des colonies le 1er décembre 1926," *Dareste* II (1926): 19.

62. See, for example, Jean Carbonnier, *Droit civil*, vol. 2, *La famille, l'enfant, le couple*, 20th ed. (Paris: PUF, 1999), 196.

63. Henry Solus, "Note sous arrêt," cour d'appel de Hanoi, *Recueil Sirey* (Paris: Sirey, 1927), 130.

64. "Note sous arrêt," cour d'appel d'Hanoi, *Penant* I (1927): 206.

65. Minutes of the general assembly of the Société d'assistance aux enfants franco-indochinois, 1927 (ANVN 1, RST, 73758).

66. Tribunal de Majunga, December 11, 1928, *Dareste* III (1930): 113.

67. Cour d'appel de Madagascar, May 30, 1928, *Dareste* III (1929): 82.

68. The FEA gouverneur général to the ministre des Colonies, April 6, 1927 (CAOM, GGAEF, 5D44).

69. "Note sous arrêt," tribunal civil de Nouméa, January 7 and 23, 1920, *Dareste* III (1920): 114.

70. The procureur général près la cour d'appel de Hanoi to the gouverneur général de l'Indochine, November 24, 1926 (CAOM, AGEFOM, 252/376).

71. Minutes of the general assembly of the Société d'assistance aux enfants abandonnés franco-indochinois, 1929 (CAOM, RST, 3890).

72. The gouverneur général de l'Indochine to the ministre des Colonies, August 22, 1926 (CAOM, CSC, 26).

73. Presentation of motives appended to the draft of the decree submitted by the gouverneur général de l'Indochine, 1926 (CAOM, CSC, 26) (emphasis mine).

74. Minutes of the general assembly of the Société d'assistance aux enfants abandonnés franco-indochinois, 1929 (CAOM, RST, 3890).

75. Minutes of the general assembly of the Société d'assistance aux enfants abandonnés franco-indochinois, 1927 (ANVN 1, RST, 73758).

76. Arthur Girault, "Rapport au Conseil de législation du Conseil supérieur des colonies," 17 (emphasis mine).

77. Conseil de législation coloniale, agenda of the 1926–27 session (CAOM, ECOL, Papiers Paul Dislère, dossier 2 Ecol 18).

78. Note from the Direction des affaires politiques, Ministère des Colonies, 4th bureau, n.d. (CAOM, ECOL, Papiers Paul Dislère, dossier 2 Ecol 18).

79. The ministre de la Justice to the ministre des Colonies, February 1, 1929 (CAOM, CSC, 25).

80. Report presented to the Conseil supérieur des colonies by Arthur Girault on the subject of observations presented by the gouverneurs des colonies following the communication of a draft of a decree concerning *métis*, January 25, 1928 (CAOM, CSC, 25).

81. The gouverneur général de Madagascar to the ministre des Colonies, May 19, 1927 (CAOM, GGM, 6[10]D4).

82. Supplement to the report presented by Arthur Girault to the Conseil de législation coloniale on the responses of the gouverneurs généraux and gouverneurs des colonies regarding the draft of a decree concerning the *métis*, February 19, 1928 (CAOM, CSC, 25).

83. Report presented to the Conseil supérieur des colonies by Arthur Girault (CAOM, CSC, 25).

84. The gouverneur général de Madagascar to the ministre des Colonies, May 19, 1927 (CAOM, GGM, 6[10]D4).

85. Report presented to the Conseil supérieur des colonies by Arthur Girault (CAOM, CSC, 25).

86. Institut colonial international, "Les métis: Mesures à prendre en vue de leur éducation et de leur instruction," Paris session (Brussels: Établissements généraux d'imprimerie, 1921), 74–75.

87. Minutes of the December 1, 1926, session of the Conseil supérieur des colonies (CAOM, ECOL, Papiers Paul Dislère, dossier 2 Ecol 18).

88. Minutes of the February 2, 1927, session of the Conseil supérieur des colonies (CAOM, ECOL, Papiers Paul Dislère, dossier 2 Ecol 18).

89. Census of *métis* conducted by the city of Hanoi in 1936 (ANVN 1, Mairie Hanoi, 3279).

90. The "renouncers" were citizens of the French settlements in India who, under the terms of the decree of September 21, 1881, were allowed to become French citizens provided they officially renounced their personal status (see chapter 4).

91. J. Mérimée, "De l'accession des Indochinois à la qualité de citoyen français" (PhD diss., Université de Toulouse, Faculté de droit, 1931), 213.

92. Speech by M. Picanon, retired inspecteur des colonies, May 2, 1928, session of the Conseil de législation (CAOM, CSC, 25).

93. Speech by Michel Tardit, conseiller d'État, May 2, 1928, session of the Conseil de législation (CAOM, CSC, 25).

94. Véronique Hélénon, "Race, statut juridique et colonisation: Antillais et Africains dans les cadres administratifs des colonies françaises d'Afrique," in *L'esclavage, la colonisation, et après . . .* , ed. Patrick Weil and Stéphane Dufoix, 229–43 (Paris: PUF, 2005).

95. Study by the Conseil d'État of the draft of a decree establishing the juridical condition of *métis* born of legally unknown parents in FWA (AN, CE, 199767).

96. Annex 3 of the arrêté of November 14, 1930 (CAOM, Aff. pol., 1637).

97. Mazet, "La condition juridique des métis," 103; and note on the nationality and status of *métis*, 1947 (CAOM, Aff. pol., 1194).

98. Study by the Conseil d'État of the draft of a decree defining the juridical condition of *métis* in Indochina (AN, CE, 196585).

99. Henri Sambuc, "De la condition légale des enfants nés en Indochine de parents inconnus," *Dareste* II (1929): 4.

100. Gutmann, *Le sentiment d'identité*, 172–73.

101. Viviane Morgand-Cantegrit, "La possession d'état d'enfant" (PhD diss., Université de Lille II, Faculté des sciences juridiques, politiques et sociales, 1993), 703.

102. Georges Lefort, "De la possession d'état en matière de filiation naturelle et modifications apportées par la loi du 16 novembre 1912" (PhD diss., Université de Paris, Faculté de droit, 1914), 96 (emphasis mine).

103. Carbonnier, *Droit civil*, 196.
104. Gutmann, *Le sentiment d'identité*, 173.
105. Lefort, "De la possession d'état en matière de filiation naturelle," 97.
106. Henri Sambuc, "De la condition légale des enfants nés en Indochine de père français et de mère indigène ou de parents inconnus," *Dareste* II (1923): 4.
107. Sambuc, "Enquête sur la question des métis," 205.
108. Gutmann, *Le sentiment d'identité*, 173.
109. Lieutenant Colonel Auguste Bonifacy, "Les métis franco-tonkinois," *Bulletins et mémoires de la Société d'anthropologie de Paris* 6, no. 1 (1910): 636.
110. On this point, see Gutmann, *Le sentiment d'identité*.
111. On this opposition, see Olivier Beaud, *La puissance de l'État* (Paris: PUF, 1994), 118–19.
112. "Les problèmes coloniaux," *Le Petit Parisien*, October 6, 1930.
113. Marinetti, "La situation des Eurasiens d'Indochine au point de vue social et politique," *La presse indochinoise*, November 26, 1937, 1, 6.
114. Records from the *tribunal de première instance* de Hanoi to the *procureur de la république*, May 17, 1938 (ANVN 1, RST, 71191).
115. Note for the preparation of the Conférence de Brazzaville by the chef du service judiciaire en AOF, 1944 (CAOM, Aff. pol., 2125/2).
116. Note on the recognition of the quality of French citizen in favor of *métis*, September 1, 1937 (CAOM, GGAEF, 5D44).
117. The gouverneur général de la Nouvelle-Calédonie to the ministre de la France d'outre-mer, April 13, 1948 (CAOM, Aff. pol., 1194).
118. Circular by the Services judiciaires on the application of the decree establishing the status of *métis* in FEA (CAOM, GGAEF, 5D44).
119. Mérimée, "De l'accession des Indochinois à la qualité de citoyen français," 215.
120. The résident supérieur au Tonkin to the gouverneur général de l'Indochine, August 1938 (ANVN 1, RST, 71191). For an account of these practices, see also the report *Les Français d'Indochine*, written by a class-3 administrator from the civil service in Cochin China, 1937 (CAOM, GGI, 53653).
121. Interview with Judge L., July 31, 1998. See, for example, Mazet, "La condition juridique des métis," 98–99.
122. Note from the *procureur de la république*, October 22, 1941 (CAOM, RST, 1154). On Vichy policies toward *métis*, see Christina Firpo, "Lost Boys: 'Abandoned' Eurasian Children and the Management of the Racial Topography in Colonial Indochina, 1938–1945," *French Colonial History* 8 (2007): 203–24.
123. Note from the Direction des affaires politiques et administratives, November 1939 (AN, GGAOF, 23G22).
124. The procureur général in Dakar to the directeur des affaires politiques et administratives au gouvernement général de l'AOF, January 28, 1936 (AN, GGAOF, 23G22).
125. Circular from the gouverneur général de l'AOF on the application of the decree establishing the juridical condition of *métis*, February 1, 1933 (AN, GGAOF, 23G22).
126. René Maunier, "Le mélange des races dans les colonies," *Annales de l'Université de Paris* 6, no. 2 (1931): 125–26.
127. See Albert de Pouvourville, "L'Indochine et ses métis," *La dépêche coloniale*, 4949, September 16, 1911. Also see the quote accompanying n. 6 in chapter 3.
128. One of the fundamental stages in this intellectual evolution was marked by the UNESCO declaration "on race and racism" in 1950. See the collection *La question raciale devant la science moderne* (Paris: UNESCO), including a text by Claude Lévi-

Strauss, *Race et histoire* (1952), and Michel Leiris, *Race et civilisation* (1951). Concerning this declaration, which contributed to the advent of a "racism without race," see Étienne Balibar, "La construction du racisme," *Actuel Marx* 38 (2005): 11–28.

CHAPTER EIGHT

1. For an example of a definitive account of the modern history of nationality law that does not ask these questions, see Patrick Weil, *How to Be French: Nationality in the Making since 1789*, trans. Catherine Porter (Durham, NC: Duke University Press, 2009).

2. The président de la Société d'assistance aux enfants franco-indochinois to the administrateur-maire of the city of Hanoi, July 13, 1938 (ANVN 1, Mairie Hanoi, 5900).

3. J. Mérimée, "De l'accession des Indochinois à la qualité de citoyen français" (PhD diss., Université de Toulouse, Faculté de droit, 1931), 215–16.

4. Decision from the gouverneur général de l'Indochine, June 27, 1939, *Journal officiel de l'Indochine française* (July 8, 1939): 1960–61.

5. Article 6 of the decision from the gouverneur général de l'Indochine, June 27, 1939.

6. Le résident-maire de Namdinh to the résident supérieur au Tonkin, May 13, 1939 (ANVN 1, RST, 71191).

7. Marginal notes on the November 17, 1938, note from the maire de Haiphong to the résident supérieur au Tonkin (ANVN 1, RST, 71191) (emphasis in the original).

8. The résident supérieur au Tonkin to the maire de Haiphong, November 25, 1938 (ANVN 1, RST, 71191). "Renouncers" were individuals and their descendants in the French settlements of India who had opted for French citizenship and renounced their local laws (see chapters 4 and 7).

9. Reply from the administrateur de la Province de Siemréap (Cambodia) to inquiry no. 4 on *métis*, 1937 (CAOM, Guernut, 97).

10. Henri Sambuc, "La condition juridique des métis dans les colonies françaises," *Dareste* II (1933): 68.

11. CAOM, AGEFOM, 252/376; and ANVN 1, RST, 71191.

12. On the racial politics of the Vichyite administration in Indochina, see Eric Jennings, *Vichy in the Tropics: Pétain's National Revolution in Madagascar, Guadeloupe, and Indochina, 1940–1944* (Palo Alto, CA: Stanford University Press, 2001), 178; and Anne Raffin, *Youth Mobilization in Vichy Indochina and Its Legacies, 1940 to 1970* (Lanham, MD: Lexington Books, 2005).

13. The président de la Fondation Jules-Brévié to the inspecteur général du travail et de la prévoyance sociale, December 19, 1942 (ANVN 1, GGI, 4809).

14. Admiral Decoux to the résident supérieur au Tonkin, April 16, 1943 (ANVN 1, GGI, 88).

15. The directeur du Bureau des affaires politiques to the directeur de l'Administration générale, December 4, 1942 (ANVN 1, GGI, 4809).

16. Christina Firpo, "Lost Boys: 'Abandoned' Eurasian Children and the Management of the Racial Topography in Colonial Indochina, 1938–1945," *French Colonial History* 8 (2007): 203–24.

17. Decree of November 24, 1943, creating the status of pupilles eurasiens d'Indochine (archives FOEFI).

18. Pierre Chauvel, "De la qualité de pupille de la nation, des prérogatives attachées à ce titre" (PhD diss., Université de Rennes, Faculté de droit, 1933).

19. Léon Bourgeois, speaking before the Assemblée nationale, cited by Eugénie Bourgeault, "Mères de famille et pétitions dans la Grande guerre: Les étapes du vote de la loi sur les pupilles de la nation" (master's thesis, Institut d'études politiques de Grenoble, Grenoble, 1997), 40.

20. René Maunier, Introduction to *Principes de colonisation et de législation coloniale: Les colonies françaises avant et depuis 1815*, by Arthur Girault, 6th ed. (Paris: Sirey, 1943), 5–6. The distinction between the two types of colonies was primarily due to Girault, who developed it at the end of the nineteenth century. He was followed by Jules Harmand, *Domination et colonisation* (Paris: Flammarion, 1910).

21. On the centrality of the notion of acclimatization for colonial doctrine, see Eric Jennings, *Curing the Colonizers: Hydrotherapy, Climatology and French Colonial Spas* (Durham, NC: Duke University Press, 2006).

22. Note from Crévost, "La question des métis est un problème social et moral" (CAOM, GGI, 7701).

23. Georges Hardy, in *La revue scientifique*, quoted by Georges Coedès during the meeting discussing the foundation of the Institut indochinois pour l'étude de l'homme, *Compte-rendu des séances de l'année 1938*, Institut indochinois pour l'étude de l'homme (Hanoi: G. Taupin, 1938), 11.

24. Michel Foucault, *Society Must Be Defended: Lectures at the Collège de France, 1975–76*, ed. Mauro Bertani and Alessandro Fontana, gen. ed. François Ewald and Alessandro Fontana, trans. David Macey (New York: Picador, 2003). See in particular the March 17, 1976, lecture.

25. The gouverneur général de l'Indochine to the ministre des Colonies, July 14, 1938 (CAOM, AGEFOM, 252/376).

26. *Le problème eurasien au Tonkin*, report in response to inquiry no. 4 of the Commission d'enquête dans les territoires d'outre-mer, April 1938 (CAOM, Guernut, 97).

27. Pierre Huard and Alfred Bigot, "Introduction à l'étude des Eurasiens," *Bulletin économique de l'Indochine*, booklet 4 (Hanoi: Direction des services économiques, 1939): 715–58.

28. Commission permanente pour la section de la France d'outre-mer pour l'organisation du concours du meilleur mariage colonial, minutes of the June 4, 1937, meeting (AN, F/12/12258).

29. Commission permanente pour l'organisation du meilleur mariage colonial, early 1936 (AN, F/12/12258).

30. Luc Boltanski, *Les cadres: La formation d'un groupe social* (Paris: Minuit, 1982), 120–28.

31. Gilbert Mury, "Le problème eurasien en Indochine," *Le courrier colonial*, March 3, 1939. See also Henri Bonvicini, *Enfants de la colonie* (Saigon: Éditions Orient-Occident, 1938), 10–11: "It has been shown that Indochina is apt to become a colony of settlement, which increasingly will be able to do without outside assistance in filling the lower and even higher cadre positions that are created there."

32. Report by Henri Planté, président de l'Amicale des Français d'Indochine, transmitted on the occasion of the Commission d'enquête dans les territoires d'outre-mer in 1938 (CAOM, AGEFOM, 252/376).

33. Christophe Bonneuil, "Mettre en œuvre et discipliner les tropiques: Les sciences du végétal dans l'Empire français, 1870–1940" (PhD diss., Université de Paris VII, 1997).

34. Conference held by the gouvernement général for the study of the "question des métis en Indochine," May 24, 1938 (CAOM, AGEFOM, 252/376).

35. ANVN 1, GGI, 4896.
36. Capitaine Henri Mader, *Les écoles d'enfants de troupe: Historique de l'institution* (Paris: Henri Charles-Lavauzelle, 1894).
37. The général de division Verdier to the ministre de la Guerre, January 18, 1936 (CAOM, GGI, 53523).
38. The ministre de la Guerre to the commandant supérieur des troupes, March 23, 1936 (CAOM, GGI, 53523) (emphasis in the original).
39. Handwritten note by the résident supérieur au Tonkin in the margin of a letter from the gouverneur to the ministre, from June 24, 1938 (ANVN 1, RST, 71191).
40. Gouverneur général Brévié to the ministre des Colonies, June 24, 1938 (ANVN 1, RST, 71191).
41. CAOM, AGEFOM, 252/376 (emphasis mine). On the prophylactic effects of the Dalat milieu, see Eric Jennings, *Curing the Colonizers: Hydrotherapy, Climatology and French Colonial Spas* (Durham, NC: Duke University Press, 2006), 38–39.
42. François de Coutouly, "Note sur les métis en AOF" (CAOM, GGAEF, 5D44).
43. The lieutenant-gouverneur de l'Oubangui-Chari to the gouverneur général de l'AEF, May 15, 1919 (CAOM, GGAEF, 5D44).
44. Robert Cornevin, "Les métis dans la colonisation française: L'hésitation métisse" (thesis, ENFOM [École nationale de la France d'outre-mer], 1941–42) (CAOM, ECOL).
45. Interview with Madame P., Marseille, June 1998. For a discussion of the interviews, see chapter 10.
46. On this episode, see Philippe Franchini, *Continental Saïgon* (1976; repr., Paris: Métailié, 1995),137–38.
47. Assemblée générale ordinaire de la FOEFI, 1950 (archives FOEFI).
48. Note on the nationality and status of *métis*, 1947 (CAOM, Aff. Pol., 1194). Since the Constitution of the Fourth Republic granted citizenship to everyone under imperial jurisdiction while continuing to distinguish between "citizens of civil status under general law" and "citizens of local status," the point of the bill was to include *métis* in the first category from the moment of birth.
49. MAE, "Sud-Vietnam," vol. 103.
50. Jean-Pierre Daumas, "Effets de la décolonisation sur la nationalité française des métis," *Revue juridique et politique: Indépendance et coopération* 24, no. 1 (1970): 35–50.
51. The Haut commissariat de la République Française au Vietnam to the ministre de la Justice du gouvernement du Vietnam (MAE, "Sud-Vietnam," vol. 103).
52. Assemblée générale ordinaire de la FOEFI, 1953 (archives FOEFI).
53. Assemblée générale ordinaire de la FOEFI, 1954 (archives FOEFI).
54. "Proposition tendant à demander au Haut conseil de l'Union française l'étude d'un statut juridique en faveur des Eurasiens," proposition no. 385 to the Assemblée de l'Union française, 1952 (CAOM, AGEFOM, 252/376). This figure is repeated by Gouverneur Oswald Durand during a workshop of the Académie des sciences d'outre-mer (see the *Comptes-rendus de l'Académie des sciences d'outre-mer*, May 20, 1955, 283).
55. Assemblée générale ordinaire de la FOEFI, 1954 (archives FOEFI).
56. Assemblée générale ordinaire de la FOEFI, 1951 (CAOM, 90 APC, 89).
57. Assemblée générale ordinaire de la FOEFI, 1954 (archives FOEFI).
58. Interview with Judge L., Montpellier, 1998.
59. Assemblée générale ordinaire de la FOEFI, 1950 (archives FOEFI).

60. Assemblée générale ordinaire de la FOEFI, 1968 (archives FOEFI; emphasis in the original).

61. Laboratoire d'anthropologie écologique des populations contemporaines et préhistoriques, *Anthropologie des métis franco-vietnamiens* (Paris: Société d'anthropologie de Paris / Masson et cie., 1967).

62. Assemblée générale ordinaire de la FOEFI, 1976 (archives FOEFI).

63. Réglement intérieur de la FOEFI, 1957 (CAOM, 90 APC, 89).

64. Assemblée générale ordinaire de la FOEFI, 1979 (archives FOEFI).

65. The président de la FOEFI to the ministre de la Justice, September 28, 1979 (archives FOEFI).

66. Reply from the Ministre de la Justice to the parliamentary question asked by M. Aurillac, November 10, 1981 (CAOM, 90 APC).

67. See Jean-Pierre Massé, "L'exception indochinoise: Le dispositif d'accueil des réfugiés politiques en France, 1973–1991" (PhD diss., EHESS, Paris, 1996).

68. Reproduction of a press release by the French Ministry of Foreign Affairs about the immigration of Franco-Vietnamese to France, *Le monde*, September 20, 1980.

69. "Les difficultés des métis franco-vietnamiens à émigrer en France et l'attitude de Paris" (text of a petition signed by about one hundred people), *Le monde*, September 18, 1980.

70. Certificate of French nationality of M.P. granted by the tribunal d'instance of the fourteenth arrondissement of Paris on July 16, 1987 (personal archives of M.P.).

71. Reply from the administrateur de Mytho (Cochin China) to inquiry no. 4 on *métis*, 1937 (CAOM, Guernut, 97).

72. *Le problème eurasien au Tonkin*, report dated April 1938 in response to inquiry no. 4 of the Commission d'enquête dans les territoires d'outre-mer (CAOM, Guernut, 97).

CHAPTER NINE

1. Response from the administrateur de Bentre (Cochin China) to inquiry no. 4 on *métis*, 1937 (CAOM, Guernut, 97).

2. The survey in question was part of the larger colonial survey conducted in 1937 at the behest of Henri Guernut, the minister of colonies under the Popular Front, known as the "Guernut survey." For an analysis of the part of the survey devoted to *métis*, see Emmanuelle Saada, "Race and Sociological Reason in the Republic: Inquiries on the *Métis* in the French Empire, 1908–1937." *International Sociology* 17, no. 3 (2002): 361–91.

3. Response from the administrateur de Kampot (Cambodia) to inquiry no. 4 on *métis*, 1937 (CAOM, Guernut, 97).

4. Response from the administrateur de Bentre (Cochin China) to inquiry no. 4 on *métis*, 1937 (CAOM, Guernut, 97).

5. Fredrik Barth, "Ethnic Groups and Boundaries," in *Theories of Ethnicity: A Classical Reader*, ed. Werner Sollors (New York: New York University Press, 1996), 299.

6. Minutes of the general assembly of the Société d'assistance aux enfants franco-indochinois, 1926 (ANVN 1, RST, 73758).

7. Minutes of the general assembly of the Société d'assistance aux enfants franco-indochinois, 1927 (ANVN 1, RST, 73758).

8. M. Rebouillat, *Les Français d'Indochine*, report for the Commission d'enquête dans les territoires d'outre-mer, Cochin China, 1937 (CAOM, GGI, 53653).

9. CAOM, Guernut, 97.

10. L'inspecteur du travail to the résident supérieur au Tonkin, January 17, 1945 (ANVN 1, GGI, 471).

11. Henri Labouret, "La situation morale et matérielle des métis dans l'Ouest africain français et la législation qui leur est appliquée," in *Compte rendu du Congrès international pour l'étude des problèmes résultant du mélange des races* (Brussels: Exposition internationale et universelle de Bruxelles, 1935), 28.

12. CAOM, GGAEF, 5D44.

13. AN, GGAOF, 21G79.

14. On the usage of the word *Algérien* in Algeria between the two world wars, see in particular Albert Camus, *Le premier homme* (repr., Paris: Gallimard, 2000).

15. Rebouillat, *Les Français d'Indochine*.

16. Pierre Huard and Alfred Bigot, "Introduction à l'étude des Eurasiens," *Bulletin économique de l'Indochine*, booklet 4, 715–58 (Hanoi: Direction des services économiques, 1939).

17. Henri Bonvicini, *Enfants de la colonie* (Saigon: Éditions Orient-Occident, 1938). In 1946, the president of the Association tonkinoise des Français d'outre-mer spoke of the steady increase of "Eurasian ethnic stock: from 16 percent in 1936, it rose to 50 percent in 1946. Soon it will far surpass other French." President of ATFO in Hanoi to ministre de la France d'outre-mer, August 10, 1946 (CAOM, Aff. pol., 1194).

18. "À nos lecteurs français," *Blanc et jaune* 1, July 11, 1937.

19. "À nos lecteurs annamites," *Blanc et jaune* 1, July 11, 1937.

20. Luc Boltanski, *Les cadres: La formation d'un groupe social* (Paris: Minuit, 1982), 82–91.

21. "Pour les Indochinois, un emploi tout trouvé: Celui d'interprète," *Blanc et jaune* 18, November 7, 1937.

22. Henri Bouchon, *Mousson du Sud: Essai sur la vie indochinoise* (Hanoi: 1942), 248–49.

23. On these two points, refer to two works by Gérard Noiriel: "Nations, nationalités, nationalismes: Pour une socio-histoire comparée," in *État, nation et immigration*, by Gérard Noiriel (Paris: Belin, 2001), and *Les origines républicaines de Vichy* (Paris: Hachette littératures, 1999), 123.

24. The président de l'Association tonkinoise des Français d'outre-mer à Hanoi to the ministre de la France d'outre-mer, August 10, 1946 (CAOM, Aff. pol., 1194).

25. CAOM, GGI, 53653.

26. "Dans l'œuvre de colonisation, pensez aux jeunes métis," *Blanc et jaune* 10, September 12, 1937.

27. See Henri Neuville, "L'espèce, la race et le métissage en anthropologie: Introduction à l'anthropologie générale," in *Archives de l'Institut de paléontologie humaine*, vol. 11 (Paris: Masson, 1933).

28. "La collaboration franco-annamite," *Blanc et jaune* 20, November 14, 1937.

29. Bonvicini, *Enfants de la colonie*, 73.

30. Jean-Loup Amselle, *Affirmative Exclusion: Cultural Pluralism and the Rule of Custom in France*, trans. Jane Marie Todd (Ithaca, NY: Cornell University Press, 2003).

31. Frederick Cooper, "Alternatives to Empire: France and Africa after World War II," in *The State of Sovereignty: Territories, Laws, Populations*, ed. Douglas Howland and Luise White, 94–123 (Bloomington: Indiana University Press, 2009).

32. See Frederick Cooper, *Colonialism in Question: Theory, Knowledge, History* (Berkeley: University of California Press, 2005)—in particular, chapter 7: "Labor, Politics and Empire in French Africa," 204–30.

33. See the claims listed by the newspaper *L'alerte* in 1937 (CAOM, GGI, 53653).
34. "Politique locale: Français d'Indochine, présents!," *Blanc et jaune* 1, July 11, 1937.
35. The président de l'Association tonkinoise des Français d'outre-mer à Hanoi to the ministre de la France d'outre-mer, August 10, 1946 (CAOM, Aff. pol., 1194).
36. This old cause was advanced by the success of Rachid Bouchareb's film *Indigènes*, which came out in September 2006. In 2010, the Constitutional Council ruled that colonial and metropolitan veterans should be paid equal pensions.
37. "Une grave injustice," *France-Indochine*, November 5, 1933.
38. The président de la Ligue des droits de l'homme to the ministre des Colonies, November 7, 1933 (BDIC, LDH, F delta rés 798/83).
39. "Politique locale."
40. The président de la Ligue des droits de l'homme to the ministre des Colonies, November 7, 1933 (BDIC, LDH, F delta rés 798/83).
41. The section de Haiphong to the président de la Ligue des droits de l'homme, December 6, 1935 (BDIC, LDH, F delta rés 798/83).
42. Report from Raoul Mary to the Ligue des droits de l'homme, August 23, 1935 (BDIC, LDH, F delta rés 798/83).
43. CAOM, Aff. pol., 1194.
44. The président de l'Association tonkinoise des Français d'outre-mer à Hanoi to the ministre de la France d'outre-mer, August 10, 1946 (CAOM, Aff. pol., 1194).
45. CAOM, Aff. pol., 1194.
46. AN, GGAOF, 21G79.
47. The gouverneur général de l'AEF to the gouverneur du Gabon, May 27, 1944 (CAOM, GGAEF, 5D44).
48. The comité directeur de l'Association philanthropique des métis français à Dakar to the ministre des Colonies, November 6, 1946 (AN, GGAOF, 21G79).
49. Pierre Rosanvallon, *The Demands of Liberty: Civil Society in France since the Revolution*, trans. Arthur Goldhammer (Cambridge, MA: Harvard University Press, 2007), 13.
50. "Le grain se lève: Indochinois, votre heure va sonner?" *Blanc et jaune* 5, August 8, 1937.
51. Minutes of the general assembly of the Société d'assistance aux enfants franco-indochinois, 1933 (ANVN 1, RST, 73758).
52. The résident supérieur au Tonkin to the inspecteur général du travail et de la prévoyance sociale, December 20, 1938 (ANVN 1, GGI, 4810).
53. Assemblée générale de la Fondation Jules-Brévié, December 18, 1939 (ANVN 1, GGI, 4813).
54. "Égalité de droits: Il nous faut des délégués aux assemblées élues," *Blanc et jaune* 27, January 2, 1938.
55. "Notre premier bilan: Quatre mois de rude lutte," *Blanc et jaune* 19, November 11, 1937.
56. Request from the Association philanthropique des métis français de la circonscription de Dakar, February 1946 (AN, GGAOF, 21G79).
57. On this point, please refer to the analyses in Gérard Noiriel, "Représentation nationale et catégories sociales: L'exemple des réfugiés politiques," *Genèses* 26 (1997): 50.
58. Michel Foucault, "The Subject and the Power," in *Michel Foucault: Beyond Structuralism and Hermeneutics*, ed. Hubert Dreyfus and Paul Rabinow (Chicago: University of Chicago Press, 1982), 212: "This form of power applies itself to immediate daily life, which categorizes the individual, marks him by his own individuality, attaches him to its own identity, imposes a law of truth on him, which he must recognize and

which others have to recognize in him. It is a form of power that makes individuals subjects. There are two meanings of the word *subject*: subject to someone else by control and dependence, and tied to his own identity by a conscience or self-knowledge. Both meanings suggest a form of power which subjugates and makes subject to."

59. See Mary Douglas, *How Institutions Think* (Syracuse, NY: Syracuse University Press, 1988). See in particular "Institutions Do the Classifying," 91–109.

60. Ian Hacking, "Inaugural Lecture: Chair of Philosophy and History of Scientific Concepts at the Collège de France, January 16, 2001," *Economy and Society* 31 (2002): 12.

61. Ian Hacking, *The Social Construction of What?* (Cambridge, MA: Harvard University Press, 1999). See in particular chapter 5.

62. To preserve the anonymity of the persons interviewed, I have changed names as well as certain dates and places.

63. Nicole Lapierre, *Changer de nom* (Paris: Stock, 1995).

CHAPTER TEN

1. Speech by Jules Ferry before Parliament, July 28, 1885, cited in *Le nationalisme français, 1871–1914*, texts selected and presented by Raoul Girardet (Paris: Armand Colin, 1966), 103.

2. See Madeleine Rebérioux, "Le mot 'race' au tournant du siècle," *Mots: Les langages du politique*, 33 (1992): 53–58.

3. See Laurent Mucchielli, *La découverte du social: Naissance de la sociologie en France, 1870–1914* (Paris: la Découverte, 1998).

4. Léon Baréty, at the first session of March 31, 1927, *Journal officiel, débats parlementaires*, Chambre des députés, April 1, 1927, 1104.

5. See Rebérioux, "Le mot 'race' au tournant du siècle."

6. On these debates, see the study by Christophe Delclitte, "La catégorie juridique 'nomade' dans la loi de 1912," *Hommes et migrations* 1188–89 (1995): 23–30.

7. Antonin Dubost, "Rapport fait au nom de la commission chargée d'examiner la proposition de loi, adoptée par le Sénat, sur la nationalité," *Journal officiel, débats parlementaires*, Chambre des députés, annex 2083, special session of 1887, 234.

8. Bill proposing to facilitate the naturalization of foreigners, presented by M. Charles Lambert (*Journal officiel, débats parlementaires*, Chambre des députés, special session of 1925, annexes aux procès-verbaux des séances, session of October 29, 1925).

9. See Elisa Camiscioli, *Reproducing the French Race: Immigration, Intimacy, and Embodiment in the Early Twentieth Century* (Durham, NC: Duke University Press, 2009).

10. Michel Verpeaux, "Le juif 'non citoyen,'" in "Le droit antisémite de Vichy," special issue, *Le genre humain* 30–31 (1996): 189–207.

11. Danièle Lochak, "La race: Une catégorie juridique?" *Mots: Les langages du politique* 33 (1992): 291–303.

12. Danièle Lochak, "La doctrine sous Vichy ou les mésaventures du positivisme," in *Les usages sociaux du droit*, ed. CURAPP, 252–85 (Paris: PUF, 1990).

13. Raul Hilberg, *The Destruction of the European Jews* (Chicago: Quadrangle Books, 1961), chapter 4.

14. André Broc, *La qualité de juif: Une notion juridique nouvelle* (Paris: PUF, 1943), 50.

15. Ibid., 53.

16. Ibid.

17. Ibid. The author added: "For example, one can very well imagine that a natural child in possession of Jewish status might ask to be recognized by one or two non-Jews or,

conversely, that a natural child recognized by two Jewish grandparents might ask a court to nullify that recognition."

18. Broc, *La qualité de juif*, 55.
19. Tribunal civil de Rabat, December 17, 1941, Raymond Lévy, report by P. Decroux, note P. Chauveau, doyen de la Faculté de droit, avocat près la cour d'appel d'Alger, *JCP* 2 (1942): 1800.
20. E.-H. Perreau, "Le nouveau statut des juifs en France," *La semaine juridique* (1941) 9, 2nd semester, study 216, 39.
21. Ibid., 40.
22. On the role of the Commissariat général aux questions juives in classifying "semi-Jews" and shaping case law in this area, see Laurent Joly, *Vichy dans la "solution finale": Histoire du Commissariat aux questions juives, 1941–1944* (Paris: Grasset, 2006), especially chapter 11.
23. Broc, *La qualité de juif*, 91.
24. Cour d'appel d'Aix (5ᵉ chambre correctionnelle), May 12, 1942, Delle Weinthal, *Gazette du palais* 2 (1942): 41.
25. Broc, *La qualité de juif*, 92. Broc is here alluding to Georges Montandon, an anthropologist used as an expert by the prefecture of police in Paris and by the Commissariat général aux questions juives, which decided "dubious" cases.
26. Joseph Haennig, "L'incidence de la séparation des Églises et de l'État sur la définition du métis juif," *Gazette du palais* 2 (1942): 32–33. "Quels moyens de preuve peuvent être fournis par le métis juif pour établir sa non-appartenance à la race juive?" *Gazette du palais* 1 (1943): 31–32.
27. Philippe Fabre, *Le Conseil d'État et Vichy: Le contentieux de l'antisémitisme* (Paris: Publications de la Sorbonne, 2001), 129.
28. Tribunal civil de Rabat, December 17, 1941.
29. Rapport Decroux, tribunal civil de Rabat.
30. Cited in Haennig, "Quels moyens de preuve," 31.
31. Tribunal de Toulouse, December 22, 1941.
32. Note sous arrêt, cour d'appel d'Aix, May 12, 1942, Delle Weinthal and tribunal correctionnel de Bergerac, June 12, 1942, Pierre Bloch, *Gazette du palais* 2 (1942): 41.
33. Haennig, "L'incidence de la séparation" and "Quels moyens de preuve." These references to German law had been noted by Danièle Lochak in her article "La doctrine sous Vichy."
34. Haennig, "L'incidence de la séparation," 33.
35. The thesis of the colonial origin of Vichy's racism was advanced in particular by Olivier Le Cour Grandmaison, *Coloniser, exterminer: Sur la guerre et l'État colonial* (Paris: Fayard, 2005). Grandmaison's primary evidence is the trajectory of Marcel Peyrouton, a high official in the colonial administration who became minister of the interior from September 1940 to February 1941.
36. This is the subtitle of the thesis of André Broc.
37. Cited by Lochak, "La doctrine sous Vichy," 274.
38. On the notion of problematization, see Michel Foucault, "Polemics, Politics, and Problematizations," in *The Essential Works of Michel Foucault, Vol. 1, Ethics: Subjectivity and Truth*, ed. Paul Rabinow, 111–19 (New York: New Press, 1997).
39. The work of Jennifer Heuer, which combined family history and the history of nationality in the early nineteenth century, is an exception. See *The Family and the Nation: Gender and Citizenship in Revolutionary France, 1789–1830* (Ithaca, NY: Cornell University Press, 2005).

40. Marcela Iacub, *L'empire du ventre: Pour une autre histoire de la maternité* (Paris: Fayard, 2004).

41. See Patrick Weil's essential book *How to Be French: Nationality in the Making since 1789*, trans. Catherine Porter (Durham, NC: Duke University Press, 2009).

42. Gérard Noiriel, *The French Melting Pot: Immigration, Citizenship, and National Identity*, trans. Geoffroy de Laforcade (Minneapolis: University of Minnesota Press, 1996).

43. Gérard Noiriel, *Immigration, antisémitisme et racisme en France (XIXe–XXe siècle): Discours publics, humiliations privées* (Paris: Fayard, 2007).

44. Anne Verjus, *Le cens de la famille: Les femmes et le vote, 1789–1848* (Paris: Belin, 2002).

45. Émile Durkheim, "Introduction à la sociologie de la famille," in *Textes*, vol. 3, *Fonctions sociales et institutions*, collected and presented by Victor Karady (Paris: Minuit, 1975), 12.

46. Michel Foucault, "Governmentality" (1978), in *The Foucault Effect: Studies in Governmentality*, ed. Graham Burchell, Colin Gordon, and Peter Miller, 87–104 (Chicago: University of Chicago Press, 1991).

47. Joshua Cole, *The Power of Large Numbers: Population, Politics and Gender in Nineteenth Century France* (Ithaca, NY: Cornell University Press, 2000). Rémi Lenoir, *Généalogie de la morale familiale* (Paris: Seuil, 2003).

48. Philip Nord, *The Republican Moment: Struggles for Democracy in Nineteenth Century France* (Cambridge, MA: Harvard University Press, 1995). For an analysis of the relationship between paternity and citizenship between 1914 and 1945, see Kristen Stromberg Childers, *Fathers, Families and the State in France, 1914–1945* (Ithaca, NY: Cornell University Press, 2003).

49. Rogers Brubaker, *Citizenship and Nationhood in France and Germany* (Cambridge, MA: Harvard University Press, 1994); and Dominique Schnapper, *La France de l'intégration: Sociologie de la nation en 1990* (Paris: Gallimard, 1991).

50. Brubaker, *Citizenship and Nationhood*, 106–8.

51. Weil, *How to Be French*, 53 (emphasis in the original).

52. Louis Le Sueur and Eugène Dreyfus, *La nationalité: Commentaire de la loi du 26 juin 1889* (Paris: Durand et Pedone-Lauriel, 1890), 69.

53. Brubaker, *Citizenship and Nationhood*, 109–10.

54. Weiss, *Traité théorique et pratique de droit international privé*, vol. 1, 2nd ed. (Paris: Sirey, 1907).

55. Ibid., 20.

56. Ibid., 21.

57. Ibid., 49.

58. Weiss's argument contradicts Rogers Brubaker's assertion that "*jus sanguinis* was never affirmed or defended on its own merits," owing to the "weakness of the ethnic moment and the correlative strength of the assimilationist moment in French understanding." Brubaker, *Citizenship and Nationhood in France and Germany*, 96, 112.

59. The neologism is Jacques Derrida's, who used it in the 1970s to describe the way in which philosophical discourse and the "Western cultural tradition" more generally were built on absolute sexual difference. See especially *Margins of Philosophy*, trans. Alan Bass (Chicago: University of Chicago Press, 1982).

60. Dominique Schnapper, *Community of Citizens: On the Modern Idea of Nationality*, trans. from the French by Séverine Rosée (New Brunswick, NJ: Transaction Publishers, 1998), 35 (emphasis in the original).

61. Cécile Laborde, "La citoyenneté," in *Dictionnaire critique de la république*, ed. Vincent Duclert and Christophe Prochasson, 116–23 (Paris: Flammarion, 2002).

62. Schnapper, *Community of Citizens*, 126.

63. For an illuminating analysis of these different exclusions, see Pierre Rosanvallon, *Le sacre du citoyen: Histoire du suffrage universel en France* (Paris: Gallimard, 1992), 393–431.

64. Laurent Dubois, *A Colony of Citizens: Revolution and Slave Emancipation in the French Caribbean, 1787–1804* (Chapel Hill: University of North Carolina Press, 2004).

65. Frederick Cooper, "Alternatives to Empire: France and Africa after World War II," in *The State of Sovereignty: Territories, Laws, Populations*, ed. Douglas Howland and Luise White, 94–123 (Bloomington: Indiana University Press, 2009).

66. Laure Blévis, "Sociologie d'un droit colonial: Citoyenneté et nationalité en Algérie (1865–1947): Une exception républicaine?" (PhD diss., Institut d'études politiques d'Aix-en-Provence, France, 2004), 142–51, 349–93.

CONCLUSION

1. Pascal Blanchard, Nicolas Bancel, and Sandrine Lemaire, eds., *La fracture coloniale: La société française au prisme de l'héritage colonial* (2005; repr., Paris: la Découverte, 2006).

2. Elsa Dorlin, *La matrice de la race: Généalogie sexuelle et coloniale de la nation française* (Paris: la Découverte, 2006).

3. "The blind spot in the thinking of the republic, of the res publica, was the notion of 'race.' It was rejected in the name of French universalism and its refusal to recognize the cultural and religious diversity of French citizens. . . . It must be admitted that the notion of 'race' defines one of the lines of cleavage in republican universalism." Nicolas Bancel, Pascal Blanchard, and Françoise Vergès, *La république coloniale* (Paris: Hachette littératures, 2006), iv.

4. On this confusion, see Gérard Noiriel, "'Color blindness' et construction des identités dans l'espace public français," in *De la question sociale à la question raciale? Représenter la société française*, ed. Didier Fassin and Éric Fassin, 158–74 (Paris: la Découverte, 2006).

5. On the way in which the law "juridicizes society in its totality," see Bruno Latour, *La fabrique du droit: Une ethnographie du Conseil d'État* (2002; repr. Paris: la Découverte, 2004).

6. Marcela Iacub, *L'empire du ventre: Pour une autre histoire de la maternité* (Paris: Fayard, 2004).

7. Gérard Noiriel, *The French Melting Pot: Immigration, Citizenship, and National Identity*, trans. Geoffroy de Laforcade (Minneapolis: University of Minnesota Press, 1996).

8. Jacques Donzelot, *La police des familles* (1977; repr. Paris: Minuit, 2005).

9. Michel Foucault, "Governmentality" (1978), in *The Foucault Effect: Studies in Governmentality*, ed. Graham Burchell, Colin Gordon, and Peter Miller, 87–104 (Chicago: University of Chicago Press, 1991).

10. Yan Thomas, "L'institution civile de la cité," *Le débat* 74 (1993): 23–44.

11. Olivier Cayla, "Ouverture: La qualification ou la vérité du droit," *Droits* 18 (1993): 3–18.

BIBLIOGRAPHY

Listed here is the entirety of sources cited in the present work. For a more exhaustive list on the subject, please consult Emmanuelle Saada, "La 'question des métis' dans les colonies françaises: Socio-histoire d'une catégorie juridique (Indochine et autres territoires de l'Empire français, années 1890–années 1950)" (PhD diss., École des hautes études en sciences sociales, Paris, 2001).

ARCHIVAL SERIES
National Archives (AN)
SÉRIE F/12 (EXPOSITION INTERNATIONALE DE 1937, PARIS)
F/12/12258: Concours du meilleur mariage colonial.

CONSEIL D'ÉTAT (CE)
196585: Projet de décret réglant la condition juridique des métis en Indochine.
199767: Projet de décret fixant la condition juridique des métis nés de parents légalement inconnus en AOF.
204047: Projet de décret réglementant dans la colonie de Madagascar et dépendances les conditions d'accession des métis à la qualité de citoyen français.
209268: Projet de décret tendant à réglementer pour la Nouvelle-Calédonie et dépendances l'accession des métis à la qualité de citoyen français.
216571: Projet de décret fixant le statut des métis nés en AEF de parents légalement inconnus.

GOUVERNEMENT GÉNÉRAL DE L'AFRIQUE OCCIDENTALE FRANÇAISE (GGAOF)
Microfilms of archives deposited in Dakar.
21G79: Associations de métis. 1939–46.
23G22: Condition des métis. Textes et documents. 1928–46.

Centre des archives d'outre-mer (CAOM, Aix-en-Provence)
MINISTERIAL COLLECTIONS
Direction des affaires politiques (Aff. pol.)
28: Abandon des enfants naturels. 1912.
1194: Métis et Eurasiens. 1918–55.
1637: Nationalité. Statut des métis. AOF, AEF, Nouvelle-Calédonie, Madagascar et Togo. 1930–38.

2125/2: AEF. Population, problème des métis. 1939–49.
3406/6: Questions politiques et administratives. AOF. Métis. 1948–55.

Série géographique, Guadeloupe (SG Guadeloupe)
133/897: Tableaux et états analytiques de la population, du commerce et des cultures.
1845–75.

Série géographique, Indochine, Nouveau Fonds (SG Indo NF)
51 bis: Protection de l'enfance. 1899–1900.
2374: Emploi des métis indochinois. 1933.
3141: Modification des statuts de l'association de protection des enfants métis. Hanoi,
Tonkin: 1925.

Série géographique, Madagascar (SG Mad)
325/843: Condition des indigènes, accession des indigènes à la qualité de citoyen français,
mariages mixtes, question des métis. 1909–38.

Service de liaison avec les originaires des territoires français d'outre-mer, 1916–23 (SLOTFOM)
VI/7: Mariages et état civil.
XII/1: Métis franco-indochinois.

Agence économique de la France d'outre-mer (AGEFOM)
252/376: Les métis et les Eurasiens. 1921–54.
900/2652: Société d'assistance des enfants abandonnés franco-indochinois. 1927.

Commission d'enquête dans les territoires d'outre-mer, dite "commission Guernut," 1937–38 (Guernut)
97: Indochine. Enquête n° 4 sur le problème des métis.

Fonds de l'École coloniale (ECOL)
Papiers Paul Dislère:
2 Ecol 18: Conseil de législation coloniale. Projets de décret sur le statut des métis.
1930–32.
Mémoires de fin d'études:
Cornevin, Robert. "Les métis dans la colonisation française: L'hésitation métisse."
Thesis, ENFOM (École nationale de la France d'outre-mer), 1941–42.
Pauchet, Claude. "Le problème des métis en Afrique." Thesis, ENFOM (École nation-
ale de la France d'outre-mer), 1947–48.

Conseil supérieur des colonies (CSC)
25: Procès-verbaux des assemblées, communiqués à la presse. 1926–34.
26: Conseil de législation. 1921–26.

TERRITORIAL COLLECTIONS
Gouvernement général de l'Algérie (GGA)
8/X/232: Monographie du poste d'El Goléa. 1955.
14/H/72: Questions concernant les indigènes. Territoires du sud. Ouvroirs des sœurs
Blanches (El Goléa; Ghardaïa). 1909–42.

Gouvernement général de Madagascar (GGM)
6(10)D4: Condition juridique des enfants métis. Société d'assistance et de protection des
enfants métis. École des enfants métis. 1903–33.

Gouvernement général de l'Afrique équatoriale française (GGAEF)

5D44: Métis. État civil. Statut juridique. Association de l'amicale des métis de l'AEF. Statut de l'association.

5D202: Politique indigène du gouverneur général Éboué. 1941–43.

Gouvernement général de l'Indochine (GGI)

1664: Au sujet d'un jugement rendu par le tribunal de Phnom Penh concernant le jeune Jean-Louis H. 1915.

2065: Métis partis en France. 1914–18.

2711: Admission des enfants métis non reconnus au certificat d'études au titre français et au bénéfice des bourses scolaires. 1919.

7700: Circulaire relative aux inconvénients résultant de la cohabitation de fonctionnaires indigènes avec des femmes indigènes. 1897–1901.

7701: Métis. Société de protection des enfants métis non reconnus. Note sur la question des métis par M. Crévost, statuts. 1896–1909.

16621: Reconnaissance judiciaire de la paternité naturelle. 1910–16.

16771: Assistance publique. Situation de la Société de protection des enfants métis abandonnés. 1912.

16772: Assistance publique. Métis abandonnés. Satisfaction donnée aux différents vœux émis par la Société de protection de l'enfance à Phnom Penh. 1917.

16773: Assistance publique. Métis abandonnés. Envoi de métis franco-indigènes en France. 1923.

16776: Société de protection des enfants métis abandonnés. Demande de rapatriement. 1923–24.

26499: Au sujet des enfants reconnus par le capitaine Gérard. 1915.

42706, 42790, 42807, 44776, 44799, 44843, 45132: Dossiers de naturalisation.

53500: Commission d'enquête dans les territoires d'outre-mer. Enquêtes sur l'alimentation, les migrations intérieures, les métis faites au Tonkin. 1938.

53523: Commission d'enquête dans les territoires d'outre-mer. Vœux adressés directement à la commission d'enquête. Vœux émis par la Société d'assistance aux intérêts franco-indochinois de Hanoi. 1938.

53653: Commission d'enquête dans les territoires d'outre-mer. Rapport de M. Rebouillat, administrateur des services civils sur les "Français d'Indochine." Cochinchine. 1937.

54220: Consulat de France à Batavia. Renseignements sur les usages commerciaux à Java et sur les métis abandonnés aux Indes néerlandaises. 1902.

65316: Textes divers, état civil annamite. 1931–40.

65319: Naissances, reconnaissances d'enfants naturels, adoption, filiation. 1924–43.

Résidence supérieure au Tonkin (RST)

1098: Demande de renseignements sur les droits de l'enfant. 1916.

1099: Métis non reconnus. Accession à la citoyenneté française. Adoptions, secours demandés. 1916–42.

1154: Naturalisations, dossiers individuels. 1897–1945.

3566: Indigènes et métis admis aux écoles de Haiphong. 1913.

3890: Projet de création de l'Assistance sociale en Indochine. 1922–30.

3920: Création d'une section coloniale du Comité national de protection de l'enfance, dirigé par Paul Strauss. 1936.

3942: Inspection du travail. 1941–42.

Résidence supérieure au Tonkin, nouveau fonds (RST NF)

3373: Engagement des métis franco-annamites dans les bataillons de la légion étrangère.

6648: Renseignements confidentiels sur Mme N., dont la fille a été reconnue par son père Georges B., légionnaire. 1940.

PRIVATE ARCHIVES DEPOSITED AT CAOM
Fondation des œuvres de l'enfance française d'Indochine (90 APC) (FOEFI)

89: Généralités sur le fonctionnement de la FOEFI.

National Archives of Vietnam, Center No. 1, Hanoi, Vietnam (ANVN 1)
Gouvernement général de l'Indochine (ANVN 1, GGI)

75: Fondation Jules Brévié. Demande formulée par le sergent B. en vue de l'éducation de son fils. 1943.

88: Fondation Jules Brévié. Recensement des Eurasiens d'Indochine. 1940–45.

89: Fondation Jules Brévié. Plan d'action en vue de l'assistance et de la formation professionnelle des Eurasiens. 1942–43.

471: Projet de création à Hanoi d'un foyer eurasien chargé de recueillir et aider les métis adolescents et adultes. 1945.

504: Fondation Jules Brévié. Nomination du président de la Société d'assistance [aux enfants franco-indochinois] du Tonkin. 1940.

4809: Fondation Jules Brévié. Société de protection de l'enfance au Cambodge. 1939–45.

4810: Fondation Jules Brévié. Éducation et placement des enfants franco-indochinois. 1938–42.

4813: Fondation Jules Brévié. Procès-verbaux des assemblées générales. 1939–45.

4896: Colonisation agricole par les Eurasiens. 1941.

6564: Naturalisation des Indochinois et des protégés français. 1910–43.

Résidence supérieure au Tonkin, Hanoi (ANVN 1, RST)

5543: Demande de subvention présentée par la Société de protection des enfants métis. 1899.

5545: Statuts de la Société de protection des enfants métis abandonnés. 1906.

5547: Société de protection des enfants métis abandonnés. Rapport annuel sur le fonctionnement et sur la comptabilité. 1907–18.

5561: Situation au point de vue du recrutement des métis franco-asiatiques non reconnus en Indochine. 1911.

8419: Liste des élèves métis orphelins ou abandonnés par leur père. 1898.

8459: Renvoi des écoles municipales des enfants métis non reconnus. 1904.

12836: Création d'un établissement agricole à Hung Hoa, à l'usage des enfants métis abandonnés. 1907.

47922: D-V-T, enfant métis abandonné.

48379: Au sujet du jeune métis V. 1920.

48405: Lettre de Mme T. demandant que le caporal L. soit mis dans l'obligation de subvenir à l'entretien de l'enfant qu'il a reconnu. 1933.

48427: Au sujet de la jeune Emma A. placée à l'orphelinat des enfants indochinois abandonnés. 1931.

71191: Enquête sur le problème métis au Tonkin. Admission des métis dans les écoles d'enfants de troupe de Dalat et Phu Lang Thuong. 1934–39.

73758: Société d'assistance aux enfants franco-indochinois. Statuts, notes sur les œuvres de protection de l'enfance. Rapports annuels sur la marche de la société. 1926–44.

79378: Dossiers de naturalisation française des Indochinois dont le nom commence par la lettre *B*. 1914–33.

79397: Dossiers de naturalisation française concernant les Indochinois dont les noms commencent par la lettre *L*. 1914–33.

81130: Demande de secours. N.d.

Mairie de Hanoi (ANVN 1, Mairie Hanoi)

3279: Recensement des métis franco-indochinois. 1938–43.

5900: Société d'assistance aux enfants franco-indochinois fondée en 1897. 1906–44.

Other Archival Collections

MINISTÈRE DES AFFAIRES ÉTRANGÈRES (MAE)

Sous-série "Sud-Vietnam." Vol. 103, Questions administratives et contentieuses. Nationalité. 1958–64.

ARCHIVES DE LA LIGUE DES DROITS DE L'HOMME, DEPOSITED AT BIBLIOTHÈQUE DE DOCUMENTATION INTERNATIONALE CONTEMPORAINE (BDIC, LDH)

F delta rés 798/83: "Problème des fonctionnaires métis."

ACADÉMIE DES SCIENCES D'OUTRE-MER

Dossier personnel d'Henri Sambuc.

BIBLIOTHÈQUE MARGUERITE DURAND

347 PAT: Presse féministe, fin du XIXe siècle.

ARCHIVES DE LA FONDATION DE L'ENFANCE FRANÇAISE D'INDOCHINE (ARCHIVES FOEFI)

No inventory available.

NATIONAL ARCHIVES OF MADAGASCAR

D130: Note sur les écoles des enfants métis.

PRIMARY SOURCES

Congresses (in Chronological Order)

Congrès colonial international. Paris: Challamel, 1889.

Actes du deuxième Congrès international d'anthropologie criminelle. Paris: Masson, 1890.

Congrès international de sociologie coloniale. 2 vols. Exposition universelle internationale de 1900. Paris: Arthur Rousseau, 1901.

Institut colonial international, rapports préliminaires: Session de Brunswick. 2 vols. Brussels: Établissements généraux d'imprimerie, 1911.

Institut colonial international, rapports préliminaires: Session de Paris. 2 vols. Brussels: Établissements généraux d'imprimerie, 1921.

Congrès de la mutualité coloniale: Session de Tunis. Bordeaux: Imprimerie de l'avenir de la mutualité, 1923.

Institut colonial international, rapports préliminaires: Session de Bruxelles. 2 vols. Brussels: Établissements généraux d'imprimerie, 1923.

Rapport général: Exposition coloniale de 1931. Vol. 5, *Les sections coloniales.* Paris: Imprimerie nationale, 1933.

Congrès international pour l'étude des problèmes résultant du mélange des races. Brussels: Exposition internationale et universelle de Bruxelles, 1935.

Periodicals

GENERAL

La revue indochinoise (Hanoi).

ANTHROPOLOGY

Bulletins de la Société d'anthropologie de Paris. Paris: Masson. Published since 1860. Becomes Bulletins et mémoires de la Société d'anthropologie de Paris in 1900.

LAW

Dareste, Pierre, ed. Recueil de législation, de doctrine et de jurisprudence coloniales. Paris: Challamel. Published from 1898 to 1939, it is commonly cited in abbreviated form: Dareste I (Législation), Dareste II (Doctrine), Dareste III (Jurisprudence).

Lois annotées, décrets, ordonnances, avis du Conseil d'état, etc., avec notes historiques, de concordance et de jurisprudence. Paris: Larose, 1911–18.

Penant, Delphin, ed. Recueil général de jurisprudence, de doctrine et de législation coloniales et maritimes. Paris: Librairie Sirey. Published since 1891, it is cited in abbreviated form: Penant I (Jurisprudence), Penant II (Doctrine), Penant III (Législation).

Recueil général des lois et des arrêts en matière civile, criminelle, commerciale et de droit public. Paris: Société du recueil Sirey. Published since 1791, it is one of the main sources for French court decisions.

Revue algérienne et tunisienne de législation et de jurisprudence. Algiers: Adolphe Jourdan. Published from 1885 until 1962, it became the Revue algérienne, tunisienne et marocaine de législation et de jurisprudence in 1912. It is divided in three parts: Doctrine et législation; Jurisprudence; Lois, décrêts, arrêtés.

NEWSPAPERS

L'alerte (Hanoi).
L'avenir du Tonkin: Journal des intérêts français en Extrême-Orient (Hanoi).
Blanc et jaune (Hanoi).
La dépêche coloniale (Paris).
France-Indochine (Hanoi).
La presse indochinoise (Saigon).
Le Tonkin républicain (Hanoi).

Published Government Documents

Gouvernement général de l'Indochine, Direction des affaires économiques. Annuaire statistique de l'Indochine: Recueil de statistiques relatives aux années 1913 à 1922. Hanoi: Imprimerie d'Extrême-Orient, 1927.

Gouvernement général de l'Indochine, Direction des affaires économiques. Annuaire statistique de l'Indochine: Recueil de statistiques relatives aux années 1923 à 1929. Hanoi: Imprimerie d'Extrême-Orient, 1931.

Ministère des Colonies, Office colonial. Statistiques de la population dans les colonies françaises pour l'année 1906, suivies du relevé de la superficie des colonies françaises. Melun, France: Imprimerie administrative, 1909.

Contemporary Published Materials

Abor, Raoul. Des reconnaissances frauduleuses d'enfants naturels en Indochine. Hanoi: Imprimerie tonkinoise, 1917.

Antonelli, Étienne. Manuel de législation coloniale. Paris: PUF, 1925.

Apchié, Charles. De la condition juridique des indigènes en Algérie, dans les colonies et dans les pays de protectorat. Paris: Librairie nouvelle de droit et de jurisprudence, 1898.

Asmis, Dr. Rudolf. "La condition juridique des indigènes dans l'Afrique occidentale française." *Dareste* II (1910): 17–48.

Augagneur, Victor. "Les femmes aux colonies." *Les annales coloniales*, January 18, 1913.

Auriol, Charles. "Du rôle de la possession d'état en droit romain et en droit civil français." PhD diss., Université de Toulouse, Faculté de droit, 1884.

Babut, Ernest. "Le métis franco-annamite." *Revue indochinoise* 61 (1907): 897–908.

Barni, Jules. *La morale dans la démocratie* [1868], *suivi du Manuel républicain* [1872]. Paris: Kimé, 1992.

Barot, Dr. Louis. *Guide de l'Européen dans l'Afrique occidentale, à l'usage des militaires, fonctionnaires, commerçants, colons et touristes.* Paris: Flammarion, 1902.

Barrès, Maurice. *Les déracinés: Le roman de l'énergie nationale.* Paris: Fasquelle, 1897. Reprint, Paris: Honoré Champion, 2004.

Bénet, Henri. *L'état civil en Algérie: Traité théorique et pratique.* Algiers: Imprimerie Minerva, 1937.

Bérillon, Dr. Edgar. "Le problème psychobiologique du métissage dans les races." *Revue de psychologie appliquée*, 4th ser., 32, no. 7 (July 1926): 114–15.

Besson, Emmanuel. *La législation civile de l'Algérie: Étude sur la condition des personnes et sur le régime des biens en Algérie.* Paris: Librairie Maresq ainé, 1894.

Billiard, Albert. *Politique et organisation coloniales: Principes généraux.* Paris: V. Giard et E. Brière, 1899.

Blot, Dr. "L'œuvre scientifique du colonel A. Bonifacy." *Bulletins et mémoires de la Société d'anthropologie de Paris*, 8th ser., 2 (1931): 9–10.

Bonifacy, Lieutenant Colonel Auguste. "Les métis franco-tonkinois." *Bulletins et mémoires de la Société d'anthropologie de Paris* 6, no. 1 (1910): 607–42.

Bonnichon, André. *La conversion au christianisme de l'indigène musulman algérien et ses effets juridiques (un cas de conflit colonial).* Paris: Librairie du Recueil Sirey, 1931.

Bonniot, R. *L'enfance métisse malheureuse.* Report presented at Congrès de l'enfance. Saigon: Imprimerie de l'union, 1940.

Bonvicini, Henri. *Enfants de la colonie.* Saigon: Éditions Orient-Occident, 1938.

Bouchon, Henri. *Mousson du Sud: Essai sur la vie indochinoise.* Hanoi: 1942.

Broc, André. *La qualité de juif: Une notion juridique nouvelle.* Paris: PUF, 1943.

Broca, Paul. "Recherches sur l'ethnologie de la France." *Bulletins de la Société d'anthropologie de Paris* 1, no. 1 (1860): 7–15.

———. "Recherches sur l'hybridité animale en général et sur l'hybridité humaine en particulier considérées dans leurs rapports avec la question de la pluralité des espèces humaines." In *Mémoires d'anthropologie.* Paris: C. Reinwald, 1871.

Brunot, Charles. *Les déclassés asolidaires, délinquants de droit commun, mécontents politiques, etc.: Notes présentées au Congrès international de l'éducation sociale.* Paris: Librairie polytechnique, 1900.

Bulletin du Comité des travaux historiques et scientifiques. Paris: Imprimerie nationale, 1897.

Chauvel, Pierre. "De la qualité de pupille de la nation, des prérogatives attachées à ce titre." PhD diss., Université de Rennes, Faculté de droit, 1933.

Chivas-Baron, Clotilde. *Confidences de métisse.* Paris: Fasquelle, 1927.

———. *La femme française aux colonies.* Paris: Larose, 1929.

"Chronique de droit civil en 1912 (filiation)." *Revue critique de législation et de jurisprudence* 42 (1913): 240–42.

Colin, Ambroise. "De la protection de la descendance illégitime au point de vue de la filiation." *Revue trimestrielle de droit civil* 1 (1902): 257–300.

"La condition juridique des indigènes en Nouvelle-Calédonie." *Dareste* II (1919): 1–16.

Danan, Alexis. "Un drame inconnu: Ces Français de hasard que la France abandonne." *Franc tireur*, no. 2292 (December 12, 1951).

Dareste, Pierre. "Les nouveaux citoyens français." *Dareste* II (1916): 1–16.

———, ed. *Traité de droit colonial.* 2 vols. Cannes and Paris: Imprimerie Robaudy, 1931.

Demontès, Victor. *L'Algérie économique.* Vol. 2, *Les populations algériennes.* Algiers: Imprimerie algérienne, 1923.

———. *Le peuple algérien: Essais de démographie algérienne.* Algiers: Imprimerie algérienne, 1906.

D'Enjoy, Paul. *La colonisation de la Cochinchine (Manuel du colon).* Paris: Société d'éditions scientifiques, 1898.

Douchet. *Métis et congaies d'Indochine.* Hanoi: 1928.

Doutté, Edmond. "Lettre à Augustin Bernard." *Questions diplomatiques et coloniales*, October 1, 1901.

Estoublon, Robert. *Jurisprudence algérienne de 1830 à 1876.* Vol. 3, *1859–1867.* Algiers: Adolphe Jourdan, 1890.

Farrère, Claude. *Les civilisés.* Paris: Ollendorff, 1906.

Fenet, Pierre-Antoine. *Recueil complet des travaux préparatoires du Code civil.* Vol. 10. Paris: Videcoq, 1836.

Furetière, Antoine. *Dictionnaire usuel contenant généralement tous les mots français et tant vieux que modernes et les termes de toutes les sciences et les arts.* The Hague and Rotterdam: A. R. Leers, 1690–1701.

Galuski, M. "Enquête sur la question des métis: Au Tonkin." *Revue indochinoise* 16, no. 4 (1913): 402–8.

Girault, Arthur. *Condition des indigènes au point de vue de la législation civile et criminelle et de la distribution de la justice.* Report published in *Congrès international de sociologie coloniale.* 2 vols. *Exposition universelle internationale de 1900*, 1:45–79. Paris: Arthur Rousseau, 1901.

———. *Principes de colonisation et de législation coloniale.* 5th ed. Vol. 2. Paris: Sirey, 1929.

———. "Rapport sur un projet de décret concernant les métis présenté au Conseil supérieur des colonies le 1er décembre 1926." *Dareste* II (1926): 17–22.

Goguey, André. "Des reconnaissances et légitimations de complaisance." PhD diss., Université de Dijon, Faculté de droit, 1958.

Gravelle, Charles. "Au directeur de la dépêche coloniale." *La dépêche coloniale*, 5040, December 18, 1911.

———. "Les métis et l'œuvre de la protection de l'enfance au Cambodge." *Revue indochinoise* 16, no. 1 (1913): 31–42.

Haennig, Joseph. "L'incidence de la séparation des Églises et de l'État sur la définition du métis juif." *Gazette du palais* 2 (1942): 32–33.

———. "Quels moyens de preuve peuvent être fournis par le métis juif pour établir sa non-appartenance à la race juive?" *Gazette du palais* 1 (1943): 31–32.

Hardy, Georges. *Nos grands problèmes coloniaux.* Paris: Armand Colin, 1929.

———. "La préparation sociale des jeunes gens qui se destinent à la colonisation: Fonctionnaires et colons." *Semaines sociales de France*, session 22, Marseille, 1930.

Harmand, Jules. *Domination et colonisation.* Paris: Flammarion, 1910.

Heuyer, Georges, and Françoise Lautmann. "Troubles du caractère et inadaptation sociale chez les enfants métis." *Archives de médecine des enfants* 40, no. 9 (1937): 553–64.

Huard, Pierre, and Alfred Bigot. "Introduction à l'étude des Eurasiens." *Bulletin économique de l'Indochine*, booklet 4, 715–58 (Hanoi: Direction des services économiques, 1939).

Huerne, André. "La nationalité de l'enfant naturel." PhD diss., Université de Paris, Faculté de droit, 1903.

Jully, Antony. "La question des enfants métis." *Revue de Madagascar: Organe du Comité de Madagascar* 7 (1905): 509–26.

Laboratoire d'anthropologie écologique des populations contemporaines et préhistoriques. *Anthropologie des métis franco-vietnamiens*. Paris: Société d'anthropologie de Paris / Masson et cie., 1967.

Labouret, Henri. "La situation morale et matérielle des métis dans l'Ouest africain français et la législation qui leur est appliquée." In *Compte rendu du Congrès international pour l'étude des problèmes résultant du mélange des races*, 17–28. Brussels: Exposition internationale et universelle de Bruxelles, 1935.

Laugier, Edmond. "À la conquête des cœurs." *La presse indochinoise*, September 6, 1926.

Lefort, Georges. "De la possession d'état en matière de filiation naturelle et modifications apportées par la loi du 16 novembre 1912." PhD diss., Université de Paris, Faculté de droit, 1914.

Leiris, Michel. *Race et civilisation*. In La question raciale devant la science moderne. Paris: UNESCO, 1951.

Le Play, Frédéric. *La réforme sociale en France déduite de l'observation comparée des peuples européens*. Paris: H. Plon, 1864. Reprint, Geneva: Slatkine, 1982.

Le Sueur, Louis, and Eugène Dreyfus. *La nationalité: Commentaire de la loi du 26 juin 1889*. Paris: Durand et Pedone-Lauriel, 1890.

Levasseur, Georges. *La situation juridique des Chinois en Indochine depuis les accords de Nankin*. Hanoi: Imprimerie d'Extrême-Orient, 1939.

Lévi-Strauss, Claude. *Race et histoire*. In La question raciale devant la science moderne. Paris: UNESCO, 1952.

"Loi sur la nationalité suivie des décrets et instructions relatifs à l'application de la loi du 10 août 1927." Nancy, France: Librairie d'administration Berger-Levrault, 1927.

Londres, Albert. *Terre d'ébène*. Paris: Albin Michel, 1929.

Mader, Capitaine Henri. *Les écoles d'enfants de troupe: Historique de l'institution*. Paris: Henri Charles-Lavauzelle, 1894.

Marchand, Dr. Henri. "Considérations sur les mariages franco-musulmans." In "Le mariage mixte franco-musulman." Special issue, *Les annales juridiques, politiques, économiques et sociales* 1, nos. 3–4 (1956): 5–23.

Marinetti. "La situation des Eurasiens d'Indochine au point de vue social et politique." *La presse indochinoise*, November 26, 1937, 1, 6.

Martial, René. *Les métis: Nouvelle étude sur les migrations, le mélange des races, le métissage, la retrempe de la race française et la révision du code de la famille*. Paris: Flammarion, 1942.

Mathieu, E. "La protection de l'enfance en Cochinchine, son œuvre, sa portée sociale." In *Semaine de l'enfance du 1ᵉʳ au 7 juillet 1934: Rapports*, 32–43. Saigon: Imprimerie de l'Union, 1934.

Maunier, René. Introduction to *Principes de colonisation et de législation coloniale: Les colonies françaises avant et depuis 1815*, by Arthur Girault. 6th ed. Paris: Sirey, 1943.

———. "Le mélange des races dans les colonies." *Annales de l'Université de Paris* 2, no. 6 (1931): 116–27.

Mazet, Jacques. "La condition juridique des métis dans les possessions françaises." PhD diss., Université de Paris, Faculté de droit, 1932.

Mérimée, J. "De l'accession des Indochinois à la qualité de citoyen français." PhD diss., Université de Toulouse, Faculté de droit, 1931.

Mersier, Émile. *Traité théorique et pratique des actes de l'état civil*. Paris: Dupont et Marescq, 1873.

Michelet, Jules. *Tableau de l'histoire de France*. Paris: Hachette, 1833.

Moncelon, M. "Métis de Français et de Néo-Calédoniens." *Bulletins de la Société d'anthropologie de Paris* 3, no. 9 (1886): 10–19.

Moreau, Paul. "De la condition juridique, politique et économique des indigènes de l'AOF." PhD diss., Université de Paris, Faculté de droit, 1938.

Mury, Gilbert. "Le problème eurasien en Indochine." *Le courrier colonial*, March 3, 1939.

"La nationalité aux colonies." *Dareste* II (1911): 9–18.

Neuville, Henri. "L'espèce, la race et le métissage en anthropologie: Introduction à l'anthropologie générale." In *Archives de l'Institut de paléontologie humaine*, vol. 11. Paris: Masson, 1933.

Paris, Camille. *De la condition juridique des métis dans les colonies et les possessions françaises: Des métis franco-annamites dans l'Indochine*. Saigon: 1904.

Perreau, E.-H. "Le nouveau statut des juifs en France." *La semaine juridique* (1941) 9, 2nd semester, study 216.

Pommier, René. "Le régime de l'indigénat en Indochine." PhD diss., Université de Paris, Faculté de droit, 1907.

Ponsolle, Paul. *La dépopulation*. Paris: Baillère et Messager, 1893.

Portalis, Jean-Etienne-Marie. "Discours préliminaire prononcé lors de la présentation du projet au gouvernement." In *Naissance du Code civil: La raison du législateur*, edited by François Ewald, 35–90. Paris: Flammarion, 1989. Originally published in P. A. Fenet, *Recueil complet des travaux préparatoires du Code civil* (Paris: Videcoq, 1836).

Pouvourville, Albert de. "L'Indochine et ses métis." *La dépêche coloniale*, 4949, September 16, 1911.

———. "L'Indochine française: Introduction générale." *L'encyclopédie coloniale et maritime*. Paris: Encyclopédie coloniale et maritime, 1936.

———. "Mariages mixtes et métis." *La nouvelle revue*, 4th ser., 7, no. 25 (May 1, 1913): 38–40.

———. "Le métis." *Le mal d'argent*. Paris: Éditions du monde moderne, 1926.

Pouzol, Abel. *La recherche de paternité: Étude critique de sociologie et de législation comparée*. Paris: Giard et Brière, 1902.

Pressensé, Francis de. "L'égalité devant l'enseignement à Madagascar." *Les cahiers des droits de l'homme* (1905): 1198–99.

Raicovicianu, Nicolae G. "La loi du 16 novembre 1912 et l'action en déclaration de paternité naturelle." PhD diss., Université de Paris, Faculté de droit, 1913.

Rapports et projets de décrets de la commission instituée pour préparer l'acte d'abolition immédiate de l'esclavage. Paris: Imprimerie nationale, 1848.

Ravoux, Médecin-commandant. "Aspects sociaux d'un groupe d'Eurasiens." *Bulletins et mémoires de la Société d'anthropologie de Paris* 9, no. 9 (1948): 180–90.

Renel, Charles. *Le "décivilisé."* Paris: Flammarion, 1923.

Renan, Ernest. "What Is a Nation?" (1882), translated by Martin Thom. In *Nation and Narration*, edited by Homi K. Bhabha, 8–22. London: Routledge, 1990.

Roseval, L. "Le mulâtre." In *Les Français peints par eux-mêmes*. Vol. 3, *Provinces*. Paris: L. Curmer, 1842.

Rousseau, Jean-Jacques. *On the Social Contract; or, Principles of Political Right*. In *Basic Political Writings*, translated by Donald A. Cress, 139–227. Indianapolis and Cambridge: Hackett Publishing Company, 1987.

Sambuc, Henri. "La condition juridique des métis dans les colonies françaises." *Dareste* II (1933): 57–68.

———. "De la condition légale des enfants nés en Indochine de parents inconnus." *Dareste* II (1929): 1–8.

———. "De la condition légale des enfants nés en Indochine de père français et de mère indigène ou de parents inconnus." *Dareste* II (1914): 1–12.

———. "De la condition légale des enfants nés en Indochine de père français et de mère indigène ou de parents inconnus." *Dareste* II (1923): 1–6.

———. "Enquête sur la question des métis." Pt. 2. *Revue indochinoise* 16, no. 2 (1913): 201–9.

———. "Les métis franco-annamites en Indochine." *Revue du Pacifique diplomatique et coloniale* 10, no. 1 (1931): 262–63.

Savatier, René. *La recherche de paternité: Étude pratique de législation et de jurisprudence.* Paris: Dalloz, 1927.

Seignobos, Charles. *Histoire sincère de la nation française: Essai d'une histoire de l'évolution du peuple français.* 8th ed. Paris: PUF, 1982.

Séville, A. "Les métis parias de l'Indochine: Appel au peuple français." *Les annales diplomatiques et consulaires* (Paris), 1st ser., 2, no. 27 (March 5, 1905): 228–31.

Solus, Henry. *Traité de la condition des indigènes en droit privé, colonies et pays de protectorat et pays sous mandat.* Paris: Librairie du Recueil Sirey, 1927.

Taridif, Georges. "Chronique métisse." *Le Tonkin républicain*, April 9, 1926.

United Nations Educational, Scientific, and Cultural Organization (UNESCO). *Déclaration d'experts sur les questions de race.* Paris: UNESCO, 1950.

Viollette, Maurice. "La promulgation de la loi sur la recherche de paternité aux colonies." *Les annales coloniales*, January 6, 1913.

———. "Rapport fait au nom de la Commission de la réforme judiciaire et de la législation civile et criminelle chargée d'examiner la proposition de loi, adoptée par le Sénat, tendant à modifier l'article 340 du Code civil (reconnaissance judiciaire de paternité naturelle)." *Journal officiel, documents parlementaires*, annexe 796, Chambre des députés, Paris (1911): 1437–44.

Vu Van Quang. "Le problème des Eurasiens en Indochine." PhD diss., École de médecine et de pharmacie de plein exercice de l'Indochine, Hanoi, 1939.

Weiss, André. *Manuel de droit international privé.* 8th ed. Paris: Sirey, 1920.

———. *Traité théorique et pratique de droit international privé.* 2nd ed. Vol. 1, *De la nationalité.* Paris: Sirey, 1907.

Werner, Auguste-Reynald. "Essai sur la réglementation de la nationalité dans le droit colonial français." PhD diss., Université de Genève, Faculté de droit, 1936.

Zola, Émile. *Thérèse Raquin.* Paris: GF Flammarion, 1970.

SECONDARY MATERIALS

Abbott, Andrew. *The System of Professions: An Essay on the Division of Expert Labor.* Chicago: University of Chicago Press, 1988.

———. "Things of Boundaries." *Social Research* 62 (1995): 857–82.

Accampo, Elinor A., Rachel G. Fuchs, and Mary Lynn Stewart, eds. *Gender and the Politics of Social Reform in France, 1870–1914.* Baltimore: Johns Hopkins University Press, 1995.

Ageron, Charles-Robert. *France coloniale ou parti colonial?* Paris: PUF, 1978.

Amselle, Jean-Loup. *Affirmative Exclusion: Cultural Pluralism and the Rule of Custom in France.* Translated by Jane Marie Todd. Ithaca, NY: Cornell University Press, 2003.

Arnaud, André-Jean, ed. *Dictionnaire encyclopédique de théorie et de sociologie du droit*. Paris: LGDJ, 1988.

Balibar, Étienne. "La construction du racisme." *Actuel Marx* 38 (2005): 11–28.

Bancel, Nicolas, Pascal Blanchard, and Françoise Vergès. *La république coloniale*. Paris: Hachette littératures, 2006.

Barth, Fredrik. "Ethnic Groups and Boundaries." In *Theories of Ethnicity: A Classical Reader*, edited by Werner Sollors, 294–324. New York: New York University Press, 1996. Originally published in Fredrik Barth, *Ethnic Groups and Boundaries: The Social Organization of Culture Difference* (Bergen, Germany: Universitetsforlag; Boston: Little, Brown and Company, 1969).

Beaud, Olivier. *La puissance de l'État*. Paris: PUF, 1994.

Beaud, Stéphane, and Gérard Noiriel. "Penser l'intégration des immigrés." *Hommes et migrations* 1183 (1990): 43–53.

Becchia, Alain. "Les milieux parlementaires et la dépopulation de 1900 à 1914." *Communications* 44 (1986): 201–46.

Bensa, Alban. "Colonialisme, racisme et ethnologie en Nouvelle-Calédonie." *Ethnologie française* 18, no. 2 (1988): 187–97.

Berque, Jacques. *French North Africa: The Maghrib between Two World Wars*. Translated by Jean Stewart. New York: Praeger, 1967.

Blanchard, Pascal, Nicolas Bancel, and Sandrine Lemaire, eds. *La fracture coloniale: La société française au prisme de l'héritage colonial*. 2005. Reprint, Paris: la Découverte, 2006.

Blanckaert, Claude. "Of Monstrous *Métis*? Hybridity, Fear of Miscegenation, and Patriotism from Buffon to Paul Broca." In *The Color of Liberty: Histories of Races in France*, edited by Sue Peabody and Tyler Stovall, 42–70. Durham, NC: Duke University Press, 2003.

Blévis, Laure. "Les avatars de la citoyenneté en Algérie coloniale ou les paradoxes d'une catégorisation." *Droit et société* 48 (2001): 557–80.

———. "La citoyenneté française au miroir de la colonisation: Étude des demandes de naturalisation des 'sujets français' en Algérie coloniale." *Genèses* 53 (2003): 25–47.

———. "Sociologie d'un droit colonial: Citoyenneté et nationalité en Algérie (1865–1947): Une exception républicaine?" PhD diss., Institut d'études politiques d'Aix-en-Provence, France, 2004.

Boltanski, Luc. *L'amour et la justice comme compétences: Trois essais de sociologie de l'action*. Paris: Métailié, 1990.

———. *Les cadres: La formation d'un groupe social*. Paris: Minuit, 1982.

———. *Distant Suffering: Morality, Media and Politics*. Translated by Graham Burchell. Cambridge: Cambridge University Press, 1999.

Bonneuil, Christophe. "Mettre en œuvre et discipliner les tropiques: Les sciences du végétal dans l'Empire français, 1870–1940." PhD diss., Université de Paris VII, 1997.

Bonniol, Jean-Luc. *La couleur comme maléfice: Une illustration créole de la généalogie des blancs et des noirs*. Paris: Albin Michel, 1992.

Bourdieu, Pierre. "Avenir de classe et causalité du probable." *Revue française de sociologie* 15, no. 1 (1974): 3–42.

———. "Le capital social." *Actes de la recherche en sciences sociales* 31 (1980): 2–3.

Bourgeault, Eugénie. "Mères de famille et pétitions dans la Grande guerre: Les étapes du vote de la loi sur les pupilles de la nation." Master's thesis, Institut d'études politiques de Grenoble, Grenoble, 1997.

Brocheux, Pierre, and Daniel Hémery. *Indochina: An Ambiguous Colonization, 1858–1954*. Translated by Ly Lan Dill-Klein, with Eric Jennings, Nora Taylor, and Noémi Tousignant. Berkeley: University of California Press, 2009.

Brubaker, Rogers. *Citizenship and Nationhood in France and Germany.* Cambridge, MA: Harvard University Press, 1994.

Bruschi, Christian. "La nationalité dans le droit colonial." *Procès: Cahiers d'analyse politique et juridique* 18 (1987–88): 29–83.

Camiscioli, Elisa. *Reproducing the French Race: Immigration, Intimacy, and Embodiment in the Early Twentieth Century.* Durham, NC: Duke University Press, 2009.

Camus, Albert. *Le premier homme.* Repr., Paris: Gallimard, 2000.

Canguilhem, Georges. "Le vivant et son milieu." In *La connaissance de la vie,* 160–93. 1952. Reprint, Paris: Vrin, 1985.

Caplan, Jane, and John Torpey, eds. *Documenting Individual Identity: The Development of State Practices in the Modern World.* Princeton, NJ: Princeton University Press, 2001.

Carbonnier, Jean. *Droit civil.* Vol. 2, *La famille, l'enfant, le couple.* 20th ed. Paris: PUF, 1999.

Cayla, Olivier. "Ouverture: La qualification ou la vérité du droit." *Droits* 18 (1993): 3–18.

Chatterjee, Partha. *The Nation and Its Fragments: Colonial and Postcolonial Histories.* Princeton, NJ: Princeton University Press, 1993.

Childers, Kristen Stromberg. *Fathers, Families and the State in France, 1914–1945.* Ithaca, NY: Cornell University Press, 2003.

Cole, Joshua. *The Power of Large Numbers: Population, Politics and Gender in Nineteenth Century France.* Ithaca, NY: Cornell University Press, 2000.

Colonna, Fanny. *Instituteurs algériens, 1883–1939.* Paris: Presses de la Fondation nationale des sciences politiques, 1975.

Comaroff, Jean, and John Comaroff. *Of Revelation and Revolution: Christianity, Colonialism and Consciousness in South Africa.* 2 vols. Chicago: University of Chicago Press, 1991–97.

Conklin, Alice L. *A Mission to Civilize: The Republican Idea of Empire in France and West Africa, 1895–1930.* Palo Alto, CA: Stanford University Press, 1997.

Conry, Yvette. *L'introduction du darwinisme en France au XIXᵉ siècle.* Paris: Vrin, 1974.

Cooper, Frederick. "Alternatives to Empire: France and Africa after World War II." In *The State of Sovereignty: Territories, Laws, Populations,* edited by Douglas Howland and Luise White, 94–123. Bloomington: Indiana University Press, 2009.

———. *Colonialism in Question: Theory, Knowledge, History.* Berkeley: University of California Press, 2005.

———. "Conflict and Connection: Rethinking African Colonial History." *American Historical Review* 99, no. 5 (1994): 1516–45.

Cooper, Frederick, and Ann Laura Stoler. "Between Metropole and Colony: Rethinking a Research Agenda." In *Tensions of Empire: Colonial Cultures in a Bourgeois World,* ed. Frederick Cooper and Ann Laura Stoler, 1–56. Berkeley: University of California Press, 1997.

———, eds. *Tensions of Empire: Colonial Cultures in a Bourgeois World.* Berkeley: University of California Press, 1997.

Corbin, Alain. "Coulisses." In *De la Révolution à la Grande Guerre,* edited by Michelle Perrot, Alain Corbin, Roger-Henri Guerrand, et al. Vol. 4 of *Histoire de la vie privée,* edited by Philippe Aries and Georges Duby, 419–611. Paris: Seuil, 1987.

Cornu, Gérard. *Vocabulaire juridique.* 3rd ed. Paris: PUF, Collection Quadrige, 2002.

Cottias, Myriam. "Le silence de la nation: Les 'vieilles colonies' comme le lieu de définition des dogmes républicains, 1848–1905." *Outre-Mers* 338–39 (2003): 21–45.

Courbe, Patrick. *Le nouveau droit de la nationalité.* Paris: Dalloz, 1998.

Daughton, J. P. *An Empire Divided: Religion, Republicanism and the Making of French Colonialism, 1880–1914.* Oxford: Oxford University Press, 2006.

Daumas, Jean-Pierre. "Effets de la décolonisation sur la nationalité française des métis." *Revue juridique et politique: Indépendance et coopération* 24, no. 1 (1970): 35–50.

Dauphiné, Joël. "Le métissage biologique dans la Nouvelle-Calédonie coloniale, 1853–1939." In *Colonies, territoires, sociétés: L'enjeu français,* edited by Alain Saussol and Joseph Zitomersky, 217–22. Paris: l'Harmattan, 1996.

Davis, James F. *Who Is Black? One Nation's Definition.* University Park: Pennsylvania State University Press, 1991.

Delclitte, Christophe. "La catégorie juridique 'nomade' dans la loi de 1912." *Hommes et migrations* 1188–89 (1995): 23–30.

Dermenghem, Émile. *Le pays d'Abel: Le Sahara des Ouled-Naïl, des Larbaa et des Amour.* Paris: Gallimard, 1960.

Derrida, Jacques. *Margins of Philosophy.* Translated with additional notes by Alan Bass. Chicago: University of Chicago Press, 1982.

Deschamps, Damien. "La république aux colonies: Le citoyen, l'indigène et le fonctionnaire (vers 1848, vers 1900)." PhD diss., Université de Grenoble, Grenoble, 1998.

———. "Les sources scientifiques et la politique indochinoise de Jean-Louis de Lanessan, 1891–1894." In *Viêt-Nam, sources et approches: Actes du deuxième colloque international Euroviet d'Aix,* edited by Philippe Le Failler and Jean-Marie Mancini, 279–92. Aix-en-Provence, France: Publications de l'Université de Provence, 1995.

Desrosières, Alain. *The Politics of Large Numbers: A History of Statistical Reasoning.* Translated by Camille Naish. Cambridge, MA: Harvard University Press, 1998.

Direche-Slimani, Karima. *Chrétiens de Kabylie, 1873–1954: Une action missionnaire dans l'Algérie coloniale.* Saint-Denis, France: Bouchene, 2004.

Domínguez, Virginia R. *White by Definition: Social Classification in Creole Louisiana.* New Brunswick, NJ: Rutgers University Press, 1986.

Donzelot, Jacques. *La police des familles.* 1977. Reprint, Paris: Minuit, 2005.

Dorlin, Elsa. *La matrice de la race: Généalogie sexuelle et coloniale de la nation française.* Paris: la Découverte, 2006.

Dornel, Laurent. "Les usages du racialisme: Le cas de la main-d'œuvre coloniale en France pendant la Première Guerre mondiale." *Genèses* 20 (1995): 48–72.

Douglas, Mary. *How Institutions Think.* Syracuse, NY: Syracuse University Press, 1988.

Dubois, Laurent. *A Colony of Citizens: Revolution and Slave Emancipation in the French Caribbean, 1787–1804.* Chapel Hill: University of North Carolina Press, 2004.

Dupâquier, Jacques, ed. *Histoire de la population française.* Vol. 3, *De 1789 à 1914.* Paris: PUF, 1988.

Durkheim, Émile. "Introduction à la sociologie de la famille." In *Textes.* Vol. 3, *Fonctions sociales et institutions,* collected and presented by Victor Karady, 9–24. Paris: Minuit, 1975.

Ewald, François, ed. *Naissance du Code civil: La raison du législateur.* 1989. Reprint, Paris: Flammarion, 2004.

Fabre, Philippe. *Le Conseil d'État et Vichy: Le contentieux de l'antisémitisme.* Paris: Publications de la Sorbonne, 2001.

Fassin, Didier, and Éric Fassin, eds. *De la question sociale à la question raciale? Représenter la société française.* Paris: la Découverte, 2006.

Favre-Le-Van-Ho, Mireille. "Un milieu porteur de modernisation: Travailleurs et tirailleurs vietnamiens en France pendant la Première Guerre mondiale." Thesis, École nationale des Chartes, Paris, 1996.

Fine, Agnès, ed. *Adoptions, ethnologie des parentés choisies.* Paris: Maison des sciences de l'homme, 1998.

Firpo, Christina. "Lost Boys: 'Abandoned' Eurasian Children and the Management of the Racial Topography in Colonial Indochina, 1938–1945." *French Colonial History* 8 (2007): 203–24.

Foucault, Michel. "Governmentality" (1978). In *The Foucault Effect: Studies in Governmentality*, edited by Graham Burchell, Colin Gordon, and Peter Miller, 87–104. Chicago: University of Chicago Press, 1991.

———. *History of Sexuality.* Vol. 1, *An Introduction.* Translated by Robert Hurley. New York: Vintage Books, 1990.

———. "Polemics, Politics, and Problematizations." In *The Essential Works of Michel Foucault.* Vol. 1, *Ethics: Subjectivity and Truth.* Edited by Paul Rabinow, 111–19, translated by Lydia Davis. New York: New Press, 1997.

———. *Society Must Be Defended: Lectures at the Collège de France, 1975–76.* Edited by Mauro Bertani and Alessandro Fontana. General editors, François Ewald and Alessandro Fontana. Translated by David Macey. New York: Picador, 2003.

———. "The Subject and Power." In *Michel Foucault: Beyond Structuralism and Hermeneutics,* by Hubert Dreyfus and Paul Rabinow, 208–26. Chicago: University of Chicago Press, 1982.

Franchini, Philippe. *Continental Saïgon.* 1976. Reprint, Paris: Métailié, 1995.

Frank, Rainer. "La signification différente attachée à la filiation par le sang en droit allemand et français de la famille." *Revue internationale de droit comparé* 3 (1993): 635–55.

Gaïti, Brigitte, and Liora Israël, eds. "La cause du droit." Special issue, *Politix* 62 (2003).

Gebler, Marie-Josèphe. *Le droit français de la filiation et la vérité.* Paris: LGDJ, 1970.

Ginzburg, Carlo. "Clues: Roots of an Evidentiary Paradigm." In *Clues, Myths and the Historical Method.* Translated by John Tedeschi and Anne C. Tedeschi, 96–125. Baltimore: Johns Hopkins University Press, 1989.

Girardet, Raoul, ed. *Le nationalisme français, 1871–1914.* Paris: Armand Colin, 1966.

Goffman, Erving. *Stigma: Notes on the Management of Spoiled Identity.* Englewood Cliffs, NJ: Prentice-Hall, 1963.

Goguey, André. "Des reconnaissances et légitimations de complaisance." PhD diss., Université de Dijon, Faculté de droit, 1958.

Goodman, Nelson. *Ways of Worldmaking.* Indianapolis: Hackett, 1978.

Guha, Ranajit. *Dominance without Hegemony: History and Power in Colonial India.* Cambridge, MA: Harvard University Press, 1997.

Gutmann, Daniel. *Le sentiment d'identité: Étude de droit des personnes et de la famille.* Paris: LGDJ, 2000.

Hacking, Ian. "Inaugural Lecture: Chair of Philosophy and History of Scientific Concepts at the Collège de France, January 16, 2001." *Economy and Society* 31 (2002): 1–14.

———. *The Social Construction of What?* Cambridge, MA: Harvard University Press, 1999.

Halperin, Jean-Louis. *Histoire du droit privé français depuis 1804.* Paris: PUF, 1996.

Hélénon, Véronique. "Race, statut juridique et colonisation: Antillais et Africains dans les cadres administratifs des colonies françaises d'Afrique." In *L'esclavage, la colonisation, et après . . .* Edited by Patrick Weil and Stéphane Dufoix, 229–43. Paris: PUF, 2005.

Hermitte, Marie-Angèle. "Le droit est un autre monde." *Enquête* 7 (1998): 17–37.

Heuer, Jennifer. *The Family and the Nation: Gender and Citizenship in Revolutionary France, 1789–1830.* Ithaca, NY: Cornell University Press, 2005.

Hilberg, Raul. *The Destruction of the European Jews.* Chicago: Quadrangle Books, 1961.

Hirschman, Albert O. *The Rhetoric of Reaction: Perversity, Futility, Jeopardy.* Cambridge, MA: Harvard University Press, 1991.

Hommes et destins: Dictionnaire biographique d'outre-mer. Vol. 1. Paris: Académie des sciences d'outre-mer, 1975.

Hughes, Everett C. *The Sociological Eye.* Chicago: Aldine-Atherton, 1971.

Iacub, Marcela. *L'empire du ventre: Pour une autre histoire de la maternité.* Paris: Fayard, 2004.

Jablonka, Ivan. *Ni père ni mère: Histoire des enfants de l'assistance publique, 1874–1939.* Paris: Seuil, 2006.

Jandot-Danjou, Colette. "La condition civile des étrangers dans les trois derniers siècles de la monarchie." PhD diss., Université de Paris, Faculté de droit, 1939.

Jennings, Eric. *Curing the Colonizers: Hydrotherapy, Climatology and French Colonial Spas.* Durham, NC: Duke University Press, 2006.

———. *Vichy in the Tropics: Pétain's National Revolution in Madagascar, Guadeloupe, and Indochina, 1940–1944.* Palo Alto, CA: Stanford University Press, 2001.

Jestaz, Philippe, and Christophe Jamin. *La doctrine.* Paris: Dalloz, 2004.

Joly, Laurent. *Vichy dans la "solution finale": Histoire du Commissariat aux questions juives, 1941–1944.* Paris: Grasset, 2006.

Jouanna, Arlette. *L'idée de race en France au XVIe siècle et au début du XVIIe, 1498–1614.* Paris: Honoré Champion, 1975.

———. "Recherches sur la notion d'honneur au XVIe siècle." *Revue d'histoire moderne et contemporaine* 15 (1968): 597–623.

Koselleck, Reinhart. *Futures Past: On the Semantics of Historical Time.* Translated from the German by Keith Tribe. New York: Columbia University Press, 1990. First published in German in 1979.

Laborde, Cécile. "La citoyenneté." In *Dictionnaire critique de la République,* edited by Vincent Duclert and Christophe Prochasson, 116–23. Paris: Flammarion, 2002.

Lagarde, Paul. *La nationalité française.* 3rd ed. Paris: Dalloz, 1997.

Lapierre, Nicole. *Changer de nom.* Paris: Stock, 1995.

Laqueur, Thomas. *Making Sex: Body and Gender from the Greeks to Freud.* Cambridge, MA: Harvard University Press, 1990.

Latour, Bruno. *La fabrique du droit: Une ethnographie du Conseil d'État.* Paris: la Découverte, 2002.

Lebovics, Herman. *True France: The Wars over Cultural Identity, 1900–1945.* Ithaca, NY: Cornell University Press, 1992.

Le Cour Grandmaison, Olivier. *Coloniser, exterminer: Sur la guerre et l'État colonial.* Paris: Fayard, 2005.

———. *De l'indigénat. Anatomie d'un "monstre" juridique: Le droit colonial en Algérie et dans l'Empire français.* Paris: la Découverte, 2010.

Lefebvre-Taillard, Anne. *Introduction historique au droit des personnes et de la famille.* Paris: PUF, 1996.

Lenoir, Rémi. *Généalogie de la morale familiale.* Paris: Seuil, 2003.

Lewis, Martin Deming. "One Hundred Million Frenchmen: The 'Assimilation' Theory in French Colonial Policy." *Comparative Studies in Society and History* 4, no. 2 (1962): 129–53.

Lochak, Danièle. "La citoyenneté: Un concept juridique flou." In *Citoyenneté et nationalité: Perspectives en France et au Québec,* edited by Dominique Colas, Claude Emeri, and Jacques Zylberberg, 179–207. Paris: PUF, 1991.

———. "La doctrine sous Vichy ou les mésaventures du positivisme." In *Les usages sociaux du droit*, edited by CURAPP, 252–85. Paris: PUF, 1990.

———. "La *race*: Une catégorie juridique?" In "Sans distinction de . . . *race*." Special issue, *Mots: Les langages du politique* 33 (1992): 291–303.

Lofgren, Charles A. *The Plessy Case: A Legal Historical Interpretation*. New York and Oxford: Oxford University Press, 1987.

Lorcin, Patricia. *Imperial Identities: Stereotyping, Prejudice and Race in Colonial Algeria*. London: I. B. Tauris and Company, 1995.

Louis, Marie-Victoire. *Le droit de cuissage, France, 1860–1930*. Paris: Éditions de l'atelier, 1994.

Lucas, Philippe, and Jean-Claude Vatin. *L'Algérie des anthropologues*. Paris: François Maspero, 1975.

Mann, Gregory. *Native Sons: West African Veterans and France in the Twentieth Century*. Durham, NC: Duke University Press, 2006.

Marcou, Jean. "La 'qualité de juif.'" In "Le droit antisémite de Vichy." *Le genre humain* 30–31 (1996): 153–71.

Martin-Fugier, Anne. *La place des bonnes: La domesticité féminine à Paris en 1900*. Paris: Grasset, 1979. Reprint, Paris: Perrin, 2004.

Masse, Jean-Pierre. "L'exception indochinoise: Le dispositif d'accueil des réfugiés politiques en France, 1973–1991." PhD diss., EHESS, Paris, 1996.

Mauss, Marcel. "Techniques of the Body." In *Marcel Mauss: Techniques, Technology and Civilization*, edited by Nathan Schlanger, 77–96. New York: Durkheim Press and Berghahn Books, 2006.

Merle, Isabelle. "De la 'légalisation' de la violence en contexte colonial: Le régime de l'indigénat en question." *Politix* 17, no. 66 (2004): 137–62.

———. *Expériences coloniales: La Nouvelle-Calédonie, 1853–1920*. Paris: Belin, 1995.

Ministère de la Justice. *La nationalité française: Textes et documents*. Paris: la Documentation française, 1996.

Morgand-Cantegrit, Viviane. "La possession d'état d'enfant." PhD diss., Université de Lille II, Faculté des sciences juridiques, politiques et sociales, 1993.

Mosse, George L. *The Image of Man: The Creation of Modern Masculinity*. New York: Oxford University Press, 1996.

Mucchielli, Laurent. *La découverte du social: Naissance de la sociologie en France, 1870–1914*. Paris: la Découverte, 1998.

Naepels, Michel. *Histoires de terres kanakes: Conflits fonciers et rapports sociaux dans la région de Houaïlou (Nouvelle-Calédonie)*. Paris: Belin, 1998.

Nicolet, Claude. *L'idée républicaine en France: Essai d'histoire critique, 1789–1924*. Paris: Gallimard, 1982.

Noiriel, Gérard. "'Color blindness' et construction des identités dans l'espace public français." In *De la question sociale à la question raciale? Représenter la société française*, ed. Didier Fassin and Éric Fassin, 158–74. Paris: la Découverte, 2006.

———. *The French Melting Pot: Immigration, Citizenship, and National Identity*. Translated by Geoffroy de Laforcade. Minneapolis: University of Minnesota Press, 1996.

———. "The Identification of the Citizen: The Birth of Republican Civil Status in France." In *Documenting Individual Identity: The Development of State Practices in the Modern World*, edited by Jane Caplan and John Torpey, 28–38. Princeton, NJ: Princeton University Press, 2001.

———. *Immigration, antisémitisme et racisme en France (XIXᵉ–XXᵉ siècle): Discours publics, humiliations privées*. Paris: Fayard, 2007.

———. *Introduction à la socio-histoire*. Paris: la Découverte, 2006.

———. "Nations, nationalités, nationalismes: Pour une socio-histoire comparée." In *État, nation et immigration*, 87–144. Paris: Belin, 2001.

———. *Les origines républicaines de Vichy*. Paris: Hachette littératures, 1999.

———. "Représentation nationale et catégories sociales: L'exemple des réfugiés politiques." *Genèses* 26 (1997): 25–54.

———. *La tyrannie du national: Le droit d'asile en Europe, 1793–1993*. Paris: Calmann-Lévy, 1991.

Nord, Philip. *The Republican Moment: Struggles for Democracy in Nineteenth Century France*. Cambridge, MA: Harvard University Press, 1995.

"La Nouvelle-Calédonie: Terre de métissages." Special issue, *Annales d'histoire calédonienne* 1 (November 2004).

Nye, Robert A. *Crime, Madness and Politics in Modern France: The Medical Concept of National Decline*. Princeton, NJ: Princeton University Press, 1984.

———. *Masculinity and Male Codes of Honor in Modern France*. Berkeley: University of California Press, 1993.

Paillard, Yvon. "Faut-il admettre les jeunes 'indigènes' dans les collèges français de Madagascar (1913)?" *L'information historique* 33, no. 3 (May–June 1971): 115–19.

Pedersen, Jean Elisabeth. "Legislating the Family: Gender, Population, and Republican Politics in France, 1870–1920." PhD diss., University of Chicago, Chicago, 1993.

———. *Legislating the French Family: Feminism, Theater, and Republican Politics, 1870–1920*. New Brunswick, NJ: Rutgers University Press, 2003.

———. "'Special Customs': Paternity Suits and Citizenship in France and the Colonies, 1870–1912." In *Domesticating the Empire: Race, Gender and Family Life in French and Dutch Colonialism*, edited by Julia Clancy-Smith and Frances Gouda, 43–64. Charlottesville: University of Virginia Press, 1998.

Pedrocini, Guy, ed. *Histoire militaire de la France*. Vol. 3, *De 1871 à 1940*. Paris: PUF, 1992.

Perelman, Chaim, ed. *Le problème des lacunes en droit*. Brussels: Émile Bruylant, 1968.

Perelman, Chaim, and Lucie Olbrechts-Tyeca. *The New Rhetoric: A Treatise on Argumentation*. Translated by John Wilkinson and Purcell Weaver. Notre Dame, IN: University of Notre Dame, 1969.

Pick, Daniel. *Faces of Degeneration: A European Disorder, c. 1848–1918*. New York: Cambridge University Press, 1989.

Rabinow, Paul. *French Modern: Norms and Forms of the Social Environment*. Cambridge, MA: MIT Press, 1989.

"Le racisme après les races." *Actuel Marx*, no. 38 (2005).

Raffin, Anne. *Youth Mobilization in Vichy Indochina and Its Legacies, 1940 to 1970*. Lanham, MD: Lexington Books, 2005.

Ranger, Terence. "The Invention of Tradition in Colonial Africa." In *The Invention of Tradition*, edited by Eric Hobsbawm and Terence Ranger, 211–62. 1983. Reprint, Cambridge: Cambridge University Press, 1996.

Rasmussen, Anne. "Le travail en congrès, élaboration d'un milieu international." In *Histoire de l'Office du travail, 1890–1914*, edited by Jean Luciani, 119–34. Paris: Syros, 1993.

Rebérioux, Madeleine. "Le mot 'race' au tournant du siècle." *Mots: Les langages du politique* 33 (1992): 53–58.

Renucci, Florence. "Confrontation entre droit français et droits indigènes: Le cas des mariages mixtes en Afrique du Nord, 1870–1919." *Cahiers aixois d'histoire des droits de l'outre-mer français* 1 (2002): 147–91.

Reynaud Paligot, Carole. *La république raciale: Paradigme racial et idéologie républicaine, 1860–1930*. Paris: PUF, 2006.

Rivet, Daniel. *Le Maghreb à l'épreuve de la colonisation*. Paris: Hachette littératures, 2002.

Rolland, Dominique. *De sang mêlé: Chroniques du métissage en Indochine*. Bordeaux: Elytis, 2006.

Rollet, Catherine. *Les enfants au XIXᵉ siècle*. Paris: Hachette littératures, 2001.

———. *La politique à l'égard de la petite enfance sous la IIIᵉ République*. Paris: INED, 1990.

Rosanvallon, Pierre. *The Demands of Liberty: Civil Society in France since the Revolution*. Translated by Arthur Goldhammer. Cambridge, MA: Harvard University Press, 2007.

———. *Le sacre du citoyen: Histoire du suffrage universel en France*. Paris: Gallimard, 1992. Reprint, "Folio histoire," 2001.

Rosental, Paul-André. "Construire le 'macro' par le 'micro': Fredrik Barth et la microstoria." In *Jeux d'échelle: La micro-analyse à l'expérience*, edited by Jacques Revel, 141–59. Paris: Gallimard/Seuil, 1996.

Saada, Emmanuelle. "The Empire of Law: Dignity, Prestige and Domination in the Colonial Situation." *French Politics, Culture and Society* 20, no. 2 (2002): 98–120.

———. "Entre 'assimilation' et 'décivilisation': L'imitation et le projet colonial républicain." *Terrain* 44 (2005): 19–38.

———. "Une nationalité par degrés: Civilité et citoyenneté en situation coloniale." In *L'esclavage, la colonisation et après*, edited by Patrick Weil and Stéphane Dufoix, 193–227. Paris: PUF, 2005.

———. "Paternité et citoyenneté en situation coloniale: Le débat sur les 'reconnaissances frauduleuses' et la construction d'un droit impérial." *Politix* 17, no. 66 (2004): 107–36.

———. "La 'question des métis' dans les colonies françaises: Socio-histoire d'une catégorie juridique (Indochine et autres territoires de l'Empire français, années 1890–années 1950)." PhD diss., École des hautes études en sciences sociales, Paris, 2001.

———. "Race and Sociological Reason in the Republic: Inquiries on the *Métis* in the French Empire, 1908–1937." *International Sociology* 17, no. 3 (2002): 361–91.

Sahlins, Peter. *Boundaries: The Making of France and Spain in the Pyrenees*. Berkeley: University of California Press, 1989.

———. *Unnaturally French: Foreign Citizens in the Old Regime and After*. Ithaca, NY: Cornell University Press, 2004.

Salaün, Marie. *L'école indigène: Nouvelle-Calédonie, 1885–1945*. Rennes, France: Presses universitaires de Rennes, 2005.

Sarraute, Raymond, and Paul Tager. *Les juifs sous l'occupation, 1940–1944*. Paris: Centre de documentation juive contemporaine, 1982.

Sayad, Abdelmalek. *The Suffering of the Immigrant*. Translated by David Macey. Cambridge: Polity, 2004.

Schafer, Sylvia. *Children in Moral Danger and the Problem of Government in Third Republic France*. Princeton, NJ: Princeton University Press, 1997.

Schmidt, Nelly. *Histoire du métissage*. Paris: la Martinière, 2003.

Schnapper, Dominique. *Community of Citizens: On the Modern Idea of Nationality*. Translated from the French by Séverine Rosée. New Brunswick, NJ: Transaction Publishers, 1998.

———. *La France de l'intégration: Sociologie de la nation en 1990*. Paris: Gallimard, 1991.

Schneider, William H. *Quality and Quantity: The Quest for Biological Regeneration in Twentieth-Century France*. Cambridge and New York: Cambridge University Press, 1990.

Schor, Paul. *Compter et classer: Histoire des recensements américains*. Paris: EHESS, 2009.

Scott, David. "Colonial Governmentality." *Social Text* 43 (1995): 191–220.

Serverin, Évelyne. *De la jurisprudence en droit privé: Théorie d'une pratique*. Lyon: Presses universitaires de Lyon, 1985.

Sibeud, Emmanuelle. *Une science impériale pour l'Afrique? La construction des savoirs africanistes en France, 1878–1930*. Paris: EHESS, 2002.

Slama, Serge. "Le privilège du national: Étude historique de la condition civique des étrangers en France." PhD diss., Université de Paris X, Nanterre, 2003.

Sollors, Werner. *Neither Black nor White Yet Both: Thematic Explorations of Interracial Literature*. New York: Oxford University Press, 1997.

Spire, Alexis. *Étrangers à la carte: L'administration de l'immigration en France, 1945–1975*. Paris: Grasset, 2005.

Spitz, Jean-Fabien. *Le moment républicain en France*. Paris: Gallimard, 2005.

Stoler, Ann Laura. *Carnal Knowledge and Imperial Power: Race and the Intimate in Colonial Rule*. Berkeley: University of California Press, 2002.

———. "Genre et moralité dans la construction impériale de la race." *Actuel Marx* 38 (2005): 75–101.

———, ed. *Haunted by Empire: Geographies of Intimacy in North American History*. Durham, NC: Duke University Press, 2006.

———. *Race and the Education of Desire: Foucault's History of Sexuality and the Colonial Order of Things*. Durham, NC: Duke University Press, 1995.

———. "Rethinking Colonial Categories: European Communities and the Boundaries of Rule." *Comparative Studies in Society and History* 31 (1989): 134–61.

———. "Sexual Affronts and Racial Frontiers: European Identities and the Cultural Politics of Exclusion in Colonial Southeast Asia." *Comparative Studies in Society and History* 34, no. 3 (1992): 514–51.

Suret-Canale, Jean. *Afrique noire, occidentale et centrale*. Vol. 2, *L'ère coloniale, 1900–1945*. Paris: Éditions sociales, 1964.

Taguieff, Pierre-André. *The Force of Prejudice: On Racism and Its Doubles*. Translated and edited by Hassan Melehy. Minneapolis: University of Minnesota Press, 2001.

Taraud, Christelle. *La prostitution coloniale: Algérie, Maroc, Tunisie, 1830–1962*. Paris: Payot, 2003.

Tarde, Gabriel de. *Les lois de l'imitation*. 1890. Reprint, Paris: Kimé, 1993.

Terré, François. *Introduction générale au droit*. 4th ed. Paris: Dalloz, 1998.

———. "Réflexions sur la notion de nationalité." *Revue critique de droit international privé* 64, no. 2 (1975): 197–214.

Théry, René. "Véritable père et paternité vraie." Paris: Juris classeur périodique, 1979.

Thomas, Yan. "L'institution civile de la cité." *Le débat* 74 (1993): 23–44.

Topalov, Christian. "Les réformateurs et leurs réseaux." In *Laboratoires du nouveau siècle: La nébuleuse réformatrice et ses réseaux en France, 1880–1914*, edited by Christian Topalov, 11–58. Paris: EHESS, 1999.

Trinh Van Thao. *L'école française en Indochine*. Paris: Karthala, 1995.

Verjus, Anne. *Le cens de la famille: Les femmes et le vote, 1789–1848*. Paris: Belin, 2002.

Vernier, Bernard. *La genèse sociale des sentiments: Aînés et cadets dans l'île grecque de Karpathos*. Paris: EHESS, 1991.

———. "Prénom et ressemblance: Appropriation symbolique des enfants, économie affective et systèmes de parenté." In *Adoptions, ethnologie des parentés choisies,* edited by Agnès Fine, 97–119. Paris: Maison des sciences de l'homme, 1998.

Verpeaux, Michel. "Le juif 'non citoyen.'" In "Le droit antisémite de Vichy," special issue, *Le genre humain* 30–31 (1996): 189–207.

Weber, Florence. *Le sang, le nom, le quotidien: Une sociologie de la parenté pratique.* La Courneuve, France: Aux lieux d'être, 2005.

Weil, Patrick. *How to Be French: Nationality in the Making since 1789.* Translated by Catherine Porter. Durham, NC: Duke University Press, 2009.

Weil, Patrick, and Stéphane Dufoix, eds. *L'esclavage, la colonisation et après . . .* Paris: PUF, 2005.

White, Owen. *Children of the French Empire: Miscegenation and Colonial Society in French West Africa, 1895–1960.* Oxford: Oxford University Press, 1999.

Wildenthal, Lora. *German Women for Empire, 1884–1945.* Durham, NC: Duke University Press, 2001.

Wright, Gwendolyn. *The Politics of Design in French Colonial Urbanism.* Chicago: University of Chicago Press, 1991.

Zerilli, Filippo M. "Il debattito sul meticciato: Biologico e sociale nell'antropologia francese del primo novecento." *Archivio per l'antropologia e la etnologia* 125 (1995): 237–73.